DEFINING MISSION

Comboni Missionaries in North America

Foreword by

Peter E. Hogan, S.S.J.

Patricia Durchholz

University Press of America,® Inc.
Lanham • New York • Oxford

Copyright © 1999 by
University Press of America,® Inc.
4720 Boston Way
Lanham, Maryland 20706

12 Hid's Copse Rd.
Cumnor Hill, Oxford OX2 9JJ

Library of Congress Cataloging-in-Publication Data

Durchholz, Patricia
Defining mission: Comboni Missionaries in North America/ Patricia
Durchholz ; foreword by Peter E. Hogan.
p.   cm.
Includes bibliographical references and index.
1. Comboni Missionaries—United States—History. I. Title.
BX3472.D87   1999 271'.9—dc21   99—30961 CIP

ISBN 0-7618-1427-2 (cloth: alk. ppr.)

Blessed Daniel Comboni: Born March 15, 1831 in Limone sul Garda, Italy; died October 10, 1881, at Khartoum, Uganda; beatified in Rome, Italy, March 17, 1996.

To Father Hamlet Accorsi and Bishop Dominic Ferrara
as well as to all the pioneers of the
Comboni Missionary Province of North America
whose hard work, sacrifices, and determination reflected
the ideals of their founder, Blessed Daniel Comboni

CONTENTS

Foreword

I write this Foreword to *Defining Mission* with both envy and regret. Let me explain. Since ordination in 1946, I have been involved in the history of the Catholic Church, particularly in the United States, and even more specifically with the African American community. It consisted of years of teaching in major and minor seminaries in the United States. There also was a semester teaching the Missionaries of St. Paul in Nigeria, preparing those who were to come and work in the mission field of the United States. I have been a part time Archivist of the Josephites since 1947, and full time one since 1964. I have been Secretary of the Chapter of Renewal of the Josephites since 1968, and all the General Conferences since then. Paper work, reports, minutes of meetings, correspondence, interviews, audio and videotapes have all been accumulated in bulk.

They were all waiting for the person who would turn them into an honest, understanding story of those who were infused with the spirit of Christ, as reflected through the founder of the Community. Such a story should tell the difficulties of strangers working in a vastly different and imperfectly understood culture. It would reflect the administrative complexities that ranged from active hierarchical support through indifference to the neglect and, at times, even opposition. It should show the dedication and heroic fortitude of the pioneers in the field, as well as the generosity of spirit of those for whom they labored. The story would describe the changing demography, the changing structures of church and State and the difficulties in adapting the basic goals of the religious founder to these changed circumstances while still preserving the true spirit.

My envy therefore arises when I see this task accomplished for the Comboni Missionaries by Dr. Patricia Durchholz. This envy encompasses not only the researcher and writer, but especially the community members who gave generously of their interest, their time, their honesty and experiences to make the work of the researcher and writer possible in the first place. The hopes of these community members, their generosity of effort, their enduring of frustration in not being able to explain the complexities of American situations to non-American authorities, their need to adapt by moving from one set of circumstances to another vastly different, all these are interestingly and sympathetically spelled out by Dr. Durchholz in *Defining Mission*.

The world of the late 1930s has become vastly different in the late 1990s. As equally changed, and to a certain extent, even more changed, is the Church of the late 1990s from the Church of the late 1930s. And yet in that change there has to remain the essentials of the Father's gift of the Son protected by the Holy Spirit. In the face of so many changes, the struggle to preserve the essentials while adapting the accidentals is never ending. Not everyone remains unscathed in the struggle, but the struggle continues. *Defining Mission* details the struggles in adapting and preserving, and most importantly, it lays the groundwork for projecting the future.

My regret comes in this projecting of the future. As an Archivist, I like to say "We put the present into the past to save the future." *Defining Mission* has done an excellent job of framing the present in the picture of the past. The saving of the future cannot be so presented in detail. However, with the track record of devotion as expressed by the founder, Blessed Daniel Comboni, by the pioneers in the North American Province, and by the continued dedication of the present members on a world-wide basis, the future has an implicit guarantee. Perhaps I should soften the feelings of regret for not knowing the details of the future to the consolation of knowing that there will be a future for the Comboni Missionaries in God's grace, especially with the help of Mary and Joseph. Too much good work has been done in Christ's name not to be held intact and growing in the future.

PETER E HOGAN, S.S.J.
Archivist
The Josephites

Preface

Over six ago, a phone call from the Comboni Mission Center in Cincinnati led to my writing this history. The story begins in 1939 as a Comboni priest, Father Edward Mason, is sent to America to find a diocese that would accept his society. War between Britain and Italy was imminent, and Comboni missionaries in black Africa were Italians working in British territory. They would be detained in prison camps if war broke out. In America, they hoped to work with black Americans. Mason was successful in his mission, and Comboni missionaries settled in Cincinnati. As pastors they began work in ghetto parishes, then in California Indians missions, discovering both the country's diversity and racism. Meanwhile, their provincials negotiated with diocesan leaders for permission to open seminaries or work in other parishes. They also found resources to build the new foundation. Each provincial had his own set of challenges and, during the period from 1939 to 1986 that this narrative covers, these challenges both in the Church and secular society were not insignificant.

Research and publication in sociology and organizational development were what I brought to this book. But despite being a lifelong Catholic, I had little acquaintance with Catholic Church history, American or otherwise. The founder of the society was Daniel Comboni, and its members were largely Italian; therefore, those who first came to the United States were essentially immigrants. Till that time, the Comboni Missionary Institute had focussed on Africa, but in the United States their work began with "the Negroes." Thus some knowledge of immigrant history as well as the history of black Catholics in America was required.

With so much to learn, the first years of work were spent searching for information and the experts who could point to it. Shortly after reading his book, *The History of Black Catholics in the United States*, I met Father Cyprian Davis, O.S.B. He graciously spent an entire afternoon acquainting me with black history, the issues he wrestled with while writing his ground-breaking book, and a number of sources I should investigate. If there has been a model for the writing of this history, Father Davis provided it. Though I lack his eloquence, erudition, and historical expertise, I hope this book reflects some of his balanced perspective.

Both Davis and others insisted that I speak with Father Peter Hogan, S.S.J., head of the Josephite Archives in Baltimore. His knowledge of church history, his willingness to share it, and the fact that he was in charge of the largest collection of black Catholic history in the United States, made a visit to his archives a priority. Not only did Father Hogan invite me to search the many rooms and files of his extensive collection, he also provided a running discourse on the history of the Catholic Church in America. Later, he read and critiqued every manuscript chapter. I am deeply grateful for this and for his encouragement and Irish humor during difficult periods of writing. His knowledge and experience in a missionary society serving black Americans provided a grounding on which to judge many of the circumstances surrounding Comboni missionaries.

The archivist who first acquainted me with archival protocol was Don Buske at the Historical Archives of the Chancery of the Archdiocese of Cincinnati. Since the Comboni Missionaries foundation in America was established in Cincinnati, the archives Mr. Buske heads was the first and most important outside source among diocesan archives. Many weeks were spent within its walls. Mr. Buske was generous in searching files and pointing to ones I overlooked. He was also available for questions, and he read some of the early chapters of this book. I feel fortunate to have worked in these archives so well managed, yet so hospitable.

Tony Dees, archivist at the Archdiocese of Atlanta, took the trouble to send documents relating to the Comboni missionaries' work in Georgia. I was grateful when he also read some chapters pertaining to the Atlanta Archdiocese. Sister Catherine LaCoste, C.S.J., then archivist of the San Diego Diocesan Archives, was gracious and helpful in locating documents on Comboni missionary work in the San Diego Indians missions. At the Archdiocese of Louisville, Vice Chancellor Florence Crawford made additional documents on the missionaries' work available. Without the assistance of the above archivists and diocesan authorities, the story of Comboni Missionaries in North America would have been greatly attenuated.

It is important to offer my gratitude to all who agreed to be interviewed, or who allowed me to use interviews they had given others. This includes close to one hundred Comboni missionaries and several dozen others. They added the eye-witness, affective, and personal dimension that documents alone cannot convey. In this regard I want to thank Comboni Father Dennis Conway, who, in the late 1980s, interviewed forty Comboni confreres and collected as many letters. He also compiled the "house diaries" of over two decades, and translated those that were in Italian. (As of December, 1998, Father Conway began serving as the ninth provincial of the North American Province.)

Interviews with Mary Luella Conwill of Louisville, and her two sons, Father Giles Conwill and William Conwill, Ph.D., added a great deal to the story of Comboni Missionaries in Louisville, black Catholics in Louisville, and other topics. Both Father Allen Tarlton, O.S.B. and Father Clarence Rivers provided the perspectives of the first two black Catholic priests from the Archdiocese of Cincinnati. References on urban renewal in Cincinnati's West End did not have the same impact as interviewing those who grew up there when it took place. Two who were particularly enlightening were Melvin Grier, a photo-journalist with the *Cincinnati Post*, and LaVerne Muldrow Summerlin, Professor of English at the University of Cincinnati.

Father Clyde F. Crews, an eminent scholar and author of *An American Holy Land*, a history of the Archdiocese of Louisville, graciously responded to my plea as another Danforth Fellow, and read both chapters on Comboni missionaries' work in Louisville. He provided information about the seminary milieu in which Louisville priests were formed and other helpful comments.

Zane Miller, Professor of History at the University of Cincinnati, on whose books and articles about urban America in general, and Cincinnati history in particular, I owe many of my observations, obligingly read an early draft of the manuscript and pointed out some basic weaknesses in its structure which hopefully have been corrected.

Several lay people went out of their way to provide important documentation. John Buse made available four decades of correspondence between Father Hamlet Accorsi and Mr. Buse's parents, John and Marie Buse. Father Accorsi's family in Verona, Italy, sent his letters to his family when he was a young priest. My thanks goes also to Clayton Emery, a fellow writer, who took time from his own work to read most of the early chapters and gave significant encouragement. Three of my adult children, Andrea, Anthony, and Theresa, took time from their work and families to read the manuscript. I must also mention the support I received from Jan Brown, the software specialist who guided me through a maze of formatting issues.

Of course this book would not have been possible without the support of the Comboni Missionary Provincial Councils in North America and the two provincials, Father Brian Quigley and Father John Converset, who served during the writing of the history. The present provincial, Father Dennis Conway, will see the history published. There were many Comboni missionaries who contributed to this manuscript by reading one, two, or most of the book's chapters. They offered a corrective perspective and sometimes prevented outright errors. Some of these wrote extensive letters and essays about their experiences in the United States. These readers included Fathers Joseph Bragotti, Oliver Branchesi, Januarius Carillo, Remus Catellani, John Converset, Walter Mattiato, and Victor Turchetti. Several prominent missionaries, including two of the provincials of North America who are very much alive at this time, Father Contran and Father Walter, have been truly heroic in allowing me to write about their work without hindrance except to correct factual mistakes. The generosity of these confreres may allow others to learn from their experience and respect their integrity all the more for their forbearance in this area.

Two Comboni missionaries who provided the impetus to begin this project, and never wavered in their support, are Father Alfred Paolucci and Father Mario Ongaro. Father Paolucci translated reams of letters, documents, and diaries for me. On his own, he had compiled a volume of biographies of all Comboni missionaries who served in the U.S., produced a translation of all obituaries of Comboni Missionaries through 1988, translated an entire diary of Father Anthony Todesco, and allowed me to use his life-journal, *My Stars.* He never failed to answer questions, and he introduced me to many former parishioners. His enthusiasm for the history and his generous sharing of resources lent the support and encouragement needed in the early years of my work. The work itself has been enriched by his contributions. Unfortunately, he, as well as Father Oliver Branchesi, died just months before the book's publication.

Father Ongaro is the Comboni missionary who first contacted me about writing this history. He subsequently worked with me in such a way that his help and advice came without interference in the work itself. With his background in library science, psychology, formation, ministry, and administration, he offered the well-seasoned advice that I often needed. Thanks to him and his fellow archivist at the Comboni Missionary Archives in Rome, the many letters that went back and forth between provincials and members of the General Administration in the 1940s and 1950s were made available. Father Ongaro translated these as well as the diary of Father Edward Mason and other documents. He did all this while maintaining the utmost fairness, diplomacy, and circumspection, allowing me to learn from his store of information, yet reach my own conclusions based on the array of facts at my disposal. Without him this history would not have been begun, much less completed.

A List of Acronyms

AAA . . . . Archives of the Archdiocese of Atlanta

AAB . . . . Archives of the Archdiocese of Baltimore

AAC . . . . Archives of the Archdiocese of Chicago

AAD . . . . Archives of the Archdiocese of Detroit

AAL . . . . Archives of the Archdiocese of Louisville

AALA . . . . Archives of the Archdiocese of Los Angeles

AAN . . . . Archives of the Archdiocese of Newark

AANY . . . . Archives of the Archdiocese of New York

CMAC . . . . Comboni Missionary Archives of Cincinnati

CMAR . . . . Comboni Missionary Archives of Rome

HACAC . . . . Historical Archives of the Chancery of the
Archdiocese of Cincinnati

SSIHM . . . . Sister Servants of the Immaculate Heart of Mary

JA . . . . Josephite Archives

SBS . . . . Sisters of the Blessed Sacrament Archives

SDDA . . . . San Diego Diocesan Archives

1. An Urgent Mission

In August, 1939, a decision was finally taken. At a meeting in Verona, Italy, the Comboni Missionaries' General Council agreed to send two missionaries to the United States. Serious talk about this had been going on for over a year. As early as July, 1938, the Superior General, Father Anthony Vignato, spoke to his council members about "a vague proposal" of the Scalabrini Fathers to open a mission in "Cincinnati, USA." But an undercurrent of resistance persisted against long-term commitments anywhere but in Africa. The rallying cry of Blessed Daniel Comboni, the Institute's founder, was "Africa or Death," but circumstances, would force a new and decisive action.[1]

WAR AND THE COMBONI MISSIONARIES

What led the Comboni Missionaries to reconsider a mission in America was the progress of events in Europe. In late 1938 and early 1939, Adolph Hitler moved his armies beyond the boundaries of Germany, annexing Austria, and demanding concessions from smaller states nearby. Hitler's belief that these demands would meet little resistance was bolstered by the "peace in our times" diplomacy of both Britain and France."[2]

While the Western world watched these events with anxiety, another drama took place in the Vatican. Pope Pius XI died, ending a seventeen year reign. In 1929, he had negotiated the Lateran Treaty with Mussolini guaranteeing independence for the Vatican State. Shortly thereafter, his relationship with the Italian dictator deteriorated. The British, who at first regarded Pius XI as a Fascist, later recognized him as a religious leader who, "denounced racialism (sic) and perverted nationalism in strong language." When the Conclave of Cardinals gathered to choose a new pope, Eugene Cardinal Pacelli was elected. Under his predecessor, he had traveled widely as the Vatican's Secretary of State. Soon after his election, German armies drove into Prague and dismembered Czechoslovakia. Pius XII immediately shifted from the outspoken policy of his predecessor. He saw this strategy as counterproductive to peace, and he believed a neutral Vatican State could negotiate a peace between the major powers.[3]

On September 1, 1939, peace prospects were shattered when Hitler's armies marched into Poland. The British demand for an immediate withdrawal of German troops was ignored, and both Britain and France declared war on Germany. Italy remained neutral, but few could predict Mussolini's next move. Most Italians were against involvement in war. But if Italy joined Germany against the British, the activities of Comboni Missionaries in British-held territories of Africa would be in jeopardy. Comboni Father Oliver Branchesi later wrote, "We could express in a sentence the predicament in which we found ourselves before the war: The Comboni Missionaries were all Italians with missions only in English colonies."

There were many factors behind the ill-will between Great Britain and Italy. A few years before, when Mussolini's troops took over Ethiopia, Britain led world opinion against him. In Italy, the Fascists were so incensed by British criticism that Christmas trees were banned as a holiday custom. Galled by what they believed were inequitable actions of their allies from World War I, many Italians, even members of the Church hierarchy, looked at the Ethiopian conquest through the eyes of nationalism. A British official in Rome, reporting on this, wrote, "The Church has proved that it is purely Italian and far from 'Catholic.'" As these comments illustrate, bad blood between the British and Italian governments also arose from the fact that one country was the center of the Church of England, and the other was the center of Roman Catholicism.[4]

Antagonism between Britain and Italy often played out in the colonies they held in Africa. When the Fascists expelled all non-Italian missionaries from Ethiopia, the British retaliated by asking Comboni Missionaries to leave the Kodok mission in Sudan. Yet throughout 1939, Comboni Missionaries continued their work in most of the British-held territories of Sudan, Uganda, and Egypt. Complicating their situation, however, was that they were then experiencing a powerful growth in vocations, and with this increase, the constraints of sending additional members to work under a foreign power mounted. It was under these circumstances that Father Vignato and his council members were persuaded to send missionaries to America. If the Comboni Institute could locate English-speaking vocations there, the survival of its missions in British colonies would be assured. Comboni Missionaries from the United States could join in the evangelization of Africa, begun over a half century before by Daniel Comboni. The man chosen to seek out an

American bishop who would accept the society was Father Edward Mason, a Comboni missionary in Africa for twelve years. He was described as a priest with "big shoulders who doesn't stop in front of obstacles."[5]

The circumstances of his appointment were later reported by Father Dominic Ferrara in Italy at the time. Vignato had invited Ferrara out for a walk. They spoke of the impending danger, and they agreed that if Italy joined the war, she would side with Germany against England and France. The English Government would then either close Comboni missions, or severely restrict their activity. Ferrara's diary reports, "It was clear that it was already late, but...we had to think of something to save what could be saved and thus avoid the total ruin of the missions." Vignato then told Ferrara of his audience with Pope Pius XII. A few weeks before, the Holy Father had suggested that Vignato turn his attention to the United States of America, 'a land fertile in vocations and always very generous in helping every good work financially.'"After telling Ferrara all this, Vignato asked, "But whom should I send?" The response was, "Why not send Father Mason?" Ferrara pointed out that he was not only then in Italy, but he was the kind of man who had the determination to begin and complete a difficult task successfully.[6] That Mason spoke excellent English had no small bearing on his selection as trailblazer to America. In July, 1939, his appointment was official.

A MAN WITH BIG SHOULDERS

With a broad dome of a head tapering to a firm chin and beard, Father Edward Mason's erect carriage lent a certain austerity to his bearing. This was a priest who could easily be mistaken as an English schoolmaster. So highly respected was he, even by British authorities, that some confreres later commented he was perhaps "a bit too British." Born in Padua in 1903, Mason proved a brilliant seminarian. As a priest he dedicated himself to furthering the education of Africans. When sent to serve at Wau in Southern Sudan, Mason's abilities were quickly recognized, and he was appointed Education Secretary of the entire vicariate.[7]

In 1938, Mason had taken leave from his Wau mission to attend a "Colonial Course" in London for leaders in education. Returning to Italy, Mason expected to leave for Wau, but instead was summoned by Vignato, and told to leave as soon as possible on an urgent mission to the United States. He must go before war spread to Italy and Africa. He must find a place where Comboni Missionaries could establish a foundation and search for American vocations. Vignato's introductory letter for Mason described his mission: "He is now sent as representative of this Missionary Congregation to the U.S. of America with a view of planning and developing useful work among the Negroes there, with the approval and blessing of the local Ecclesiastical Authorities....I may respectfully say that H.E. Cardinal P. Fumasoni-Biondi, Prefect of Propaganda Fide, and H.E.R. Ch. Rossi Prefect of the Concistorial (sic) C. have favorably and warmly encouraged our Congregation to this proposal." Vignato hoped Mason would be assisted in this new aim "that we have considered for the sake of the souls' salvation, to the Glory of Almighty God, and trusting in the abundant riches of the Sacred Heart of Jesus."

Mason was not a man to hesitate in carrying forward an assignment. He obtained his visa and other papers, and on October 19, 1939, he stopped in Rome to pick up the recommendation for ministry in America from Carlo Raffaello Cardinal Rossi of the Consistorial Congregation. However, the recommendation he received was not what he expected. His diary reports, "Really we had requested a recommendation for the ministry among the Blacks, but this was not given to us. Perhaps for...Roman reasons." [Emphasis not added.] And he mentioned another disappointment, "Even Cardinal Fumasoni-Biondi [Prefect of Propaganda Fide], who had been requested kindly for the same, did not wish to give us that recommendation, even though, when he heard of the news of the decision of the Society to go and establish itself in the United States, he said, 'Only now you are thinking about that!'"[8]

Reticence on the part of Rossi and Fumasoni-Biondi is not surprising. Pietro Cardinal Fumasoni-Biondi had been Apostolic Delegate to the United States only a few years before. There he witnessed the meager attention American clergy gave the Negro. As for the Consistorial Congregation, it had for decades advocated on behalf of Blacks in America. Rome's disappointment with the American hierarchy's lackluster performance was hardly a secret. The Vatican had pushed American bishops to seek out missionaries for the evangelization of Blacks and development of black vocations. American bishops resisted the ordination of young black men; and they turned to religious societies for ministry among Blacks.

Thomas Wyatt Turner, founder and leader of the Federation of Black Catholics, expressed frustration about the Negroes' exclusion from mainstream Catholicism. In 1931, he addressed a letter to the American hierarchy calling for "every bishop to see that the doors of every Catholic institution be opened to black Catholics, every school, hospital, college, university and seminary." Rome was aware of demands Catholics like Turner were making, and the Vatican had been sympathetic to many of them. Cardinals Rossi and Fumasoni-Biondi might hesitate, therefore, to explicitly support foreign missionaries going to the United States to work among Negroes at a time when young black men were being,denied entry to Catholic seminaries. In suspecting "Roman" politics, Mason failed to understand that the Cardinals' refusals might be connected to the policies of the American hierarchy regarding black Catholics.[9]

In November, 1939, the city of Naples was still untouched by a war spreading across Eastern Europe. The crowded port, lying beneath the smoking peak of Mount Vesuvius, anchored one end of the curved harbor. It was a familiar sight to Mason and his confreres who passed through Naples on their way to foreign ports. Here, on the fifteenth of November, Mason boarded the *Conte di Savoia*, a famous passenger ship that sailed under the Italian flag. Despite warnings that German nationals were detained at Gibraltar by the British, Mason's passage was free of interception. He continued his carefully documented diary with the goal of his trip as explained by Father Vignato. It included two levels, "Manifest - to look for missionary work among the Blacks in the States; Real: to find a base on which to establish the Society overseas for recruiting of vocations, and in order to find means, possibly beginning with work in a parish." This clandestine approach to his mission was perhaps an "open secret" among those who approved it. The Pope, aware of his society's dedication to Africa, understood that the spread of war put its work in jeopardy, and that a safe haven for Comboni Missionaries was best located in an English-speaking country. The Vatican knew that black Catholics' call for inclusion in mainstream American Catholicism was largely ignored, and perhaps Comboni Missionaries, with their experience in Africa, could bring another perspective to the American Negro missions. This service would be a legitimate means of preserving their society if its main body were trapped on the continents of Europe and Africa.

As he suffered no seasickness, Mason had considerable time to think about the five suggestions Father Vignato gave him. They were: 1) not to accept work that was in debt; 2) not to accept work requiring donations from Italy; 3) to find a place in one of the great cities, but not around the Lakes or too far South; 4) an ideal center might be Cincinnati, Ohio; and 5) that he should present himself to everyone, ask for work among the Blacks, give talks in colleges and parishes, and ask for Mass intentions. On November 23, he arrived in New York. Who he met, what he saw, and the information he collected established the direction that Comboni Missionaries' work in America would take for years to come.[10]

AMERICA IN FIFTY-EIGHT DAYS

As Philip Gleason reminds us, even Thomas Jefferson, author of the Declaration of Independence, believed the Roman Church could never flourish in the free air of America. Many Americans believed that "Catholicism was intrinsically irreconcilable with Americanism...."[11] Those with fewer philosophical ideals had even less tolerance for Catholics. In the mid-nineteenth century, when waves of Irish immigrants arrived, the Ku Klux Klan, the American Protective Association, and the Guardians of Liberty stirred up rivalry, bigotry, and enmity against the Irish that led to open violence. In 1834, Irish Catholics lost their lives and property in Charleston, Massachusetts, and ten years later such losses also occurred in Philadelphia. Some abatement of violence began during the Civil War when disproportionately large numbers of Irish served in the Union's ranks.[12]

Since being recognized as an American was imperative to acceptance as an individual, a worker, and a citizen of the United States, the Catholic hierarchy was extremely sensitive to the need to prove Catholicism compatible with democracy and with being an American. Most of the clergy and hierarchy involved in this adaptation had been, or were born to, Irish immigrants. The Irish, therefore, were significantly involved in "Americanizing" Catholicism, a strategy designed to adapt the Church to characteristics of American life such as social equalitarianism, separation of church and state, religious freedom, and a willingness to cooperate with other religions in social and civic activities. In the late 1800s this led to accusations from Rome of "Americanism" which Cardinal James Gibbons of Baltimore denied, writing, "I do not believe that there is a bishop, a priest, or even a layman in this country who knows his religion and utters such enormities..."[13] The Irish had an advantage over most immigrants who followed them. They not only spoke English, but they were extraordinarily adept at using it. In contrast, Italian immigrants came to America without benefit of the English language. Large numbers were from the poorest region of Mezzogiorno, east and south of Rome, long after the Irish were well established. The Irish and Italians were also separated by old European enmities concerning papal politics. Only after the Concordat was signed by Mussolini and the Holy See in 1929 did the issue of the temporal power of the Pope evaporate. Till then, most devout Catholics, especially the Irish, viewed the Pope as a prisoner in the Vatican and blamed the Italian government and its people.[14] Franciscan Father Leonard Bacigalupo concluded, however, that the issues between the

Irish and Italian should be blamed on both groups. On the one hand, the Irish had dominated the Church in America and were slow to adjust to the needs of other ethnic Catholics. On the other, Italians, with their close proximity to church politics over the centuries, were often indifferent to attendance at Mass, harbored a degree of anti-clericalism, and did not believe the Church and its schools were in need of financial support.[15]

On Thanksgiving Day, Father Mason arrived in New York, a city celebrated as a refuge for immigrants. He was a guest of the Scalabrini Fathers at Our Lady of Pompei. Father Cavicchi, the superior, helped him make contacts, and Mason began by trying to see Archbishop Francis Spellman of New York.

While waiting for news from Spellman's secretary, Mason visited two black parishes in Harlem. One was Saint Mark's served by the Holy Ghost Fathers. Its pastor was Father Michael Mulvoy, said to be "the blackest white man in Harlem." Mason heard that results were very good. Baptisms varied between forty to one hundred a year, and this was generally true in other parishes of the United States.[16] At St. Charles Church, the pastor was Monsignor William McCann who gained fame for purportedly winning 200 black converts a year throughout the 1930s. He told Mason about the changes in American cities as the relatively rich Whites left the business centers of downtowns areas. Mason's diary notes, "He spoke of how property values then decreased as a few Blacks moved in, and eventually poverty levels were such that "living quarters of Blacks are dirty, dilapidated, overcrowded. The case is not rare that Blacks do not go to church because they do not have decent clothes, or because they have to stay in bed on cold days since they don't have what is necessary to protect themselves from the cold..."[17]

On November 28, Mason was received by Monsignor James McIntyre (later named Archbishop of Los Angeles) to have his *celebret* approved. Mason wrote, "My reception is rather cold...he tells me, 'But Father, why did you come to New York?' And so he continues to ask me questions five or six times every time I try to explain things to him. He tells me that there are other African Missionaries...who established themselves in New Jersey...then they come into the diocese to <u>collect</u> funds, and 'we cannot control them!' He added that they already have too many diocesan priests, and they do not know where to put them." Mason admitted he had difficulty keeping himself from telling McIntyre that he, " had not come <u>to steal his bread</u>." [Emphasis not added][18] Adding to Mason's frustration was his failure to get an immediate interview with Spellman. Due to travel arrangements he made, Mason asked for a later date, but was told he would have to write directly to Spellman.

Mason commented in his diary, "Naturally I do not write, and everything evaporates."

What Mason did not know was that Spellman was then taking part in negotiations between the American president and Pope Pius XII to permit an American representative to the Vatican. From October to December, 1939, Spellman traveled to and from Washington, D.C. as he and the Apostolic Delegate, Amleto Cicognani, acted as intermediaries in these negotiations. The result was the appointment of Myron Taylor as the president's personal representative to the Vatican.

VISITING THE SOUTH.

On December 3, Mason left for Baltimore as the guest of Father Louis Pastorelli, Superior General of the Josephites, a society dedicated solely to work among the American Negro since 1893. Mason's diary tells us, "Father Pastorelli gave me such good advice, especially with regard to not accepting any place in the South or in the West where one cannot make a living because of the poverty of the inhabitants. He says the missionaries of Lyons made that mistake...Father Gillard, an authority on the problem of the Blacks in America, also gives me interesting advice and information."[19]

John T. Gillard was Pastorelli's personal secretary described later as "his most articulate spokesman." Gillard took Mason to schools, churches, and other institutions for Blacks in the Baltimore area, one of which was served by the Oblate Sisters of Providence; another was the academy run by the School Sisters of Notre Dame where black resident students of Saint Frances Academy were giving a band recital to visiting white students. Mason wrote that Gillard made "similar excursions for promotion reasons and in order to remove racial prejudice and arouse feelings of acceptance and brotherhood between blacks and whites. " It is necessary, Gillard told him, "to work on two fronts, that is, ignorance, prejudice, fanaticism, and distrust of the Blacks on one side, and the aversion, and racial prejudice of the Whites on the other." Mason questioned this, "I get the impression that Father Gillard talks too much of race on the natural level. And it seems to me...this will reinforce and rekindle the preconceived aversion that is instinctive...it gives me the impression he was not speaking of equality in Christ, but rather of equality on the natural level..."[20] That Mason made a distinction between spiritual and natural equality is surprising since, in his *Plan for the Regeneration of Africa*, Daniel Comboni, founder of Mason's society, emphasized a connection between evangelization and human improvement.

On December 6, Mason visited the Apostolic Delegate, Archbishop Amleto Cicognani in Washington, D.C. When he arrived at the delegation, Cicognnani quickly appeared and greeted him warmly, "What do you wish me to do for you?" he asked. Mason replied, "Your Excellency, I would ask you to give me a letter of recommendation for the bishops I will visit."

Cicognani responded, "But I have no direct authority over the bishops. And a general letter does not amount to much. Every bishop thinks that another bishop will help you, and thus you risk receiving help from nobody." Cicognani told Mason he would give him a letter of recommendation for Monsignor McNicholas, Archbishop of Cincinnati, whom he knew quite well. McNicholas, he said, was open to religious orders, and if he could not accept Mason's society, Cicognani would then ask him to recommend Mason to some other bishop.

Satisfied, Mason visited black churches and schools in Alexandria, Virginia, where he saw "the segregation between the races, and the Blacks on trains and buses have their coach or section , or they have to stay in the back." He was told that priests working among Blacks in the South had to conform to segregation directives in order not to upset the Whites and make it impossible to continue their work. Schools and churches were segregated, and Blacks attending a "white church" had to sit in the rear. Lacking a balanced historical perspective of America's history, Mason wrote, "The racial prejudices...rampant in the South... are inconceivable in a democratic society like the United States. The fault, many say, was a little bit with Lincoln, who wished to abolish slavery all at once, and to give the same rights to the Whites and the Blacks. And so it happened that where the majority were Blacks, the Whites had to suffer such great injustices at the hands of the Blacks who were set in charge that they still remember it today with much rancor..."[21]

IN THE NORTHEAST.

Mason returned to Washington to collect his recommendation from Cicognani, then traveled to Philadelphia where Father Walsh, pastor of a black church believed there might be a need for priests. But the ministry in question had already been given to the Redemptorists. Mason also visited the convent and one of the schools founded by Mother Katharine Drexel noted for her extensive financing of African American and Indian causes. He then spoke to several lay organizations in Philadelphia, New York City, and Metuchen, New Jersey. In Newark, Father Stanton , the diocesan Director of the Propagation of the Faith, told Mason, "You missionaries do not seem to realize that we are under orders to send everything to Rome, You just walk into the office and ask for help. " Mason wrote, "I apologize and make a thousand excuses and protests. He lets me go, promising that some help would be forthcoming. And, as a matter of fact,...he will send me thirty-five dollars for Mass intentions."

On December 14, Mason met with Bishop Richard J. Cushing, then Director of the Propagation of the Faith in the Boston archdiocese. Mason described him as a kind and gentle man, "...without hesitation he promised me: 1. Fifty dollars as his personal Christmas gift for a typewriter... 2. A hundred dollars for a hundred Mass intentions every month to be sent to Father Zanini for our missionaries for all of 1940." Cushing explained he could give no more due to a commitment to a young missionary from the Hudson Bay in desperate need of medical attention. The clergy of his archdiocese, he said, gave most generously of their surpluses "due to the personal contact that he [Cushing] was able to establish throughout the diocese..." Cushing believed "he should not be removed to avoid seeing this successor in difficulty, or the offerings decreasing..."[22] And in fact, Cushing would remain in Boston as Archbishop, succeeding Cardinal William Henry O'Connell in 1944.

At Lynn, Massachusetts, Monsignor McGlinchey introduced Mason to the economics of the parochial school system. Mason was amazed that. "He requires that the Catholic boys attend parochial school and [he] asks the parents to pay the expenses, and they...pay and send their children...while they could instead send them to a public school which is very close, has magnificent buildings, school materials to throw away, and doesn't cost a penny."

Back in New York City, Father Edward Kramer, Director of the Commission for Catholic Mission Work among the colored People and the Indians, greeted him with kindness, but was "serious, dry, almost embarrassed..." He told Mason he thought Mason's superiors had given him "a bad job," that he should have written first and been invited by the bishops to come. Mason wrote, "And to think that other people had given me the very opposite advice, not to write, but to present myself personally and ask outright because American people, even in their own kindness, are very volatile, and we should not give them the time to change the good decisions that they might take..."

Mason's next stop was Buffalo, New York. It was a few days before Christmas. The bishop was leaving for Florida, so nothing could be done. A visit to the Director of the Propagation of the Faith brought no better results.

Mason now realized the poor timing of a visit during the holidays. An entire month had passed since he arrived in America, and there was no sign of progress, only growing evidence that he would fail. Those he spoke to were not encouraging. Even Italian pastors in Buffalo were short of resources and refused him funds. Buffalo, on the shores of Lake Erie, is known for its brutally cold winters. Several feet of snow on the ground in December is not uncommon. People were busy with plans for Christmas, but Mason could not have been rejoicing. He decided to visit Niagara Falls, perhaps to meditate on his predicament.[23]

OPPORTUNITIES IN THE MIDWEST.

Mason headed west to Cleveland, Ohio, where a friend helped him prepare a circular to distribute to over one hundred Italian pastors. Bishop Joseph Schrembs was "very kind," but he had just permitted the White Fathers to establish in his diocese. Monsignor Tracey, at the Office of the Propaganda for the Faith, was " a little rough" at first, but he told Mason, "Since you are Italian...I cannot turn you down," and he wrote Mason a check for one hundred dollars. Like other Comboni Missionaries, Mason began his mission with virtually empty pockets, and he received Tracey's check with a "thanks be to God." Word came from Detroit that Cardinal Mooney would not be able to meet with him. At this point, the words of Mason's superior not to seek a place "around the Lakes" must have seemed prophetic. Mason continued to Chicago for an appointment with Bishop William David O'Brien, President of the Extension Society. O'Brien was one of two auxiliary bishops to the recently deceased Cardinal George Mundelein. The other was Bishop Bernard James Sheil. The late cardinal had adversaries on several important issues, but the one that irritated some members of the American hierarchy the most was his outspoken support of President Franklin Roosevelt. Although Bishop Sheil had been favored by both Mundelein and Roosevelt as successor to the Cardinal, this favoritism would work against him. It was during the interregnum period after Mundelein's death that Mason met with O'Brien, Sheil's close associate.

Mason learned from O'Brien that the Extension Society collected funds for home missions and had an account "of various millions from which every year it distributes among various dioceses and missions to the Indians and Blacks of the South." O'Brien made Mason some forthright and generous proposals. He agreed to give lodging to two priests in his own house and to obtain all the faculties for them to work temporarily in the diocese. He said that the two fathers would have to stay in Chicago until the new ordinary could give them one of the twelve parishes that were being transferred from the Whites to the Blacks.. If this could not be done in Chicago, O'Brien would help find a place among bishops who were his friends. Mason wrote in his diary, "He advises that I telegraph the Superior General immediately so that he may send the two fathers."[24] Mason sent the following message to Verona:

"PLACE FOUND CHICAGO LETTER FOLLOWS"

Due to this salutary encounter, Mason decided to leave for Italy on January 13 instead of January 20 as previously scheduled., and he wrote to the two fathers who would follow him, Fathers Accorsi and Ferrara, to wait for him in Italy. He then traveled to Des Moines, Iowa, where he met Monsignor Luigi Ligutti, the Executive Secretary of the National Catholic Rural Life Conference. Ligutti gave Mason a tour of his parish and experimental school outside of Des Moines which Mason called a "model of an agrarian school both elementary and high." In St. Louis, Mason visited seventy-eight year old Archbishop John J. Glennon, described in the diary as a "tall person, old, somewhat dry, but kind. He listened to me standing up and concludes that for the time being, he does not see a way to help me..." At the Director of the Propagation of the Faith Office, Mason was told that two missionaries had already visited Monsignor Carroll, and on leaving the office, Mason passed by a Jesuit from China waiting his turn at the door.

Although recommended by his superior as the ideal place to visit, Cincinnati was Mason's last stop. He stayed with the Scalabrini priest, Father Molinari, pastor of Sacred Heart Church. Molinari described what life was like for priests in America. His view, shared by other Italian clergy, was that American priests' spiritual lives were neglected due to the bishops' greater interest in money. Parish account books received more attention than the spiritual welfare of souls, "Much is said about the duty to support the church, to go to Mass, and to practice abstinence," Mason noted in his diary, "but modesty and any personal control are less known."[25]

THE CINCINNATI PROPOSAL.

Cicognani had kept his promise. His letter to Archbishop John T. McNicholas of Cincinnati had said that, while he had never before met Mason, he knew the missionaries he represented and, "This Congregation has done excellent work in Africa, and desires now to plan and develop useful work among the Negroes here." Although Mason should consult other members of the hierarchy, Cicognani asked McNicholas "to interest yourself in advising Mason" and to "assist him in meeting the Bishops who could welcome this Congregation into its Negro missions."[26]

A Dominican, John T. McNicholas came to Cincinnati with an exceptional resume. Ordained in 1901, and groomed by his provincials for leadership roles, he received his Lectorate in Sacred Theology at the *Collegio San Tommaso* in Rome and gained fluency in the Italian language. Sent to New York in 1908, he built a national identity for the Holy Name Society, and in 1916, he was appointed *socius*, or counselor, at Dominican headquarters in Rome. There McNicholas made friends with powerful members of the hierarchy including Dominican Cardinal Tommaso Boggiani who assisted in a major reformulation of procedures for the selection of American bishops. Boggiani introduced McNicholas to Pope Benedict XV who often called upon him as an unofficial advisor on American affairs. In 1918, McNicholas was appointed Bishop of the Diocese of Duluth in Minnesota where he had a reputation as an authoritarian administrator, but one intensely interested in the intellectual formation of his priests. In 1925, by a quirk of fate, McNicholas was chosen to fill the Cincinnati See when Bishop Joseph Chartrand refused the appointment.[27]

Events moved quickly in Cincinnati. On his arrival, Mason spoke to Monsignor Freking, the Director of the Propagation of the Faith, who invited him to lunch. Following lunch, Mason met with Mc Nicholas. The archbishop apologized for not answering his letter containing Cicognani's endorsement, but he assured Mason he would help him. But first he asked Mason if there had not been "some other more important city" in which Mason's confreres could settle. Mason noted in his diary, "I answered that after contacting almost all of the bishops of the East and Midwest, as I had been advised by Father Pastorelli, he was now the last resort after all the negative replies received." McNicholas told Mason to meet with the pastors of the five black parishes in Cincinnati, After that, if he still wanted work in Cincinnati, the archbishop would meet with him again. Father Backhus, one of the priests referred to by the archbishop, made arrangements to pick Mason up the following night.

At this meeting, there were six diocesan priests representing five black parishes. For two hours they discussed their parishes. They told Mason that though poor, Blacks were generous and able to meet most of the expenses for church, school, rectory, and convent. However, subsidies were needed for extraordinary expenses, and these were provided either by the Bishop, the Extension Society, the Indian and Negro Missions...or by pastors' friends who allowed a collection to be taken up in their parish. For this reason, a pastor who worked among the Blacks could not provide for his old age. The priests spoke about the sad case of the newest parish established in June, 1939,[28] among the city's middle-class Blacks (professionals and white collar workers). The present pastor of that parish volunteered that "after visiting over sixty families, he had not been able to get a single registration for catechism class. It was agreed this was because, when the church was inaugurated the previous June, one priest was heard to say, 'Tell those niggers to shut up...' Members of the black community overheard this, and it created general resentment and malcontent." Despite this setback, the pastors told Mason, the work was rewarding and giving good results represented by forty to one hundred conversions a year. When Mason asked the priests if they had any objection to his asking for a parish for the Comboni Missionaries, "Three priests stood up and offered their own!" The meeting then ended with "refreshments and good booze..."

On January 8, 1940, after being interviewed by a reporter from the *Catholic Telegraph Register*, Mason had lunch with the archbishop. With him was Father Rigo, presumably a Scalabrini. Also at lunch were a doctor, the Archbishop's secretary, McNicholas' brother, and the bishop of Denver, Colorado. Later, McNicholas withdrew with Mason into his private office and asked him what he had learned from the previous evening. Mason said he thought the situation in Cincinnati was not very different from what Comboni Missionaries experienced in Africa, and this would be an asset in America. McNicholas responded with an offer of a parish, but the two Comboni fathers who would come to Cincinnati should act as assistants until they learned the local customs. Later, they could receive full responsibility if they worked in harmony with other pastors. Mason promised to do this "even at the cost of personal gain..." adding that his confreres would be "grateful for any advice from the chancery, the neighboring pastors, or the Archbishop."[29]

A SERIES OF SURPRISES

Without noting whether or not he communicated McNicholas's offer to his General Administration, the diary reveals that Mason left Cincinnati on the evening of January 9, 1940, and headed for Washington, D.C. There he thanked the Apostolic Delegate, then stopped in Philadelphia to say good-bye to the Italian priests. Finally he left for New York in order to leave for Italy since he expected Fathers Accorsi and Ferrara to wait for him there. But Verona had already acted. At New York, Mason found Father Hamlet Accorsi waiting for him. After receiving Mason's telegram from Chicago, his superiors had arranged to send Accorsi to America. Since Mason makes no mention in his diary of informing Verona about McNicholas's offer, his superiors were probably not aware that Cincinnati was an option. It is assumed that the two missionaries' decision to then leave for Chicago was in obedience to their superiors' expectations. Telegraphing Bishop O'Brien to expect their arrival, Mason and Accorsi boarded a westbound train. At the Extension Society's office, they found that O'Brien was out of town, and Mason wrote, "And, therefore, I will no longer be on time to leave with the *Rex*."

During this delay, Bishop Francis C. Kelley, of the Diocese of Oklahoma City, invited Mason and Accorsi to a meeting. Kelley, the founder of the Extension Society, offered Mason "a parish among the Whites, originally German, at Manchester, which is one hundred fifty miles from Oklahoma City...I thank him, and then I mention to him the offer I have received from Cincinnati." Kelley advised him to take the Cincinnati offer without hesitation. Mason wrote, as if it had no bearing on the matter, "then he [Kelley] goes on to speak of something else: politics and history."

On January 16, Bishop O'Brien received the Comboni priests. About this meeting, Mason reported, "*Quantum mutatus ab illo*!!!" ["How changed from his earlier self!!!"] O'Brien asked Mason whether he had accepted Kelley's offer. Mason said he "would like to take advantage of his [O'Brien's] hospitality...and after some months, if no opening is possible in Chicago, I would go to Cincinnati." Upon hearing this, O'Brien reportedly said with some excitement that, "he is sorry, but that there must have been some misunderstanding, that he could not possibly introduce new priests in the diocese at a time when there was no ordinary, that his house was not very big, that they were always busy, that he would not be able to obtain faculties and so on..." Mason wrote, "I was dumbfounded! (This was one more case to confirm that saying about Americans changing with their climate, and you must take them at their word on the spot)."

While Mason smarted from this rejection, O'Brien made arrangements for Accorsi to stay at a local Catholic hospital. He said he hoped they did not believe he had changed his mind or reneged on his commitment. His offer had been only in case they received no other. Mason wrote, "He was advising me to grab the proposal from Cincinnati." Mason added that he left O'Brien with "words choked in my throat." He could not know that O'Brien undoubtedly had discovered that it was not his co-auxiliary, Bishop Sheil, who would be the next Archbishop of Chicago. Displeased with President Roosevelt's open endorsement of Sheil, the Vatican instead appointed Archbishop Samuel Stritch from Milwaukee, Wisconsin, to fill the Chicago See.[30]

Accorsi stayed in Chicago as a guest of the Sisters at the hospital, and Mason proceeded to New York where he hoped to find McNicholas's formal offer. The Archbishop's letter of acceptance said that the Comboni Missionaries were accepted to work among "our poor Negroes per modum experimenti" (by way of experiment), and that "If it seems advisable to open a Juniorate in a Diocese like Cincinnati, I shall further encourage your Fathers to undertake this work if their parochial endeavors are successful..." Mason copied the letter to Accorsi, and wrote a note thanking McNicholas. He told him that Father Accorsi, who had "long experience...in southern Sudan and in Ethiopia...would proceed the following week to Cincinnati."[31]

It is left to the reader of Mason's diary to sort out questions left unanswered, for example, why did Mason tell McNicholas that Cincinnati was his last chance when he believed O'Brien had made him an offer in Chicago? As it will be seen, Mason wrote at least part of his diary after leaving the United States. It is possible that he kept some notes during his visit here, made others on board the ship back to Italy, and in putting these together, some inaccuracies in chronology were made.

AFTERTHOUGHTS

On board the *SS Vulcania*, Mason tallied the statistics of his trip -22,082 kilometers (approximately 13,801 miles) traveled by train, ship, car, tram, and subway; --13 "important" cities and 9 smaller ones; -visits to 11 bishops and archbishops; letters to 10 more; -received 21 no's, 2 yes's, 1 doubtful (responses); -visited 10 directors of the Propagation of the Faith; -wrote to 125 Italian pastors for offerings; and spent $866.00 and collected $950.00. Americans, he thought, were indeed generous and a truly democratic people. Attendance at Sunday Mass in large cities was "far above that of the best cities in Italy." The priests in the U.S. were zealous "in their own way...to us they may give the impression of being not so strongly based spiritually." He admitted his conclusions could be flawed, but Catholic practice in America seemed to consist of "not committing sin, observing the laws of the Church, [and] asking sacrifices of money for one's church...Prayer, mortification, sacrifice do not seem to be talked about much."[32]

Mason's views on American Catholicism reflected those of Father Molinari and other Italian priests. His conclusions about racism were somewhat flawed due to his limited knowledge of slavery in America. But his diary leaves an indelible picture of a man with courage to explore a country virtually unknown to him, with the necessary audacity to present his case to major leaders in the American Church, and with the determination to persist despite incredible odds. Mason would return to America, but only because of the men who followed him. Father Hamlet Accorsi who confronted the rigors of African mission life, would admit later that these were minor hindrances compared with establishing a foundation in America.

2. The Cornerstone

When Archbishop McNicholas's official invitation reached him, Father Hamlet Accorsi left Chicago for Cincinnati. Arriving on January 24, 1940, in the middle of a snowstorm, he joined two diocesan priests at Holy Trinity Church, Raymond H. Backhus, the pastor, and Father Charles E. Ford, an assistant.

Along with an apology for not accompanying him to Cincinnati, Mason sent Accorsi the journal he kept with its candid commentaries on the bishops, priests and others he visited. Accorsi was advised to keep these opinions to himself since, formed in haste, they could easily prove inaccurate. Mason said he warned the Institute's General Administration "not to look for money" from America, but whatever became available should remain with the new foundation. He added, "I told [them] at Verona that on you rests the burden and honor of the foundation..."[1] With these words, Mason conveyed his confidence in the man who would provide the major thrust to the new province. Not just in Cincinnati, but on the East Coast, West Coast, and many states between, people would be captivated by Accorsi's colorful stories from Africa, his obvious sincerity, and his total dedication to the missions. He would become, therefore, the cornerstone of the Comboni foundation in America.

THE MYSTERY OF ACCORSI

Comboni missionaries who knew him paint a rather forbidding picture of Accorsi. They claim he led an extremely ascetic lifestyle, and maintained a cold and aloof air when approached by younger priests for advice. He spoke only when necessary and then was often caustic and critical. The picture lay people draw of Accorsi is of another man altogether. They recall their children gathering round him to hear his stories, and they remember him as devoted to his society but at home with their families. When lay people and Comboni missionaries' views are combined, Accorsi appears as both courageous, yet cautious; generous to the missions, yet exacting of himself and confreres; witty and charming in public, yet brusque to confreres. Examining documents from his seminary and early mission days shows Accorsi to have been far more complex than many suspected.

Accorsi was never strong as a child, and when he entered the seminary at the age of ten, he was quite thin, and his complexion led the other boys to call him "Darkie." His mother, Venusta, operated a home industry making shoe parts while also caring for her children and household tasks. His father, Benedict, a director of road maintenance in the Bologna province; was a man of unqualified integrity and courage who thwarted a plot by local communists to disrupt devotions at a nearby shrine. He has been described as a stern father who, with one whistle, gathered all his children around him like little soldiers.[2]

Accorsi's devotion to this family is documented in a brief diary that begins with his birth date and ends a year after going to mission. Two crises are mentioned. One occurred in March, 1919, when he was sixteen years old and "fell seriously ill" with an unnamed malady. He was forced to return to the hospital several times, finally undergoing an operation in February of 1920. A second crisis was the death of his five-year-old sister when he wrote, "Dear Valentina died on...the feast of the Solemnity of St. Joseph. 'Little angel, I will never forget you.'" His visits to his home are remembered as experiences of "affection and holy intimacy." After ordination, and before he departed for Africa, there were a series of goodbyes as family members met him at Martignone, Mirandola, Como, Milano, and Brescia. Once at his Tonga mission, Accorsi described these scenes to Mr. Accorsi: "Dear Father, I lived once more in these days the painful experience of our separation, and I found myself in your midst, very sad against my will, and you in so much in pain. I still hear the noise of the car...coming to take me away...and then the last embrace...and the departure in that rainy and gloomy fall morning...I left you and mother... sustained only by that strength the Lord gives to the ones He calls." To his sister and little brothers he wrote, "How beautiful is family life... I think that if the Lord had not wanted me to live here, I would have liked to live all the intimate sweetness of family life..."[3]

Accorsi was no longer the frail youth he once had been. He was then in a territory scorched by an equatorial sun and converted into swampland by torrential rains. Swarming mosquitoes forced him and his confreres to cover every inch of skin, and locusts blackened the skies. This marsh-like, roadless earth was home to the tall, proud Shilluks, a fierce tribe whose warriors rarely put down their weapons. Accorsi not only survived the climate, the insects, the heat, and the swamps, he was a priest who could kill and eat crocodiles, and travel long trails to visit the sick in distant villages.

Accorsi's love for the Shilluks grew, and years later, when the young priest's leg became infected, he risked his life by delaying treatment, so reluctant was he to leave this new-found family. He was not forgotten by this family. A young Shilluk boy later wrote to Accorsi, "Is your stomach bitter with the country of the Shilluk, or did your head forget us?" And as late as 1977, a Comboni missionary heard old people among the Shilluks talking about "Abuna Cursi" (Father Accorsi).

In 1936, after recuperating from the leg infection, Accorsi studied English in England, then was assigned to Ethiopia as a military chaplain. It was an assignment complicated by political, social, and religious changes.[4] Accorsi's life was rife with difficult assignments. One of these was to begin a new Comboni foundation in America. But his devotion to his family and to the Shilluks foreshadowed his work in the United States. He would gravitate to people who reminded him of those he left behind.

MCNICHOLAS AND HIS "NEGRO APOSTOLATE"

The first Comboni missionaries in America knew little about the history of slavery, the United States, or African American culture. They expected that serving African Americans would be similar to serving Africans. What they did not understand was what Carl Fisher, an African American bishop, later observed: "...slavery in North America was unlike any other experience of slavery in that the actual humanity of the person was denied."[5]

Cincinnati had been one of the first cities black migrants from the South passed through on their way to better jobs in the North.[6] By the 1920s, its Negro population was estimated as 7.5% of the city's total, a significantly higher rate than in most northern cities. During the Civil War, the Ohio River had served as the boundary between the slave state of Kentucky and the free state of Ohio. The impact of this was still apparent as late as 1949 when a Cincinnati priest wrote, "Thousands of people live in the river cities of Kentucky...but commute to work in Cincinnati. It is therefore impossible, so they say, to [hire] a Negro bank clerk because it might 'offend' the Kentucky customers."[7]

Shortly after his 1925 installation, the Archbishop of Cincinnati, John T. McNicholas, heard from the pastor of Holy Trinity Church that the exodus of German parishioners from his West End parish was followed by an "influx of Negroes." The pastor reported that "Within a radius of five block[s] there are more that (sic) 3,000 colored children attending the public schools, which would lead us to believe that the colored population...numbers more than 10,000...I think not more than 20 are Catholic. Therefore we may conclude that this is a real missionary field."[8]

Soon after this, McNicholas issued a pastoral letter proclaiming, "To the colored people in the vicinity of Holy Trinity Church, we extend a cordial invitation to attend divine service there..."[9] Reverend Leo M. Walsh was named the new pastor, and the following year, the Sisters of the Blessed Sacrament staffed Holy Trinity School at which 300 African American children were enrolled.[10] Two years later, Father Walsh opened Madonna High School, the first and only secondary school for black students in Ohio at that time. This was also staffed by the Sisters of the Blessed Sacrament.[11] In 1927, at the "Greatest Holy Name Meeting" in the archdiocese, six hundred people gathered to "see for themselves the wonders that have been wrought" now that it was a "Colored" mission. These "wonders" included 140 baptisms, 200 confirmation candidates, and 125 children preparing for First Communion. Prominent black Catholics met the delegates, a black band performed, and a black poet, Raymond Dandridge, wrote a poem, the last lines rejoicing that:

Yes, we'll sing a glad Hosanna/ To the Holy Name, Divine,
Marching 'neath the righteous banner/ Where there is no "Color Line"

McNicholas was proclaimed "the redeemer to raise the Colored people from the deplorable condition into which they are plunged by reason of being segregated into the worst districts" of Cincinnati.[12] But his battle against racism had barely begun. Father Walsh raised disturbing issues concerning racism in the Cincinnati archdiocese. First, two prominent and educated Catholic Negroes had been refused admission to the commercial high school of Saint Xavier. Second, St. Joseph's Cemetery Board had refused to sell burial lots to Negroes. Third, Negroes had also been barred from Good Samaritan Hospital, and Negro publisher William Dabney was about to publish affidavits to that effect in his newspaper, *The Union*. Furthermore, Walsh reported that retreats could not be held for the "Colored men of Cincinnati," since the majority of the men's work demanded their presence late at night and early in the morning, even on Saturday and Sunday.[13]

In 1937, Cincinnati suffered a disastrous flood when the Ohio River spread through the main business district. This spurred interest in a master plan that would end flooding and invigorate the central business district. As this plan gathered support, it became clear that Cincinnati's West End was targeted for "slum clearance." Faced with this prospect, pastors of its black parishes were more likely to neglect expensive repairs. Effects of the Great Depression had already made it difficult to raise the funds needed to operate schools, pay nuns' salaries, and repair aging physical plants. But before Accorsi came to Holy Trinity, there had been courageous priests in Cincinnati who took up the challenge of serving African Americans. Among them were Leo Walsh at Holy Trinity; Clarence Schmitt at St. Edward's who cashed in his life insurance policy to keep his parish going;[14] and Raymond Backhus who welcomed the Comboni priests to Holy Trinity. These men were among a cadre of diocesan priests who volunteered to serve in the poorest black parishes of Cincinnati. Given these conditions, it is not difficult to understand why, when Edward Mason asked them if they objected to his asking for a black parish in Cincinnati, three offered him their own.

IN A CINCINNATI GHETTO

From the steps of Holy Trinity Church, one could barely see Fountain Square and the Carew Tower, the center of downtown Cincinnati. In the Square, the Tyler-Davidson Fountain graced a tree-lined park, the lights of the Albee theater's marque beckoned, and gracious dining rooms, mahogany-paneled hotels, and upscale retailers were available to all but Negroes. A few blocks west of this, Holy Trinity Church was surrounded by tenements. To its south, train tracks wound around warehouses near the Ohio river. Depots of the Chesapeake and Ohio, the Baltimore and Ohio, the Cincinnati, Columbus, and Cleveland, and the Cincinnati, Dayton, and Hamilton lines all converged here.[15] Damage from the movement of trains was reported by a pastor as early as 1925, "The brick work of the tower above the struts has been jarred so much that it has loosened, cracked, and bulged; at least two layers of brick...can be seen."

Accorsi found that some of Holy Trinity's former parishioners continued to visit the church and contribute time and money to the "Apostolate of the Negro." Several members of the Buse family were among these benefactors, and in January of 1940, two of them met the newly arrived Comboni priest. On leaving the moderate temperatures of Ethiopia, Accorsi had no thought of the winter climate of Midwest America or its January temperatures that hover near 0°F.[16] When Carl and Marie Buse met him, Accorsi had no coat, hat, gloves, or any necessities for the frigid weather. Without hesitation, Mr. Buse took him shopping. His son John still remembers the Comboni priest returning to their home wearing his new attire, a modestly tailored black raincoat: "'Look at this,' Father Hamlet said to my mother showing off the new coat. He was so pleased." To Marie and Carl Buse, Accorsi was like a member of their family. Carl introduced him to his circle of contacts among businessmen. Marie held teas for him so women actively involved in church and community groups could meet him. For the rest of his life, Accorsi maintained contact with the Buses, often addressing his letters to them with "Dear Mother" or "Dear Dad."[17]

While Accorsi was getting settled in Cincinnati, another Comboni priest was preparing to go to America. Father Dominic Ferrara, who had advised his Superior General to send Mason to America, was himself directed there. After a brief visit with his elderly parents, Ferrara boarded the ocean liner *Rex* on February 7, 1940. At New York City, he contacted Accorsi, but received word there was no room for him at Holy Trinity's rectory, and that it might be better if Ferrara returned to Italy. In a letter from Mason to Accorsi in February, this delay in Ferrara's journey to Cincinnati takes another slant. Mason wrote, "I suggested to Father Ferrara that, before he comes to Cincinnati, he stop for some months at Metuchen [New Jersey] to practice English so...he will not face some language difficulties in the diocese...I leave to your prudence to do everything in such a way that Cincinnati will not realize that the Apostolic Delegate, who had asked McNicholas for help, had essentially promised that the fathers he would send would have previously stayed in England!!!" Mason had carried the letter from Cicognani to McNicholas endorsing the Comboni Missionaries. He knew that the Apostolic Delegate had written, "The fact that it ["The African Missions of Verona"[1]] has some houses in England and that a number of its members speak English must be mentioned..."[18]

Ferrara made friends easily while on board ship, and they found him lodgings in New York. After a short stay with the Scalabrinis at St. Joachim, he remained with the Brothers of the Sacred Heart at Metuchen, New Jersey, for several months. In April, He received an offer from the Scalabrini Superior General in New York. Father Cavicchi advised him that "a beautiful house on the shores of the Hudson [River] not far from New York" could be donated to a religious congregation. Ferrara found it to have "the beauty of our 'Lago Maggiore,' a nice castle in the town of Poughkeepsie, situated on the top of a little hill...Every room was furnished... everything was in perfect

---

[1] The Comboni Missionaries, then known as Verona Fathers.

order..." In his diary, Ferrara wrote, "I informed Father General of the deal, letting him know that he was still in time to send all the fathers who were still in England, and who would certainly be confined in a concentration camp in case of conflict between England and Italy...I didn't receive an answer." Ferrara later discovered that his proposal had been considered, but the General Administration delayed action on it. As Ferrara ruefully commented, "This decision was fatal." It was fatal because Mussolini entered the European conflict in late May of 1940, and his declaration of war on June 10 ended all hope of bringing Comboni missionaries from England to America. A few days before hostilities broke out, Italian priests were invited by the authorities to leave their residences and were confined on the Isle of Man. And so, as Father Ferrara commented in his diary, "...a precious occasion was allowed to escape us!"[19]

A Humble Resistance

In response to questions from Accorsi, Mason wrote back from Italy, "I think that it is rather strange that the Archbishop would entrust to us foreigners the best parish for the Blacks in Cincinnati." But to take charge of Holy Trinity seemed like too much responsibility. He advised Accorsi, "I think it would be better to have a parish of less importance where we could more easily succeed in fulfilling the expectations of the people and of the local clergy." He praised Accorsi for his caution for "if we jump into a parish now, we would not give a good impression to the local clergy."[20]

In mid-July, Ferrara was called to Cincinnati as an assistant at St. Edward/St. Ann's parish, a merged African American church.[21] Later that summer, Accorsi was informed that Trinity's pastor, Father Backhus, would be moving to St. Edward's, and Father Ford would remain at Holy Trinity until Accorsi could take over.[22] In McNicholas's eyes, Accorsi was excessively cautious. In November, 1940, the Apostolic Delegate asked the archbishop's opinion on Accorsi and Ferrara. McNicholas was positive about their work, but had a few caveats. "The Italian Fathers...seem to be earnest good priests. They are...timid up to the present." McNicholas blamed this on language problems. Accorsi worked hard preparing for sermons and instructions, but hesitated to give regular instructions to children or adults. Father Ferrara had a greater handicap with the language, but "seems extraordinarily gifted in music." He was teaching the children and adults to sing, and had more success than anyone else in the fifteen years of the Negro Apostolate. This pleased the archbishop for he had been "very keen about having our Negro children and adults trained as singers." He ended with this comment, "I have been anxious to make Father Accorsi *Vicarius Oeconomus* of the parish in which he is residing, but with real humility and also with an excessive fear of the work, he has asked that this appointment be delayed." None of these concerns of McNicholas prevented the Apostolic Delegate from sending his blessing to Accorsi.[23]

On the eve of the new year, Superior General Anthony Vignato sent congratulations to Accorsi and Ferrara for gaining so much good will, affection, and esteem in their new environment. He said that in mid-December he had an audience with the Holy Father, and that Pope Pius XII, "showed his kind interest in your work, knows Cincinnati and Archbishop McNicholas well, and appreciates the cordial welcome he gave you because of your zeal for the conversion of the Blacks. Paternally and affectionately, he blesses you and your benefactors. The Cardinal Prefect congratulates you also." In late 1941, Father Ford was assigned elsewhere, and Accorsi was named pastor of Holy Trinity, with Ferrara appointed his assistant.[24]

UNITED STATES CATHOLICS AND THE WAR

It was not until the bombing of Pearl Harbor on December 7, 1941, that the debate ended on whether or not the war on the Continent should involve the United States. Americans were still harboring disillusionment about World War I which they had expected would bring lasting peace; going again to the aid of what they considered unrejuvenated European aristocrats and politicians was as politically popular as communism. For American Catholics, communism appeared to be the real threat. A letter to the Archbishop of Baltimore from a man belonging to the "Christian Front" expressed the view that "the treachery of the Communist forces in their midst [and the] War party [was dragging] our peaceful country into a war that is not of our making."

The Christian Front was a national association formed by Father Charles Coughlin in Royal Oaks, Michigan. Coughlin's earlier radio broadcasts had supported President Roosevelt and the labor movement. But later, he criticized the President, believed unions were of communist origin, turned anti-Semitic, and voiced the opinion that "warmongering was a weapon of the communists." Members of the American hierarchy were powerless to do anything that could be viewed as censorship.[25]

Coughlin represented one extreme of Catholic attitudes on the European conflict. But after Germany invaded Russia, Roosevelt's decision to send arms to Russia was opposed even by moderate Catholics. A poll taken by Lord Halifax, British Ambassador to the United States, revealed that ninety percent of American Catholics opposed aid to Russia. A major roadblock to such aid was a papal encyclical that, if literally interpreted, prohibited cooperation with communist Russia. Archbishop Mooney of Detroit urged the Vatican to reconsider this interpretation. On September 9, 1941, Roosevelt's envoy, Myron Taylor, took a letter from the President to Pope Pius XII asking that the encyclical *Divini Redemptoris* be modified due to the exigencies of the war. The Holy Father agreed that American Catholics could be relieved of their concern about military aid to Russia, but he wanted an American bishop to offer this interpretation of the encyclical. Chosen for this task was Cincinnati's Archbishop McNicholas since "he was known for his reserve and political neutrality, and he could not be accused of having succumbed to government pressure."

In a pastoral letter, McNicholas turned to Pius XI's encyclical *mit bremender Sorge* which drew a distinction between Nazism and the German people, and he extrapolated such a distinction between communism and the Russian people. The pastoral was widely distributed and accepted. After the Japanese attacked Pearl Harbor, and Germany and Italy declared war on the United States, the bishops offered Roosevelt their support, and the debate about the war was ended.[26]

BLESSINGS AND BENEFACTORS

The two Comboni priests in Cincinnati were little affected by war expanding to America. They had to register with the authorities, be fingerprinted, and their travel was slightly restricted. Communication with confreres abroad was difficult (the Vatican and the Red Cross were the only channels of contact with confreres in Italy and those detained in camps by the British). But, with the help of new friends and the local clergy, Accorsi and Ferrara's circle of supporters gradually increased. As his English improved, Accorsi gave talks to clubs and other organizations about missions in Africa. Due to the war, numerous Italian ships were stranded in American ports, and confiscated by the government, their crews confined in detention camps. The Comboni priests visited these detainees at Reading, Pennsylvania, and in Missoula, Montana, where the hall for mass was always packed. Confessions were so numerous that Bishop Gilmore from Helena, who spoke Italian, assisted with the sacraments.

Back in Cincinnati, the two priests were intensely involved in parish work. Besides saying masses and hearing confessions, numerous meetings were scheduled for the large number of parish organizations. In addition, house to house visitations were standard practice for the two missionaries, and this was in addition to sick calls.[27]

Archbishop McNicholas was so pleased with the missionaries' work that, in 1943, he addressed a letter to "all High Schools of the Archdiocese of Cincinnati" asking the principals to welcome Father Accorsi. He told them, "His Congregation...is devoted exclusively to the work among the Negroes...It is our manifest duty to encourage these good Fathers..." McNicholas hoped Accorsi would "secure some good young men who want to dedicate their lives wholly to the Negro Apostolate in his Congregation." This letter granted Accorsi a rare privilege. While it assured the school administrators that Accorsi would not visit their institutions for financial help, the archbishop's enthusiastic support signaled his approval for financial assistance from the Catholic population in the archdiocese.[28]

McNicholas's generosity bordered on paternalism, but it was a benevolent one favoring the Italian missionaries. When he discovered that they were without an automobile, he wrote them that "in America, cars are not just conveniences, they are necessities." He sent Accorsi $500 toward a car's purchase, adding, "I think it is very important that you purchase a new auto, rather than a second-handed one. If you do not have sufficient funds...please let me know, and I will help you out..." Like a father to a young son, the archbishop cautioned, "It is important that you have a secure place to keep your car at Holy Trinity and that you carry sufficient insurance on it...Please do not fail to go to some school where you can be taught by expert men how to drive." After taking driving lessons, Accorsi reported to McNicholas that he could not find a car for less than $1,300, and that seemed too much. At this point, Carl Buse introduced Accorsi to his brother, Ray Buse, a long-time contributor to the "Negro Apostolate." Ray Buse had contacts among automobile dealers, and he told Accorsi, "you choose the car...and I [will] pay the rest above the $500..." Accorsi was amazed at this unsolicited generosity.[29]

Although Holy Trinity parishioners were generous according to their means, and the archdiocese paid for the priests' salaries and for major repairs, credit for the financial viability of Holy Trinity must be shared with benefactors among lay people. They ran bazaars, organized festivals, and supported the missionaries whether at Holy Trinity, or at later assignments. By 1944, both Accorsi and Ferrara's work had gained the attention of the broader community. A "noted lady pianist of Cincinnati," Mrs. Ann Meale Di Girolamo, was about to undergo an operation that could end her career, but before she entered the hospital, she gave a benefit concert for the two missionaries' work. It was organized by a citizens' committee on which Carl Buse sat, and it included a dozen other prominent Cincinnatians, including a councilman. This event alone earned $1,200 for Holy Trinity.[30]

Accorsi and Ferrara tended to draw friends from different populations. Accorsi attracted the Irish and German-Americans: the Buses, Detzels, Gormans, Hinkles, Kramers, Millers, Penkers, Reardons, Shoenbergers, Willenbrinks, and Williams. He spoke at their business and social functions, and he could quickly drive the attention of his audience to his point, invariably the African missions. Ferrara, on the other hand, was more at ease with Italian Americans, visiting their homes, their stores, their produce markets, and at Music Hall. He was a friend both to the poorest, most recent immigrant, as well as to those who were well established: the Di Girolamos, Ginocchios, Palazzolos, Spertis, Valerios, and Vellas. "We needed these two different people," a Comboni priest later said, "to introduce the Comboni Missionaries to America."

Ferrara's success at teaching music at Holy Trinity led Archbishop McNicholas to ask him to develop a "real Colored Choir" at other black parishes, one to "give the Negroes a certain prestige and lay emphasis on the work that the Church is trying to do for this neglected race." Ferrara's extraordinary efforts to bring beauty and fine music to Holy Trinity attracted some uncommon friends. Metropolitan Opera stars performing in Cincinnati frequently appeared at Holy Trinity. Crowds would fill the old church to hear Licia Albanese, Vivian Della Chiesa, Giovanni Martinelli, Salvatore Baccaloni, Virgiliao Lazzari, and both Mr. and Mrs. Landi, sing at Sunday Mass. Father Oliver Branchesi, who arrived in the U.S. in 1946, remembers that the famous singers "would have excited any congregation...but our distinguished guests were never applauded, even when their Ave Marias shook the window panes of that huge church...for they were not coming to be applauded. They came to see their friend Father Ferrara.[31]

Ferrara told the Blessed Sacrament nun who taught him English, Sister Gervase, a story that explains these contacts: "Father had studied to become an opera star, but before graduation [he] heard Jesus calling him to the priesthood [and] answered the call. He had a close friend also who studied opera with Father Ferari. (sic) His friend was broken-hearted about the separation...years passed by. Fr. Ferari (sic) heard his friend was singing in a nearby city. Father called on him but was told by a friend that he was at a board meeting and could not be disturbed under any circumstances. Father sat down, and shortly stood up, went to the doors where the meeting was in session, and began singing the last part of the opera [they had] sung before they parted. The door opened with his friend also singing--they clasped each other's arms and finished the opera song together."[32]

THE AFRICAN INFLUENCE

Commenting later on why Accorsi and Ferrara captivated people in both the white and the black communities of Cincinnati, a Comboni priest said it was due to their African experiences. Before they had arrived, he contended, American Catholics tended to look toward the East: Jesuit missions in Patna, India; Maryknoll missions in the Philippines; Marist missions in New Guinea. He thought that stories from Africa that Fathers Accorsi and Ferrara told opened up new horizons to the curious and generous Americans.[33]

While Accorsi and Ferrara were serving at Holy Trinity, two future black priests attended Holy Trinity and St. Ann's schools. Fathers Allen Tarlton, O.S.B., was the oldest of three children belonging to Mrs. Smith, Holy Trinity's housekeeper. Father Clarence R. Rivers, a student at St. Ann's, and later De Porres High School, would become Cincinnati's first black diocesan priest. The vocation decisions of these two priests did not result simply from Accorsi's and Ferrara's influence. But because the Comboni Institute believed that evangelization of Africa depended on indigenous vocations, Accorsi and Ferrara were open to an African priesthood, and this carried over to support African American vocations.

Young Allen Tarlton frequently served mass for Accorsi, and he remembers going with him to serve Benediction at a nearby convent school. He recalled how Dominic Ferrara turned holy day services into breathtaking liturgical celebrations, and how at Christmas, the church was resplendent with flowers, candles, tinsel, and festive greenery. A carefully rehearsed choir and Christmas pageant attracted people from all over the city. Tarlton remembers, "Even when temperatures dropped below zero degrees, and ice slicked the streets, Midnight Mass was packed with people."[34]

In 1952, Tarlton wrote Father Julius Rizzi, then Comboni provincial in America, asking permission for Father Accorsi and (then) pastor of Holy Trinity, Father Alexander Nardi, to come to St. John's Abbey in Collegeville, Minnesota. The occasion was the ceremony at which Tarlton would take his vows as a Benedictine monk. Tarlton told Rizzi, "Father Accorsi was the first one to help me begin my study for the priesthood, and I feel I owe him a special debt of gratitude for being in every sense a true spiritual father to me. I would deem it a privilege to have them both here on the day of my solemn profession as a monk."[35]

Father Clarence Rivers, as a ninth grade student at Madonna High School, had Ferrara as a choir teacher. Now a renowned composer and liturgist, Rivers will never forget the day when Ferrara pulled him out of the boys' section of the school choir and placed him among the sopranos. He later said, "At age thirteen, that was the most embarrassing thing that ever happened to me." After the choir practice, Ferrara asked him to remain behind. Accompanying him at the piano, the Comboni missionary instructed Rivers to sing the scales. When Rivers finished, Ferrara turned to the Blessed Sacrament nun standing nearby and said "I wish I had a dozen voices like this one.!" Father Rivers recalled that, with those words, all embarrassment faded away. Ferrara, he believes, by recognizing his gifted voice, was one of several people who made an impact on the direction of his life. As a result, Ferrara's is one of the names that appear in the dedication of Rivers' first published work, the *American Mass Program.*

"The Comboni Fathers understood," Rivers claims, "at a time when many people including Blacks did *not* understand, that Americans of African descent were specifically that, of African descent, not some new creature. I suppose they made that link because of their work in Africa, their first love."[36]

A BITTER WAR ENDS

In June, 1945, Archbishop McNicholas offered Accorsi another West End parish, leaving Ferrara as pastor of Holy Trinity. Months later, Ferrara's diary reported, "On the 13th of August, 1945, about 6 p.m., we heard the long awaited news of the end of the war. The bell-ringing was almost deafening and lasted more than an hour, which showed the joy at the end of the nightmare that had kept us anxious for too many long years. People of many different faiths came to church for a thanksgiving prayers."[37]

In Italy, the war touched people with more than anxiety. From the beginning, the alliance of Italy with Germany was an uneasy one, and Italians were shocked by the cruelty of Nazi Germany. Early in the war, Italians fought bravely in their country's defense, but when Sicily was invaded by the Allies, and areas around Rome were bombed, the people were ready to rebel. In July of 1943, a motion of "no confidence" in Mussolini was passed at a meeting of the Gran Consiglio, and Mussolini's dictatorship collapsed. But the German army was still deeply entrenched in Italy, and heavy bombing continued. American bombers conveyed most of this destruction and misery to Italians citizens. In 1943, due to bombardment, Comboni scholastics at Verona moved to Rebbio near Como, and the students of philosophy took their courses at Venegono. Comboni seminarians had to abandon Brescia due to the "dangers of war," and in 1944, the Comboni house at Padua was hit by shelling. But the bombs that fell in Verona between the mother house and the statue of Saint Joseph remained unexploded.[38]

Father Oliver Branchesi was then in Florence, Italy, "I was teaching at our Fiesole Seminary seventeen hours a week and studying at the University of Florence...we did not have books, some professors had disappeared because they were Jews, air raids frightened us almost every day. During the alarms, I took refuge inside the Cathedral of Florence hoping that...at least that monument would be spared..." Father Alfred Paolucci remembers that, as a young priest, "We traveled by bicycle...there was nothing else since the Germans had taken the rest. The [Allied] airplanes came in at low altitudes, shooting up everything on the road. I'd jump off my bike and hide in a ditch...First fascists, then Germans...confiscated everything...when Germans came for inspection [and] looked at our places at Venegono (we had them full of good food so we could secretly supply the poor) they never found a thing. It was an old castle, and old castles have many hiding places."

After the war, forgiveness was needed on both sides for many innocent Italians died during Allied attacks on retreating German armies. Paolucci's hometown of Urbania, a sparsely-populated mountain village, was hit on a Sunday in early 1944. People were gathering after mass to exchange news in the town square when a huge squadron of American bombers roared over and dropped bombs that destroyed the entire center of the town. Four hundred people were killed or injured, ten percent of the populace.[39]

Before the war ended in America, Father Vignato sent Accorsi a letter,"I am waiting for a letter from you riassuring (sic) me of the good state of health of you two, and giving me some account of the development of your plans on behalf of the Negroes in Cincinnati...as well as for our Congregation in the U.S." Vignato said there was no loss of life among Comboni Missionaries at home or in the mission field. "This long war has not effected (sic) our development...I personally think we are now strong enough to...extend our apostolic activity in Africa and among the U.S. Negroes as well, if only the door be opened." Accorsi was told to see Archbishop McNicholas about sending more Comboni priests to America and opening a school for aspirants. Vignato said he could send Fathers Branchesi, Colombina, and Paolucci, and he thanked Accorsi for sending Mass stipends..."it is a demonstration of the high spirit of charity which keeps us always united in *Corde Jesu* (Heart of Jesus)."[40]

When he received his superior's letter, Accorsi reported to Vignato his suggestions for work in the United States: 1) send a priest to act as the General's representative; 2) send a priest who knows English well enough to speak in Catholic schools about vocations; 3) send "a few good scholastics to study in Cincinnati and form a community to attract vocations; 4) the congregation should look for work in other places, "particularly...in some of the big Eastern cities with a large Catholic population"; 5) each "mission-parish" should have a seasoned missionary and a young priest. Accorsi said that he recently sent $2,125 in offerings for mass intentions to Father Bombieri, the Comboni General Procurator. He inquired about Father Frizzero, detained in Canada during the war, who used his confinement to complete a bachelor's and master's degree at Assumption College.

In a year that promised to end on a positive note, a tragedy befell Accorsi and his family. In October, Accorsi's younger brother, Ferruccio, also a Comboni missionary, died in Africa of blackwater fever. He had shown great intellectual and spiritual promise. Mc Nicholas sent a substantial offering in his memory to Angelo Negri, Vicar Apostolic of Equatorial Nile. An acknowledgment of this gift was sent to McNicholas with a letter from Accorsi. Typical of his official persona, Accorsi's letter lacked any sentiment regarding his brother's death.[41]

3. The Architect

Archbishop McNicholas's letter to Father Accorsi about St. Henry's parish warned him to keep its contents private: "My present plan is to ask you to go to Saint Henry's, assuming [the] responsibility of pastor. It is hard telling what may happen to Holy Trinity. I assume, however, that Father Ferrara can take care of affairs there until decisions are reached..." The archbishop told Accorsi that he should not say St. Henry's was a "Colored" parish, but should simply invite everyone in the neighborhood to come to it. The same strategy would apply to the school: "We shall again open the school. We shall not say it is a Colored school, but we shall invite the children of the neighborhood to attend it." McNicholas promised to "make the most generous provision we can for the Colored children..."

This letter suggests that the parish still had a viable but dwindling white presence; otherwise, there would be no need for secrecy. Notes from previous financial reports confirm that white parishioners were slowly disappearing from St. Henry's located approximately a mile west and north of Holy Trinity. The yearly reports also testify to the general attitude toward the new migrants who were replacing them:- "1939, The flood of 1937 not only chased away the majority of our families, but was the cause of the influx of many non-desirable people. The pocket book is not safe any longer." - "1940, Black population increasing, and Whites are rapidly declining." - "1941, Black population steadily moving in. - "1942, The Old White families are steadily supplanted by the Blacks, and other people of the lower class. - "1943, White families have practically disappeared. -"1944, St. Henry school has been discontinued for lack of pupils, by order of the Archbishop. - "1945, Practically no Catholic is left at St. Henry. Sunday Masses are attended by 175-180 people, and weekly Mass by 4-5 people."[1]

McNicholas's doubts about the fate of Holy Trinity referred to ongoing discussions about Cincinnati's Master Plan at City Hall. Priests working in the Negro Apostolate heard Monsignor August Kramer announce that, due to legislation still under discussion, "...certain slum areas might be blighted by law and turned over for clearance or industrial purposes." Kramer told the group that no construction of new housing for the people in the West End was foreseen, yet slum clearance was a certainty. The priests were advised that "only necessary repairs be made on existing parish plants in the basin area." When Cincinnati's Master Plan was made public in 1948, it called for massive slum clearance, nonresidential redevelopment, and a new urban expressway system, all of which would eliminate what was then the West End neighborhood. It would displace thousands of lower income people, mostly Negroes. While the city recognized the need to relocate those whose homes would be razed, the Ohio Supreme Court's decision against tax exemption for public housing made it difficult to do so.[2]

SAINT HENRY'S NEW ROLE

In 1873, the West End's rapid growth had led to the establishment of St. Henry's parish. After flood damage in 1883 and 1884, it was rebuilt by its German parishioners in 1893, and dedicated to the German Emperor, Saint Henry, and his wife, Saint Cunegunda. The church was 173 feet long and 58 feet wide, could seat 900 people, and was located between Flint and Cortland Streets. When Accorsi became its pastor, it was within walking distance of the Union Terminal train station to the west and the Sisters of Mercy Academy to the east.

Though Accorsi found few white parishioners at St. Henry's, those who remained formed a small cadre that staffed the bingo, played the organ, and generally kept existing functions running. It was left to Accorsi's personal skills to introduce and welcome black families into St. Henry's, while also maintaining the good will of the white parishioners. Accorsi went into the streets to meet people, knocked on their doors, and spoke to the children playing on the sidewalks. His ingenuous manner was difficult to rebuff. He distributed fliers that promised programs to address issues such as, "Do Catholics Adore Idols?" as well as "The Catholic Church and Racial Discrimination." Assurance was given that there would be no admission charge or collection taken up.[3]

Middle-class black professionals lived on the northern edge of St. Henry's parish. Many others lived in a nearby public housing project opened to African Americans after repeated protests by those professional Blacks. But a large proportion of African Americans in the West End lived in miserable tenement conditions, their crowding increased by the migration of defense workers during World War II and the general relaxation of building codes. Father Paolucci, who joined Accorsi in 1946, witnessed conditions that a few reform-minded citizens of Cincinnati, and the Better Housing League were also reporting. Families were crowded together in two-room flats without shower, toilet, or central heating.[4] Paolucci related what he saw on home visits, "We walked up and down dark flights of steps; entered overcrowded rooms which were at times both bedroom and kitchen for a family of ten or so. Beds, kitchen stoves, tables, and chairs all contended for the corners and walls of the same room or hallway. There was hardly enough space for your feet to wedge their way in. Other families shared old attics long since uninhabited, or lived in damp and windowless basements."

Accorsi's contacts produced results. After spending the long hot summer of 1945 canvassing the neighborhood as well as painting and cleaning the school, he was rewarded when fifty children enrolled at St. Henry's School in September. These fifty were spread over the first four grades. One child was White, six were Catholic.

PREPARING THE WAY

When Vignato congratulated Accorsi on receiving a second parish in Cincinnati's West End, he also saw it as a sign of Archbishop McNicholas's trust, and he told Accorsi to obtain the permits for the ones who are...to come." This permission was difficult to obtain since post war America now feared fascist infiltration. Vignato left it to Accorsi to find a way around new legal restrictions.[5] Accorsi had no better ally than Archbishop McNicholas, a highly respected and conservative member of the American hierarchy. Judging from McNicholas's later correspondence to the Cardinal Prefect of Propaganda Fide in Rome, the archbishop's letter to the U.S. Consul gave generous amounts of praise, "I am happy to report," he wrote, "that the Italian priests who came to Cincinnati at the suggestion of Your Eminence (Missionari di Verona) are doing exceptionally good work among the Negro people of Cincinnati. I can only praise them in the highest terms. I have just written today to the Consul General at Naples asking that he give visas for five other Fathers whom the Superior General is willing to send to us..."

The archbishop believed the Comboni Missionaries could "do a great deal for the Negroes of the United States," and they would receive every encouragement from him.[6] Meanwhile, like many immigrants before them, Accorsi and Ferrara made arrangements to pay the fare of those coming to America, saving money from their salaries and friends.

Father Vignato had also asked Accorsi to begin the promotional work needed for the society's main objective which he clearly stated as: "simply the foundation of a seminary for the recruiting of vocations..." Accorsi was to look for property for a seminary and urged to profusely thank McNicholas "for all the graces and favors" he had granted the new foundation.

For close to a year, Accorsi and Ferrara had both worked without assistants. Accorsi also carried the responsibilities of vocation promoter, treasurer, and superior of the American foundation. It is not surprising that when he wrote Vignato the following February, he said, "The coming personnel...will be able to do many things for the Glory of God....I do not wish any of them the sufferings and headaches I had to overcome during these last few years." By early 1946, Vignato wrote Accorsi that he had found someone to lead the American foundation (Accorsi had refused). This man, whom Vignato said had his complete trust, was Father Julius Rizzi who would come with the status of "Visitator." Again Vignato stated the purpose of the congregation in America: "The principal reason that our Institute intends to establish itself in the United States is determined from the first as: to recruit American personnel for our missions in Africa and to lend ourselves in favor of the black people in America."[7]

BORN TO GIVE ORDERS

Julius Rizzi was described as a man who was "born to give orders." Tall, handsome, charming, with a vibrant voice and resolute manner, Rizzi was the polar opposite of Accorsi. Whereas Accorsi's health was never strong as a child, Rizzi had an athletic youth, competing in sports, and becoming a champion swimmer. While not poverty stricken, Accorsi's parents worked hard to provide for their children; Rizzi's family, on the other hand, sent him to a private elementary school. If Accorsi wrote letters to his family filled with love and poetic narrative, Rizzi dreamed of action and glorious deeds, telling his friends when he heard about mission life: "Bologna, Romagna, Italy...are all too small; let us go to Africa." It was at the regional seminary in 1919, that he discovered his vocation to the missions. But he was forced to delay this call when he was asked to compete for a scholarship to the prestigious Lateran Seminary in Rome. Gifted with an acute intelligence, he easily won the scholarship, thus assuring his request for mission work would be denied. Rizzi was later drafted into military service and assigned to an artillery post in Rome. Years went by before he was finally able to act on his earlier inspiration. Sometime near the end of 1923, he appeared at the

Comboni novitiate in Venegono in full military uniform. "From the barracks to the novitiate," a confrere later wrote.

Ordained in 1928, Rizzi was later assigned to the Comboni Missionaries' Cairo community. In 1936, he was entrusted with a new mission in Ethiopia, and with five other missionaries (including Hamlet Accorsi), Rizzi began as superior of the new community at Gondar in Ethiopia. Typically, his projects were ambitious. They included a school for artisans and an experimental project to teach the natives modern agricultural practices. The Gondar mission was so successful it was named an Apostolic Prefecture by the Sacred Congregation of the Oriental Church. Comboni Father Pietro Villa was elected Prefect Apostolic on July 28, 1937. In 1941, bombs began falling on this Italian territory, and by March of 1942, Fathers Rizzi and Di Francesco (who later came to America), were interned in a prison camp in Sudan. On his release at the end of the war, he was Vignato's choice to head the American province.[8]

Father Victor Turchetti, treasurer for the province who worked closely with Rizzi and Accorsi, commented on the roles they played in building the American foundation: "We can hardly speak of Father Rizzi's role in America without associating him with his friend, Father Hamlet Accorsi. They complemented each other. Rizzi was by nature an enthusiast, always planning great things, often carried away by his vivid imagination, but invariably ready to cut down his plans to the size of Father Hamlet's more concrete perspective." By late May, 1946, Rizzi and two more Comboni priests arrived in Cincinnati: Father Bruno Colombina, a professor of philosophy from Florence, and Father Zelindo Marigo, just released from a Russian prison camp. Colombina recalled that he and Marigo had "secured a place in a 'Liberty' ship returning [to America] after it carried wheat to starving Italy." After a perilous voyage, the two arrived safely in New York and took a train to Cincinnati. In July, 1946, Fathers Oliver Branchesi and Alfred Paolucci followed their confreres. Paolucci took up residence at St. Henry's with Accorsi, Rizzi, and Marigo. Branchesi stayed with Ferrara and Colombina at Holy Trinity. The new arrivals brought fresh energy to the small Comboni foundation. And with McNicholas pressing the missionaries to open a seminary, Rizzi conferred with his Superior General. His six-page, single-spaced report summed up the assets and liabilities of the new foundation:

Accorsi and Ferrara had done good ground work. Comboni Missionaries in America had a generous archbishop who even helped them look at other important centers such as New York, Boston, and Chicago. Local clergy welcomed them. But many other religious congregations were in the

Cincinnati area. Had Comboni Missionaries come too late? Perhaps not. Accorsi had reopened St. Henry's school where there were mostly black students, but the parish needed bingo to support itself. Holy Trinity's activities were well organized, but there were too many for just two priests (Fathers Ferrara and Colombina) since they also had to give marriage instructions and hold convert classes. Rizzi had only praise for Accorsi. The others, he said, had language difficulties, and adjusting to the new customs required time. Archbishop McNicholas had promised to help the new community settle in a good location, preferably near the diocesan minor seminary. But neither black nor white people in America were very sympathetic to African missions. A public relations man was critical to recruitment and Accorsi was perfect for the job. But someone else familiar with English needed to be sent to replace him since he was "tied to the parish."[9]

Vignato was undaunted by Rizzi's concerns. On the contrary, his General Council had received Rizzi's news with gladness. The entire General Administration believed meeting Archbishop McNicholas was a blessing from God. Their reason for believing this is revealed in an interview Rizzi had with a reporter from *The Catholic Telegraph.* The subsequent article reported that Comboni Missionaries had one major and three minor seminaries for native diocesan students in Africa, several colleges and a boarding school at Khartoum in Sudan, and that graduates from these colleges were accepted without question at Oxford and Cambridge Universities in England. Despite this, their presence in Africa was now threatened. The Apostolic Delegate to Uganda, Monsignor Methew (sic),[10] had told them that the British were serious about ousting Italians. He said that "the desire of the [British] Colonial Office is that, within a ten year period, the personnel of Latin origin be substituted with Anglo-Saxon personnel..." Now obtaining American vocations was critical to a Comboni Missionary presence in Africa. Rizzi admitted to the reporter that the task of locating and educating five hundred American or English priests and several hundred American or English brothers for the African missions within ten years' time would be difficult. But with so many more Catholics in America than in England, Vignato and his administration believed their future lay largely with success in America.[11]

Even though Rizzi was firmly established in the leadership role, he continued to seek Accorsi's advice in administrative decisions. With Paolucci and Marigo at St. Henry's, Accorsi could help in the search for property. The two priests followed leads in the suburbs of Western Hills where many of their benefactors lived, among them pastors like Monsignor Reardon at Saint William's in Price Hill whose piety, popularity, and talent were matched only by his greatness of heart. Other Price Hill pastors at St. Theresa, St. Lawrence, and Our Lady of Grace welcomed the services of Comboni priests where as many as six daily Masses were celebrated. McNicholas, however, turned Rizzi's attention to Forestville, a rural area fifteen miles east of Cincinnati, and the two priests' focussed on a fifty-six acre estate owned by the widow Krug. The property's main house was of nineteenth century Victorian vintage. It had a spacious parlor, dining room, kitchen, and storage area. Bedrooms on the second floor were large enough to divide into dormitories. Behind the main house were several outbuildings, a garage, and a swimming pool.

Only a few houses dotted the largely open countryside around the estate, and the land was flat and rectangular in shape. The house was once home to a wealthy merchant, then later a nursery. Rows of maple and beech trees stood on both sides of a thick grove of pine trees. Nearby was a large stand of blackberries and an orchard of wild pears. Fields of grass had remained uncut for many seasons, and there was everywhere a general sense of neglect. But the main building was essentially sound.

On August 29, Archbishop McNicholas inspected the property. He found it so agreeable he pledged $5000 toward the $71,000 sale price. Indeed, if he had not enthusiastically endorsed its purchase, Rizzi and Accorsi may have found the house too ornate for their tastes. But the Krug estate was only two miles away from St. Gregory's Seminary. On September 29, Rizzi put a $5,000 deposit on its purchase. For the rest, he had to struggle, and the figures he sent to Father General Vignato reveal why. The new Comboni foundation, largely through Accorsi's contacts, had been blessed with a bequest of $20,000. Benefactors had raised another $5,000. McNicholas said he might contribute another $10,000 for a total of $40,000. Rizzi explained all this to secure his superior's approval for a loan of $30,000 which the Archdiocese of Cincinnati was willing to make.[12]

The approval was granted. But there were a few details to dispose of, and McNicholas saw that his chancery office and its legal advisors resolved them. First, the lawyers completed the procedures so that not-for-profit status was granted the missionaries. Second, proper legal procedures were taken: title search, property surveys, etc. Third, Father Rizzi was prevented from becoming a victim of a squatter's ruse. A man pasturing horses on the Forestville property tried to persuade Rizzi to give him five years of free rent on an outbuilding, free pasturage, and rights to the income from hay he would grow on the property. He promised to erect a barn (for his horses), build a road from the barn (he would use), and see that the front lawn of the property was mowed (to feed his horses). He obviously counted on Rizzi's naivete. But a strongly worded letter from the law office of Dempsey and Dempsey foiled the squatter's plans.[13] This affair, however, delayed the missionaries' move to their new residence.

Meanwhile, Father Frizzero arrived from his wartime hiatus in Canada, and the holidays were upon the Comboni missionaries. At St. Henry's, a Christmas musical was reported as "unquestionably the best in town." The school's enrollment had grown to eighty children, entire families were receiving religious instruction, and with benefactors' help and government funding, there was a school lunch program. Fathers Rizzi, Frizzero, Accorsi, Ferrara, Branchesi, Colombina, Marigo, and Paolucci all gathered at the home of their friends the Vellas, where Mrs. Vella had prepared a turkey dinner.

In January, the Chancellor sent Rizzi the original and carbon of the petition the Comboni Procurator General was required to present to the Holy See asking permission to incur a $30,000 debt. Both Fathers Rizzi and Accorsi signed a demand note for this amount on which the Comboni Missionaries would pay the Archdiocese of Cincinnati three percent interest on the principal twice a year. A month later, the man with the horses was gone.[14] Rizzi wrote Vignato that everything was successfully concluded, and publicity for the new seminary was appearing in all the Cincinnati papers. The Archbishop promised to ask all local clergy to support the new enterprise, and Father Marigo was busy preparing a pamphlet about it.[15]

In the Catholic Telegraph, banner headlines announced the new seminary and described it as located on "state route 125 in Forestville, Hamilton County, about two miles beyond St. Gregory's seminary..." A subsequent article in the *Telegraph* reported Rizzi as calling for vocations not only from "eighth grade graduates of this year" but also from high school boys, college students, and veterans taking graduate work "in Cincinnati, Hamilton, Middletown, Dayton, Springfield, and all the smaller cities and towns of the Archdiocese of Cincinnati," as well as "the youth of the entire United States, to seminarians, and even to priests..." Fathers Rizzi and Branchesi would be the first two members of the seminary faculty, and the article called for "generous financial support which the opening of their new seminary warrants."[16]

The *Cincinnati Times-Star* described the property as having two large houses, one of twenty-two rooms, and the other with eight. The *Cincinnati*

Enquirer reported that the Comboni Missionary Society consisted of "1000 priests, students for the priesthood, and lay brothers...its territory in Africa extends to almost the whole of Sudan and part of Uganda..." The *Mt. Washington Press* added the practical news that "At present [the missionaries'] most pressing need is for furniture with which to furnish the two houses on the seminary property...the present [postwar] shortages is making it difficult to find suitable furnishings."

On February 24, 1947, Fathers Rizzi and Branchesi prepared to take possession of the first Comboni seminary in America. They loaded a truck with furniture and pots and pans contributed by friends. Rizzi's car, full of suitcases and packages, led the way. Branchesi accompanied a borrowed truck, its driver, the son of a friend, John Fiasca.[17] "It was terribly cold, and then it began to snow" the house diary tells us, "Our sense of contentment was at its peak. Fr. Rizzi, while waiting for Fr. Branchesi, lighted a fire; then he went out to find wood, but locked himself outside. He was forced...to enter through a window, helped by the sacristan of the nearby parish. Even inside, it was so cold you couldn't stand it. Fr. Branchesi arrived with the truck; they unloaded it, and he left for a second trip."

An attempt to light the boiler of the furnace failed, and a call to the city water department led to the discovery that the water pressure was too low at the street, but two days later the entire house could be heated. It was the day after this that Branchesi and Rizzi were racing along Columbia Parkway: "We must have looked like two happy junk dealers to the policeman who stopped us for speeding....Father Rizzi tried to explain, but because of his English, he was not understood, so the officer cut him short and said, 'If you have anything to say, say it in court.'" When Rizzi returned from court the next day, he was horrified. He told Branchesi, "As I entered the court room, an usher pointed to a bench, and told me sternly to sit down...At the very instant I was sitting down, I read a huge sign over my head saying 'CRIMINALS.' I almost fainted."

The kindness of friends, however, quickly made up for minor ordeals. While Fathers Rizzi and Branchesi were moving into the new seminary, the rector of St. Gregory's Seminary invited them to take meals there. The two Comboni priests were grateful for this invitation, but primarily, as Fr. Branchesi noted, "because at St. Gregory's we met many experienced priests and learned so much about seminary life, the Archdiocese, and Church life in the U.S.A."[18]

REPORT TO VERONA

In April of 1947, Rizzi was the first Comboni missionary to fly the Atlantic Ocean. The occasion was the convocation of the General Chapter at Verona, Italy, a meeting at which delegates from every region of the Comboni Missionaries would elect a new Superior General.

In his report, Rizzi described the scope of his mission in America as, 1) work among the American Blacks; 2) recruiting English-speaking vocations: results were few (they had applications from two young men for the following fall); 3) locating financial help for mission work. Rizzi was completely candid and even blunt about ministry among African Americans: "...We ask the following...Is it only a means to achieving the other two points, or is it an end in itself? It is necessary to take a definite direction because this problem is not completely clear....It is our opinion, however, that only by working effectively for the Blacks in America can we achieve the other two goals....Other questions we could ask are....how are we to act about the vocations that may come from the Blacks? Do we have to say expressly and definitely that we work for the Blacks and the African missions, or leave the issue behind and speak of missions in general? It is a fact that Blacks in the African missions are not very attractive to the general public in America, but we cannot play on ambiguity forever." In asking these questions, Rizzi was addressing issues that would vex the American province for decades. What response he received could only be inferred from documents that followed, but explicit answers were decades away.

Rizzi proposed: -that the Institute begin work in other areas such as the big cities of the East; -that more personnel were needed for promotion and a magazine and Comboni brothers were needed to renovate the old house and clear the grounds; - that scholastics were needed to provide a youthful community, one that would attract American students. This was the first General Chapter held after the war. None had been possible during the hostilities. When Accorsi and Ferrara first came to the United States, Europeans did not consider America a major factor in the war. But by this General Chapter, the United States had moved to the center of the world's stage as an international power, and most of Europe had suffered major destruction. Only months before the Chapter, President Roosevelt's representative to the Vatican reported, "A new hunger wave is sweeping through European countries this winter...Italy is one of the chief sufferers..." In France, food was so scarce that children were emaciated, and tuberculosis, rickets, and anemia were commonplace. Notices in diocesan papers in

America reported thousands of Germans still "starving, cold, and dying from diseases brought on by malnutrition."[19] Another year would pass before the United States Congress enacted legislation for the Marshall Plan that allocated the impressive sum of $17 billion for Europe..

. It was against this background that Rizzi's confreres at the General Chapter listened to his proposals. At the same time, thirty-two new Comboni priests were being ordained in Italy, the society was determined to expand missionary work in Africa, and one hundred missionaries were preparing to go to missions. Rizzi wanted to know how many of these would go to the United States. Would his confreres accept the fact that there were indeed poor and neglected people to serve in America as well as in Africa? Could his Italian confreres, who had survived the tragedies that World War II inflicted on their homeland, believe in the spiritual neglect, isolating prejudices, and depth of poverty that afflicted America's black citizens? Would a newly elected Superior General support an American foundation? Rizzi made a powerful case for sending more Comboni Missionaries to America. But this effort took its toll on his health, and when it was found he had ulcers, he was forced to remain in Italy for several weeks of treatment.[20] However, the newly elected Superior General, Anthony Todesco, and his General Council, decided in favor of development in the United States. Before 1947 was over, Rizzi's requests for personnel were honored.

HELP ARRIVES

When Rizzi returned to America, he brought back two more priests: Angelo Barbisotti and Alexander Nardi. The three priests arrived in time for the official inauguration of a chapel at Sacred Heart Seminary presided over by Auxiliary Bishop George J. Rehring. Present were many friends including members of the Mission Apostolate of the Sacred Heart, or MASH. MASH was the group of volunteers that Archbishop McNicholas had urged to support Comboni Missionaries. Thanks to MASH, much of the new chapel was furnished, and when Comboni students arrived from Italy, MASH members took on the tasks of ironing and mending their clothes. In 1947, eighty women were counted among its members.[21]

The first Italian scholastics to go to America were astounded by this order. As one reported later, "It was the spring of '47. We had been studying very hard. One day the Superior came to me and said: 'You'll have to get some documents together, your baptismal record and others. You are going to the United States.'

'You must be kidding. What for?' 'To study."
The student thought this strange since no student had ever before left the country until he was ordained. "My parents were dumbfounded," he said, "It didn't go over well with them." This student had only a course or two in English. When he tried to listen to it on the radio, he could not understand a word. In Cincinnati, he was not even aware that a professor called his name until his classmates began staring at him.

When Comboni students left Italy in 1947, postwar reconstruction had hardly begun. To buy train tickets at Verona, they stood in water next to a temporary structure. The railroad depot had been totally obliterated, and the pavement, storm drains, and all that was once a street, had vanished. The train to Naples was so crowded that one of the students stood for over four hours with one foot on the floor of the train and the knee of his other leg resting on a suitcase. Because conventions and meetings in Naples had filled all lodging facilities, six students, two lay brothers, and their superior, Father Gabriel Chiodi, spent a night sleeping on the pavement of the harbor. They embarked for America on the *Marine Perch*, a Liberty ship once used to transport American troops. Few Italian liners were in seaworthy condition, but Liberty ships were purchased by Italian merchants at large discounts from the United States and converted to carry passengers "in bulk."[22] "Bulk" meant that, in third class accommodations where the students bunked, sleeping was available only in open dormitories. Bathroom facilities were also open, separated only by sex. For the sheltered students who maintained personal privacy even in their own company, this experience was the most difficult trial of all. Since Liberty ships were never known for speed, and the weather was worse than expected, the trip took twelve days instead of the usual eight. People were so sick from the rolling motion of the tub-like boat, they seldom appeared for meals. The ship finally docked at New York, but no one was there to meet the group. Father Mario Ongaro recalls, "We disembarked separately. An immigration officer asked me where I was going to study. I said, 'St. Mary's of the West.' The officer looked for it in his book. 'There is no such school,' he said, and I was put in another room. The others had already left the ship. An hour went by. Finally, Father Accorsi came on board. He explained to the authorities that I was going to *Mount* St. Mary's of the West. Then we left the ship, and all of the students and Father Chiodi boarded a train for Cincinnati."

In Cincinnati, Branchesi had desks, a study room, and a dormitory ready. Three days later, the students began classes at Mt. St. Mary's. The drive back and forth to classes normally took thirty to forty-five minute from Forestville to Norwood. But when winter brought snow and ice, or the spring thaw flooded lowlands near the Little Miami River, the students would hardly arrive at their classes before it was time to leave.[23] Father Hugo Riva remembers that during his first school days there were no texts available. Students arose at 6:00 a.m. for prayers, followed by Mass, meditation, breakfast, then housecleaning. When they arrived at class, many of them were falling asleep at their desks. "For awhile," Riva remembers, "we were the joke of the class...Then our theology professor began to speak to us in Latin." Students from that time agree that if they had not been fluent in Latin, successful study in the new culture would have been impossible. Father Archimedes (Archie) Fornasari, who came as a student in 1948, remembers that Father Timothy McNicholas (nephew of the archbishop) asked him, "Do you know English?" "No," Fornasari replied. McNicholas laughed and said, "Well, you had better learn it." Fornasari recalled, "Necessity sharpened the mind. The first time my name was called, and I stumbled out an answer in English, the whole class applauded. I knew that the history class was enjoyable only because everyone was always laughing. When I began to grasp English, I understood why. The professor expected you to read the history part in the book. In class, he told all the anecdotes, what the menus were at the Council of Trent, who was fighting with whom, etc. I remember another professor was talking about Price Hill. He must have seen my bewilderment. 'You don't know what Price Hill is?' he asked. I said, 'No.' He said, 'Price Hill is the earthly paradise of Catholic priests in Cincinnati.'"

One of the students' first tasks was clearing out wild pear trees. Much of the wood had to be piled and burned. Supper at 5:30 or 6:00 p.m. was followed by an hour of recreation, then study time was allotted until 9:30 p.m. After this were prayers and lights out Fornasari remembers that when a conflict arose between how things were done in Italy and how they were done in America, Father Rizzi always adopted the most rigorous of both countries. If in Italy students were allowed to sleep a little longer in summer, that was an Italian custom, not for America. But when the hot and humid summers of Cincinnati called for short sleeved or cotton shirts, the students could wear nothing but long sleeved nylon ones that had been donated.

ACCORSI'S NEW ROLE

Accorsi's meetings with lay people were rarely forgotten. Charles Curro, for many years Vice President of Central Trust Bank in Cincinnati, recalled, "There was a joke that Father Accorsi came at dinner time on purpose. He knew that if he arrived between four and six o'clock, he would catch people when they were eating. We all came to know this, and that he would make himself right at home. He was before his time, for he let people know that he was human." Others remember being put off their guard by Accorsi's Roman collar and black suit when they first found him at their door. He would take advantage of this moment by asking for a glass of water, or if he knew the person, ask for a toothpick and a glass of water. The general reaction of people Accorsi visited was one of being honored by a man so openly candid in his strategy, and so genuinely humble in his approach. Whatever the gift of rapport he had with lay people, he was rarely turned away.[24]

Rizzi was convinced that Accorsi should be assigned to promotion activities, and Accorsi finally conceded to accept this role because, as he told his Superior General, there were no others prepared to fill it. In September of 1947, Accorsi was freed from pastoral duties, and Father Alfred Paolucci was named pastor of St. Henry's.[25] The combination of Julius Rizzi at the helm negotiating with the General Administration for personnel, and Hamlet Accorsi scouting the Midwest and the East for vocations and support from lay groups, was a potent one for the growth of the new foundation. The synergy of this partnership would never be duplicated. But new men were coming to join them. And many would play pivotal roles in the development of the Comboni Missionaries in North America.

4. The Foundation

Seldom in the history of the Comboni Missionaries in North America was there a period of greater creativity, enthusiasm, and productivity than in the years 1947 through 1952. Well over thirty priests, brothers, and scholastics contributed to this era. Two more bishops invited the Comboni Missionaries into their dioceses, a novitiate was established, and plans were made for a new building to house increasing numbers of personnel from Italy. Father Zelindo Marigo sent articles for publication to Italian language magazines in the U.S. and launched a full-fledged magazine similar to those other missionary societies produced. But these goals were not achieved without obstacles.

Before leaving office in 1947, Vignato made it clear to his missionaries abroad that financial requests to the American foundation had to halt until seminary work there was more fully established. But news of success in the American foundation spread quickly, and a flood of requests for funds poured in. Accorsi commented to Father Vignato that "if you had to take into consideration all [these] requests, we wouldn't have enough [Mass] intentions to send the Mother house..." Petitioners were asking him to send donations directly to them instead of to the General Administration which was against the rule. Accorsi mentioned the name of a provincial who had asked him to do this, adding laconically, "If you were to give him a few hundred MI [Mass intentions], you can imagine how happy I would be."[1]

When Father Marigo wanted to publish a magazine, Accorsi did not favor it, preferring a simple newsletter instead. But Marigo, who had been in both African missions and Russian prison camps, forged ahead. Once an introductory letter from Archbishop McNicholas arrived, the first issue of *Frontier Call* went to press. When he received his first copy, the archbishop visited Rizzi to offer his congratulations.[2]

Getting permission from the chancery for the publication had required diplomacy. The chancellor had said it was important to have "a very good title," and advised Rizzi to choose a name "by which your community may be popularly known in America..." Rizzi had already obtained his Superior General's permission to identify his society in terms of "Foreign Missions" instead of "African Missions." But the chancellor, Clarence G. Issenmann, believed that using "Foreign Missions" would confuse the Comboni Missionaries with the Maryknoll Missionaries "which also used the term 'Foreign.'" Issenmann worried that readers of the Comboni publication would think that Rizzi's confreres were *only* foreign missionaries, and that this would limit their appeal. The chancellor suggested the name "Maryville Fathers in America" as more suitable than "Verona Fathers" (the name by which Comboni Missionaries were then known). "Maryville Fathers," he thought, combined a reference to Our Lady with a reference to the location of the Comboni seminary, Forestville. Over the chancellor's signature was the imperative "By Order of the Most Reverend Archbishop."

It took Rizzi six weeks to muster up a reply. With gracious and careful wording, he informed Issenmann that he had given the matter great thought, but was unable to consult with his new Superior General who then was touring Comboni missions in Africa. He had, however, consulted Monsignor Freking, the archdiocesan Director of the Propagation of the Faith, and others in the Cincinnati Archdiocese. They all agreed on the title *Frontier Call*.[3]

Once launched, the fate of the publication remained in peril. Marigo was working on the second issue when he was assigned to Mexico. With Marigo going, and Accorsi arguing for a simple newsletter, debates about the magazine resumed. When Father Branchesi witnessed how disheartened Rizzi was at losing the publication, he wondered if he could attempt the job. He knew that this was a "bizarre" thought since he had barely mastered English. Approaching Rizzi on the matter, Branchesi was asked how he could manage such a task. He told Rizzi he was willing to write every line, set up a mailing list, and use his bedroom as an office, the porch as his mailing room." He would not publish anything without having it thoroughly checked by someone with perfect English. Rizzi warned him, "We have no money to hire the secretary you need; Father Hamlet will never let us do that." "Find me a volunteer," Branchesi replied. And despite his previous reservations, Accorsi found one, Helen Detzel, a reporter for *The Cincinnati Times-Star*. Branchesi maintained there was nothing epic, glamorous, or controversial about *Frontier Call*, but when Superior General Vignato received a copy, he was a bit puzzled, "...To promote vocations to the missionary life, we usually print the holy picture of St. Joseph the worker, but you are using the photo of a cowboy happily riding a horse in the Far West..."[4]

THE GENERAL INSPECTS HIS TROOPS

On March 12, 1948, Ferrara traveled to New York to greet Father Anthony Todesco, the new Superior General of the Comboni Institute. This was the first time a head of the society visited America, and preparations for the event were extensive. Todesco was nearly forty-eight years old when he succeeded Vignato as General. He was ordained in 1926, then sent to England to study English which he learned to speak with elegance. Having been novice master for ten years prior to his election as General, his lifetime ambition was to cultivate in members of the institute a love for the interior life and a faithful adherence to the rules of the Institute. One of his first acts as Superior General was to establish a Scholastic Council charged with the proper running of seminaries.

In early May, after visiting Holy Trinity parish, Todesco left for New York with a gift for the new seminary of Viseu, Portugal, his next stop."[5] Left behind was a twelve page evaluation of the American foundation consisting of minute remarks and directives on the spiritual formation of religious life and the Canon Law that dictated these concepts. Todesco charged members of the American foundation to "adhere to the spirit of their rules and not let themselves be overcome by the worldly fashions that surround[ed] them." He wanted a community schedule devised with bells rung for rising, prayers, eating, and all the day's activities, and no time wasted in "wandering around or in idle talk." Everyone was to master the English language, and refrain from speaking Italian. "Above all," he said, "there should be a strong attachment to our society and to the superiors."

Todesco sent another set of regulations regarding finances that were unlike those of his predecessor, Father Vignato. The latter's conciliatory policy regarding the American foundation's financial obligations came to an abrupt halt. Confreres in America were to increase contributions to the mother house by intensifying domestic economy and promotion. They were to seek ministry in different parishes and avoid hiring outside workers. Among other demands, Todesco set the quota of funds required from the Delegation of the United States at $20,000 a year. There would be no financial help for the U.S. foundation, and all trip expenses to America would be charged to that province. Gifts to the General Superior above the required quota were encouraged.[6]

To be fair, Todesco's demands must be viewed in the context of the times and the goals of the Comboni Institute as he perceived them. Italy was emerging from the ruins of war, and there was a fervor of renewal that was increasing vocations with the accompanying ambition to expand the society's mission fields. In the twelve years that Todesco would hold the position of Superior General, the number of Comboni communities expanded from 66 to 190, and the number of members increased from 663 to 1,210.[7] No one ever faulted Todesco for being fainthearted in expanding the missionary efforts of his Institute.

IN SEARCH OF A NOVITIATE

The new financial obligations that fell on the province came when it already had heavy debts from building a seminary. Not only were there young men entering the high school seminary, Rizzi even had candidates for the novitiate, and novices at that time required an isolated environment.

Before the Second Vatican Council, minor seminary students experienced their first taste of a prayer schedule and the demands of religious community life. But, except for separation from their families, their lives were not too different from daily life at home. If they persevered in their calling, and were evaluated as ready to go on, they spent the next two years as novices learning the rules of religious life in a heightened way, with all its demands and rigors. The novitiate was essentially a spiritual boot camp, not unlike that which a military organization imposes on its recruits.

After the death of Daniel Comboni, his successor, Bishop Sogaro, asked Italian Jesuits to help him form a religious missionary society, and they developed rules that reflected the rigors of military life advocated by their founder, Ignatius Loyola. These rules were intended to indicate to a young man whether or not he could live as a Comboni missionary. For example, could he say "yes' to being sent anywhere in the world as a missionary? If his superior told him to continue a task that seemed impossible, would he accept the challenge without complaint? Passing these tests, he had learned the vow of obedience. Could he live without owning anything, without ever making a gift of significant material value, or spending a dime without asking permission? If so, he had begun to understand the vow of poverty. Could he, in his late teens or early twenties, promise to live a celibate life and deny the natural desire to father a family? Then he had begun to understand the vow of chastity. Learning to discipline oneself was not a feat to be disdained, and even young men who left the novitiate often agreed the experience had been valuable. During this period of testing, Comboni novices had to be separated from all other personnel as well as from outsiders. Only their novice master and the superior of the novitiate could have contact with them.

Rizzi had candidates for the novitiate, but no appropriate environment in which to house them. By the end of 1948, Sacred Heart Seminary was housing approximately twenty men and youths in Forestville, including priests, brothers, scholastics, and high school students. To comply with novitiate rules, Rizzi and Accorsi began searching for another property. They first looked for a place on the East Coast that could also welcome American friends as well as Comboni missionaries who were traveling to and from the Americas. Rizzi met with a Monsignor McMahon who offered some hope for an opening, but nothing developed. Accorsi, who traveled constantly, also searched for a place to house novices. At Columbus, Ohio, he sent a postcard to the Buse family saying he would be there for a week. This trip was probably connected to a "momentary hope" when the Bishop of Columbus, Michael Joseph Ready, was taking a personal interest in a Comboni novitiate. By the end of November, Accorsi visited at least five other promising locations, but difficulties arose at every one. In the diocese of Hartford, Connecticut, Chancellor John J. Hayes denied a request to open a house due to the fact "that so many have come here during the last few years..."[8] He did grant Comboni Missionaries the right to appeal for funds in four parishes the following year. About that time, Accorsi, a man the community believed was made of iron, spent eight days in the hospital with an unnamed illness.

In January, 1949, Rizzi received news that the Columbus property was no longer available. The donor wanted it to go to a contemplative order. Over the following months, Rizzi continued corresponding, and Accorsi persisted in his contact work. The results were more refusals from dioceses in the East. In February, Rizzi called for a novena to Saint Joseph. Not only was he having trouble finding a place for the novitiate, but his superior, Todesco, was wavering on the idea of permitting it even if a place were found. In mid-March, Rizzi wrote Father Leonzio Bano, in Verona, "I heard that the Superior General mentioned my name regarding the opening of a novitiate. I could plug the hole for the time being, but I don't feel like doing this permanently...we have five postulants: a pilot, a chief steward, a bricklayer, and two clerks...all finished high school, and we promised to the first two that investiture would take place after six months. They have already suffered enough being alone with strangers and holding on faithfully in the middle of defections of the rest...it will be a question of our word of honor and of our future success.... it is absolutely necessary to start [the novitiate] if we do not want to face failure with those who [are] promising young men..."[9]

Two weeks later, Rizzi wrote to Vicar General Gaetano Briani, "...You are wondering why I have not notified you about the result of the deal with Columbus. Dear Father, if we have to judge what our future will be from all the difficulties we are now encountering, we would have to say that we will be waiting a long time." He was told that at Columbus, the bishop had been favorable to their request for a house for sale in the Columbus area which "was ready and was furnished with everything, even to the radio and the food for one month which the owner had provided..." But then, Rizzi told Briani, a letter from the bishop informed him "...that he does not believe that it is opportune, etc., and wishes that we find something better somewhere else." Meanwhile, Rizzi planned to open the novitiate near Cincinnati where permission from McNicholas was available. Then another obstacle appeared. Rizzi confided to Briani that a letter from Superior General Todesco told him to wait to open a novitiate until the following fall. "This," Rizzi wrote, "was like a bolt of lightening to us and put us in great distress." How could he wait? He had already promised two postulants their habits on the feast of Saint Joseph after Todesco had granted him the faculty to do so. Rizzi appealed to Briani to intercede with Todesco. This appeal apparently succeeded, and a search for a novitiate continued.[10]

Rizzi sought Archbishop McNicholas's advice about a novitiate. A memo of encouragement was returned by Vice Chancellor Henry J. Vogelpohl with the archbishop's message, "Do not permit the experience in Columbus to discourage you...Perhaps a gift would have been too easy and we must do things the hard way!" McNicholas told Rizzi to keep trying, "Your progress in this country has been phenomenal in these few years as it is. Things are not always going to move as quickly." But in April Rizzi asked McNicholas for an outright favor. He reminded him, "Some time ago...you offered to make a tentative approach to the Cardinal of Detroit for a possible establishment of our novitiate in that diocese..." Rizzi understood that this was a delicate undertaking, but said he would be grateful for any help the archbishop could give. A letter from McNicholas told Rizzi what to do. "Will you kindly write to His Eminence, Most Reverend Cardinal Mooney, about your interview? You can say in your letter that the Archbishop of Cincinnati informed you that His Eminence was willing to receive you. You can then ask that the Cardinal indicate the time which would suit his convenience. It would be well to get this letter off immediately to His Eminence..."

When by June he had not heard from Detroit, Rizzi was again told how to proceed. The Cincinnati Chancellor advised, "the Cardinal has many things to occupy him...Perhaps, inasmuch as you wrote to the Chancery in Detroit, and have no answer, you may drop a little note of inquiry, discreetly asking that perhaps your previous letter went astray...and asking the chancery to instruct you to this end." The strategy met with success. On July 1, 1949, the Vicar General at Detroit, Stephen Woznicki, sent a brief note to Rizzi: "I am giving you official assurance that His Eminence, Edward Cardinal Mooney, gives permission for the Sons of the Sacred Heart to establish a religious house in the Archdiocese. It is understood that this religious house will have a novitiate for the training of their subjects, and that it will be located within the county of Monroe, Michigan."[11]

Little time was left, and Rizzi asked McNicholas for permission to establish a temporary novitiate in the Cincinnati archdiocese. Sensing Rizzi had only cursory knowledge of church politics, Chancellor Issenmann expressed concern that, by not accepting Mooney's invitation speedily, the hard-won battle to establish in the Detroit Archdiocese could be lost. Any kind of foundation in Monroe would suffice, not necessarily a novitiate. Without one, Issenmann said, Mooney was apt to believe that Rizzi was not pleased with what was offered. Moreover, McNicholas wanted to caution Rizzi "not to put too much faith in letters. Permissions may be revoked. Persons pass off the scene of their labors, and their successors may think quite differently...accept the invitation by a response in setting up a foundation, no matter how small, or how few members make up the house at the beginning..." Rizzi could not realize how deeply this advice was then understood at the Archbishop's house when McNicholas's health, unknown to the public, was quickly failing.

Issenmann had Rizzi's assurances he would take his advice. An intra-office memo from Issenmann, presumably to McNicholas, reported, "...I think he [Rizzi] is impressed that the Society should snap up Cardinal Mooney's permission." Issenmann then reported that Rizzi planned to set up a temporary novitiate near Cincinnati. The chancery official wondered why a permanent one had to be outside the Cincinnati archdiocese. One reason, he thought, might be that Rizzi "is fearful of the expenditure to purchase - they [the Combonis] are tapping the bucket locally in putting up the seminary." Issenmann's last comment referred to the ongoing plans for building the first wing of the new seminary at Forestville that involved a loan from a bank for $125,000.[12]

There was great indecision concerning where to open a temporary novitiate. In correspondence between Rizzi and the Archdiocese of Cincinnati, sites near Amelia, Ohio, Milford, Ohio, and on the Sacred Heart Seminary grounds were mentioned. Desperation increased as the summer passed and candidates were due to arrive. In early August, Rizzi, Accorsi, and Father Gabriel Chiodi, the novice master, visited a small summer camp owned by the Franciscan Sisters of Mary. This congregation taught in one of the black parishes in Cincinnati, and their members took their students to the camp during the summer. It was located in West Harrison on the White Water River in a remote and tranquil place thirty miles west of Cincinnati. There were three houses on the grounds. The Comboni priests and the Franciscan Sisters of Mary quickly reached an agreement about renting the camp, and there was great relief that the novitiate could open on time. But overlooked was an important detail. The town of Harrison, Ohio, was in the Archdiocese of Cincinnati, but Camp St. Joseph was in West Harrison, and within the jurisdiction of the Archdiocese of Indianapolis. A letter from Sister Mary of St. Hedde, F.M.M., local superior of the Franciscan Sisters of Mary, and two visits from some embarrassed Comboni missionaries, gained the permission from the Archbishop of Indianapolis, Paul C. Schulte.

In early September, Father Chiodi and four postulants took blankets, sheets, cooking and eating utensils, pots and pans, and other necessities donated by the St. Peter Claver Seminary Guild and left for West Harrison. Documents arrived from Propaganda Fide in Rome canonically establishing the novitiate, and Father Innocenzo Simoni joined the small group as confessor and treasurer while also assisting at a parish in Harrison. In November, the investiture of three new novices opened the novitiate. Admittedly, the camp was in a choice setting for the fall display of forest color, but it was never intended for winter use. The walls of the houses had no insulation, and only minimal heating was available. Work began on wrapping exposed water pipes and installing heating stoves. With those measures taken, the novices settled in for the winter in true pioneer style. Meanwhile, Rizzi met with Cardinal Mooney in Detroit, and in October, returned with news that he purchased sixty acres of land in Monroe, Michigan, for a future novitiate.[13]

BRICKS, MORTAR, AND THE SWEAT OF SCHOLASTICS

When Rizzi asked for additional personnel in 1947, priests and scholastics were dispatched to the U.S.. But for construction he needed skilled

Comboni lay brothers. He stated his case to Todesco on the basis of wages in the United States, "The cost of labor here [in the U.S.] is enormous. Just think that a plasterer costs $22 a day, and a bricklayer $26, plus overtime pay and double pay on Saturday." If Superior General Todesco thought labor was expensive in Italy, he should think about the savings that could go to "the general works of the society" if Comboni lay brothers came to work in America. In early 1949, Rizzi's request was granted, and the lay brothers who later worked on the novitiate began to build a first wing of Sacred Heart Seminary.

On July 31, 1949, the cornerstone for a new Cincinnati seminary was blessed by Bishop George J. Rehring, and many of the city's prominent leaders were present: the Mayor of Cincinnati, Albert D. Cash; the Knights of Columbus, and good friends among local priests and lay people. "This is the day we see our dreams coming true." Accorsi declared.[14]

While Rizzi, Accorsi, and other priests worked to make the new seminary possible, the brothers and scholastics literally labored in the trenches. They spent their summer vacation digging ditches for the foundation and new sanitary system. They carried concrete blocks for the masons. Father Hugo Riva, among the first students to come to America, remembers these summers, "After working eight to ten hours on the first wing of the seminary, we had to... say our prayers, make our visits to the Blessed Sacrament, say the rosary, and do the spiritual readings. We didn't have time to even breathe." The students wore donated nylon shirts with long sleeves while working during Cincinnati summers with humidity at 80% and temperatures hovering around 85°F. If a student rolled up his sleeves, Rizzi was scandalized, and no amount of pleading changed his mind. Even after working in the hot sun, students were not allowed to go into the kitchen for a cold glass of water.

Father Archie Fornasari also worked on the seminary. He recalled, "When we started, there were two types of activities: work and work, or study and work. So sometimes we would ask for just a half hour off to walk around. We didn't walk around. We caught up on some sleep." On the occasion of his sub-diaconate, he was part of the crew that cleaned up for the festival. Later, when he and Riva were ordained as deacons, they thought they had escaped work since, on their return to the seminary, the cinder block had been laid up. But Fornasari was given water sealer to spread on the first floor blocks, and Riva had to spread it on those of the second floor.

As the construction was nearing completion, new financial problems surfaced. That Rizzi was searching for money is confirmed by an internal chancery memo noting that he had visited the chancery desperate for cash.

The bank would not assume the mortgage on the seminary until a number of bills were paid. Rizzi needed $80,000, but $40,000 would help greatly. Paul F. Leibold, the new chancellor, typed in a cryptic memo, "They have difficulty...borrowing for they are new, all holdings in Italy, have nothing that can be mortgaged...He said he asked you in June - you replied that that (sic) time you had nil to loan - he was inquiring about now..." Leibold's question was: Could Rizzi make a three or four month loan in order to avoid the higher rates that some of the banks were asking? In ink on the memo was written "No." Leibold wrote a polite note to Rizzi saying the treasurer of the archdiocese had refused the loan.[15]

On April, 1950, the Comboni house diary recorded, "Forestville Seminary (first 'L' shaped section) completed after a lot of hard work both doing the building and finding the finances to pay for it. A large part of the cost was paid for by money loaned to us by the local diocesan clergy at interest rates well below the going rate. This show of support was very encouraging." The novices had returned to the big frame house in Forestville after seven difficult months in West Harrison. In temperatures that frequently dropped to 0^0 F, they had only one space heater to each of the three houses. The White Water River had flooded, and the mud clogged up their water pump. This meant they went without drinking water seven times. Short circuits had been common occurrences. Some novices had been seriously ill, one with food poisoning and two needing the services of a hospital. They left West Harrison with no regrets. After scholastics and novices moved furniture from the old house to the new seminary, the novices moved their equipment from West Harrison to the house. On Easter Sunday, the first high Mass was held in the new building.

In late March, ordination of the first Comboni seminarians in the United States had taken place in Cincinnati. They were John DeBernardi, Archie Fornasari, Guido Gori, and Ugo Riva. The four new priests wrote a joint letter to Archbishop John T. McNicholas: "On the eve of our ordination to the priesthood, we want to express to You our gratitude for all You have done to (sic) us and to our society. It is through Your Grace's interest and generosity that today the Sons of the Sacred Heart have their first four priests in the United States.[16]

It was true. By the spring of 1950, ten years after Accorsi's arrival, the Comboni Missionaries had purchased property, expanded it to meet their growing community, located a place for their novitiate, launched a magazine, and brought the first four young men through to their ordination. McNicholas had a part in each of these steps, even providing free tuition for Comboni students attending Mount Saint Mary's of the West seminary. It seemed as if he were waiting for these milestones to be reached. On the evening of April 22, shortly after the move into the new seminary and the ordination of the first Comboni priests in America, a phone call came to the Forestville seminary informing the Comboni priests, brothers, and students that they had lost their very good friend and mentor. After twenty-five years as head of the Archdiocese of Cincinnati, John T. McNicholas had died.

MONROE: ANOTHER MILESTONE

On July, 1949, Rizzi wrote to a diocesan priests in Rochester, New York, that he received approval from the Detroit Archdiocese to open a Comboni novitiate in Monroe, Michigan, and that the archdiocese wanted three Comboni priests to assist local clergy. But efforts to locate property had failed. Two months later, Rizzi wrote him that he had paid $14,000 for 60 acres of land not far from downtown Monroe,[17] and Fathers Remus Catellani and Walter Mattiato were assisting at Monroe parishes. Situated on Lake Erie, Monroe is approximately twenty miles north of the border between Michigan and Ohio. The sixty acres Rizzi purchased included forty cleared for farming and twenty in thick woods. Father Walter Mattiato described it, "The general location was good, but that particular place was not ideal. There were trees and open fields, but the trees stood in very low land that tended to be full of water...Father Rizzi was fond of trees, so that's where he wanted the Seminary built. The first time we went into the woods to measure the building site, water was up to my ankles."

Unable to use creditors established in Cincinnati, Rizzi asked Cardinal Mooney for advice. "With the proceeds of our early summer festival and some appeals in parishes here and there, we have on hands (sic) about $30,000..." He estimated that with this cost estimate he would need another $25,000-$30,000. Rizzi asked the Cardinal, "Would Your Eminence be in a position to advance such an amount to our Society, or to assist us in obtaining a loan at satisfactory rates?" Rizzi was told to have plans drawn up and get bids. The Cardinal could not advance a loan for any building other than a diocesan institution or parish facility, but Rizzi was to contact the president of City Bank who would name an insurance company that offered a mortgage at reasonable rates.[18] Acting on Hickey's advice, Rizzi found the low bid at $150,000, more than double what he had calculated. An appeal to St. Joseph brought an extraordinary number of donations, and construction could begin.

By the spring of 1951, Father Mattiato began to work with Brothers Ciccarese and Bianchi on the Monroe property. He recalled: "Our goal was to prepare a suitable accommodation for more brothers and priests while building the new Seminary. The three of us found accommodations in a barn in Carleton where we slept in the hayloft. Downstairs there was a little place where I could say Mass every morning before work. The only water we had to drink and to wash in was a little fountain on the side of the barn. By the beginning of the summer, a place to live in was ready, and more Brothers came with Father Turchetti to supervise the work. Father Frank Di Francesco came as Spiritual Director."

Rizzi could report to Todesco that an entrance road was built and foundations dug. "We have cut many big oak trees, and we have the trunks ready to saw into planks.!" The people in Monroe were enthused about the project; they had no other religious priests in Monroe.[19] Over the following year, eight brothers worked with Turchetti on construction. They were: Brothers Sebastiano Bello´, Dino Bianchi, Pierino Ciccarese, Giovanni Colussi, Victor De Gasperi, Leone Montini, Salvatore Puggioni, and G.B. Volpato. These men, who in other missions acted as skilled artisans teaching and supervising work, literally dug ditches in swampy terrain and rain. Cement blocks were chosen so a roof could be in place before winter weather arrived, but the cold was so bitter in November that fires were lit to prevent mortar from freezing. Work continued six days of the week, and as long as the daylight held out, in order to beat the weather deadline.

People in Monroe were impressed with priests and religious who slept in hay lofts, said Mass in barns, and worked at heavy manual labor in miserable weather. The Verona Mission Club was organized with twenty men, and Donald Wolfe was elected president. Club members prepared an elaborate celebration for laying the cornerstone on September 16, 1951. Leading a procession was the platoon guard of Navy Air Base Sailors from Grosse Ile and the Fourth Degree Knights of Columbus. Present were virtually all the clergy of Monroe County, representatives from the Sisters, Servants of the Immaculate Heart of Mary, a host of friends from the neighborhood, from Detroit, and from Cincinnati. Monsignor Warren Peek blessed the cornerstone in which was put a copper box containing three 1951 coins, copies of *Frontier Call*, and the local newspaper. In all, close to a thousand friends showed support for the hard working missionaries, and six skilled workers volunteered their work on Saturdays to help with construction. It was an interfaith group of Catholics, Masons, and Protestants.

Monroe citizens not only contributed to the construction of the novitiate, they campaigned to prevent deportation of Comboni lay brother workers. This required passing a special bill in the United States Congress that would extend the Brothers' stay in the U.S. At the end of 1951, the Monroe Postmaster, A.C. Maurer, told Sister Andrea of the Sisters, Servants of the Immaculate Heart of Mary, that he had written such a request to all the Michigan Congressmen. Her superior, Mother Teresa, also wrote to the Detroit Congressmen and to the two Michigan Senators. Both Senator Blair Moody and Congressman Louis C. Rabaut responded favorably to H.R.3155. Maurer heard from the Bureau of Immigration that the bill had passed in the House, but would need watching when it reached the Senate. Mother Teresa and Mr. Maurer told Senator Moody that four of the Comboni Brothers had already received deportation notices. In June, H.R.3155 was passed by the Senate, and signed into law by President Harry S. Truman. Now the Brothers could remain in the United States. Ironically, a number of them did not accept the privilege. They said they had never worked so hard anywhere else in the missions, and despite their admiration for the people and the country, they preferred to go back to Africa.[20]

In Cincinnati, novices, scholastics, faculty, and provincial administrators, despite the new seminary wing, were still stepping on each other's toes in the old house. Wardrobe and storage rooms were packed to overflowing, the smallest desks were purchased for students, and the priest faculty's rooms housed the library as well as used by day as classrooms. Then a near disaster in Cincinnati emphasized the need for haste in building at Monroe. As a temporary measure, workshops built in an outbuilding were converted into dormitories and study areas for the scholastics. Father Marino Perghem, then a scholastic, later described the unexpected consequence: "It was the night of December 2, 1951. Twelve of us were sleeping in the garage dormitory. It was a particularly cold season, and we had no central heating, only a gas stove, and we let it run for days. During the night, I woke up to make sure all the doors were closed....We had beds [that were] low, some high, others you reached with a ladder. Lockers were scattered around....As soon as I put my feet on the floor, the dormitory began spinning at fantastic speed, and I fainted. Luckily for me, and the others, I fell against an iron locker with such a noise that everyone jumped out of bed. Three others fainted from the carbon dioxide. We threw open the doors and windows, then passed the night around a bonfire under a star lit sky. Somebody up there took pity on us. A few more hours and we would have started a journey of no return."

After this episode, it is not surprising that Rizzi said the communities in Forestville had a rather depressing atmosphere."We are waiting anxiously for the Monroe construction to be completed."[21] In August, 1952, the walls and roof were in place, and the novices moved in. There were no floors, windows, ceilings, or doors, but they lived in the building that would keep them dry if it rained. Father Chiodi, Superior of the house and Master of the Novices, later described this beginning, "We gladly went to occupy our permanent residence...The woods had poison ivy and poison oak, but the work of those early days was full of enthusiasm." Left unmentioned were the clouds of mosquitoes in the swampy surroundings or the Spartan conditions of an unfinished building. Instead, Chiodi remembered the many kindnesses received: "Divine providence sent along... Mrs. Laura Adams and [her].sisters who saw a sign on Telegraph Road, drove in...and were touched by our poor beginnings. We were given a tremendous donation. The Pellerito family from Detroit...was drawn by the seemingly Italian name then of 'Verona Fathers,' and offered all the necessary items for the new chapel...."

Never forgotten was that, from the beginning, the nuns from the Sisters, Servants, of the Immaculate Heart of Mary convent saw that food from their farm, including milk, butter, fresh vegetables, was delivered to the novitiate.[22]

CAMPAIGNING FOR EXPANSION

As his province was growing, Rizzi repeatedly asked Todesco for more personnel. In June, 1951, after repeated requests were ignored, Rizzi "exploded, "The last two years we were not treated well. It seems...that after all the effort we have engaged in to help everyone, and the development that we have given to our works here in America, without asking for a penny from Verona, on the contrary, sending much money, our work of growth here may still find opposition and people opposed to a certain generosity for us. All of the confreres in the States would be surprised to know of this opposition." Minor seminaries in Italy, England, and Portugal, he said, had eight to ten priests each, but American seminaries were without "even one priest for the scholasticate and two for the minor seminary." The American Province was not only supporting itself, it was contributing to other foundations. He added, "As a matter of fact, one Apostolic Prefecture is surviving with funds from America... Believe me...the efforts that we are making to economize, in many cases, is greater than what is done in Italy." Students in America were working in order to economize and to help the development of the province.

Even while Rizzi was "exploding" about personnel, he continued to seek entre to the dioceses of Indianapolis; Los Angeles; Mobile, Alabama; New York; Pittsburgh; Rochester, New York, and others. From September, 1952, to the spring of 1953, he corresponded with Father S.M.D. Gillen and Father J.B. Tennelly of the Bureau of Catholic Mission. The latter were anxious to discuss his taking over the Blackfoot Reservation in Browning, Montana. Rizzi visited the reservation in May of 1953, but nothing conclusive developed.[23]

On another front, Rizzi contended with confreres from other missions who saw America as an unending source of funds. To Todesco, Rizzi expressed concern that one such confrere, the head of an African Prefecture, "cleared $30,000, almost all of it in Cincinnati by going door-to-door to our friends." There were others coming, and Rizzi feared conflicts would arise between them. He wrote, "If we were to work together, everybody would benefit...." What were Todesco's thoughts about this? Rizzi wanted Todesco to create a protocol among the superiors of the Institute. But this would not happen for either him or his successor.

A look at the Comboni Missionary Institute in the early 1950s provides some answers to why Todesco remained uncommitted regarding personnel and financial monitoring. After Daniel Comboni's death in 1881, and the tribal insurrection destroyed his African missions, [24] Comboni Missionaries could not reenter Central Africa until 1900, then it took ten years to gain a hundred converts. But 1953, however, this number had grown to 300,000, and this achievement did not escape the Vatican's attention. Along with the American foundation, four other regions were juridically established as provinces of the Institute in 1950: England, Mexico, Mozambique, and Mupoi (Sudan). Pope Pius XII noted "not withstanding the present difficult situations, Divine Providence watches over your enterprises and over your Missionaries. God will foster a Society which does so much good...." The Pope himself did a great deal to foster the society's expansion. Although an offer from the Vatican to enter South America was first refused, in 1952, the Comboni General Administration learned that the Holy Father had entrusted to them missions in Brazil and Ecuador. These obligations required training centers in both Spain and Portugal as well as maintaining mission and educational institutions in Egypt, Sudan, Ethiopia, Uganda, and houses of study and the General Administration in Italy. To a large degree, Rizzi's superiors were in a situation similar to Rizzi's: a shortage of personnel and funds to support new obligations. Financially, it was natural for the Comboni Missionary Institute to look to the U.S. for support. It was the United States that largely helped Italy begin its financial recovery after the war. In 1946, the U.S. waived fees for supplies and equipment, and lent money to the Italian government. By 1947, it had contributed 1-3/4 billion dollars of foreign aid to Italy. This caused serious inflation until the Marshall Plan went into effect.[25] Before the war, other European countries contributed heavily to the missions. But they were also in a recovery mode. It was an era when religious institutions looked to the generosity of the American people to continue humanitarian and missionary work. And they were rarely disappointed.

A determined and imaginative leader, Rizzi was capable of forging ahead on many fronts at once. During his last years as provincial, he consolidated the opening of the Monroe novitiate, improved and enlarged Sacred Heart Seminary, and presided over an expansion of his province in the United States. Rizzi also assumed a substantial debt. When he left America in 1953, the era of greatest growth in the Comboni Missionaries' American province was reaching its peak. His partner in all this, Father Hamlet Accorsi, would maintain its momentum with determination.

5. In the California Missions: 1948-1953

A ROUGH START FOR COMBONI MISSIONARIES

In the spring of 1948, Anthony Todesco, the Comboni Superior General, interrupted his tour of the American province to meet Bishop Buddy of San Diego. Todesco needed a base in the San Diego diocese to supply the new Comboni community in Baja (Lower) California, Mexico. Bishop Buddy, with an expanding diocesan population, needed priests. At this meeting Buddy agreed to place Comboni priests as assistants in parishes, and later assign them as pastors. Father Rizzi sent Father Angelo Barbisotti, a 16 year veteran of the Central African missions.[1] This marked a critical milestones in the history of the Comboni Missionaries in America, and the beginning of their members relationship with Bishop Buddy, at times volatile. It encompassed both good fortune as well as adversity. On the one hand, Buddy' left no doubt about who was running his diocese. On the other, he gave his blessing to those who brought it achievement and recognition.

The Most Reverend Charles Francis Buddy became the first bishop of the newly-formed Diocese of San Diego in October of 1936. A native of St. Joseph, Missouri, he was born to Annie Farrell, a well-educated Irish-American, and to Charles Allen Buddy, a commission merchant of German-Alsatian lineage. While in Rome studying to be a priest, his father sent him a letter warning him against his "one special predominant passion -- that of a quick-tempered disposition as well as an inherited spirit of aggressiveness." While this temper could lead him to an abrupt or arbitrary decision, Buddy's interest in the poor and neglected was never denied. He first demonstrated this in his home town of St. Joseph when, during the Great Depression, he established the St. Vincent Cafeteria for the hungry and homeless. As Bishop of San Diego, his episcopate spread over four California counties: Imperial, Riverside, San Bernardino, and San Diego. At the time when the entire country was in the grips of a depression, Buddy's first diocesan funding campaign exceeded its goal by over $300,000.[2]

In August, 1948, a letter from Buddy to Rizzi praised Barbisotti's work in the Brawley, California, parish. He told Rizzi that the Franciscans Fathers were giving up the San Diego Indian missions "on account of their commitments [in] China....The central point of this missionary work would be at Santa Ysabel." On October 23, Buddy offered Rizzi a second mission territory, the San Antonio de Pala Mission. Rizzi raised a question of an agreement. At issue, were "the economic conditions of the Missionaries" as well as the need for a residence so Comboni missionaries could practice their rule of community life. Buddy wanted to wait to build a rectory until everyone could better "decide on precisely the most practical place..." He agreed to give each priest a stipend of $80 a month, but this was only to be used as a subsidy if collections from the parish proved insufficient.[3]

Copies of an agreement must have passed between Buddy and Barbisotti several times, but Rizzi did not see all of them. Indeed, he did not see the one that almost lost the California assignments. Barbisotti, perhaps influenced by Todesco's call for financial support of the General Administration, inserted in one version of an agreement a clause about seeking funds in the San Diego diocese. Buddy sent back a letter saying no such permission would be given as "the needs of this missionary jurisdiction are urgent and acute...the Indian parishes...will not be able to donate beyond the support of their own churches." However, the Comboni missionaries in California could contribute to their mother house and novitiate from "the $110.00 a month each Missionary will receive." Barbisotti must have read this increase in subsidy as a bargaining ploy, and he turned the bishop down.[4] Buddy's temper flared. He fired a message off to Rizzi asking him, "Do you come for funds or for souls?" Rizzi, undoubtedly shaken, replied immediately by telegram and letter assuring Buddy that he was "disappointed and indeed chagrined" by Barbisotti's actions, that he had just received Barbisotti's version of the agreement, and was in the act of signing and sending back Buddy's version, with an apology, when the bishop's telegram arrived. As far as finances were concerned, Rizzi had only intended to make clear that 1) The Comboni Missionaries did not want to make money from the Indian missions, but that 2) They had no money to devote to such missions. With more apologies, Rizzi even suggested recalling Barbisotti, and said he would go to San Diego soon to assure the bishop of his society's good intentions. To emphasize his commitment, Rizzi's telegram announced the arrival of more Comboni missionaries:

"YOUR EXCELLENCY'S PROPOSED AGREEMENT IS ACCEPTED WITH SINCERE GRATITUDE. THREE FATHERS WILL BE AT SAN DIEGO DECEMBER 15."[5]

On December 11, 1948, four men boarded a train in Cincinnati headed for San Diego. Fathers Bartholomew (Bart) Battirossi, Januarius Carillo, Luigi Crotti, and Brother Erminio Pilia made the four day journey with a total of $120 in their pockets. It was a great deal of travel money for Comboni missionaries, Carillo later admitted, "but in those days they didn't serve fifty cent breakfasts on trains like you could find in restaurants." Carillo was 32 years old and had taught Canon Law before going to the United States. Battirossi, or Father Bart as his confreres called him, was also 32. He had taught at the Carraia seminary in Tuscany, Italy, where, during the war, he and his confreres had been trapped between German and Allied Lines.[6] Crotti, at 28 years of age, had been ordained only three years earlier. Brother Pilia was on his way to Mexico. Of the four missionaries, only Carillo could speak passable English, and the fact of the recent dispute between Buddy and Barbisotti had to weigh on his mind as he and his confreres crossed a vast country they never expected to visit. The five were met by Barbisotti in San Diego, and taken to Buddy for the obligatory presentations. They were given a "practically new" Dodge to take to the Santa Ysabel mission territory where Fathers Carillo and Battirossi would serve. After accompanying them to Santa Ysabel, and seeing Brother Pilia off to Mexico, Barbisotti and Crotti planned to go to the San Antonio de Pala Mission.

What little knowledge the three newcomers had about California probably came from Barbisotti. Before the agreement was signed between Buddy and the Comboni Missionaries, Barbisotti had inspected the Pala mission. But this was just one of eighteen mission chapels for which his society would be responsible. Given a lack of American history, the prejudice of Anglo-Americans, and the negative stereotypes about Indians, it is unlikely that Comboni Missionaries had any authentic knowledge about Native Americans. For all practical purposes, these four Italian-born priests knew virtually nothing about the bishop, the region, or the people they were about to serve.

A HERITAGE OF VIOLENCE

Close to two hundred years earlier, the course of history changed drastically for California Indians. In 1769, two highly disparate cultures met in California, the one Spanish in origin, the other Native Californian. The largely Hispanic culture was part of an authoritarian empire, widespread and with a complex society of almost constant warfare and conquest. The Native Californians or Indians lived in groups of 50 to 500, and spoke as many as 300 dialects. Thus organizing for war was difficult for them. After the Spanish settled in California, Native peoples were often compelled to forced labor and changing nutrition. They were devastated by disease and epidemics; between 1769 and 1850, the California Indian population dropped from nearly 300,000 to 100,000. When data was collected in 1871, only 16% of the original population had survived.[7]

Following a war for independence, Mexico inherited California from Spain. From 1835 to 1845, the secularization of Franciscan missions began, and the land was taken over by Mexicans. The plight of the mission Indians was desolate. An ex-neophyte Indian from Mission Dolores observed, "..my people were once around me like the sands of the shore... They have died like grass...gone to the mountains....I am all that is left of my people."[8]

In February, 1848, the Treaty of Guadalupe Hidalgo ceded California, Arizona, New Mexico, Nevada, and Arizona to the United States. This brought new misery to Native Californians. Anglo colonists flooded Indian Homelands. The Gold Rush of 1849 brought lawless and ruthless men seeking their fortune. Anglo rule brought outright slaughter of Indian communities, which in California was often provoked by nothing more than a desire for Indian property. In 1850, one such venture was led by Capt. Nathaniel Lyon who, with soldiers and boats, crossed Clear Lake in northern California, and massacred virtually the entire Pomo population, killing men, women, and infants by gun and knife.[9]

After the Gold Rush, new labor laws changed the Indian's status from peonage to virtual slavery. In 1863, an investigator of "auctioned" or enslaved Indians at a San Pablo ranch in Contra Costa County reported, " I found seventy-eight on this rancho...they were there most of them sick, all without clothes, or any food but the fruit of the buckeye...eighteen had died of starvation at one camp...These...are the survivors of a band who were worked all last summer and fall, and as the winter set in...broken down by hunger and labor, without food or clothes, they were turned adrift to shift for themselves.[10]

It was not until January 12, 1891, that acquisition of land for Indian reservations was authorized by an Act of Congress. It led to the purchase of nearly all 17 reservations in California. The amount of land granted the "Mission Indians" was large, but nine-tenths of it was barren, and without enough water to support the population for which it was intended.[11] However, the Bureau of Indian Affairs (BIA) was slow to protect Indian land and water rights. White law-breakers were seldom prosecuted, and they frequently infringed on Indian land rights.

From 1925 till the Great Depression, civic groups had some success in thwarting the worst policies of the Bureau of Indian Affairs. Though many benefits that came from this were lost in the 1930s, President Franklin D. Roosevelt's New Deal agencies preserved some changes favorable to Indians. During World War II, employment opportunities opened up for Indians. They learned new skills at war plants, and were members of the armed forces. But after the war, when employment waned, some returned to the reservations to work the land. Without the money of wealthier ranchers, they often returned to employment, and reservations could become the refuge of the unemployed or the retired. The public then began stereotyping Indians as lazy and without a work ethic.[12]

TAKING OVER FROM FRANCISCANS

"I always said that if we had known what was going on between him [Bishop Buddy] and the Franciscans, probably we would never have accepted to go [to San Diego]." The Comboni priest saying this had worked in the Pala and Santa Ysabel missions for many years, and it was these two missions, and their surrounding chapels, that the Franciscan Fathers served before the arrival of Comboni Missionaries. Father Julian Girardot, O.F.M., had been pastor at Pala Mission, and Father Bonaventure Oblasser, O.F.M., was pastor at Santa Ysabel. The latter was apparently also the spokesman for his provincial.

In early 1945, Oblasser described his ministry to Bishop Buddy: "the greater part of the native population is still addicted to paganism in varying degrees...To eradicate gradually what is harmful in the old system, and to incorporate what is good in the Catholics scheme of things is the fundamental duty of the missionary." Doing this required years of missionary experience, Oblasser said, therefore his order needed "a guarantee of permanene in the field" which meant that the missionary centers of Pala and Santa Ysabel and Fort Yuma, "be entrusted to the Franciscan Fathers by a *'beneplacitum apostolicum'*" (e.g., "at the pleasure of the Holy See").[13] Not long after that Bishop Buddy offered three more missions, and they were accepted. Oblasser tried to build a rectory at Santa Ysabel, but finances proved difficult during a period of inflationary prices. Trying to eke out money for construction discouraged the Franciscan priest. Buddy apparently tried to encourage him, and Oblasser set about making plans for the rectory. Meanwhile, he began placing Indian children in Catholic schools, but was frustrated by lack of tuition monies.

In the summer of 1948, Oblasser stopped receiving his subsidy for car expenses from the diocese, and he inquired about this. Buddy replied, "In response to your esteemed letter of October 1, please be advised that under date of July 2, 1948, your Very Reverend Provincial wrote me to the effect that his Council was of the opinion that the Franciscan Fathers could not longer take care of the Indian Missions in this Diocese, that their providing so far for these people was only to help us out during the stress of the war. This decision forced me to contact other Religious Orders..."

Oblasser received the news with a generous heart, and was thankful that "these poor missions were not to be divided among the neighboring parishes, as stepchildren, but were to be entrusted to one association and to be treated as missions."[14] Soon after Father Carillo and Battirossi arrived at Santa Ysabel, Oblasser showed up to take them on a tour of their new mission. When he bid farewell to Carillo and Battirossi, he said, "Don't worry. Everything will be okay." But in the weeks that followed, Carillo, now pastor, found only bills coming in and no money to pay them. But he and Battirossi were too busy to worry. An immediate problem was the lack of a place to sleep as Santa Ysabel had only a sacristy and chapel. Carillo took $20 a friend gave him, bought a little lumber, and with a few spare boards, the two priests partitioned off part of the sacristy into a tiny office, with a couch for Battirossi, and a space for a cot behind a partition for Carillo. A sink brought cold water from a dam. It was dirty, but they drank it for six months. Someone donated a propane gas stove. The fact that they arrived in midwinter, however, did not make a lack of sanitary facilities easy.[15]

Comboni priests at both Pala and Santa Ysabel found Indians who identified themselves as Cahuillas, Cupeños, Ipai, and Luiseños. When Battirossi tried to learn their language, the difference in dialects made it difficult. Some mission chapels were located on reservations, but some served both Anglos, Hispanics, and Native Americans. A priority for Carillo and Battirossi was to organize catechism classes for all the mission chapels, but this was more complicated than expected. Except for the chapel at Santa Ysabel, none had any facilities or place to sleep, and all ten of them varied in distance from 24 to 160 miles away. Mesa Grande, Warner Springs, Los Coyotes, and Imaja were closer to Santa Ysabel and were served by Carillo. Barona, Baron Long, Campo, Jamul, Manzanita, and Sycuan were further south and were served by Battirossi. On Wednesday, Thursday, Friday, and

Saturday, Battirossi went to the six reservations in the south to teach religion, say daily Mass, and visit families. On Sunday, after Mass at three of the missions, he returned to Santa Ysabel to help Carillo until the following Wednesday. Together the two priests covered as much as 2,500 miles a week.

When snow and ice covered the roads, reaching mountain missions was virtually impossible. Before a second car was available, Carillo would pick up Battirossi at the Campo mission. But in 1949, the winter was severe, and even Pala Mission experienced its first snow in sixty years. One Sunday, the snow-covered roads near Campo (a few miles from the Mexican border) prevented Carillo from reaching Battirossi. This was during the time that everyone fasted from water and food from Saturday midnight till after receiving Communion on Sunday. When Carillo finally reached him on Monday, Battirossi had had nothing to eat or drink for close to two days. It was a cold experience for Father Bart, and a few wooden chairs from the Campo Chapel met the flames to keep the waiting missionary alive. At the end of February, Bishop Buddy donated a second car, and Battirossi and Carillo could work independently.[16]

Battirossi quickly made friends among the Indians. One, an elderly chief, Ramon Ames, had attended mission school in San Diego. Ames had worked to get the Barona and Baron Long ranches for his people when the government moved them off their El Capitan Grande reservation in order to build a dam. When Battirossi first arrived, Ames took him to all the reservations and introduced him to the people. Knowing the mission chapels had no sleeping quarter, the chief offered Battirossi a room in his own house. When the idea of a modest residence for the priest at Barona was suggested, the chief was the first to offer his tractor and labor for the project.[17]

Father Carillo was concerned that his parishioners had no place at which to meet. The Indians of Santa Ysabel were reticent about participating in parish groups, and those who lived in the mountains often avoided contact with Euro-American institutions. Carillo felt the need for some generous gesture. He and Battirossi began visiting and blessing all the homes. They were well received, and the visits continued on an annual basis. Then Carillo heard that Buddy had received $5,000 from the Negro and Indian Missions Commission for a rectory, but that he had balked at the cost of one previously proposed reportedly around $14,000. On the Sunday of May 1, Carillo felt ill on his way to say Mass at Mesa Grande, and he went to Santa Ysabel Ranch where he passed out. The pastor of Ramona, fifteen miles away, was called to administer Extreme Unction, and Comboni priest was rushed to the hospital. Water out of the Santa Ysabel faucet from the contaminated dam was suspected, and he was hospitalized for several days. Parishioners who visited him said, "The two of you cannot continue the way you are living. Something has to be done." They offered their support for a proper residence and the use of heavy-duty equipment as well as their own labor. A plan was drawn up for a modest rectory that could be built for $6,000 to $8,000.[18]

Bishop Buddy had been in Rome when Carillo took ill, but on his return, he promptly visited the recuperating missionary. The subject of the rectory was brought up. "Fine," Buddy responded, "but how much will it cost?" Carillo said, "Well, bishop, if we can get $5,000, the people guarantee me that we will be able to build it." The bishop agreed, and with the generosity of the parishioners, even a garage was included. Both priests pitched in to assist the carpenters, and Rizzi sent Brother John Volpato to help. Buddy visited Santa Ysabel in September, 1949, to bless the new "monastery" and confirm a group of children. The people were faithful to their pledges, and a list of names of those who contributed included employees of the Santa Ysabel Ranch and their foreman Cauzza; a Mr. Davis; the Kitchins; the Morettis; the Indians and their spokesman; and the "Non-Catholics who cooperated with enthusiasm. Along with the rectory, a new well was dug and a telephone installed. [19]

To make up a shortfall in funds, Carillo organized a barbecue, and by December, 1949, the Santa Ysabel mission had electricity in the church, pads on the kneelers, and a new heating stove. It was packed at Christmas, and Bishop Buddy wrote a complimentary article in the diocesan paper, *The Southern Cross*. People donated a new refrigerator, an electric heater, a sofa, chairs, and tables for the rectory. Carillo wrote Buddy that even the Indians brought gifts, and he added, "May I expect a picture of Your Excellency to hang on the wall of the living room?"

In June, 1950, Carillo was building again, and Father Rizzi promised him the continued assistance of Brother Volpato. Buddy was pleased with the chapel Volpato was constructing at Los Coyotes, and he agreed a rectory should be built at Barona. With the help of parishioners, the Los Coyotes chapel was completed in four weeks. By August, Volpato and Battirossi started the rectory at Barona. With all this construction, it was fortunate that the September barbecue was an even greater fund-raiser than the one held the previous year.[20]

A strong current of good will developed between Buddy and Carillo. The financial agreement finalized between the Bishop and the Comboni provincial had provided only $80 a month for each Comboni missionary which had to cover all food, clothing, and residential expenses. But Buddy sent additional support that year as well as donations to the Comboni General Administration in Verona, Italy. With the poverty of the Indian missions, Buddy's help was critical. Some Sunday collections amounted to only a few dollars which could not cover car repairs and maintenance of chapels. Getting started at the Santa Ysabel mission led its Comboni priests to a new and deeper appreciation of the vow of poverty.

In 1951, Carillo and Battirossi increased their efforts to develop the spiritual life of the mission. A week-long retreat was given in the mountain areas of Los Coyotes. In early fall, a catechetical center was built in Warner Springs near a public school that sixty Indian students attended. On All Soul's Day, the priests blessed the Indian cemeteries. It was one of the most important ceremonies for Native Americans who held their ancestors in reverence long before the coming of the padres.[21]

In the spring of 1952, Carillo's parishioners helped with a huge landscaping project at Santa Ysabel which was virtually invisible from the main highway. With the loan of a "mastodonic" bulldozer, parishioners cleared, leveled, and laid down a direct road from the highway to the church. They planted trees on either side that eventually provided a picturesque and shade-covered entrance to the mountain mission. When Bishop Buddy came for Confirmation, Carillo and his parishioners proposed that a parish hall be built and dedicated to Father Edmond La Pointe, a Canadian priest whom the Indians remembered as a priest who walked or rode a mule to visit them. The cost would be $6,000. Buddy agreed to match any funds up to $2000. Novenas to St. Joseph resulted in several thousands of dollars for the hall. By September, the walls were up, and not long after, a monument to Father La Pointe was dedicated. Carillo told Buddy that friends came from far away (especially Indians) "who felt a spiritual uplift in the remembrance of the Father of their souls." On November 2, 1952, Buddy blessed Father La Pointe Hall. Its official inauguration occurred on Thanksgiving Day . Carillo believed, "The hall seems to have broken the barrier some put before us because they like[d] the Franciscans who were here before us...they all seem united in celebrating their efforts together."[22]

In the midst of the enthusiasm about the new hall, the parishioners received the news that Father "Bart" Battirossi was called to Cincinnati to serve at the seminary. Carillo described to Buddy the Indians' reaction. Battirossi was a priest "whom the Indians loved very dearly. He could speak to them in their own language. At Barona and Baron Long, they improvised a farewell parties (sic) for him. Everyone went to Confession and Communion in the morning. In the afternoon and evening they presented him with...useful gifts, and expressed their affection more with tears than words..."

Indeed, they also expressed it with words as a petition to Bishop Buddy demonstrated, "[Father Battirossi] is the only Priest we have loved so much since the late Rev. Fr. La Pointe. He has spent all of his time among the Indians in the Southern District, visiting each family...Our children love him more than we can express. He makes visits to our Mission twice a week...has also started the Alter (sic) Society, something Indians have never had on this Reservation...we want him to complete his tasks." Forty-one signatures were on this testimony to Battirossi.[23]

PALA MISSION, 1948-1953

"Pala" means water in the Indian vernacular, and the Mission received its name from the San Luis Rey River that runs through the valley near it. The friar who discovered the valley reported the ample running water, unlimited timber, plenty of stones, firewood, and good pasture land. A thriving assistencia, or little chapel, was established in 1816, and an entire quadrangle was built around it.

From 1834 to 1836 the Mexican government secularized virtually all twenty-one of the Franciscan missions and the assistencias attached to them, and they fell to the avarice of the *rancheros* and white settlers. Tiles and timbers torn from their roofs were carted away for construction elsewhere, the rain deteriorated the unprotected adobe walls, and before long, the mission and chapel buildings were in ruin. But as Carillo wrote, "during those dark days, the light dimmed over Pala Mission, but it was not extinguished." It was the only mission in California which, from its founding was never abandoned.

In 1903, Cupeño Indians were driven from their ancestral lands in Warner Springs and relocated on the Pala Reservation established when Congress bought the 3,500 acres for Indian relocation. They were left to camp on the river banks. They went months without housing before the federal government brought in prefabricated one-room houses from New York, costlier than the adobe or frame homes available locally. A resident priest was then assigned to the Pala Mission Chapel.[24]

The chapel's interior is narrow and dark, and three windows allow only the dimmest light on the white walls that range in thickness from 24 to 42 inches. Despite the dim light, bright red, brown, and gold designs on the walls illuminate the dusky interior. Outside, the campanile, or bell tower, stands apart from the main building. Its two-bell niches rise fifty feet into the sky, with a cross on top against a blue sky and a rugged hillside landscape. Next to the cross is a cactus. Legend claims the mission's founder, Father Peyri, planted the cactus as a symbol of the cross conquering the wilderness, but another legend states that when Peyri set the cross into the soft adobe, a bird dropped a cactus seed onto it.[25]

In December, 1948, after seeing Carillo and Battirossi settled at Santa Ysabel, Barbisotti and Crotti proceeded to the Pala Mission. Attached to Pala were chapels at Cahuilla, La Jolla, Pauma Valley, Pechanga, Rincon, Santa Rosa, and Temecula. From the beginning, Barbisotti was the spokesman for his confreres, and he was a concerned pastor. In 1949, when a parishioner complained of the cold seeping in from the chapel's unsheathed roof tiles, Barbisotti saw that repairs were made. When an elderly Sacristan of Pala died, Barbisotti presided over a funeral with appropriate solemnity, and two nights of vigil were observed instead of the normal one. Prayers were said in English, Spanish, and the tribal language.

The Pala Mission's finances were sounder than Santa Ysabel's. It had a few hundred dollars in its account, and the June Corpus Christi fiesta raised additional funds. Rizzi arrived to preside at the fiesta's mass, and there was a grand procession with three benedictions, each announced by pistol shots. All this was captured by the Los Angeles and San Diego newspapers.[26] In September, 1949, Barbisotti petitioned the Marquette League for funds to build a rectory at Pala. He also launched a passionate plea in this petition for a Catholic school at Pala. A rectory, he said, could wait. Without a Catholic education, "The rest - including the building of rectories and churches - is secondary." There is no indication that any monies were forthcoming for either a rectory or a school.[27] But prominent citizens and Hollywood notables contributed to the Mission. Mr. Thomas Leavey, President of Farmers' Insurance Group in Los Angeles, supplied uniforms and supported the softball teams for the grade and high school children. Ramon Novarro, an actor famous for his portrayal in "Ben Hur" and other films, attended daily mass at the Pala chapel. North Hollywood friends donated a film projector put to use at the next Fiesta with a showing of "Our Lady of Guadalupe."

After Father Todesco visited America in 1951, his report to his General Council expressed his own and Bishop Buddy's opinion of Comboni missionaries stationed in California, "...The bishop is very satisfied with the...zealous activity of the fathers. He praises very much the missionary spirit that they seem to exhibit. I think I can say that they could not do more....The fathers...are not envied by the [diocesan] clergy, but are admired for the enthusiasm that they put in their apostolate." Todesco said that Barbisotti had not been well accepted because of "certain acts of imprudence" with the bishop and his lack of diplomacy with him. On the other hand, the bishop was very pleased with Carillo "because of his work, his imagination, and submission to the curia [chancery] and the bishop."[28]

In the fall of 1951, Monsignor Anthony J. Brouwers, head of the Los Angeles Archdiocesan Office of the Propagation of the Faith, asked Father Rizzi if Father Crotti could work with his office on mission movies. Rizzi and Accorsi welcomed this entree to Los Angeles. Crotti began as an assistant at Precious Blood Parish, meanwhile taking courses in cinematography, mentored by the cinematographer, Dr. Gino Stiller. Rizzi invested $5,000 in equipment so Crotti could produce films for vocation and mission promotion. The first focussed on Pala Mission; it was a new experience for the mission's Indians. When the film premiered at Pala, they immediately conferred stardom on one another. Rizzi reported that it had not gone so well during production. The actual filming found them with little enthusiasm, but the response to the film, he thought, boded well for the future.

Father Alfio Mondini, who had been transferred to Pala from Cincinnati, returned from his diocesan assignment at Fallbrook, California, to the Pala Mission in 1951. He had been well received in Fallbrook, and had written a series of articles for the local newspaper. He also was the priest who allegedly brought about the decision of the film director Frank Capra to solemnize his marriage, a ceremony that took place at Pala the following spring.[29]

Seeking a Catholic education for Indian children, Barbisotti first took the route that Oblasser, the Franciscan, had followed. He purchased a small school bus so some could attend the Catholic school at San Luis Rey. But school fees and the lack of a lunch program presented difficulties. Many Indians were not prepared for, and could not afford the new expenses. That generous benefactors provided for this need becomes clear in a report Barbisotti gave Bishop Buddy at the end of the year. One donation was for beginning a school fund, and from this Barbisotti was able to buy a Chevrolet Suburban to transport students going to San Luis Rey. It also paid some tuition, books, and uniforms for the poorer children.[30]

Barbisotti was the first with plans for a school at Pala. After speaking to the Indians, he prepared drawings for a kindergarten, a parish hall, and a residence. In the fall of 1952, he decided to present these to the bishop. Hearing that Buddy would be at San Luis Rey High School, Barbisotti went there and asked to see the bishop. Moments later, Buddy appeared and said he did not want to talk business. But in the next breath, he asked to see the plans. Barbisotti entered their exchange in the Pala Diary. It took five minutes, he wrote, and "His Excellency does not feel he can make a loan to Pala. It is not expedient to look for help outside the diocese, nor...within the diocese. With this nice encouragement, we will sit down in our cave for another generation or two.!" There wasn't even time to explain [that] the plan...would have decreased the cost by about two-thirds (the free work of the architect, of the foreman, of the carpenter, and of our own [missionaries]. So be it."[31]

MAKING CHOICES

For several years, the Bureau of Indian Affairs had declared its intention to "terminate" all government services to Native Americans, do away with the reservation system, and divide tribal assets among individual Indians. A great hue and cry among the Indians and their supporters eventually prevented a wholesale give-away. But in 1952, this issue was not yet resolved, and Rizzi believed Indian reservations would be disbanded. He saw Pala as an attractive center to which visitors would eventually come, and thought it might provide a foothold in a diocese for a future seminary. He hoped to ask Bishop Buddy for permanent control of the Pala mission in return for an offer to assume all expenses and contribute the labor of Comboni brothers. In retrospect, his hopes do not seem different from those of the Franciscans.[32]

Rizzi did not want to approach Buddy with this request until he could determine whether or not his requests to enter the Los Angeles Archdiocese would be answered. When they were not, he informed Todesco of this and said he was also, "waiting to see how the situation in Los Angeles and *the question of the fight with the Franciscans* is going to develop." {Emphasis added] The "fight" to which he referred was apparently between the Franciscans and Bishop Buddy. On July 23, 1952, Buddy sent a telegram to Rizzi that read, "Franciscans will release St. Thomas Parish, Fort Yuma, July 29. Could you send much needed zealous missionary to take charge? Letter follows, Cordial Respects. S/Bishop Buddy." Buddy added that the mission had run down for years since the Franciscan Father in charge had health problems.[33]

Buddy made no threats if his offer were rejected, but Rizzi was afraid if he refused it, the bishop might bring in another society, thus diminishing prospects for gaining control of Pala or opening a seminary in the San Diego diocese. Rizzi's concerns seem overblown since the bishop explicitly stated that if his society could not accept St. Thomas, he would appreciate their sending someone temporarily. In the end, Rizzi refused St Thomas Parish. [34]

Not long after Rizzi appointed Barbisotti pastor at the Pala Mission, he began having doubts. First there was the blunder Barbisotti made in negotiating with Buddy. By 1950, Rizzi and Todesco both were planning a move. Rizzi wrote, "...we must substitute Barbisotti, as you say..." In 1951, Rizzi suggested sending Battirossi to substitute for Barbisotti "when we will be able to move Fr. Barbisotti to a new foundation." Finally, in 1952, Rizzi told Todesco, "Fr. Barbisotti is always the kind of confrere we know. Good, intelligent, but not a patient organizer." [35]

If Barbisotti was not a good organizer, he had his own gifts. In Sudan, he taught at the seminary of Okaru from 1931 to 1947. He overcame serious health problems to study English, and he succeeded so well that an Englishman at Okaru stopped by a window of the missionary school to listen to him read and talk. Barbisotti was credited for saving Comboni schools in Sudan when the English looked unfavorably on Italian missionaries. It was later said that Barbisotti's main difficulties stemmed from a personality sometimes beginning too many initiatives at once. Those who worked with him in California said the Indians loved him. But administration and external affairs were not his forté. Two issues persuaded Rizzi to move Barbisotti. First, Rizzi envisioned Pala Mission as a promising center for the Comboni Missionaries. It had already proved it could draw people from as far away as Los Angeles. With some major investment and imagination, Rizzi believed it could provide more support for the Indians and attract vocations and mission support. Second, Bishop Buddy favored Carillo for his administrative and fund-raising skills. Barbisotti was a good pastor and a willing worker, but the Bishop of San Diego and Rizzi wanted someone who could organize big projects with resources and people behind them.

As a senior member of the American foundation, Barbisotti was elected to attend the Comboni General Chapter held in Verona in 1953. After the Chapter, he was appointed Regional Superior in England, and later named Apostolic Administrator, then Vicar Apostolic, of Esmeraldas, Ecuador. Barbisotti kept up a lively correspondence with Bishop Buddy for years after leaving California, and he received substantial support from the San Diego bishop for his Esmeraldas mission. [36] In the summer of 1953, Rizzi transferred Father Carillo to Pala Mission as pastor. (See "Pursuit of a Dream")

6. Confronting Racism

When Archbishop McNicholas arrived in Cincinnati in 1925, 10,000 people escorted him to his residence. Heading the procession was a tall, dignified Negro, Charles B. Lobert, carrying the American flag. Decades later, when the *Catholic Telegraph* interviewed Lobert, he said he was convinced that the hope of the Negro population was with the Catholic Church, and that the Negro population represented an enormous opportunity for conversion to the Catholic faith. But he saw little progress in race relations. "As a matter of fact," he told the reporter, "I think prejudice is on the increase.....employment opportunities World War II gave us are disappearing. No Colored men are appointed to the Fire department. There are no Colored motormen, conductors, or bus drivers....there have been no Colored interns at the city-owned Cincinnati General Hospital. Since white people [do not associate with blacks]...many of them...judge Negroes by the actions of a few. And I am afraid the public press has always devoted more space to our crimes than to our accomplishments."[1] The first Comboni missionaries arriving in America lacked a true understanding of the "peculiar institution" of slavery and its consequences.

Black parish issues and the heritage of slavery in the United States were poorly understood by the Comboni General Administration. Even Father Accorsi seems to have treated work in black parishes much as he would have treated work in a poor white parish. His articles in *Frontier Call* concentrated on African, not African American missions. Against this background, one can understand that a Comboni missionary might experience a certain uneasiness when first serving a black parish. Caught between the biases of Whites and the needs of Blacks, they could find the truth difficult to discern in the undercurrents of racial politics. The one conviction they could rely on was that they were serving people in the United States who were among the "poorest and most abandoned," and this was a principle criterion their founder, Blessed Daniel Comboni, laid down for members of his congregation.

ONE PRIEST'S PASSAGE

Ordained in 1940, Father Alfred Paolucci came from that sturdy stock of Italian people who nourished themselves more with religious faith then with an amplitude of material goods. In 1946, he was assigned to America, and he remembers that a generous pastor from Corona, New York, treated him to a short tour of the American metropolis. There the young priest saw "the tallest skylines, the longest bridges, the largest steaks and portions of ice cream in the entire world." Arriving in Cincinnati, he confronted a different perspective of America At the train terminal he could see the city's West End where he would work. Row houses crowded close to narrow streets, and a thick layer of smog covered a valley that stretched from the business district to the east to the hilltop suburbs in the west. Behind him, train tracks led north to the Mill Creek Valley, and south to the Ohio River. When a Comboni missionary picked up Paolucci, he pointed to a tall steeple nearby. It was St. Henry's Church where Paolucci would spend his first six years in America.[2]

The young priest was pleased with the atmosphere in the United States. He commented, "It was not long before I was sold on the American people. Because of my experience in a dictatorship, I considered it ideal that everybody could express his or her own opinion. Even more was the fact that the people were generous. They were respectful of other people's opinions. And they respected their priests. [But] I was able to understand only a few words and to pronounce even fewer correctly." Sister Veronica, an elderly Sister of Mercy, was assigned to teach Paolucci English. She rehearsed the young priest for his sermons, each time encouraging him to do it with less arm-tossing saying, "I wonder how Italians would talk if they had no hands!"[3]

A year after his arrival in the U.S., Paolucci was summoned by Father Rizzi to the Forestville seminary. Twirling his pencil rather nervously, his superior told Paolucci, "I want you to take over at St. Henry's as pastor." Paolucci blurted out, "You are crazy!" But he caught himself and said, "Excuse me, Father, but I cannot be the pastor!" He listed his inexperience, his youth, and his language difficulties. For over an hour, Rizzi countered these arguments and explained why the assignment was critical to the province. Father Accorsi was needed for mission and vocation work, and Paolucci's English was the best among the Comboni priests available for ministry. There was no alternative. On September 18, 1947, Paolucci was appointed pastor of Saint Henry's parish.

Opened to African Americans by Accorsi, virtually all the children in the school were black, but former white parishioners still provided most of the school's money. Paolucci learned how politically sensitive the situation was, even for a seasoned missionary. One day a white woman, who had weathered through three former pastors, shook her head at Paolucci and said, "You will have a hard time, my young man, filling your predecessor's shoes." Paolucci already knew this. At thirty-one years of age, he was the youngest pastor in the entire Archdiocese of Cincinnati. But with over a hundred students enrolled in St. Henry"s school in 1947, and a huge parish plant to oversee, there was no time for self-pity.[4] Paolucci came face-to-face with the demands of an aging physical plant. The church basement needed plastering and painting. An old pipe system in the church hall was falling apart. Although the church steeple was solid enough, in early 1949 it suffered wind damage. Then a routine fire department inspection led to replacing all the wiring in the church hall. The bingo money permitted the basement to be remodeled for the children, but other costs forced Paolucci to dig into parish savings.[5]

Registered Catholics at St. Henry's were few, but a hundred people attended nightly rosary services in May. By July, St. Henry's Legion of Mary was officially recognized, and Father Alfio Mondini joined Paolucci to work with young people and direct the choir. Since Blacks were restricted from most parks and all swimming pools in Cincinnati, during the summer, school children were transported to the camp in Indiana run by the Franciscan Sisters of Mary. That fall, for the first time since reopening, students were enrolled in all eight grades as well as kindergarten.

When the Diamond Jubilee of St. Henry's parish approached, Auxiliary Bishop George J. Rehring, a son of the parish, offered to celebrate a Pontifical High Mass for its present and former parishioners. Many of the latter lived only a few miles away and were expected to fill the church. As preparations were underway, it was suggested to Paolucci that the school children, virtually all of them black, be placed in the back pews or balcony in order to leave the front pews for white visitors. Paolucci vetoed the idea. With assistance from the nuns, he saw that students were outfitted with new uniforms and shoes. On the day of the celebration, they marched proudly up the aisles to seats reserved for them at the front of the church. Close to 700 former parishioners joined in celebrating mass with Bishop Rehring presiding. "For one day," Paolucci wrote in his diary, "the church was filled with the joy of an integrated community." The following year, St. Henry's School had 201 students; it was the youngest and largest black Catholic school in Cincinnati at that time.[6]

Coming from the Italian countryside, Paolucci worried about the neighborhood children playing in narrow streets and sidewalks. With no parks, no open areas to run or play ball in, no trees to climb, the summers were hot and confining for them. A steady bulldozing of buildings created a dismal and risky environment. As the winter of 1950 progressed, and repairs to the church roof took $5,000 from parish savings, Paolucci knew he had no money for the children's recreation. His diary reports, "The children's desire to get out was matched only by our desire to get them out. As hard as I thought, I saw no substitute for money to build a bridge between what was then termed the asphalt jungle and a real forest jungle for these children of God. Transportation, equipment, allocation of grounds...all cost money."

In March, a meeting of parents was called, and they organized a Fathers' Club, its goal, raising funds for extra-curricular activities for young people. The new club members lent their energy to a weekly social with prizes, crates of tomatoes, bags of potatoes, baskets of strawberries, apples, oranges, and cans of food of every kind as well as modest amounts of cash. Admission was fifty cents. They hoped to attract 2,000 patrons a week from more affluent neighborhoods. The social began in June as a Thursday night bingo, but success was not easily won. A fire started when an altar boy put away an "unlit" piece of charcoal intended for the altar censor. Soon smoke began pouring into the hall and sent bingo players out to the street, their money refunded. On another Thursday, storms flooded the basement with six inches of water, and five hundred dollars were refunded. But Fathers' Club members persevered.[7]

A catalyst to a rapid increase in the bingo's success came in the person of an employee of the Powell Valve Company in Cincinnati. Paolucci met him after speaking to the Knights of Columbus about St. Henry's children and the Fathers' Club's work. Mr. Koester, with a background in accounting and promotion, outlined a strategy to increase attendance and boost income. The size of the prizes would be augmented by soliciting them from prominent businesses. The Fathers' Club bingo would give away not only crates of food, but television sets and large cash prizes as well. The carpentry services of Brother Victor De Gasperi were enlisted in order to help club members enlarge the school's basement. Fliers about the new prizes were printed and distributed. Members of the Fathers' Club, Koester, a local bank manager, Price Hill volunteers, and St. Henry's teenage boys and girls, helped run concession stands, serve guests, and generally make the expanded bingo operation successful. Attendance jumped from two hundred players at the beginning of the summer to two thousand the following fall, and income more than doubled.

Such "gambling" was frowned on by some in the Cincinnati community. But it was extremely popular in the black neighborhoods where it was recognized as a major support of West End parochial schools. It also offered an inexpensive social outlet for neighborhood adults. A University of Cincinnati professor, LaVerne Muldrow Summerlin, who grew up in Holy Trinity parish, remembers bingo as her mother's only source of recreation after a long work week. For a dollar or two, she could relax with friends at bingo. At a time when movie theaters, restaurants, and other "public" entertainment in Cincinnati were segregated, bingo provided inexpensive entertainment for African Americans. Summerlin recalled, "I can remember when there was a bill on the ballot to tax bingo proceeds. You could see bumper stickers all over town that read, 'Keep Your Grandmother Off the Streets: Vote for Bingo!'"[8]

There is no doubt that bingo kept the school running and that it provided 150 children an escape from city pavements during the summer. There were picnics, softball and kickball games, athletic competitions, swimming and boat rides. Paolucci's assistants, Fathers Walter Mattiato and Archie Fornasari, drove school boys to a swimming pool in Dayton, Ohio, seventy-five miles north of Cincinnati. Other children were sponsored for a ten day stay at Camp St. Joseph where a small pool was available. Eventually, Paolucci acquired a bus from the Forestville community, and members of the Fathers' Club put it back in working condition. Between outings, there was a program for the altar servers and a sewing class for the older girls. Films were shown twice a week. Revenues from the bingo covered expenses for these programs, including uniforms (shorts and dresses the mothers sewed), picnic and excursion costs, Camp St. Joseph tuition, movies, Singer sewing machines and good conduct prizes.[9]

When summer came to an end, Bishop Paul F. Leibold, chancellor of the archdiocese, wrote Father Rizzi, Paolucci's superior, "'perhaps many of us sin by defect in not sufficiently praising good work and cooperation that is given us. Lest we fail seriously in this matter, we wish to bring to your attention the fine work that has been accomplished by Father Paolucci at St. Henry Parish during this past summer. We have before us a report on his work, particularly, from the young people of the St. Henry district, and also a report of commendation of his work from the local Catholic Youth Office."

Statistics from 1951 show the increase in students and converts at St. Henry's parish from 1945 to 1951. Over that six year period, the number of students increased from 50 to 201, or 400%, and the number of Catholics increased from 6 to 54, or 900%. But as the number of students increased, the percentage that were Catholic did not keep pace, rising only from 12% to 27%. This was a clear sign that St. Henry's was still a mission parish although the total number of adult converts had increased from 5 in 1945 to 129 in 1950, an encouraging indicator of future success. In sending these figures to Bishop Leibold, Paolucci wrote with some foresight, "right now the history of this parish is at a turn that one may wonder what hardships are lying ahead.[10] Perhaps without realizing it, the Comboni priest put his finger on an issue that had consequences far beyond what would occur at one parish. In the early 1950s, two forces were gaining momentum, and the archdiocese was not adequately prepared for either of them. The first was that urban renewal was disrupting community life in the West End, forcing African Americans out of their homes and parishes, The second was the growing aspirations of African Americans for education, better jobs, and access to better housing and living standards. Negro men who had served in the nation's armed forces that pledged democracy to the world thought it was time to practice it in the United States. Incidents like the one at Springlake, Kentucky, were the kind that sensitized Blacks and some Whites to these facts.

A MATTER OF COLOR

The story of the camp at Springlake, Kentucky, began with an act of generosity. Paolucci described the circumstances, "Through a tireless good friend and the generosity of the president of a railroad in Louisville, we secured a ten-acre piece of land in the State of Kentucky in the locality of Springlake near where the Licking River merges into the Ohio. The spot was beautiful. Magnificent cedars and oaks lined an open, level patch about the size of two Little League baseball diamonds. We found an old cistern on the premises and reactivated it, whitewashing its lining and spraying it with vinegar. Then we had city water dumped in it."

Members of the Fathers' Club, Paolucci, and others began to build a "Camp St. Henry." A pump was bought for the cistern. Weeds were cut, grass mowed. But a shelter was needed for the children. The bus used for outings began carrying cement blocks, sacks of cement, lumber, and members of the Fathers' Club. Men and women rode the bus two or three times a week to Camp St. Henry's sitting on water coolers, furniture and cement bags. Accompanied by Paolucci, they worked for weeks on the shelter and outhouses. Women brought kitchen utensils, patio furniture, and curtains to furnish a staff room and kitchen. It was estimated that between one and two thousand hours went into this project.[11]

But events took an unfortunate turn. Paolucci's diary explains: "The crash program to make St. Henry's Camp functional...did not quite work out. Snags of every kind stood in the way of our strongly determined men. But our human inadequacy was not the only drawback....There was another ugly human factor from outside that gradually gained momentum. Like a pack of dogs alerted by a danger signal, first a few, then a swelling rank, the population around our new premises raised its attention to the new developments at Springlake. Not that those peace-loving people had any prejudices against Blacks. Not that they did not consider them as humans. But just for some inexplicable reason, they did not want them in their community...a thin curtain of resistance grew into a solid wall of opposition. A spokesman from our group was invited by the all-white town council to their official Town Hall meetings. I deliberately sent a white man. The matter was brought up, and unanimously, the town councilmen [passed] a motion that no colored person should cross their roads on the way to our Camp. They said, 'And we came to this conclusion with regret, for your own safety, lest your bus be stoned, and somebody get hurt.' Frustrated, humiliated, embarrassed by his own race, Clarence [Koester] related the meeting to me, tears of deep anger in his eyes."

The first reaction was they could never go back. In his diary, Paolucci explains, "We were not looking for a confrontation. We were only looking for a place...where the children could, for a few hours, escape from the hot ghetto tenements." But, in fact, they did slip back to camp, not often, and not conspicuously. But eventually they had to forego these visits. Others in the West End community wanted to go, and they wondered why they could not. Paolucci and his parishioners never told them about the "racial unacceptance of the Springlake population" for fear of increasing racial tensions, but their neighbors' insistence, Paolucci wrote, "compelled us to finally lock up the Camp once and for all."

It was a long time before the events of September, 1951, were forgotten. When school opened, children were honored for summer program achievements with a day trip to the shrine of Our Lady of Consolation, and Father Mattiato took others to Lake Saint Mary at Maria Stern, a shrine one hundred miles north of Cincinnati. Another group visited Fort Ancient, an Indian burial grounds tucked in the hills along the Little Miami River. Paolucci believed that, "Events...injected into everybody not only the will to look for better things, but a real disposition to enjoy them...We pulled together toward a better world to live in, not necessarily straining to change the world, but consistently exerting an effort to change ourselves...Things were good in those days at St. Henry."[12]

Students and parishioners achieved notable successes. They collected trophies in basketball, softball, and baseball. St. Henry's had regular CYO (Catholic Youth Organization) and Boy Scout affiliations. "Our teams were second to none," Paolucci maintained, "'Where is this new generation coming from?' everybody was asking. All who came in contact with our kids automatically stopped saying that Blacks 'should stay in their place.'" But racial barriers continued. Leading Catholic hospitals in Cincinnati would not accept two students from St. Henry's in their nursing programs, so Paolucci turned to institutions outside the city. When these two young women graduated, they were the first black registered nurses in Cincinnati. In another area, vocations to religious life were nourished at St. Henry's school, but as Paolucci reported, "Equipped with most of the qualifications of any boy or girl, two young ladies applied to enter a religious community, and two boys to our mission seminary. The women religious communities (there were three of them) were not quite ready to meet the 'problem,' and our girls never made it to the doorsteps of a convent. The boys were accepted at...Sacred heart Seminary and proceeded as far as college graduation..." In 1963, one of these former seminarians, Daniel Billings, would carry a cross on his shoulders in the Washington, D.C., Peace March.[13] By the summer of 1953, a Mr. Pierce, who owned a funeral home, offered another property for the use of the school children. The academic and athletic achievements of the parish school continued to gain attention, baptismal classes grew to 60-70 adults a season, and the parish fund-raiser was known as the "best bingo in town."

All this raised expectations, and sometimes even envy. In his six years as pastor of St. Henry's, Paolucci gained an understanding of the cultural prejudices of America, and he witnessed these in the daily lives of his parishioners. Neither he nor they were yet sure how to free themselves from the effects of racism. But the Comboni priest knew change was taking place even if he could not name its ingredients. It was a mix of many things, he believed, "a questioning of the past, a new wave of permissiveness, and a challenge to color barriers."[14]

To give an example of the changes to which Father Paolucci discretely referred, from 1952 to 1954, a number of Protestant clergy and lay people were demonstrating against discrimination at a major amusement park in the Cincinnati area. This amusement park refused to admit Negroes, and some of the demonstrators were subject to violence and arrest. As was not uncommon in the early days of the civil rights movement, there were those who accused such demonstrators of being communists, and this was the opinion of some Catholics and even church leaders.

When Paolucci was transferred from St. Henry's, Father Bart Battirossi was appointed pastor. The following year, his name and that of his assistant, Father Archie Fornasari, appeared on a list of religious leaders who signed a petition addressed to the owners of the amusement park in question. It asked them to admit Negro patrons. Battirossi was questioned by someone from the Archdiocesan chancery about how his name, and that of his assistant, appeared on the petition, the only two Catholic priests listed. Battirossi replied that he had not signed the petition, but the week before, someone had called Father Fornasari and asked him if he was in favor of "Negrores (sic) going to Coney Island," Because Fornasari was working with "colored," he responded affirmatively. Battirossi said Fornasari had no "idea he was working with any groups of preachers on any project, etc. etc."[15]

7. Holy Trinity: Beginning of a Black Diaspora

BLACK CATHOLICS AND THEIR CHURCH

Since the last part of the nineteenth century, black Catholics in America wanted to increase their participation in the life of the Church. Few, if any, Blacks were represented in the clergy, and Catholic institutions, including schools, were segregated by default. As Father Giles Conwill, a former Comboni student, pointed out, even black Catholics in mission parishes tended to be separated from both decision-making and ceremonial roles.[1]

In 1919, Thomas Wyatt Turner founded the Committee Against the Extension of Race Prejudice in the (Catholic) Church. He was one of the first black Catholics to raise the question about increasing participation of blacks in their church.[2], In her biography of Turner, Marilyn Nickels notes that, despite his being a professor of biology at Howard University, Turner lived with the race problem daily. It surfaced when he boarded a train to go to a convention and was forced to a separate compartment, or when he was asked to take a separate elevator to the convention room itself. He knew that it was not necessarily true that if a black man lifted himself out of poverty and ignorance he would be treated as an equal by his fellow white Americans."[3]

Turner wanted Blacks to have access to every role in the Church that Whites enjoyed. He wanted black Catholics to obtain this status without having to collaborate with white priests toward this end. One of these priests was John LaFarge, S.J., who launched the Catholic Interracial Council. These Councils did effect change in the American church through the backing of white clergy and religious like LaFarge. But efforts to achieve equality for black Catholics remained inadequate well into the 1950s.[4]

But in 1954, the United States Supreme Court ruled that segregation in public schools violated the fourteenth amendment of the U.S. Constitution, and in 1955, Blacks in Montgomery, Alabama, boycotted segregated city buses, a new leader, Rev. Martin Luther King , Jr., stepped forward, and the Civil Rights movement was born. Three years later, American bishops stated for the first time that, "The heart of the race question is moral and religious.

It concerns the rights of man and our attitude toward our fellow man. If our attitude is governed by the great Christian law of love of neighbor and respect for his rights, then we can work out harmoniously the techniques for making legal, educational, economic, and social adjustments. But if our hearts are poisoned by hatred, or even by indifference toward the welfare and rights of our fellow men, then our nation faces a grave internal crisis."[5]

Even as America began to address civil rights in the 1960s, African Americans were discovering strength and solidarity in their fight against segregation.[6] Black Catholics began revisiting the separatist versus collaborative modes at issue between Turner and LaFarge. They wanted black leadership and a liturgy deeply rooted in black culture and identity. The move African Americans made from a relatively passive acceptance of their role in the Church to one of criticism and a growing sense of ethnic unity took most white Catholics by surprise. White Catholics had assumed that integration, i.e., acceptance of white culture as the standard, was the goal blacks should and would embrace. The story of African American parishes in Cincinnati's West End, and how they were lost, offers an example of why an acceptance of white culture and control did not always serve the best interests of black Catholics.

WINNERS, LOSERS OF URBAN RENEWAL

Beginning in the 1950s, the work of Comboni missionaries in black parishes was increasingly frustrated by plans to redevelop the West End. A wholesale and chaotic diaspora of black Catholics began as one church after another, one house after another, was leveled. The forces behind this destruction were many and complicated, but four of them were: 1. Overcrowding in congested and neglected neighborhoods. 2. Determination of Cincinnati's business leaders to improve the Central Business District. 3. A strong current of racism that a real estate lobby cultivated to its advantage. 4. Rejection by white citizens of Blacks as neighbors due to property value fears.

A Master Plan for downtown Cincinnati was published in 1948. It included flood control, recommendations for "high-speed transportation," and new business sites. Only a short paragraph was devoted to an admission that "Cincinnati has retrogressed in providing suitable living accommodations" and a satisfactory solution to this was necessary. But a solution was complicated by the fact that although federal monies were available for public housing, on June 3, 1942, the Ohio Supreme Court ruled that authority-owned housing projects were private activity and therefore taxable. This ruling halted any federal monies for such projects in Cincinnati for ten years. Although the Housing Act of 1949 provided money for public housing as well as slum clearance, by default, the Ohio State Supreme Court ruling favored the forces supporting slum clearance.[7]

However state and federal monies were available to raze old buildings and provide new infrastructure, and the city could paid very little for the properties that it condemned. Once cleared, and a new infrastructure constructed, the city believed it could sell the new "improved" property to business and industry and thus, it was argued, increase the tax base. But overlooked were the facts that a) state and federal funding was also taxpayers money, and b) that a good many of the "tenement" buildings were solidly built and very often capable of renovation simply by improving sanitary facilities and making up for deferred maintenance.[8]

In 1948, the Cincinnati Community Development Company (CCDC) arranged for a company to build a 208 unit project as well as other projects. But in the South Cumminsville and College Hill neighborhoods north of the West End, a Realtor circulated petitions claiming that public housing would increase crime and decrease property values. According to one report, those passing out petitions unabashedly asked homeowners, "Do you want N-----rs in your backyard?" In 1952, a group of Realtors tried to pass a public referendum on public housing that would require voter approval of all new public housing projects, and the Home Builders Association and the Home Savings and Loan Companies joined the campaign. Opposing them were those eager to begin construction of the Mill Creek Expressway; the Citizens Committee on Slum Clearance; and the three major newspapers. On November 6, 1952, the referendum was defeated by a substantial majority.

Despite this early victory, community after community fought public housing within its boundaries, and the CMHA (Cincinnati Metropolitan Housing Authority) was forced to retreat from its goal of building in the suburbs. From Delhi Hills on the west of Cincinnati, to the city of Sharonville in the north, suburbanites claimed that mass housing projects would crowd schools, congest traffic, and lower property values. What they were unwilling to state publicly was their desire for a homogeneous community limited to white middle class families.[9]

THE PASSING OF HOLY TRINITY

Holy Trinity, the oldest black parish in the West End, established by Archbishop McNicholas in 1926, was the first in his "Negro Apostolate." McNicholas's Apostolate was so successful that it expanded into other West End churches. A dozen churches and schools were opened to Blacks, among these were the first black Catholic high school in Ohio,[10] and (later) separate black Catholic high schools for girls and boys. A 1950 issue of the *Apostolate of the Negro* newsletter noted that the Negro Apostolate then included five black schools in the West End serving 749 black students. It also reported there were 100,000 Negroes living in the Archdiocese of Cincinnati which constituted "a mission field right here at home." This newsletter was forthright in its discussion of race issues, and in its last issue, it deplored hiring practices that discriminated by color, and it took issue with landlords' neglect of property.[11] No subsequent issue of this newsletter is believed to have been published.[2] After the death of Archbishop McNicholas in 1950, and the virtual end of his Negro Apostolate and its newsletter, a vacuum existed that local pressures could exploit.

In 1949, Father Dominic Ferrara, Comboni pastor at Holy Trinity since 1945, was transferred to Africa as the first Prefect Apostolic of Mupoi in the Sudan. His parishioners raised $927 at a festival and added their own money for his future mission post. The archdiocese also collected $5,700 for Ferrara from pastors and the Indian and Negro fund. Replacing him was his assistant, Father Alexander Nardi, who that year had opened a parish Family Club offering services that included films, a lending library, job search assistance, health care, food, clothing, and legal advice. The interior of the church and its large congregation was the site of many Comboni ordinations. At one, Bishop Edward Mason ordained Fathers Aldo Cescatti, Xavier Colleoni, Aristide Guerra, and Marino Perghem.

Holy Trinity was an important center of Comboni Missionary activity. But what it represented to black Catholics in the West End was suggested by Professor LaVerne Muldrow Summerlin , "When Mother moved to the West End, she was working as a domestic and had four children to raise. She believed Catholic schools would give us a quality education. When we moved

---

[2] Five issues of this newsletter were collected by the author and placed in the Josephite Archives as well as in the Historical Archives of the Chancery of the Archdiocese of Cincinnati.

there, I was in the fifth grade. The twins went to the first grade, and the youngest was in kindergarten. We liked going to school because it was a safe place. We were often there even before the nuns arrived...Going to church was stressed, but we had many extra-curricular activities: plays, teams of all kinds. These were open to both children at Holy Trinity and to [those] not going to Holy Trinity. Amazingly, we were always in the team play-offs, amazing since our parents worked, and couldn't get home till late. Father Ferrara, and later the younger priests, instilled in us an appreciation for four-part music. The Comboni seminarians who came down to sing with us were so good, we felt we had to measure up to them.

"Our whole family converted to Catholicism when I was in the eighth grade: our mother, grandmother, my two sisters and brother. When Father Branchesi was editor of the Comboni magazine, he would get us to help him. He paid us with those orange and green mint slices, the ones that were kind of like jelly on the inside with sugar coating. But to us it was more like working in a home away from home, especially with the recreation room in the basement. Working with the magazine, proofreading, labeling, putting stamps on, putting it together...we did a lot of reading."[12]

Melvin Grier, now a photographer with *The Cincinnati Post*, is a former Holy Trinity student who believes that the kind of discipline and education students found at Holy Trinity school is a lost art: "What was remarkable was that you could go into a classroom, and you wouldn't hear a pin drop. There was such an aura of discipline. The Blessed Sacrament Sisters lived in a house on Dayton Street. They were driven by Mr. Carl Bates in an old Nash. Every morning the nuns would come and pile out of this car. When those four nuns got out...oh my...school had started!...They were *in* charge. Their authority was unquestioned even though that neighborhood was rough and tough.. It was so tough that once, after the school had already closed, we were out on the old playgrounds, and we saw a guy running toward us between the two old school buildings, and we saw puffs of smoke off the wall. The cops were chasing and shooting at him. But whether you were Catholic or not, in those days, everybody respected the nuns. You wouldn't dare not show respect for the nuns. It was unthinkable. They tolerated no nonsense. I remember Sister Julienne in the first grade. She had a way of taking hold of you. If you misbehaved, Sister Regina would put you under her desk... And the Comboni priest would come in and say, 'Are you being good?' You're darned right you were being good."[13]

On the 150th anniversary of Ohio's statehood in 1953, a Missal covered in velvet with brass corners was discovered in a "dusty corner of Holy

Trinity's attic." Dated 1843, there was an inscription written inside from the American Consul in Vienna on the occasion of Holy Trinity's dedication as the first German Church in Cincinnati.[14] Ironically, 1953 was the year of the first dismantling of the old church. A report to the Archdiocese explained that an inspection of the church tower revealed that fractures in its terminal masonry buttresses had increased. Bids for repairs came in with several options, a) repairing the tower and church, b) removing the tower, and c) razing the entire church to the ground. Estimates for razing the entire church were virtually equal to the cost of repairing the tower.

   In reporting these bids, Father Nardi also gave the archdiocese his views on a suggestion [evidently made by the chancery] to merge Holy Trinity with St. Anthony's, another black parish in the West End. Nardi's letter throws light on both churches' circumstances, "...St. Anthony's is too far out of the way, next to the railroad tracks and coal yards. Holy Trinity has more transportation facilities and is centrally located. Moreover, Trinity has always been *remarkable in the West End for [its] religious and recreational activities.*" [Emphasis added] Nardi enumerated a litany of Trinity's activities: the Holy Name and the Altar Societies, the St. Catherine Society, the Legion of Mary, the Club for High School Students Boy Scout Troop, two Girl Scout Troops, five teams who now belonged to the Catholic Youth Council, the Red Cross courses in civil defense, and the recently opened Holy Trinity Family Club.[15] Even this list is not complete.

   In early May, Monsignor Leibold granted Nardi permission to remove the church tower. He gave explicit directions on how to lower the bells, how to prepare the school auditorium as a chapel, and how to fix the school basement for social purposes. When the demolition of the tower took place, other parts of the building were found to be deteriorating. The cost of repairs appeared prohibitive, and the archdiocese decided to raze the entire church.[16] The decision was reported in a local newspaper: "One of the venerable landmarks in Cincinnati's West End, the century-old Holy Trinity church, will be torn down this summer....Decision to raze the structure was made after an examination revealed that the steeple, ceiling, windows, and other parts of the building had deteriorated to such an extent that it was felt that the cost of renovating it would be prohibitive....After the wrecking operation begins, church services will be held in the school auditorium. Father Alexander Nardi...said an altar would be erected on the auditorium stage and that a moveable partition would separate the sanctuary from the auditorium when the hall would be used for other than church purposes. The rectory, which adjoins the rear of the church, will be left standing. The three church bells will be sent to St. Catherine's Church, Cincinnati."[17]

The parishioners of Holy Trinity contributed generously to the renovation of the school auditorium. Father Nardi noted in his house diary, "The City of Cincinnati... has various plans about the general refixing of the area... it will take years before things are settled... it is beautiful to see how the poverty of our situation does not discourage our parishioners, nor does it cause the non-Catholics to take their children out of our poor school [even] when there is a nice new public school not too far away and the education there is free.... At the end of last year [June, 1953], there were 185 students in Holy Trinity school, half of whom were non-Catholics."

Students could not officially join the Church unless one of their parents was Catholic. Otherwise, a child had to wait until he or she reached an age of responsibility, generally considered 12 years. Melvin Grier, as a student at Holy Trinity, found himself in that situation. His Catholic mother had died, and his father was not Catholic. Yet his father never missed a PTA (Parent Teacher's Association) meeting at Holy Trinity. Grier said, "He told me that my mother's dying words were, 'Don't send that boy to [the public] Jackson School,' And this, even though we could literally look out our window and see Jackson School. I had to wait till eighth grade to become a Catholic because there were no Catholics in my family, but my father never dreamed of letting me miss Mass."[18]

In 1954, when Nardi was transferred to Monroe, he summarized the achievements of students attending Holy Trinity. The boys of the elementary school had won the city championship in basketball. Three of four scout masters from Cincinnati who won the Boy Scouts' Silver Beaver award were Holy Trinity parishioners. There was a substantial apostolate to the sick and poor with the pastor visiting the sick in the hospital, in the "old folks homes," and in the home for the blind. One 'quintale' [220 lbs] of clothes had been distributed, and a parish St. Vincent de Paul Society was organized. A census carried out by the Legion of Mary had found 10,000 people. Nardi and his assistant, Father Dominic Pazzaglia, were visiting those whose marriages needed "straightening out," and children of such marriages were being baptized. In 1954, Holy Trinity was still a parish with a lively spiritual and communal life.

BEGINNING OF A BLACK DIASPORA

When Nardi was transferred to Monroe in 1954, Father Oliver Branchesi added pastoral work at Holy Trinity to his duties as editor of *Frontier Call.* For six months he did this alone until Father Aldo Cescatti arrived from Italy to take over the magazine work. In 1955, Archbishop Alter sent Branchesi a notice that, "With the growing shortage of available teachers and the changing complexion of the territory around Holy Trinity...it has become necessary to decide on the closing of Holy Trinity School at the end of this...year." Although the number of students at Holy Trinity was closer to 187, Alter believed there were only 150, and they could be easily absorbed in other black schools: St. Anthony's, St. Edward's, and St. Henry's.[19] Branchesi was to tell his people about the closing after the school year ended. Informal communication from the chancery advised Branchesi that the archdiocese would eventually replace several West End parishes with a new church and school. Students of Holy Trinity, he was told, were to be assigned to different parishes, not moved as a unit.[20] Obviously, this was the most convenient method of absorbing so many students for the other parishes, but it nonetheless initiated one of the first "scatterings" that would rend the Holy Trinity community, and leave its members confused and abandoned.

Grier recalled his thoughts as a child when his parish connections were severed one by one, "I remember the day they took the bells out of our church. And we cried. We really cried. Then I remember when they started tearing the church down. We were in class when they pulled down one of the walls. It scared us. We jumped up and ran from the window. And I remember when they told us they were going to close the school. We cried again. When you remember the way things were, and you think about how it was taken away from you...But then we were passive about these decisions. We thought, 'This is a decision of the archdiocese, and the archdiocese must be doing what is right.' Now I think we would fight it! We would fight it."

Even after the school closed, the parish maintained one of the highest number of conversions, and over one hundred parishioners demonstrated their loyalty by pledging regular donations over two and a half years toward the building of a new church. As Branchesi noted, "the amounts are comparable to the donations of any other parish in the city in spite of [the parishioners] economic disadvantage." On June 12, 1955, the first black priest from Cincinnati, Father Allen Tarlton, celebrated his first Solemn High Mass at Holy Trinity. Tarlton, a Benedictine monk, was ordained a priest on June 4 in the Cathedral of St. Cloud, Minnesota. His Superior from the Benedictine monastery at Collegeville, Minnesota, and five other monks (four of them black), accompanied Tarlton to Cincinnati. There, Holy Trinity's auditorium was festively decorated and packed with people who witnessed this historical event. Father Accorsi, who had encouraged Tarlton in his vocation, assisted at the Mass; Father Branchesi acted as deacon; and Clarence Rivers, destined to be the first African American priest from Cincinnati to serve in the Archdiocese, acted as sub-deacon.[21]

A parish is a community with a common purpose, and that purpose is of the highest nature, to seek the way of the Lord. When such a community is broken up, something much greater than a collection of individuals goes with it. Branchesi sensed this in the last days of Holy Trinity, and he wrote about it many years later, "When I went back to Holy Trinity in 1954, urban renewal was underway, old tenements were coming down, expressways were being built, a new bridge [was going up] on the Ohio, and the Third Street distributor was being built. Old St. Peter in Chains Cathedral was regaining its splendor. I was like a man coming home who could not find his own people. Going through the baptismal records, I found that 1,000 people had been baptized at Holy Trinity since it was designated a black congregation [in 1926]. But no more than 150 of them were still living within the parish limits. I was determined to find the other 850, and I succeeded in finding all of them. Most had moved into twenty-one different parishes within the city; some were in Old Folks' homes; a few were at the cemetery where I said a prayer over their graves. The Legion of Mary and the St. Vincent de Paul Society,...found many still living around the parish, in attics and basements, alone, waiting for the bulldozer to decide their future."

Yet in that dying neighborhood, Branchesi said, there was still a lively faith. There was Linda, a member of the Junior Legion of Mary, who shopped for a blind lady, cleaned house for an old woman, and did other works of mercy. Linda's story appeared in the *Catholic Telegraph,* and it was the topic of a local radio "talk" show when call after call commended her performance. Then there was Bennie Rogers, an elderly man who often went with Branchesi in search of former Holy Trinity members. One day, Bennie came to the parish office with a Holy Water sprinkler in his hands and said to Branchesi, "I've got a surprise for you. Come and bless it." Bennie had bought a used car for the Holy Name Society in order to help "go around the city and find our brothers." This he did, faithfully reporting his visits and never accepting any money for expenses. There was also Miss Aman who, after retiring from a government job due to ill-health, devoted herself to teaching catechism to shut-ins in the West End. Somehow, she found her way through dark alleys and up cluttered stairways to cramped and dirty attics, talked for hours to lonely, blind, and often crippled people without friends or relatives. By the time Branchesi closed Holy Trinity, he had baptized the one hundred and fifteenth person that Miss Aman prepared to enter the church.

It all ended in 1958. The Comboni Provincial, Hamlet Accorsi, wrote his superior in early September of that year, "The archbishop here called me last week to tell me he intends to close Holy Trinity, and he was proposing to give us St. Anthony on Budd Street. This is also an old church that is to give up the ghost. In any case, after consultation, we have decided to accept..."

Afraid that vacated facilities might be condemned if they deteriorated, the archdiocese' chancellor wrote to Branchesi, "I am reliably informed that it will be a year before the City is prepared to go into that area for Kenyon-Barr purchases -- meanwhile we are responsible for the upkeep of the place." The solution, he thought, was for Branchesi to remain in charge of Holy Trinity buildings even while he acted as pastor of St. Anthony's parish, a mile away. He suggested that, after boarding up the house, cutting off the water, etc, the school might be used for bingo by St. Anthony's parishioners or by other churches or nearby schools.[22] When, in 1960, the City of Cincinnati purchased the Holy Trinity property, the archdiocese accepted an offer of $79,000.

Father Branchesi moved to St. Anthony's in 1958. Its physical plant, he said, was in good shape,"if you didn't mind the [coal] dust that's been piling up for 25 years or so, or the fact that it was bordered by train tracks and coal yards." With former Holy Trinity parishioners coming to it, five hundred people attended Mass on Sunday. It now had the highest number of converts of any parish in Cincinnati. The school, run by the Franciscan Sisters of Mary, had 170 students.[23]

St. Anthony's, Branchesi discovered, was close to celebrating its centennial. With the help of friends, including an owner of a neighborhood factory, the huge interior of the church was painted, and a Centenary Committee formed that included former parishioners, both Irish and German. The church had a seating capacity of 1,000, but the committee believed even more people could be expected. A suggestion was made to have a separate Mass for the former parishioners, or else keep all the black parishioners in the choir loft. Branchesi had a different solution. He purchased all the grey, white, and navy blue cloth he needed from army surplus at practically no cost. Then a Jewish friend who owned a clothing factory was willing to make new uniforms for St. Anthony's students. Finally, Don Shafer, the factory owner who helped pay to paint the church, bought new shoes and socks to match the uniforms. Branchesi described what happened, "We kept everything secret. At the Centennial Mass, the church was bright with fresh paint and flowers, and it was packed with people. When the time came for the service, leading the procession before the Archbishop were 150 school children walking slowly, two by two, down the aisle. They genuflected before the altar, turned back, split, and continued down the side aisles to the choir loft where they sang a polyphonic Mass with Comboni seminarians."

Father Paolucci returned to the West End to care for the parish when Branchesi was transferred. In 1962, the *Catholic Telegraph* announced: "Ninety-six year old St. Anthony's church, Budd Street, Cincinnati, will be removed to permit work on the Queensgate Urban Renewal Project, an announcement by city officials revealed last week....The city has agreed to pay $360,000 for the church property...St. Anthony's parochial school has been discontinued, and the Franciscan Missionary Sisters of Mary... have returned to their provincial house in New York."[24]

St. Anthony's was the second black Catholic church in the West End closed for demolition. The site it stood on remains, abandoned and undeveloped. Former Holy Trinity and St. Anthony parishioners were sent to St. Henry's parish a mile away. When this, too, was claimed by the wrecking ball, no thriving business centers replaced it.

REFLECTIONS ON A LOST COMMUNITY

St. Edward/St. Ann's parish in the West End was served by diocesan priests. It was the successor of St. Ann's, in 1866 the first black parish in Cincinnati. This historical monument to black evangelization was closed even before St. Henry's. Not all of these parishes, and the neighborhoods they served, were torn down due to their poor condition or the need to construct an expressway. Some were simply victims of a poorly conceived plan to replace residences in the West End, with commercial business and industry. The city planner, Ladislas Segoe, commenting on the lost opportunities of Cincinnati's urban renewal said: "That was...a very tragic error made by the city, when they moved in there with their bulldozers... and demolished most of those [buildings] in the hope, believe it or not, of getting some multi-story industrial buildings...thinking that maybe history [would] repeat itself....This, of course, did not materialize, and in the process they have done away with an awful lot of well designed, solid buildings that could have been rehabilitated. The social tragedy of this was no provision for the reception of the people who have been displaced..."

Professor Zane L. Miller, of the University of Cincinnati, added to Segoe's critique of West End renewal, "...most of the West End...was a slum, but it was neither stagnant nor yet doomed to indefinite decline....Its population was appallingly poor, disproportionately old, and discouraged by the petty criminality and drunken dereliction. The small middle class residue was terrified...by their lack of control and the prospect of forced removal into a new neighborhood....they organized and insisted through the West End Community Council and Queensgate II Club, the only channels open to their grievance, that their neighborhood be...preserved. Desperately afraid, they could not afford the luxury of a riot. Their fate...rested with the outsiders who met regularly in City Hall...and the Old Vienna, a restaurant across the street from City Hall."[25]

Most of the former parishioners of Holy Trinity, and the other Catholic churches that were demolished, made their way into parishes in the next tier of suburbs around the city. They went in small groups, and were often treated as intruders. In the process of being cast out not only from their churches but also from their homes, many felt betrayed by the white community, including church officials. Those interviewed for this history said church attendance became less important to some of their fellow Catholics, and a good number joined other denominations. Virtually all the former Holy Trinity parishioners interviewed wondered what happened to the money they donated to build a new church to replace Holy Trinity. The only one rebuilt in the West End was St. Joseph's, a parish not listed among those in McNicholas's Negro Apostolate.

After serving his country in the air force, and attaining a reputation as a noted journalist and newspaper photographer, Melvin Grier still ponders on what is left of his old neighborhood, a place where African Americans owned their own businesses, had their own movies, and could meet their black heroes at the local clubs:

"People got into fights. People went to jail. I remember a riot out in the middle of the street at Fifth and Mound. They weren't ideal times, but it was in balance. I have childhood friends who were murdered, but I also have childhood friends who are successful attorneys, who have done well in politics and in business. Pete Randolph was the first black attorney in Cincinnati. And there were many others....if you look at aerial photographs of the West End as it was, and look at [new ones to see] what has been removed for... expressways or what-have you, [you have to ask], "Where did those people go? What happened? Well, what happened was Holy Trinity disappeared, St. Henry disappeared. St. Anthony disappeared. [St. Edward]/

St. Ann disappeared. St. Joseph as we knew it disappeared. St. Mary's Hospital and Mercy Academy disappeared.... And it makes a difference. It makes a tremendous difference....A major aggravation in my life, for which I can forgive no one, is that I don't have any of my childhood I can go back to.."[26]

Father Timothy McNicholas, nephew of the archbishop, observed that since Comboni Missionaries accepted ministry at three of the four black parishes that were razed, they were stigmatized in Cincinnati's clerical circles as priests "who closed churches." The Archdiocese of Cincinnati was the only diocese in which this was the case. In other dioceses, Comboni Missionaries left them as prospering and spiritually vital institutions. Former parishioners of West End churches understand this about Comboni pastors. As Grier pointed out, "The Church should serve people....and they might have been Italian priests, they might have been [Blessed Sacrament] nuns, but they served the people. That was the difference. They lived in our community. They were part of us. And you knew that. And that's why you respected them..."[27]

When Father Hamlet Accorsi took over as head of the American province in 1953, he was convinced that he would not receive ministry in any viable black parish in Cincinnati. This undoubtedly affected his actions in his search for new ministry in the United States.

8. Opening in Louisville

By the early 1950s, Fathers Rizzi and Accorsi had reason to believe that black ministry in Cincinnati was limited. Both priests had searched diligently for such ministry in dioceses all over the United States. But as the end of his provincialate drew near, Rizzi had no offers. The Comboni vocation recruiter Father Charles Busetti, however, had made a friend in Louisville: Father D. Autheman, a diocesan pastor of an Italian parish. Autheman was so impressed with Comboni missionaries that he approached Louisville's Archbishop Floersh, and asked for a Comboni priest to serve as his assistant at St. Michael's parish. When Auxiliary Bishop Maloney spoke to Rizzi about this, he also offered to give Comboni Missionaries the opportunity to open a new black parish in Louisville. In the spring of 1952, only months after arriving from Italy, twenty-eight year old Father Robert Erbisti, went to Louisville to assist Autheman at St. Michael's Church.[1] That same fall, Autheman submitted his resignation to Archbishop Floersh. Erbisti was the first Comboni priest to serve at St. Michael's, a challenging assignment for a young priest only a few months in the United States. Soon thereafter, he was called back to Cincinnati to teach at Sacred Heart Seminary and Father Frank Di Francesco replaced him at St. Michael's.[2] A seasoned missionary, Di Francesco was named administrator of St. Michael's. Floersh wrote Rizzi about efforts to acquire property for the black parish. Not long before he left for his society's General Chapter in Italy, Rizzi was asked to inspect property purchased in Louisville's West End for the new parish. Rizzi learned that the church, school, and rectory would be built under one roof, and partially financed by the Archdiocese.

In August, 1953, Floersh sent a copy of a decree establishing the parish of the Immaculate Heart of Mary (IHM) to those pastors whose parish boundaries would be affected. The parishes were Christ the King, Holy Cross, St. Benedict, St. George, and St. Denis churches. James J. Maloney, at Holy Cross, wrote Floersh that establishment of the new parish would "take care of a great spiritual void in this part of the City. You are to be congratulated upon selection of the site you have chosen."[3]

SLAVERY, SEGREGATION, AND BLACK CATHOLICS IN LOUISVILLE

Louisville, approximately one hundred miles southwest of Cincinnati, was settled on the south side of the Ohio River, a river that marked the boundary between slave and free states in the Civil War. During the years of slavery, Negroes fleeing from the South knew that, if they could safely cross the Ohio, they had a chance to escape slavery. Many perished in this desperate bid for freedom. Those who survived sought sanctuary in the "underground railroad," a series of safe havens among white abolitionists who risked fines, loss of property, and prison if fugitive slaves were found on their premises. In the 1850s, Harriet Tubman, born a slave herself, led over three hundred men, women, and children across the waters of the Ohio River from Kentucky, risking her own freedom nineteen times on these trips.

Near the end of the 1700s, Western Kentucky became a center for black Catholics as their Catholic masters from Maryland migrated to Nelson County and adjacent areas. The first bishop of Bardstown, Kentucky, Benedict Joseph Flaget (1763-1850), owned slaves, and there were slaves in the seminary of St. Thomas founded by Flaget. Slaves from Maryland had been subjected to more than a century of toil under Maryland's slave code. It was the first to establish the perpetuity of slavery and extend the definition of slavery to those "any freeborn English woman" produced by a Negro slave."[4] In Kentucky, the slave system was seen as necessary means to support priests and nuns on the American frontier. An historian writing about the use of slaves to work the land around St. Thomas Seminary remarked, "But the [slave] system was vicious, and calculated to hold the Church back.... until slavery was abolished and the support of the Church was thrown directly and unavoidably upon the people, there were not more than twenty priests laboring in the country [side] and small villages of the Diocese of Louisville."

The Emancipation Proclamation issued by Abraham Lincoln took effect on January 1, 1863. It freed the slaves in all states and territories still at war with the Union. In 1866, the Archbishop of Baltimore, Martin Spalding, formerly Bishop of Louisville, called a council "to discuss the future status of the negro (sic). Four million of these unfortunates are thrown on our Charity..." he declared, "It is a golden opportunity for reaping a harvest of souls, which neglected may not return."[5] The Second Plenary Council opened on October 7, 1866. It threw the American hierarchy into a bitter debate about whether or not a separate episcopate should be established for Catholic Negroes. Little that was positive resulted in the way of ministry to African

Americans. A decision for the status quo was taken, and each bishop could decide for himself what was best for black Catholics in his diocese. A pastoral letter published by the Council recognized that a "most extensive field of charity and devotedness" was opened to the American prelates, but they believed it would have been better if, "...in accordance with the action of the Catholic Church in past ages, in regard to the serfs of Europe, a more gradual system of emancipation could have been adopted, so that they [the slaves] might have been in some measure prepared to make a better use of their freedom, than they are likely to do now..." The failure to form a coherent policy for ministry and evangelization of former slaves has been called, "one of the tragedies of American church history..."

The Third Plenary Council in 1884 established an annual collection for Indians and Negroes, to be taken up in all dioceses on the first Sunday of Lent and sent to the Commission for Catholic Missions Among the Colored People and Indians. The amount collected by this Commission was never exceptionally generous, but it was a source of funds for building and maintaining schools and churches intended for black Catholics. Even before these funds were available in Louisville, St. Augustine's was established for Negroes in 1868. In 1871, St. Augustine's School for Colored opened. This was the only church with a school for Negroes in Louisville.[6]

In 1896, the United States Supreme Court, in its decision on *Plessy vs. Ferguson,* permitted "separate but equal" facilities for African Americans, thus bestowing its blessing on segregation. Black Catholics who attended segregated churches in and around Louisville in the early 1900s recall such segregated practices. African Americans were relegated to the back of the church, often with standing room only; and they were only allowed to receive Communion after white Catholics received it. Segregation was extended even in death by burying black Catholics in the rear plots of Catholic cemeteries. Such practices were not isolated to southern states like Kentucky. Cincinnati, as well as other cities in the North, adopted similar practices lasting well into this century. All this tore at the pride of African Americans, persuading some who were Catholic to prefer separate churches where they would not be embarrassed at worship.[7]

Although Blacks in Louisville could vote without interference, as late as the 1940s and 1950s, most restaurants, hotels, theaters, occupations, professions, and parks were still closed to them. Until 1950, both the public and parochial school systems were segregated as well as the university and most of the library system. Finally, in 1950, the Kentucky Legislature, through an amendment, repealed the infamous 1904 Day Law. By doing so, it killed the legal underpinnings of school segregation. Amendments to the law, however, stated that in institutions of higher education, the schools' elected officials had the right to decide whether or not to integrate. To their credit, the Catholic colleges of Louisville, Bellarmine, Nazareth, and Ursuline immediately announced that their doors were open to all races. Catholic elementary and secondary schools followed suit.[8]

Against this background, the question arises concerning why Archbishop Floersh decided to open a virtually exclusive black church. The answer may lie in the experiences black Catholics still had when they attended "white" churches. First, there were no churches in the West End of Louisville specifically for black Catholics. According to Mrs. Mary Luella Conwill, whose family lived in Louisville for generations, there were only two churches for black Catholics in that area, St. Augustine's near the border of the West End at 13th and Broadway, and St. Peter Claver, a very small church on Lampton Street. Mrs. Conwill and her mother attended Mass daily, but going to the white church close by home could be humiliating. During her third pregnancy, Mrs. Conwill went to mass at St. Louis Bertrand's, only four blocks from her home. But on taking her seat, a man tapped her shoulder and said, "You'll have to move. You don't belong in this pew," and he pointed to the back rows of the church. When the Conwill family moved within a short distance of another Catholic church, they were treated so poorly that they preferred to travel to the all-black church of St. Augustine's several miles away.[9] Racial bias still ran high in Louisville, and Archbishop Floersh did not want black Catholics exposed to it in church.

GATHERING THE FLOCK

When Father Alfio Mondini first came to the United States in 1948 at the age of 32, he served at St. Henry's in Cincinnati, then at the Indian mission at Pala. But his desire to serve Blacks ran so high, that he was never fully satisfied in California. In 1953, he was selected by Father Rizzi to be the first pastor of the new parish in Louisville, which was to be known as Immaculate Heart of Mary (IHM). At Louisville, Di Francesco took Mondini to visit Archbishop Floersh. The only document Mondini brought with him was a letter from Rizzi announcing that he would stay temporarily with Di Francesco "where you will eat well while waiting to start the new parish." The archbishop laughed when he heard this, for it was obvious to him that Mondini was a "string bean" of a man. Floersh warned him, "Yes, you better put some flesh on your bones." On September 7, 1953, Floersh sent a copy of the decree to Mondini officially establishing the IHM parish and announcing his appointment as pastor. Floersh gave the Comboni priest his blessing, but warned him, "When you go there, Father, you might [only] find four or five Catholic families in all."[10] While at St. Michael's, Mondini made daily visits to his parish neighborhood in order to take a census. On his first trip, he hired a taxi and gave the driver the address of the future church at 34th and Southwick Avenue. "Oh, you don't want to go there, Father," warned the cabbie, "That's over in Little Africa. You won't like it." "Little Africa, is it?" Mondini pondered, "Oh, I think I will like it very well."

Mrs. Conwill, who lived in the new IHM parish boundaries, remembers the Comboni missionary's first days, "The first I heard about Father Mondini was that he was walking around the parish gathering information on the Catholics in this area. He walked everywhere, met people, and was directed to others. It was an inspiration to all of us because he was so wrapped up in his vocation. The people loved him from the beginning because he was so caring. He came with an interest and love that I'll never forget." When the census was complete, Mondini found not four or five Catholics in his parish, but one hundred fifty families in which at least one member was Catholic.[11]

The land around the new parish was swampy and the roads muddy. Government housing projects were rising on the horizon. A single-resident housing project called Alpha Gardens was more attractive than the projects, and it offered those in the multi-family projects an opportunity to buy their own homes when their economic circumstances improved. When Immaculate Heart of Mary parish was established, the neighborhood was integrated, and many of the black and white families were long term residents. As Mondini was exploring his parish, a ceremony was held in honor of opening one of these new housing projects. A Protestant minister said an opening prayer, and Mondini said a closing one. Mondini prayed, "that the 650 families in the project would grow to be as one big family, governed by the laws of love of the Ten Commandments, and blessed by the care of the Blessed Mother." At the ceremony's conclusion, the Mayor of Louisville approached Mondini, took hold of his hand, gestured toward the people, and said, "They are yours now Father. Please take care of them."

It was November when Mondini took up residence in his parish. Before moving in, someone telephoned him that the archbishop had an old car for him. His new address was a vacant white house with no furnishings inside. Both black and white parishioners soon combined efforts to clean the house and bring the necessary furniture. In local news, Mondini was described as a "tall, thin man, with greying hair, eloquent hands and a dream." He was quoted as saying that, while he had visited many places and met a host of good people, he had never met more generous people than those in Louisville, Kentucky. One of the parishioners, remembering her first impressions of this Comboni priest, said, "You could tell that [he] lived in the spirit of poverty. I remember finding Father Mondini walking around in his overcoat inside that house to conserve on utility bills. 'What are you doing?' I said to him, 'You need heat in here.'"[12]

A week after moving, Mondini celebrated Sunday Masses in an improvised chapel at the house. When people attending these Masses overflowed into the kitchen, Mondini moved them to the auditorium of a nearby housing project. At Christmas, an old but large nativity scene was donated. With a little painting and a few repairs, it was set up in a barn next to the parish house. Father Walter Mattiato, who assisted Mondini at the time, recalled, "When Father Mondini first went there, there was nothing. We didn't have a housekeeper, a secretary, a janitor, or money, but the people were good to us..Our Catholics did not mind... kneeling in a barn. That Christmas, the place best resembled the very first one in Bethlehem..."[13]

The barn on the parish property still had stalls in it, a dirt floor, no electricity, and a leaking roof. But Mondini envisioned a new use. Together with volunteers, hard work, and his own perseverance, a transformation took place. The primitive outbuilding was turned into a temporary chapel. William Conwill, later a Comboni Missionary student and now a clinical psychologist, was nine years old at the time. He explained how this could happen in a parish where weekly collections rarely amounted to more than a few hundred dollars, "[Mondini] was someone who was always scraping things up, bringing in wood, bringing in supplies. He would beg anything: bricks, siding, roofing, shingles, whatever it took." In this way, Mondini and his volunteers removed stalls, poured cement floors, installed lights, and put a substantial roof on the barn. Work continued through the cold winter nights of 1953-1954. By April, when the weather permitted, the unheated "barn" served as a chapel until construction of the new church was completed. Mondini recognized that those who gave materials for this chapel often gave them at some sacrifice. But they did this as members of a new community. He said, "The stable may be poorer [than the housing project's auditorium], but at least we are at 'home.'"

Financial help began coming to the new parish. On January 27, the Ladies Auxiliary of the Italian-American Brotherhood gave a spaghetti supper to benefit IHM, and IHM ladies worked in the kitchen with high school girls serving as waitresses. Holy Cross parish donated $10,000 in bonds through the archdiocese. Mondini spent time speaking at local Catholic schools on behalf of Blacks and Indians. In addition, he was giving adult instructions twice a week, and private instructions to those confined to their home.[14]

ST MICHAEL'S: A "TEMPORARY ASSIGNMENT"

St. Michael's parish in Louisville was the first white church accepted by Comboni Missionaries in America. Accepting it was not viewed as a total compromise with the original mission to African Americans since it led to establishing Immaculate Heart of Mary for Blacks. And St. Michael's did fit the Comboni criterion of ministry to the "poorest and most abandoned." Located in a neighborhood suffering the same misfortunes as black parishes in Cincinnati's West End, urban renewal was gradually eroding what was once a neighborhood. The difference in Louisville was that the people being displaced were white, not black. Father Di Francesco described the area in his house diary: "It is made up of the nearly poor and blue collar workers...They live in huge apartment buildings for five dollars a week...some Syrian and Italian families consider themselves the stable nucleus of the parish, that is, until they have the money to buy a home on the outskirts of the city....In the school, I have about 50 students, of whom about one third are Protestants who prefer our school to the public one...the Monsignor Secretary of the School Board came twice to propose that I close the school because of the scarcity of nuns. I insisted that we keep the school open as an important means of approaching families and to exercise a good influence on the neighborhood. The last time, I spoke clearly to the Monsignor: 'I want to have the school to be able to do a bit of good for these poor families, not because I love to have headaches. But if the bishop wants to close it...' The Monsignor replied, 'I am sure the bishop won't close it.'"

Di Francesco was not a priest to budge from his convictions. In 1954, when he wrote this, he was 41 years old, had served in the African missions as early as 1939, was a military chaplain in 1940, volunteered to serve in a prison camp a year later, and in 1946, was in Palestine caring for prisoners in the Gaza Strip. He had an air of gruffness about him that intimidated younger students when he taught in the seminary, but he never minced words when he believed he was right.

In 1955, Di Francesco lost his battle for St. Michael's school, but gave up only after a letter came directly from the archbishop. In that same year, he had taken on ministry duties at a new Jewish hospital which had many Catholic patients and nurses. On one occasion, he was called to the hospital to prevent a suicide. He succeeded where the doctors and nurses could not. Hospital work required frequent visits every week as well as emergency calls. Jewish doctors often called upon DiFrancesco for advice about Church teachings when it came to "certain operations."

Urban renewal persisted relentlessly around St. Michael's, just as in Cincinnati at that time. Old buildings were torn down, and a huge open air market moved out of the city. New industries developed as property zoning changed, and this affected the atmosphere of the neighborhood. Older Italians, Di Francesco wrote, were disappearing one after another. But those who took their place still loved to attend the little church because it was "always clean and recollected, where you can pray with devotion." In 1956, he reported, "We are in this parish more than four years, and it was supposed to be only a temporary assignment while waiting to do a work among the Blacks more in keeping with our missionary vocation....but the superiors have not seen fit to withdraw the father from this parish because the Archbishop who had shown himself so kind and pleased with us, would not like it."[15]

BUILDING A BLACK PARISH

While the days of St. Michael's parish were numbered, at Immaculate Heart of Mary, Mondini was deeply involved with opening a new parish plant and learning about its finances. The archdiocese, he was told, paid approximately $30,000 for the church property, and it was planning to pay an additional $20,000 toward construction of the physical plant. The remainder of the cost would be borrowed and paid off over time. As construction began, a note was sent to the Louisville Gas & Electric Company advising it to allow for three separate billing entities under the one roof of the structure: a parish church, a school, and a priests' home or rectory. Mondini's thoughts about the size and type of building were solicited. On January 8, a bulldozer leveled the ground for the church and school, and on February 1, the foundation was poured. Construction continued throughout the spring and summer.

At one point, a conflict arose between Mondini and the contractor, and the contractor eventually complained to the chancery. His electrician had obtained incandescent fixtures that were used from a public school at no cost. As he began installing them in the school, Mondini raised objections, saying that only fluorescent fixtures should be installed. The electrician argued with him, and Mondini told him that, if the used incandescents were installed, the cost would double. He would remove them within a week and replace them with fluorescent lighting. Hearing this from his electrician, the contractor joined the argument against Mondini, telling him there were "better ways to spend extra money than on these fixtures." But he did not persuade the priest. "Fr. Mondini," the contractor told the chancery, "feels that his people will feel that they are being given the other fixtures because of their color." The difference in cost amounted to only $600, and the chancery office decided in Mondini's favor.[16]

Soon after going to Louisville, Mondini began a search for nuns to staff the new school. Mother Anselm of the Blessed Sacrament Sisters regretfully turned him down for lack of available teachers. In mid-August, 1954, IHM was visited by the Mother General of the Dominican Sisters, but she could not promise any teaching nuns until after Christmas. Discussing this with Archbishop Floersh, Mondini was concerned that another year would go by before the school could open. Monsignor Pitt, Director of the Catholic School Board, arrived at IHM a week later, and announced that four grades at IHM school could open using lay teachers, at least until Christmas. Due to the lateness of this decision, there was concern that parents would continue to send their children to public schools. On the September 2 registration day, a member of the archdiocesan school board stopped by to check on how many had registered. He found the names of forty students. The opening day, the school found Mrs. Mary Luella Conwill and Mrs. Minnie London teaching sixty-one pupils. By February, 1955, the Dominican nuns arrived, and Mondini and Mattiato turned the residence over to them. For their own living quarters, they partitioned off a spare classroom.[17]

Mondini did not count numbers when it came to accepting converts into the Catholic Church. He told a confrere, "We need first-class Catholics, of the heroic kind...those who have the courage to live, with the help of God's grace, a thoroughly Christian life." Mondini did not limit the hours it took to prepare such converts either. At Christmas, he recorded twelve baptisms, six of which involved adults whom he had instructed twice a week for an entire year. A High Mass celebrating the Christ Child's birth was still held in the crowded barn.

There were times when Mondini was discouraged and times when he was weary especially if fewer people attended a service than expected. But then he was cheered if, during a Forty Hours service, someone was present in the church at all hours or local clergy came to closing services. In the summer of 1955, Mondini took a visiting confrere around his parish. They drove over old, rough, unpaved streets onto new paved ones. They saw old shacks near modern structures. A great deal had changed in two years. "The city,"

Mondini noted, "is showing signs of effective interest in the improvement of this area."[18]

That fall, IHM school opened with 115 students. An additional Dominican Sister came to teach a fifth and sixth grade, and construction finally came to an end. On the morning of December 4, 1955, Bishop Charles G. Maloney officiated at the ceremony dedicating the church. That afternoon, Archbishop Floersh led the ceremony dedicating the school. Father Mattiato worked continuously on the Christmas Crib in the hall, hooking up lighting effects and a recording of the Nativity story. Visitors from around Louisville agreed it was the best Nativity scene in the city.

By the summer of 1956, parish activities were growing as more and more people participated in them. A Parent Teachers Association collected money to refinish the classroom floors. Two more bedrooms were added to the convent to accommodate additional nuns, and a fence constructed around it. One hundred and fifty students enrolled that fall, and Mattiato remembers this as a time when the parish was building a strong community base with an Altar Society, an Altar Boys Club, and a St. Peter Claver Society. At the center of these activities was Mondini whom his assistant, Mattiato, recalled was "loved and respected, but as strict with others as he was with himself. The people cooperated with him because he was always fair. The parish was poor, but its members were good Catholics, and with help from outside our parish, the school continued to go on."

One day, a little girl tugged on Mattiato's coat to get his attention. When he noticed her and asked, "Yes?" she looked up at him and said, 'Father, you talk funny!' He later laughed about this, "Leave it to children to tell you the truth."[19] But an unsigned, undated letter sent to "Dear Archdiocese" was more blunt than the girl. It read, "Why can't we have someone we can understand...it is not that we don't like him Mondini (sic) but we they (sic) ask me what did he say, and all I can say is I don't know..." A year later, when Mondini was told by his provincial, Father Hamlet Accorsi, that some of his parishioners had trouble understanding him, he was crushed. He wrote Archbishop Floersh, "It is rather shocking news which throws to the winds all my four years of work among them. I have at least one instruction...two sermons on Sunday...people seemed to enjoy it. I teach Religion, music, gym. I prepare them... to (sic) First Communion...and if all is done in the dark.... I love these people too much to betray them..."

Mondini asked the archbishop to be recalled by his provincial, "Better to sacrifice one man than let all the people perish..." Floersh declined his request; Mondini stayed at IHM another four years.[20] William Conwill later commented on this, "You have to understand something about Mondini. One of the things I remember very well, because it went on for years, was how he managed to get government surplus foods and store them in the school building: butter, flour, beans. If you needed food, you could come to him. Anyone in the community could ask. He made himself an asset to the community. He understood the notion of speaking first to people's inner needs. So if he was known as a person you could go to when you had trouble, you eventually trusted him. It didn't matter if you didn't understand everything he said."[21]

A CHANGING CLIMATE

At St. Michael's, Italians still called on Di Francesco when they were sick or for special occasions. Once a month, Mondini joined him for a day of recollection and to discuss difficult moral cases. Di Francesco never knew what new situation would arise at St. Michael's. There was the case of the seventy-year-old Italian who finally made his First Communion. He had delayed all his life because he was afraid he would have to dress up in a white suit like a youngster and walk with them, and a language barrier kept him from inquiring about this. By 1959, Di Francesco recorded in his diary, "St. Michael's, a temporary assignment since 1952, with the same pastor... is slowly losing ground. The houses are being destroyed and the Italians are getting old and disappearing because they are shut-ins or have died. Only the Jewish Hospital, and during Lent the noon Mass [that show] some numbers." Accepting St. Michael's was not a mistake. Its parishioners had helped Immaculate Heart of Mary thrive and Comboni Missionaries could recruit vocations and preach mission appeals there. In August, 1960, the archbishop closed St. Michael's for lack of parishioners. Di Francesco left with the archbishop's praise for work well done.

At IHM, Mondini had informed the Louisville chancery in January, 1957, that a new influx of students required construction of another classroom and another teacher. If the classroom he and his assistant were occupying was needed for the school, then perhaps a rectory had to be built. That same month, the Comboni priest began recording the transformation taking place in his neighborhood. "'Little Africa' around IHM is changing...The narrow roads, full of mud during the winter and dust in the summer are being populated with new houses...The city has bought and destroyed tens of old buildings and huts, and is replacing them with new popular apartments for over 400 families. There is already one in the area for over 600 families. It is the struggle of the citizens of the slums." Mondini disagreed with the politicians who saw this as the best solution for people. He wrote, "There are too many people in too small a space...The police are always busy in the area, even if they only take interest in a few cases.[22] Meanwhile, funds would not permit IHM to build a rectory for many years, but the archdiocese kept the parish running. At the end of January, Mondini received an analysis of the debt situation. His parish owed four notes to the archdiocese totaling $45,000. Only on $20,500 of that amount was IHM paying interest.[23] In early 1958, more schoolrooms were necessary due to yet another housing project. Bishop Maloney called in the original contractor for the addition. The cost was $20,613.58 of which "the Board of Colored and Indian Missions" paid $5,500. By April, Mondini reported other changes in the neighborhood: Due to the transient population, there was concern at the school about students who often appeared or disappeared in the middle of the school year. Mondini wrote, "The children are lost and confused. The teachers don't know what the new students have studied elsewhere. Discipline is harder to keep. We don't know how many teachers we will need as the school year progresses. But if these families are Catholic, we certainly don't want to reject their children."

Some newcomers were a different kind of white family than the neighborhood had known before, he added. They were disproving the false theory of white supremacy both materially and morally, and their children were suffering from the results of their upbringing. The teachers at IHM wondered why it was so difficult to teach them.[24] Again in April of 1959, Mondini spoke of the social changes wracking his parish: "While the neighborhood grows in number because of the increase in public housing projects, the families are very mobile, staying only a short time before moving again. Often they are thrown out by the police for not paying their rent which is supposed to be very low, but many times it is not low at all. The northwest part of the parish is being 'improved"...for modern buildings, shops and entertainment places. This means many families are forced to sell their houses to the city at ridiculous prices and move away without enough to buy another place of their own. A few of these find some place to live close enough to remain in the parish, but most we never see again."

Despite these changes, in the fall of 1959, IHM school enrolled 285 students in 8 classes taught by 4 sisters and 2 lay teachers, a tremendous teaching load. Mondini wrote, "We consider this educational effort to be one of the most important things we are doing. Given the family situation...of the children, we sometimes feel discouraged, but the moral and spiritual teaching, [and] basic education the children receive in the school, is great."

The new housing projects in Louisville, he said, had borne little good fruit. There were no fights yet, but he expected some since he assessed the new white tenants as not of the highest moral development. He said, "some [people] are frightened to come out of their apartments, a few even refuse to come out during the day time." He tried to attract them to the church, but without success. Boy Scouts and Girl Scouts were organized, "but without much spiritual effect since there is no priest available here to work on that level..." Mondini then had only one priest from Trinity High School to help with the third Mass on Sundays.[25]

How did Mondini carry the heavy load of work in a large parish area, and do it alone? Again, William Conwill, who knew something about religious life from his seminary years, provided insight on this question: "Basically, Father Mondini was somebody who was very, very serious and prayerful. You saw him in church all the time even when no one else was there. He spent a great deal of time meditating. I don't think the work he did could have been done without that. The task was just so impossible because there were no resources to speak of. He had to scrape everything up. He was one of those who really understood the message of the founder of his order, Daniel Comboni, to go into uncharted areas, and not only carry a message, but be the medium of that message. You *are* that message... He set an example, and you could actually see somebody who, beyond the rhetoric, beyond the 'listen to what I say and not what I do', was a living example...."[26]

In 1961, Mondini was transferred to the Monroe novitiate. Later, his dream of serving Africans was realized. In 1978, when the Immaculate Heart of Mary parish celebrated its Twenty-Fifth Anniversary, the parish paid Mondini's air fare from Africa to come to their celebration. Meanwhile, other Comboni missionaries served the people of IHM parish. When IHM was finally returned to the Archdiocese of Louisville (See "Expanding Black Ministry"), it was so it could play a central role in Louisville's West End, and a diocesan priest, Father Anthony Heitzman, was named pastor. In a 1994 interview, Heitzman recalled the Comboni missionaries who pioneered Immaculate Heart of Mary parish as "tremendously gutsy," and he cited Father Mondini as having "served from the heart." For years before leaving the United States, Mondini worked for Sudanese refugees in the United States. In 1974, he left for missions in Tanzania, and in 1990, he began serving in Kenya. He died there in a car accident, crossing railroad tracks, in 1991.[27]

Sacred Heart Seminary opened in this house located at Beechmont (State Route 125) and Nagel Avenues in Cincinnati. It was purchased in January, 1947, by Father Julius Rizzi and Father Hamlet Accorsi for the Comboni Missionary Institute. In 1967, due to its deteriorating condition, the house was burned down as a practice for the area's fire department. (CMAC)

Holy Trinity Church and School, West Fifth Street, Cincinnati, circa 1896. (Courtesy of the Historical Archives of the Chancery, Archdiocese of Cincinnati.)

St Henry Church and School, 1056 Cortland St., Cincinnati. It was founded as a white parish in 1873, opened to Blacks in 1945, closed due to urban renewal in 1972. Photo by Father Alfred Paolucci.

Monroe Seminary, Monroe, Michigan. It opened as a novitiate in 1953; became a high school in 1968, and was sold to the Brothers of the Holy Cross in 1987 (Photo from Comboni Missionary Archives, Cincinnati.

LEFT: Hamlet Accorsi (1903-1978).

RIGHT: Julius Rizzi (1902-1983).

RIGHT: Anthony Todesco, (1902-1979).

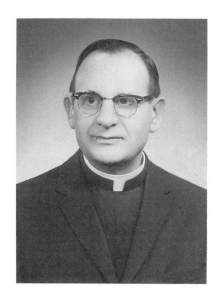

LEFT: Sergio Contran (1926-).

LEFT: Charles Busetti (1920-1980).

RIGHT: Charles Walter (1940-).

Sacred Heart Seminary faculty members and sixty-six students in 1955. (CMAC)

Sacred Heart Seminary in the early 1960s before it was faced with brick. The first 'L' shaped section was completed by April, 1950. The last section of the building was completed in the mid-1960s when Fr. Todesco was provincial. The building is now operating as a Comboni Mission Center. (CMAC)

Member of North American Province meet to discuss renewal and Vatican II decrees , November 1966. FRONT ROW: Fr. John Buetler, Fr. Adelmo Spagnolo, Fr. Archie Fornasari, Fr. Innocent Simoni, Fr. Anthony Todesco, Fr. Remus Catellani, Fr. Kenneth Dahlen, Fr. Dominic Ghirotto. SECOND ROW: Fr. Ugo Riva, Fr. Januarius Carillo, Fr. Francis Didoni, Fr. Gabriel Chiodi, Fr. Aldo Cescatti, and Fr. Peter Premarini. THIRD ROW: Fr. Frank Di Francesco, Fr. Gino Doniney, Fr. Peter Tarquini, Fr. Joseph Bragotti, Fr. Mario Ongaro, Fr. Walter Mattiato, Fr. Charles Busetti, Fr. Joseph Zelinski. FOURTH ROW: Fr. Sergio Contran, Fr. Dominic Pazzaglia, Fr. Oliver Branchesi, Fr. Alfio Mondini, Brother Jerry Charbonneau, Fr. William Crouse, Fr. Benedict Paletti, Fr. Joseph Valenti, Fr. Raymond Pax, Fr. Kenneth Gerth, Brother Eugene Miller. TOP RIGHT: (Unknown), Fr. Paul Donohue. (*Frontier Call*, March-April, 1967, CMAC.)

The Campanile or Bell Tower of Pala Mission. Completed in 1816 by Franciscan Father Peyri, the original bell tower was destroyed by floods in 1916. It was rebuilt that year to mark its one hundredth anniversary, and it still retains its original bells. (Photo from Comboni Missionary Archives, Cincinnati.)

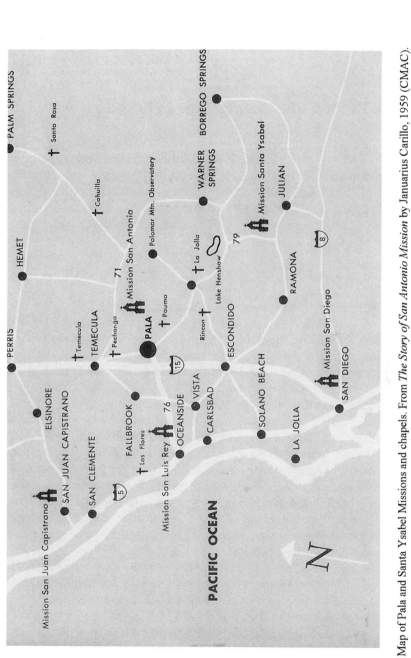

Map of Pala and Santa Ysabel Missions and chapels. From *The Story of San Antonio Mission* by Januarius Carillo, 1959 (CMAC).

9. Pursuit of a Dream: The Pala Indian School

As pastor of Pala Mission, Father Carillo confronted what appeared to be an "impossible dream." Some of his confreres thought it would interfere with the "real" goal of Comboni Missionaries, i.e., supporting African missions. Carillo later said that, without Father Hamlet Accorsi's strong support, he would never have been able to pursue the possibility of building a Pala Mission school.

A QUESTION OF TRUST

San Antonio de Pala Indians wanted their children educated in their own faith and within the tribal community's setting. Their faith was a heritage from the Franciscan Padres, and their desire for local control was partly a reaction to the federal and state's attempts to assimilate Indian children into mainstream culture. One method used was the boarding school based on one founded in Pennsylvania by Richard Henry Pratt. It advocated taking Native American children away from their tribal environment since, as Pratt believed, "the sooner all tribal relations are broken up...the better it will be." The industrial school was used as a model. Boys learned farming and trades; girls learned domestic skills. Students were sent to work on farms and in households, and their wages were sent directly to the school. Essentially Indian youngsters worked for this kind of schooling.[1] The Bureau of Indians Affairs' (BIA) boarding school system was attacked for inadequate food, overcrowding, poor medical service, unsuitable teachers, and harsh discipline, and reports of children dying while trying to escape these schools became a symbol of the system's outcomes.

The "day school" was also instituted in Southern California under newly established Mission Agency reservations. Its success was limited. Sickness spread quickly in the small, ill-ventilated school rooms which resulted in a high rate of absenteeism. The BIA reacted by eliminating all schools with fewer than 20 students. Opposition to day schools grew so strong that several were burned down, one at Pechanga in 1895.[2] After 1900, the Indian Service moved to de-tribalization of California Indians through enrollment in public schools. But racial prejudice against Indian children was widespread, and some school districts practiced segregation.[3] In 1965, data from the Division of Labor Statistics and Research discredited the entire history of Indian education in California. It showed that 5% of all rural or reservation Indians had received no schooling, 43% were not educated beyond the eighth grade, and as many as 57% had completed less than one year of high school. A Senate investigating committee denounced public education for American Indian youth, claiming it reflected white middle-class values and exhibited racial and cultural bigotry.[4]

It was into this historical setting that Father Carillo stepped. At his first meeting with Indians in 1953, Robert Lovato, chief and spokesman of the Indians, laid down the challenge, "Well, when are we going to get a school? Father Angelo [Barbisotti] promised that we would have it this very month. Where is it?" The school of which Lovato spoke was the centerpiece of a larger project: the reconstruction of the entire Pala Mission quadrangle. Barbisotti had drawn up plans, but could not pull together the resources to implement them. Against him, too, was the question of a general store, leased by the San Diego Diocese, that took up part of the quadrangle and blocked reconstruction north of the chapel. When Bishop Buddy visited the mission in 1949, Barbisotti mentioned that the store's lease was due to expire. But he failed to connect a need to close the store with any large scale building project. He simply said the priests needed more room. Buddy thought the store provided a service to the Indians, but he released one of its storerooms to the mission. The matter became a face-saving issue when a parishioner sent Bishop Buddy a letter offering to pay the $75 rent fee if he would release the store to the Comboni missionaries. The bishop took this as a personal affront, and the question of ending the lease was closed for another five years.

The Indians knew all of this, so when they confronted him, Carillo said, "You know we cannot even touch the property until 1955....meanwhile, the priests here do not have a decent place to stay. Let's do something about that." The Indians agreed, and Carillo laid out a plan. The store was on the north side of the chapel; its entrance, like that of the chapel, faced west. A rectory could be built on the south side of the mission behind the chapel. Carillo suggested using adobe bricks. They would match the old style and could be made on site. If the Indians would provide wood from Palomar Mountain, they could begin building. The Indians owned the Palomar timber, and they agreed to supply it.

Carillo had developed a working relationship with Buddy from his experience at Santa Ysabel, and he approached the bishop directly about a rectory, Buddy wanted to know the cost. Carillo believed he would have $1,500 from the Corpus Christi Fiesta, and he had $2,000 in the bank. He told the bishop, "I can count on approximately $5,000." Buddy gave him permission to start. In Carillo's mind, the new rectory was simply a first step in reconstructing the entire mission quadrangle. To fit the rectory into this reconstruction, Larry Weir, of Weir Construction, went over its design. Brother Carmelo Praga came from Mexico to help build it,[5] and shifts of Indians made adobe bricks. The young worked during the day, and their elders came in the evening after farm work. By nightfall, adobe molds were filled with the mixture of mud as well as the road oil required to prevent crumbling. Carillo employed his skill as a cook so that day and evening laborers found hamburgers, beans, and soft drinks waiting for them.

In the spring, when wild flowers bloomed on Mount Palomar, the Indians began cutting the trees, largely cedars. They had promised one hundred and fifty for the rectory, and the first load began arriving from Morgan's Hill. Reporter Ed Ainsworth of the *Los Angeles Times* described how Carillo joined in the labor, "One day he is on the Mission roof laying tile. The next he is on Mt. Palomar hewing cedar timber." News about the reconstruction spread throughout Southern California.[6] A year later, when asking Bishop Buddy to bless the new rectory, Carillo told him about other donations he had received. A man who was not even Catholic had donated half the materials for a parish hall at the outlying chapel at Temecula, and a contractor had pledged free labor to build it. Buddy sent a check for $1,000 as a loan toward the Temecula construction and wrote, "You have my cordial permission to proceed with the construction...You have done very well indeed..."[7] On May 8, 1955, the new rectory representing a 3,000 square foot restoration of the old mission was blessed. An article and photos about this appeared in the *Los Angeles Times,* and other papers followed suit, bringing a sizeable increase of visitors to the mission.

THE CORPUS CHRISTI FIESTA

In California, religious and secular fiestas uniquely blend Indian, Spanish, Mexican, and California frontier customs and beliefs.[8] At Pala Mission, the feast of Corpus Christi has been a religious fiesta since the founding of the mission in 1816. Because of the solemnity and romance of the event, it has attracted thousands of visitors.

For days before the Fiesta, Pala Indians clean and decorate the streets and houses of their village and place flowers on the altars and little shrines that border the processional area. On Corpus Christi morning, the people gather around the famous bell tower for the celebration of mass. Then Indian men on horseback lead a solemn procession to the many little shrines, and the priest carries the Blessed Sacrament. Representatives from each reservation follow, carrying banners emblazoned with pictures of their chapels' patron saints. Old Spanish hymns are sung by a choir while the crowd behind prays. At each shrine, the procession stops, and the priest blesses the crowd. At a given signal, an Indian who has gone ahead discharges a pistol. This brings forth a rapid ringing of mission bells. When the procession reaches the last shrine, the pistol signals the climax and end of the ceremony. Then Indian hosts and visitors gather under the shade of old pepper trees and enjoy a California pit-barbecue. They listen to Mexican music, watch Indian dances, and participate in the singing and dancing. In the evening, the ancient Native American game of Peon may be in progress; it is basically a guessing game between two teams accompanied by Indian chants. At one time, this game continued for days.

The 1955 fiesta attracted more tourists and pilgrims than anyone expected. A motion picture based on a script by Ainsworth, the Los Angeles reporter, began production of "The Man Who Shot the Devil." A.P.I.A. Films told the Indians who were serving as extras that the producers would donate income from the movie's premiere to the mission. This Fiesta was so successful that Carillo could pay off some debts to the chancery; one was a check for the University of San Diego that the Bishop was building. Carillo had cautioned the diocesan chancellor that his parishioners' contributions might be small since there were large families at Pala who were "nearly starving." But he said that his parishioners were proud to contribute what they could, "even if it were only a small amount."

Carillo was so respected by Bishop Buddy that he asked the Comboni missionary to perform a delicate bit of diplomacy. A strip of property near the new university's entrance was owned by two elderly brothers. The bishop's agent had made them an offer, but had failed to reveal the diocese as the buyer. Carillo discovered that it was because of this that the two brothers did not sell the property. They were afraid someone was only interested in making a profit at the diocese's expense. Their lawyer, a Mr. Janeway, knew Father Carillo, and he gave him assurances that the bishop would have the first opportunity of purchase. The lawyer kept his word.[9]

A DREAM TAKES SHAPE

One of the impediments to a Pala school continued to be the general store attached to the chapel and adjacent small rooms. But on July 28, 1955, Bishop Buddy, while visiting Pala for a funeral, told Carillo that the store would be returned to Pala Mission, thus permitting the possibility of a school. The first move was to restore rooms in the west wing of the store, and Paul Cunningham, an artist from Los Angeles, designed them as a museum for Indian arts, crafts, and mission relics. Next, the store and adjacent ruins were excavated, and remnants of the original mission were revealed. This work led to new tourist interest. Funds accumulated for a garden around the mission which made it even more attractive to visitors. Seeing this progress, Buddy gave his official approval to the school construction with the stipulation that sufficient money had to be raised and nuns found to staff it.[10]

Publicity brought the Pala Mission side benefits. It was now on the schedule of the mobile X-ray machine; a Mr. Beading donated $500 to paint Pala houses; the Mission Valley Country Club fashion show raised $900 for the school; and the premiere of "*The Man Who Shot the Devil*" brought crowds to Pala from Los Angeles and San Diego. At this last event, a barbecue served on the back patio of the mission, and demonstrations of Indian crafts and dances contributed to significant growth of the school fund. That year's Corpus Christi Fiesta drew a larger crowd than ever. Twenty-five hundred people ate steaks, Mexican food, hot dogs, and hamburgers.

A new sense of responsibility for past actions surfaced among Anglo-Americans. On August 19, 1956, Carillo set up a memorial to Juan Diego in the Keyhole cemetery. Diego was memorialized in Helen Hunt Jackson's novel, *Ramona*. This was the story of an heroic Indian's defense of his wife and property in the late nineteenth century. Murdered by those who coveted his land, Diego symbolized the violence suffered by the Native-American under Anglo-American rule. Descendants of Diego's wife, *Remanet*, were present for the ceremony. A considerable number of white people came to give witness to past injustices.[11]

By the end of 1956, the school had neither sufficient funds nor nuns to staff it, but Carillo began working with an architect. The architectural firm, Comeau and Brooks of Sherman Oaks, California, had worked on church projects in Redondo Beach, Pomona, and Phoenix, Arizona. It had experience in reconstructing old missions, including those in San Fernando, San Gabriel, and San Juan Capistrano. Earl G. Brooks wrote Bishop Buddy that the company volunteered its services to Pala Mission because of its "special appeal." In early 1957, after a parish novena to St. Joseph, another generous offer was made. Mr. and Mrs. Thomas Leavey from Los Angeles, while visiting the mission, announced a substantial contribution. Described as a "family project," they promised $40,000 to be given over 1958 and 1959, and some funds could be anticipated during the current year through loans. Meanwhile, prospects for staffing the school brightened. Carillo's superior, Father Accorsi, had corresponded with the Sisters of the Blessed Sacrament whom he knew from Holy Trinity in Cincinnati. But his efforts appeared unnecessary when the Sisters of the Precious Blood offered to staff the school. Now both issues required to proceed with construction were resolved, and Buddy gave his wholehearted approval. He wrote the Leaveys of his "deepfelt appreciation" and added, "Your long range charity stimulates every one of us in this uphill work."

Before large-scale operations could begin, more money was needed. Meanwhile, the parishioners joined Carillo and his assistant, Father Mario Ongaro, in other projects. On evenings, men and women painted and tiled the floors of the museum and other rooms of the mission. Volunteers knocked down the remaining walls of the old store to prepare for digging the school's foundation. In early March, Bill Magee brought his bulldozer for more excavation, and this unearthed new evidence about the earlier mission's size which prior researchers had been unable to determine. There was increased attendance at Lenten services at all the chapels, and after another novena to St. Joseph, a check for $5,000 was received from the Catholic Indian Mission Bureau which promised another $5,000 later that year. Now construction could begin, and a date to bless the cornerstone was set.[12]

May 19, 1957, was the kind of day one would expect for a celebration orchestrated by Father Carillo: a rough beginning and a salutary end. Morning clouds and rain canceled a procession, but at the 11 o'clock Mass, Auxiliary Bishop Richard H. Ackerman was ready to confirm the children. By noon, the sun was shining for the laying of the cornerstone. A crowd of friends and the group called the Restoration Committee were present. The latter's signatures were on the document: (Colonel) Irving Salomon, a friend of President Eisenhower; Mr. Frank Capra, the film director; Mr. Ben Dixon; Mr. Jim Sullivan; Mr. Chester Comeau, the architect; Mr. Ramon Novarro, the film actor; Mr. Charles Weseloh; Mr. Lawrence Weir, of Weir Construction; Mr. Charles Considine; Dr. Eugene Vinograd; Mrs. Frank Riley; and Mr. John Cunningham.

After the ceremony, the bishop, his secretary Father Campion, Father Anthony, O.F.M. from San Luis Rey Mission, and friends with their spouses, had lunch at the rectory. Dr. Vinograd told how, for three years, the committee members had worked with Carillo to build a school. Colonel Salomon recalled how his contact with the Leaveys led to their contribution to the school, and he reminded the group that twice that sum was needed to complete the project. He then made an immediate donation of five hundred dollars. Bishop Ackerman left the meeting impressed.

Members of the Restoration Committee were an elite group. But other benefactors included businessmen, skilled laborers, Native Americans, people from Los Angeles, San Diego and other parts of California. They made up a unique group of benefactors from many ethnic groups and all walks of life. Carillo's ability to attract such a wide spectrum of support was commended in a report on his Canonical Visitation. Buddy praised him for his "excellent administration..."[13]

RISING FROM THE RUINS

In late July, the process of making 30,000 adobe bricks for the school began, but when fires broke out in Southern California, Pala's volunteers were not available. Weir Construction then joined the construction, and real progress began. When the company's workers began laying bricks into walls, they discovered damage by termites and burrowing animals. A complete fumigation was necessary, and a friend offered to do this at little cost. Carillo's resourceful supporters turned the fumigation into a media opportunity. They announced that the largest fumigation in the history of San Diego County was about to take place. The story appeared in all the newspapers, but television crews arrived too late to cover it. However, dead mice and rats were found everywhere. At the fall meeting of the Restoration Committee, another fund-raising barbecue was planned for the school.[14]

In early 1958, Comboni Brothers John Volpato and Vincent Dall' Alda arrived from Cincinnati to work on the school, and they joined Indians in cutting lumber on Palomar Mountain. The timbers were cut from the same spot where those for the original mission were taken. When rain interrupted construction, Larry Weir used it as an opportunity to build a new shrine on the mission grounds. One side was dedicated to the Crucifixion; the other to Our Lady of Lourdes. Weir had supported the reconstruction from its beginning, and building the shrines was his way of honoring it. The donor of most of the materials for the shrines was Ramon Novarro who had a ranch only a few miles away. One of the first benefactors of Pala Mission, Novarro was born Jose Ramon Gil Samaniegos in Durango, Mexico, one of ten children. When his father died, he became the chief support of his family, and it moved to the United States in 1917. Hard work, good looks, and an excellent singing voice helped Novarro to rise to Hollywood stardom in the film *The Prisoner of Zenda.* In 1926, he had the starring role in *Ben Hur.* He made a better transition from silent films to the "talkies" than many contemporaries, but by 1957, Novarro's film career had passed its zenith. It was then that Novarro renewed his zeal as a Catholic, even receiving the sacrament of Confirmation from Bishop Buddy in a private ceremony. It is said that he even considered becoming a priest. When the new shrines that Novarro funded were blessed, it seemed fitting that the shrine of the Crucifixion be dedicated to the actor's deceased parents.[15]

In February of 1958, the Superior of the Sisters of the Precious Blood inspected the construction's progress. She was optimistic about members of her society staffing the school, and Buddy agreed it could open that fall. With a date for opening the school now set, the mission turned into a whirlwind of activity. Carillo described it in his book on Pala, "Men and women, Indian and White alike, worked side by side. They nailed the sheeting on the roof. They plastered, painted, and...cleaned. Their laughter, shouts, and rollicking songs attested their high spirits in doing a monumental and important task." In the midst of these preparations, the Superior of the Precious Blood Sisters advised Carillo that she could *not* staff the school. She said that the novitiate at San Luis Rey had not given expected results, and she could not promise anything for the future. The news sent a shock wave through the Pala community. When Monsignor Brouwers in Los Angeles heard it, he moved quickly. As founder of the "Lay Mission Helpers" group, he knew some of his lay missionaries were unable to work outside the United States, and they were willing to staff the school in the fall. Meanwhile, Brouwers appealed for additional teachers in the Los Angeles archdiocesan paper *Tidings* and in the nationally circulated *Our Sunday Visitor.*[16]

By the end of May, a last push was made to finish the exterior of the school for the Corpus Christi Fiesta. The Bonsall Lions Club nailed boards on the roof. Rest rooms were finished; classrooms shaped up. A history teacher, Ben Dixon, archivist and director of the Serra Museum in San Diego, volunteered himself and his students for an exterior project. With permission of the Pala Indians (to whom the property belonged), they began building a stone wall around a little park in front of the mission. It took 400 sacks of concrete, and when students could not return to the project, the Indians and Comboni lay brothers finished it. That June, three thousand people marched in the Corpus Christi Fiesta procession. Monsignor Brouwers celebrated the

Mass, and by 2 p.m., 3,500 guests had eaten all the barbecue, hamburgers, hot dogs, and Mexican food available. Jose Torres and his Strolling Troubadours furnished the music. The Lions Club had organized the afternoon festivities, and they were congratulated for this and for the fact that the fiesta was so successful both in enjoyment and fund-raising.

The Pala School opened on September 10, 1958. Those attending the celebration of a High Mass could hardly believe it was happening, and that fifty-seven children were enrolled. As yet some doors and windows were not in place, chalkboards were missing, and floors still not tiled. But a lunch program was operating, and leading benefactors took time out to celebrate. Mrs. Fenton, a member of this group, threw a barbecue party at Bandy Canyon Ranch. Colonel Salomon, who had recently been named a U.S. delegate to the United Nations, was there; also the Leaveys, Novarro, Dr. Vinograd, the Weirs, and Bishop Buddy, who expressed his thanks. But even this gathering had a financial goal. With the film star Jack Haley (the Tin Man in *The Wizard of Oz*) acting as Master of Ceremonies, everyone enjoyed themselves, and a donation of $1,500 was collected for the school.[17]

In October, Carillo entered the hospital with a double hernia, and complications kept him there longer than expected. His assistant, Ongaro, was transferred, and Father James Francez arrived to take his place. After months of writing to communities of nuns, in November Carillo heard from Accorsi that the Blessed Sacrament Sisters were favorably considering Pala School. Carillo wrote a grateful letter to Mother Mary Anselm, the congregation's Superior General. He told her that 90% of the students at Pala were Indian. Now there was the question of a convent. The Leaveys had volunteered a contribution of $10,000, but no plans were drawn up.

At the end of a demanding yet satisfying year, Carillo gave thanks for the new choir loft at Rincon Chapel and the kitchen at the Temecula church hall, but above all, he was thankful for the Pala Mission School. It's opening was making a difference in the students' academic work and conduct.[18] Christmas always brought parties for Indian children. The girls of the St. Joseph's Cathedral High School held one both at Pala and at the Rincon reservation. The women marines from Pendleton Marine base gave another one for the school children. Theirs was the Marine base that had sent a large crane to lift cedar poles into place at the mission. People came from all over to see the nativity crib, a hallmark of the Comboni missionaries wherever they serve.

The dedication of Pala School was scheduled for April. At a last meeting of the Restoration Committee, a Mr. Rollins announced he would pay for a year's publicity for the mission, and an article was already prepared for the

May issue of the *San Diego Magazine*. A Press Party would take place in April, a TV program before the dedication, and other public relation strategies. The Press Party drew twenty representatives from newspapers, radio and television stations to the mission. They were told its history and about the upcoming dedication and Fiesta. Members of the press were impressed with the students' work. They commented on the artful roof tile designs by the Mexicans José de Jesús, Murillo, and Hilario Cuevas. At a barbecue dinner, they were hosted by Ramon Novarro and Mrs. Fenton. This hospitality was repaid. The story of the Pala School appeared in all the newspapers, and it ran several evenings on television's Channel 8. The new mission school so engaged the media that even the blessing of a fountain was published. Three days before the school's dedication, Carillo appeared with five Indian children on Channel 10 television to talk about the school. The next day, his book, *The Story of Mission San Antonio de Pala"* came off the press.

Carillo wrote Buddy he would like to recognize "those persons who have so generously helped us out..." He noted the large sums donated by the Leaveys and Novarro, then said, "In our conversation, I mentioned the name of an Indian lady, who has been most helpful...Financially speaking, she has given...generously according to her means..." But her contribution had gone far beyond monetary assistance. She had been a prompt and constant worker for the Church, and was well known for her leadership in the Oceanside deanery. The Indian woman Carillo referred to was Julia Calac, whose husband Macario had also worked for the Comboni priests and the mission.[19]

On April 26, 1959, Carillo wrote in his diary, "This is the most important date in the history of our Missions in modern days. It is the day we have been preparing for a long time." At noon, members of the Restoration committee, Father Accorsi, the school's teachers, and a few others who donated substantial labor or resources were treated to dinner. At 3 p.m. Bishop Ackerman administered confirmation and prepared to dedicate the school. He brought with him Father Campion, his secretary, as well as Father Meehling, a Navy chaplain. All priests in the area were invited. Those who came were: Monsignor O'Leary from the parish of the Holy Spirit; Monsignor Trivisonno; Monsignor Behane with Fathers Nolan and Gurity from Oceanside; the Franciscan Fathers Ronald, Anthony, and Geoffrey from San Luis Rey; Father Lawlor of Escondido; Father Ullman of Fallbrook; Father Meagher of Fontana; Father Ross from Remanet; Monsignor Brouwers from Los Angeles; and the Comboni Fathers Dominic Pazzaglia from Santa Ysabel and Zelindo Marigo from Irwindale.

Tours of the mission were conducted by Macario Calac, Henry Rodriguez, Vivian Banks, and Sam Pouvall. After Confirmation and Benediction of the Blessed Sacrament, Ackerman blessed the school. He then entered the auditorium that Mrs. Fenton, Mrs. Rollins, and Mrs. Jeffries had painted (Jeffries painted the delicate murals of Native American women on the mission's exterior walls). The bishop uncovered the dedicatory plaque, and blessed the fountain in the patio. The children opened a short program by singing the "Magnificat."

On the stage were Bishop Ackerman, Fathers Accorsi, Ullman and Meehling, Mr. and Mrs. Thomas Leavey, Jack Haley, Ramon Novarro, Dr. Vinograd, Colonel Salomon (who postponed his departure as U.S. delegate to the United Nations), Mrs. Fenton, and Mrs. Julia Calac. Carillo introduced each one, but when Colonel Salomon was called upon, he was too overwhelmed to speak. Then Julia Calac rose. With simple but elegantly expressed words, she thanked the benefactors for helping the Indians and, in the name of the Tribe, she promised to repay them with prayers. The silence in the audience reflected the sincerity of her speech.

In the fall of 1960, ninety students enrolled in the school. People contributed catches of yellowtail and other fish to the lunchroom. Carillo's assistant, Francez, even leveraged large quantities of beef from the Temecula slaughterhouse. And Father Angelo Biancalana interrupted duties as mission promoter to organize a CYO (Catholic Youth Organization). During that year, Bishop Barbisotti came back again from Ecuador to baptize the new baby in the Frank Capra family, and Father Girardot, the Franciscan pastor at Pala till 1948, stopped for a visit to the reconstructed mission. There was much for which to be grateful. Then on December 1, Mother Anselm promised four Blessed Sacrament Sisters as teachers for the following school year.[20]

Carillo was honored for his work on several occasions. One of these was a breakfast meeting with benefactors that turned out to be a city-wide gathering in his honor. The Mayor of San Diego presented him with a gold key to the city for his work with Native Americans. The Supervisor of San Diego County presented him with miniature flags of the United States, the State of California, and the County of San Diego. All this was televised on Jack Linkletter's *On the Go* program that also featured the Pala School choir and a contribution of a complete set of Encyclopedia Britannica to the school's library.

A DIPLOMATIC GAFFE

Once again with the convent, obtaining land for construction was a major obstacle. Blessed Sacrament Sisters traditionally lived close to their work; this meant a convent had to be constructed on land owned by Indians. Marian Scott Arenas owned the largest block of land which she inherited from her Luiseño mother. Her husband had descended from the Keyhole Indians of Warner Springs. They both agreed to sell the land for the convent, but there were other parcels of land involved. The Indians who owned these, Innocence and Silverio Blacktooth, also committed to sell. But Native Americans could not sell their land outright. The sales had to be approved by the Bureau of Indian Affairs. In April, Carillo explained to Mother Anselm, " ...the Bureau of Indian Affairs [moves] very slowly. They could have sent the deeds to the Indians three months ago....I was really upset about it. Talking to Ramon Novarro and to another friend of mine...they suggested that I bury a statue of St. Joseph in the field that we want to buy. I had already decided to start a Novena....So, on the first day of the Novena, I buried a little statue. On the day of the feast of St. Joseph [March 19] ...the Indians received the deeds...The whole process is very simple, but you never know when the Bureau is going to move..."

By June 12, 1960, one deed had still not arrived. Necessity determined that the convent's cornerstone had to be laid, with trust that St. Joseph would not let his friends down. The Leaveys were asked to choose the convent's patron saint, and they selected Saint Theresa of the Child Jesus. The convent itself was named after Mother Katharine Drexel, the recently deceased founder of the Blessed Sacrament Sisters. Two weeks later, the last legal title to the land arrived.[21]

In late June, a worried letter from Colonel Salomon of the Restoration Committee reached Bishop Buddy's desk: "Only yesterday word arrived that our good friend, Father Carillo, will be transferred in approximately two months....This is sad news to us...not only because of our personal feelings in regard to Father, but also because of our concern over the fate of the Mission Indian School at Pala....the Convent has yet to be built for the Sisters who will arrive in September, the sources of funds for its construction...are only partially collected, and Father Carillo's efforts and friendship will bring this to fruition....the new Father might be able to cope with the above, but he must be a unique man indeed to...walk into this singular situation cold, and carry it off. Would an extension of Father Carillo's stay [be possible]? We all consider it quite essential...to surmount the last major hurdle and establish the Indian School..."

On July 1, a curt note from Bishop Buddy's secretary, Reverend Michael J. Byrne, was sent to Carillo. Buddy had heard that Carillo would be transferred shortly, and "The Most Reverend Ordinary would appreciate it if you would advise him as to whether this is correct, and if you would give him an official statement regarding it..." The next day, apologizing to Buddy, Carillo said he had not mentioned his transfer because he was told not to. He added that the Comboni father, Dino De Grandis, would arrive in August to replace him, and that his newly appointed provincial, Father Anthony Todesco, said he would write about this to Buddy "in due time." Notice of his transfer had come at the end of his retreat, with warning to keep it confidential, but when he returned to Pala, he found that many people already knew about it, even before he did. When Carillo was granted an interview with the bishop on July 5, whatever else transpired, one outcome was a check for $5,000 "to liquidate the bills related to your construction program, including the convent." A letter was also sent to Colonel Salomon telling him that there was nothing anyone could do to interfere with the decision of the Comboni Missionary's superiors.[22]

Why Father Todesco ignored a basic rule of church diplomacy, i.e., that of consulting the head of a diocese about personnel changes is a mystery. It was a serious breach of protocol. Not until July 25 did Todesco send Buddy a letter announcing changes at both Pala and Santa Ysabel Missions. However, on August 18, when Father De Grandis arrived at Pala Mission, he brought a letter deferring Carillo's transfer until the convent was completed.

With construction behind schedule, Carillo arranged for the nuns to live in one of the rental houses belonging to the Ray Considine family. The Considines furnished a porch as a temporary chapel in their largest house. But the Blessed Sacrament nuns were concerned that Considine's "ranch" would be like those in Hollywood movies complete with cowboys, guns, rattlesnakes, and wasteland. Mr. Considine called Mother Anselm, the Superior of the Blessed Sacrament Sisters, and asked her to contact the Superior of Franciscan nuns in Minnesota who had stayed at his ranch in order to be reassured about safety.

This contact served its purpose. The four teaching Sisters who arrived at Pala on August 27 were: Mother Infante, the superior of the community and principal of the school; Sister Marina; Sister Marie Duschene; and Sister Thaddeus Marie. A welcoming party was held at the Considines' ranch for both Father De Grandis and the Sisters. Mother Anselm, the Superior General of the Blessed Sacrament Sisters, and Mother Jerome, Vicar General of the congregation came to help the nuns get settled. On their first day at the school, they found 100 students waiting for them.[23]

In late September, Carillo reported to Buddy that he could pay most of the convent's expenses, but he needed a $15,000 loan to pay the workers and the end of month bills, and to complete the job. He also informed Buddy that Superior General Briani would be in San Diego any day, and he wanted to visit the bishop. Monsignor James T. Booth wrote back that "to be perfectly frank with you, the money is not available at the present time..." Carillo, he said, should go back to his benefactors. Carillo replied that he contacted benefactors, but they could do no more. He understood the financial difficulties of the diocese (the University was straining its resources), but he had "gone ahead with the plans with the approval of His Excellency and His promise that we could borrow up to $15,000..." Buddy denied this promise. He claimed the $5,000 check sent in July was to balance the books between the chancery and the mission. When Colonel Salomon heard of Carillo's predicament, he told him to ask permission to make a loan from benefactors. Salomon promised to lend $2,000, and Mrs. Fenton said she would lend the same amount. Carillo waited for the right moment to approach Buddy.

When Briani, Todesco, and Carillo visited Buddy, the bishop praised the Comboni fathers. This was the moment Carillo anticipated. He presented his case on the convent's finances, saying the Sisters were living uncomfortably in one room at Valley Center, and could not move to the convent at Pala if "a few things were not completed." The Bishop said he had no idea the nuns were not already at Pala. He not only approved loans from the benefactors, but he, himself, provided Carillo with a loan for $6000 for outstanding bills.[24]

Before leaving California, Carillo reported to Buddy that all the mission's accounts and reports were completed through November, but that he had been unable to get an appointment with the bishop. He thanked Buddy for his great kindness and above all for his friendship. On December 2, Buddy sent back a letter which, given the incident over the loans, was laced with irony, "Even though my heavy schedule precluded the consolation of thanking you, in person, for your zealous apostolate in this Diocese during the last twelve years, now you have the distinct advantage of having it down in writing...You did get into a missionary field here and transformed it by dint of hard, persevering, and selfless work. What you have achieved here shall always be a consolation for you to recall..."[25]

10. The Founder as Provincial

In 1953, Fathers Rizzi and Accorsi joined Father Angelo Barbisotti at their Society's General Chapter. Rizzi was appointed Vicar General of the Comboni Missionary Institute, and Accorsi returned to America as provincial of North America. Now, with missions fields expanding overseas, Superior General Todesco and Vicar General Rizzi urged Accorsi to carry an even heavier burden. Ministries and public relations in America had to expand to support not only growth in America, but in the rest of the Institute. Accorsi began holding meetings with friends on how the problems of the missions could gain more of the public's attention and how to make better use of the press in this regard.[1] Accorsi's forté was his ability to learn from others' how to succeed financially, but he was less effective in negotiating with diocesan officials or dealing with the internal affairs of the province. Despite these deficiencies, what Accorsi achieved between 1953 and 1959 is a testimony to his tireless pursuit of duty.

An issue he inherited from Rizzi was a lack of personnel, and this proved a major obstacle. Statistics taken from the *Annuario* (the Annual Directory of the Comboni Institute) show that between 1954 and 1958, the number of scholastics increased by 70%, novices increased by 142%, and "houses" or communities of Comboni personnel increased by 50%. But the number of priests increased by only 40%, and the number of brothers actually decreased by 38%. This was taking place between 1953 and 1960 when minor seminarians increased 300%. Meanwhile, Accorsi received offers from the dioceses of Georgia, Los Angeles, and Newark, New Jersey. But providing confreres for these assignments was another matter.

NEEDED: A FEW GOOD MISSIONARIES

While the vocations of Comboni seminary students in the United States were developing, Accorsi had to rely on personnel from abroad. But competition for personnel intensified as new missions developed in Africa,

Mexico, and Ecuador. After asking Todesco for priests in early November, 1953, Accorsi followed with greater insistence, "I have no news from New Jersey yet [from the Archbishop], but on the one hand, I am not sorry because we are not ready with the personnel." Accorsi heard that the Mexican Provincial, Father Patroni, was given orders to send someone to help in America. But Patroni claimed he had no such orders. Accorsi addressed Todesco sharply about this issue, "...you see how long it takes to get people into the States.....Don't you think it is necessary to give orders immediately...? If we wait to start the process when we are called to [somewhere], *it is not going to happen*...[emphasis not added] Father Rizzi was urgently asking me to push the idea of Los Angeles, but how can we propose such an idea when we are so short of personnel?"[2]

Not only did Accorsi want priests for ministry, he needed Italian novices to create a sense of community with the few Americans seminarians, "I have gone to Monroe where I found a deserted place. Three students and two lay novices. Even Father Chiodi was somewhat discouraged. He hopes for the arrival of two Italian novices and two Mexican postulants." Accorsi also reminded Todesco that two more priests had to be sent for new ministries expected to open.

Todesco blamed delays on paper work required by the U.S. Immigration Service. He asked, "Is it possible that, even after so many years, we haven't found the way [to get them through immigration], and that we bump into difficulty after difficulty for this blessed visa?"[3] One reason for the red tape was the change in the political climate of America. Immediately after the war, the federal government feared fascist elements would infiltrate the country. But by the early 1950s it was more concerned with communists infiltrating the country. If there was any optimism in Accorsi's reports to his superior, it was about the future of Sacred Heart Seminary. He told Todesco, "I am more and more convinced that our promise for the future is in our minor seminary." The Increase in enrollment at the Forestville seminary was largely due to the efforts of Father Charles Busetti. From 1949, when he began work as a recruiter, until 1954, the number of minor seminarians increased tenfold from five to fifty-eight. By 1959, the number doubled.

AN INVITATION TO GEORGIA

When Accorsi took over as provincial, his society had six mission parishes in America: Holy Trinity and St. Henry's in Cincinnati; Immaculate Heart of Mary and St. Michael's in Louisville; and the Pala and Santa Ysabel mission in the San Diego area. Three of these were black missions, two were Indian, and one was an Italian parish in Louisville that would soon close. Father Rizzi had searched diligently for black parishes from New York to Los Angeles before returning to Italy in 1953. That same year, Holy Trinity's church was torn down, and Accorsi was aware that virtually all black parishes in Cincinnati's West End would close. Any hope he had of serving Blacks in Cincinnati or anywhere else was fading, and if he were going to increase work in ministry, the Comboni Institute would have to compromise its original goal of exclusively serving African Americans. It had already made an exception with the Indian missions in San Diego due to a need for a supply center for Baja California missions, and under Accorsi, the society again reached a point at which expediency determined mission orientation. This choice received sharp criticism from many confreres for years thereafter. But what critics chose to ignore was that, when these priorities changed, the General Administration fully supported them. It depended on the financial fruits they provided for work outside North America.

Shortly after assuming his role as provincial, Accorsi promised Todesco he would contact Auxiliary Bishop Francis E. Hyland in Georgia, and try to contact the Archbishop of Newark, Archbishop Thomas A. Boland, who had work with Puerto Ricans in mind. As for Georgia, Rizzi had already visited the Savannah-Atlanta diocese before leaving for Italy. At the top of a copy of his letter to Bishop Hyland, a handwritten memo refers to his visit to the diocese, "On Oct., 1952, I saw Bishop Hyland - he offered us [the opportunity] to send a priest to Elberton, Ga, where there is a nice stone Church (sacristy +one room) - around 60 families - almost all Italian (Sicilians) - most of them lost their faith..." The letter itself was Rizzi's report to Hyland about the visit. Rizzi told him he had celebrated mass in Elberton, spoken to members of the congregation, and discussed the "local situation" with them. But a decision on the bishop's offer had to be deferred until after his society's General Chapter.

Hyland pushed for a larger proposal. In March, he offered Rizzi seven counties in Northeast Georgia: Hart, Elbert, Wilkes, Lincoln, Taliaferro, Warren, and McDuffie. Sunday masses were currently being said in the towns of Washington, Sharon, and Elberton, and in Thomson and Hartwell, it was offered in private homes. Attached to the chapel in Washington was an orphanage for boys conducted by the Sisters of St. Joseph. On its grounds were two small cottages; one could accommodate a chapel constructed for private "spiritual exercises." Hyland's offer included the chaplaincy of the orphanage and the spiritual care of seventy orphan boys. As far as the Bishop knew, the entire area contained only 150 Catholics, but he suspected there were more who no longer practiced their faith. Another society was interested in this offer, but Hyland believed the Comboni Missionaries should have first chance to accept it, and he understood that a final decision had to come after the General Chapter. Rizzi's confreres could be assured this was "genuine 'mission' work. It will not be easy, and it will demand many sacrifices..."[4]

This is how the offer stood when Accorsi contacted Hyland in November of 1953. The two concluded an agreement in Chicago while at the Fiftieth Jubilee of the Director of the Extension Society, Bishop William David O'Brien. Plans were made to renovate one of the Washington, Georgia, residences so it could house a second missionary. The construction took time, but in early May, Accorsi left for Georgia with two of his priests, forty-five year old Alexander Medeghini and thirty-two year old Gino Doniney. Arriving in Athens, Georgia, at 9:00 p.m., they were met by the diocesan Father Walter J. Donovan. The next day they continued to Washington and were warmly received by Father John Crean. who saw their arrival as his chance to retire. Later, when the Comboni priests were able to visit an old Catholic cemetery, it proved that many more Catholics had once lived in the area. Their number dwindled due to a lack of priests, the need to relocate to more prosperous surroundings, and through conversion to the Protestant sects that dominated the area.

Fathers Medeghini and Doniney provided religious assistance at St. Joseph's Orphanage Home, and organized small groups of Catholics for Sunday Mass. Father Donovan and his assistant Father Francis were good friends to the two missionaries, and when Medeghini and Doniney called a meeting with Hartwell Catholics to discuss building a church, Donovan was there with the eighty people that attended. Most were Bohemian immigrants. The meeting focussed on purchasing a house to convert to a chapel. A large six-room home on seventeen acres of land was available for $8,500. Donovan inspected it, immediately called Bishop Hyland, and received verbal approval to purchase it. Two days later, a check arrived for the house, and the Catholic population in Hartwell had a solid base on which to grow.

This fact was not welcomed in some quarters. People began writing to the newspapers with amazement that Catholics were going to build their own church, and maybe even their own school, hospital, and cemetery! By August, the Hartwell house/chapel was well on its way to completion, and mass was celebrated for the first time on the August 15, the Feast of the Assumption.[5]

Accorsi began viewing expansion in Georgia as attractive. The diocese had a bishop who was intelligent, accommodating, and generous, and Hyland was pleased with the work of the Comboni missionaries. Even before an invitation came from Hyland, Accorsi asked Todesco to send more priests for Georgia because "we are anticipating the request from Georgia where that large territory, seven counties, has to be covered by two priests. They are already building two small chapels for better assistance."[6]

Todesco replied, "You are asking me to prepare two fathers for Georgia. Do you really intend to develop our work there? Would it not be more useful to go elsewhere in locations more suitable for PR work? Todesco had good reason to question this move. Georgia had few Catholics, and there were no urban centers nearby where promotion or recruitment could flourish. Accorsi, on the other hand, was thinking about the increasing competition among religious societies in populated areas. He explained to Todesco, "The possibilities for PR work are becoming more and more difficult because every institute intensifies its efforts...and we are always the "foreigners', the "Italians." Accorsi saw that in Georgia there was little competition, and being a foreigner or Italian there was no worse than being a Catholic.

That Accorsi did some plotting to expand in Georgia is supported by a priest there at the time. He recalled that Accorsi had been looking at possibilities, "They wanted something in Atlanta, or a place with contact with more people. [He] went around [looking at possibilities]...but the bishop was not so anxious to give up a parish [in Atlanta]..."[7] The word "they" that Donini used undoubtedly referred to Fathers Accorsi and Medeghini. As pastor of Washington, Medeghini took a lively interest in diocesan affairs and had many friends among the priests. He was, during this same period, scouting for a place to house the Comboni scholastics. When Todesco came to Georgia as part of his scheduled visit to America, he was taken to the five chapels the Comboni priests were serving. Then he surveyed Toccoa, where small groups of Catholics lived in the surrounding mountains without a priest. It was said that Todesco "was very pleased with what he saw, and when he met Bishop Hyland in Savannah....he officially requested that Toccoa be entrusted" to his Institute.

To Bishop Hyland, Accorsi explained what may have appeared an abrupt decision on Todesco's part, "Considering the distance and the relative isolation of our two priests now in the Washington area from any community of ours, the Superior Gen. thinks that it will be very advantageous to their spirit...if they have a few more confreres working in an adjacent territory....After talking this matter over with my counsellors, we came to the conclusion to make a formal application, in line with the suggestion of our Superior General..."

The bishop's reply to Accorsi was quite amiable, "That area of our diocese [Toccoa] has been on my mind for sometime, and it is a great relief to know that our few scattered Catholics there will soon have your good Fathers to minister to their spiritual needs.... According to present plans, the following six counties will be assigned to the Toccoa mission area: Towns, Rabun, Habersham, Stephens, Banks, and Franklin..." Accorsi wanted two priests for Toccoa, but there were only accommodations for one. In April, Hyland agreed to "1) immediately begin construction of a Toccoa rectory, 2) send $200 monthly to the fathers there, 3) [provide] two cars, 4) [provide] Mass Intentions," adding, as Accorsi's note on the letter indicates, that the "Fathers have to take care of own meals... [but] if money is not enough, to let him know."[8]

Father Turchetti, treasurer for the American foundation for years, was sent to Toccoa as its pastor. Anxious for work in ministry after many years as treasurer, he was the right man for the job, not least because of his construction experience. Meanwhile, on November 8, 1956, Bishop Hyland was installed as the first Bishop of the new, autonomous Diocese of Atlanta. The Apostolic Delegate, Amleto Cicognani, gave an official discourse at this installation, and he did not forget to commend the work of the Comboni missionaries.[9]

During Todesco's visit to America in late 1955, he had been questioned by confreres who were bewildered by his decision to expand ministry in all-white mission territories of Georgia. Before returning to Italy, the Superior General gave a talk at Sacred Heart Seminary. In this speech he included admonitions and directives about religious life, charity, poverty, and other subjects. Then he addressed the questions about white missions: "The Most Reverend Superior General, having been questioned on the purpose of the development of the society in America, gives the following clarification: 1. To extend the society by means of new and good vocations, and to contribute financially within limits, to the general works of the society. 2. To dedicate oneself to the Apostolate among the Blacks and other *comparable* groups with parishes, schools, centers of instruction, etc. [Emphasis added] 3. To accept also the apostolate among the Whites, but especially in activities that will be within our missionary vocation, that is, parishes that do not enjoy an easy economic situation, but that do require work that resembles the missionary condition." Todesco encouraged American citizenship to his missionaries and urged everyone to be more faithful in speaking the English language.[10] A copy of this speech was sent to every Comboni community in America.

A FOOTHOLD IN LOS ANGELES

The first contacts with the Los Angeles Archdiocese were made by Father Julius Rizzi. "Please keep us in mind" he wrote Cardinal James Francis McIntyre in 1952, and he followed with similar correspondence on several occasions. Accorsi followed Rizzi's lead in 1954 by asking McIntyre for a parish so Comboni priests in Los Angeles could act as "procurators" for priests "far away from stores ....[those in Baja California]" Accorsi also asked for the privilege of making mission appeals and of opening a vocation center.[11] Auxiliary Bishop Timothy Manning wrote that nothing new was available. But when he did ask for Comboni priests as assistants, Accorsi had just given the only two available to Georgia. Roles reversed the following year when Accorsi again asked about entry into Los Angeles. Manning told him that now his request was too late.[12]

Throughout the remainder of 1955, Accorsi continued to press Manning for ministry in Los Angeles, but with little success. Finally, Todesco, on a visit to the American province, spoke with Manning and put this into writing to him, "The specific end of our Society is to carry on mission work among Negroes in Africa or in any other Mission field; and to pursue similar apostolic work among poor and difficult (sic) people in any land." With these words, Todesco clearly stated that black mission work was not the Comboni missionaries' exclusive calling in the U.S.. Perhaps he believed this was no longer a concern since Comboni missionaries abroad were serving those who were not black in Latin America.

In 1956, the long awaited letter arrived from Manning, "...I write to advise you that the Fathers of your community may take over the assignment of the care of souls at the mission of Our Lady of Guadalupe, Hermosa Beach, beginning Saturday April 7th. It is understood that this assignment is of a tentative and temporary nature until such time as a final determination is made about the development of that territory, and pending the approval of the Holy See..."[13] Father Zelindo Marigo, back from Mexico, was sent to Hermosa Beach as pastor. With him was Father Seraphim Meneghello from Santa Ysabel Mission. Marigo described Hermosa Beach as a "lovely little city on the Pacific about 25 kilometers from Los Angeles." It had been a mission for Mexicans, but plans were being made for it to become a full-sized parish. When Marigo and Meneghello arrived in 1956, there were 120 Mexican families and no Anglos attending masses, all of which were celebrated in Spanish. Archdiocesan officials wanted priests who could speak

Spanish but introduce English, and they were looking for those who could begin organizing the mission into a parish. Before long, Marigo and Meneghello were saying one mass in Spanish and two, then three, in English every Sunday. Catechism classes were reopened, special care was scheduled for the sick, and classes were held for those to be married in the Church. Groups essential to a parish were organized: the Holy Name Society, the Altar Society, the Legion of Mary, cultural and sports programs. Fifty children and ten adults were confirmed by the end of the year.

The chapel was adequate for only 130 people, and it was in poor repair, but not as poor as the rectory which accommodated only one priest. To house a second, parishioners built another room and an office. The atrium of the chapel was repaired and redecorated, and most of the land for a school purchased. At this point, Auxiliary Bishop Manning visited and complimented the Comboni missionaries on their work. In his house diary Marigo wrote, "Fiestas rendered both a spirit of cooperation and financial returns. The finances of the parish improved considerably in that first year; after all the improvements, there was a surplus of $13,000. But in two more months obedience would send us away to an even poorer mission."[14]

Accorsi wrote Todesco, "Are you aware that we are being moved from Hermosa Beach? It is already official. Here there is a new Catholic high school that is being directed by the [Franciscan] Conventuals. To them is entrusted the new parish...started here, but it will also take care of...the Whites. We are being given a Mexican mission...in the Northeast of the city at the foot of the Sierra Madre. There is a little church that is better than...at Hermosa. But no residence, no hall, only the church...but the church is choked without any ground around it. When I visited Bishop Manning, I tried gently to show him the inconvenience of this. He cut me short in the customary manner for which he is known and told me, 'What do you expect" If you don't like that place, I'll give it to someone else. There are many communities that are asking to come into Los Angeles...' It was useless to...explain that we did not have any expectations..." Todesco wrote back that he was sorry his missionaries had to leave Hermosa Beach, "I especially do not understand the expression made by Manning in our regard after all the expressions of satisfaction made to Father Marigo on his visit to our church and for the work and organization achieved."[15]

When Father Meneghello was transferred from Los Angeles, Father Gino Doniney left Georgia to assist Marigo. Doniney leaves a description of the Irwindale mission area: "there was a chapel and a lot of holes, but very few decent houses...houses were in bad shape, like a place abandoned by God."

It was when he and Marigo reported this to Accorsi that their provincial went to Manning and was rebuffed. From Marigo's diary we discover that when they arrived in Irwindale, he and Doniney found a church, but no house, not even a room. "The pastor of Azusa, the next town over, had been entrusted by the archdiocesan curia to find a house for us. Upon our arrival, he stated 1) although he had looked for two months, it had been impossible to buy or even rent a house. 2) it would be better if we put ourselves temporarily in a house in Glendora, because there was no room in his rectory. This meant we would be staying fourteen kilometers [close to nine miles] away from Irwindale. It was already night so we made do with the four cold bare walls...When they [knew] of our situation, friends from Hermosa Beach came to our rescue with essentials like food, blankets, linens, and money...Father Nardi [serving at Santa Ysabel Mission] came for a visit and was so impressed by our situation that he went home, and that same night sent us a generous donation to buy food."

It was a difficult start, but two weeks later, Marigo found a house to rent less than a mile from his chapel for which he paid $65 a month. But the week's collection at the chapel amounted to only $18. When the owner told the missionaries they had to vacate, Doniney had to substitute for another Comboni priest on vacation, and Marigo was alone and without lodging. The priest at Azusa permitted him to return to Glendora, but not for long, he said, for it was going to be remodeled for a new pastor. Marigo wrote, "I'm sure my readers who do not know the area and the situation won't believe my adventures. I could hardly believe them myself. I had to keep in mind the suffering of Africa and those in Russia and prison camps to help me bear these. More than once, I had to open the poor box to be able to buy a couple of sandwiches...the coffee they gave me free."

Finally, tired of wandering around, Marigo decided to build a room in a little space behind the chapel. He called a Mexican worker, and the two worked eight hours a day and finished in three months. They kept the style of the old church which was built early this century from rocks and stones dug by Mexican field workers. Marigo said, "it was admired by the people, the Curia, and the pastor of Azusa, They called it the miracle of Irwindale, because it was begun without a dime on hand."[16]

THE NEWARK, NEW JERSEY, CENTER

A series of chancery memos record the first contacts between the Newark Archdiocese and Comboni Missionaries. They indicate that Archbishop

Thomas A. Boland met with Father Accorsi on May 5, 1953, and again in October of that year. The following spring, Accorsi explained his understanding of their meetings to the archbishop, "I was told that You would notify me as soon as possible when a suitable residence could be found for our priests, so that they would help the Porto-Ricans (sic). I had promised that they [Comboni missionaries] would have been available for any kind of work possible to them."[17]

In May, 1955, Accorsi, still thinking of serving Puerto Ricans, inquired whether he should send two Comboni priests to Newark. That fall, he apologized to Monsignor James F. Looney, the Newark chancellor, for being a "nuisance, but said he felt compelled to write since the Archbishop promised to find a place "where two priests of ours could work for the Porto Ricans (sic)." A piece of property for sale in Glen Ridge, Accorsi said, was to have been investigated by someone from the chancery. In fact, Father Eugene Gallagher of St. Paul the Apostle Church, had inspected it, and found it to be "a fine buy for anyone who can make use of so large a house." Gallagher also looked at property on High Street in Montclair, a 150' x 300' extending to Nishuane Road, with 16 rooms, 5 bathrooms, a finished attic, and a three-car garage for $35,000. Because of the depth of the property, some could be sold off."

Whatever transpired off-record, Accorsi persisted in his pursuit of the Newark Archdiocese thinking that the archbishop was delaying his decision. In late 1955, he summarized the situation to Boland, "In April, 1953, Your Excellency very graciously accepted...our priests working for the Porto-Ricans(sic) in the Archdiocese, and very generously promised to provide a residence for them...Since 1953...I inquired about this residence as I was keeping two men available...Did I misunderstand Your Excellency...?"[18]

Boland replied that there was a misunderstanding. "My intention originally was to permit you to purchase a residence in the Archdiocese...to be a convenient stopover for your priests in transit, etc. I promised to let you know if we learned of any place...When the subject of Spanish-speaking fathers came up, I asked you if you had any who could help in our work with the Porto-Ricans (sic). You spoke of the probability of two. I said we could furnish a residence for them in neighboring parish rectories." Boland added that when Accorsi wanted to keep his two priests together, he (Boland) had suggested that whatever conveniently located residence Accorsi found could house the two Comboni missionaries. As for the assignment to Puerto Ricans. the Minor Conventuals and Jesuits were now serving them.[19]

Accorsi apologized for his mistake. He asked if his society still had permission for a residence in the Newark Archdiocese. Boland's response let him know he had this permission all along. Hearing that Newark was still open, Todesco wrote, "Don't waste time. Send somebody immediately (that is, two fathers). It may be a temporary appointment, but open officially a community..." By August, 1956, Accorsi made arrangements to purchase the High Street property. [20]

Why so much confusion arose between Accorsi and the Newark Archdiocese remains a mystery. If the Newark chancery had, as a Comboni priest claimed, the greatest percentage of Catholics in any American archdiocese, the sheer volume of work could have interfered with communications. However, Accorsi's workload was so heavy that his attention to these affairs may have lapsed. He was not only the primary contact for his society in the United States, he had to contend with some difficult internal situations between confreres, search for a permanent scholasticate, and be ready for a quick response to benefactors, one of which was requiring a great deal of time. It was a complicated role to fill, and Accorsi was even typing his own correspondence and traveling to communities scattered all over the United States. This burden of work, and the fact that Father Accorsi assumed responsibility for much of it made his search for a scholasticate an arduous task.

11. Accorsi and the Houses of Formation

Critical to the future of the American province was its houses of formation, historically the first established outside of Italy. From the first American seminarian to enter Sacred Heart Seminary, to the first scholastics from Italy who took up residence there, to the first candidates for the novitiate assembled at West Harrison, Ohio, the success of the Comboni venture in America hinged on the vocations these "houses" nurtured.

In 1954, one year into his first term, Accorsi reported to Todesco that Sacred Heart Seminary had fifty-eight minor seminarians, and their classrooms were squeezed into the first wing of the new seminary. Eleven scholastics and twelve members of the teaching and administrative staff were also "falling over one another" in the old farmhouse next door. He repeated the situation in his next letter, "Financially, if we did not have the debt with Verona of $40,000, we could start building immediately. The need is urgent, and we do not know how to accommodate the increasing number of students."[1]

Crowding promised growth, and this prompted Accorsi to think of moving the scholastics to a new location.[2] The Monroe novitiate also needed to expand as a natural outcome of success at the high school level. Vocational growth in the United States was then phenomenal, and Accorsi and Todesco viewed the American foundation with great optimism. Providing for the minor seminary, the novitiate, and the scholasticate would occupy Accorsi at least as much as opening new ministries.

THE HIGH SCHOOL SEMINARY

No one doubts that Father Charles Busetti was a Comboni vocation promoter par excellence. Arriving in the United States on January 4, 1949, he took over recruiting from Father Branchesi.[3] From 1949 through 1954, Busetti was responsible for an eleven fold increase of students at Sacred Heart Seminary.[4] It was his work that produced its overcrowding. Those recruited by him have trouble isolating exactly how he persuaded them to join the Comboni Missionaries. It often came down to his exuberance and faithfulness in responding to letters. As a high school freshman, David Baltz was hiking along a country road in St. Louis County when Busetti's car slowed down beside him. The Comboni missionary had already signed up Baltz's younger brother, but David was thinking of joining the Jesuits. Baltz recalled, "He had this horrible accent, and when I couldn't understand him, I just kept saying, 'Yes Father, Yes Father.' He must have been asking me if I wanted to join the Comboni missionaries. When I got to my house, I asked my mother, 'Who in the world was that?'"[5]

Other priests recruited by Busetti spoke of his infectious enthusiasm. He had no secretary, only a desk for his work, yet he kept in touch with every boy who contacted him throughout the school year and vacation.[6] He spent most of the week on the road, and his schedule was described by Father Walter Mattiato who began working with him in 1958. On Sunday afternoons, Mattiato started out from Monroe, Busetti from Cincinnati. Between the two of them, they covered the Midwest, Great Lakes area, and the East, taking in three or more states at a time. At least two or more talks were given at Catholic grade schools in a day. The two priests lodged at a rectory or a Catholic hospital, and offered their services to the pastor or chaplain in recompense. Mattiato returned to Monroe to say Sunday Mass.[7] Busetti's trips could keep him on the road for more than a week.

Meanwhile, Sacred Heart Seminary's rector, Father Remus Catellani, moved ahead on state accreditation. A library campaign began, and many members of the faculty studied for masters degrees. On April 14, 1955, H.G. Jones, Inspector for the State of Ohio, visited the seminary, approved the school, and graciously accepted an invitation to dinner. The Archdiocese of Cincinnati's Superintendent of Schools was amazed that a school directed by foreigners was recognized in so short a time.[8] Credit for this was due not only to Father Catellani, but to other staff members including the Spiritual Director, Father Dino De Grandis, Mr. Singer, and Fathers Louis Buffoni, Ken Dahlen, Robert Erbisti, and Archie Fornasari,.

As students increased, the seminary's main entrance area and chapel were completed, private rooms for staff added, and space beneath the sanctuary opened up for basketball practice. Later, outdoor tennis courts and a roller rink were constructed. The art work in the chapel was designed and executed by Fathers Innocent Simoni and Xavier Colleoni. Father Victor Turchetti said the first Mass in the chapel on a marble altar donated by his parents in Brescia, Italy. A bronze statue of the Good Shepherd placed above the chapel's entrance was donated by the pastor of Martinengo, Italy (Busetti's birth place). Brother Dino Bianchi's craftsmanship was evidenced in the chapel's woodwork and doors.[9]

In 1955, when a friend left the Comboni Missionaries a bequest close to $50,000, Accorsi wanted to build the east wing of Sacred Heart Seminary. Todesco offered him an alternative, "Did you ever think of taking the scholasticate to Canada near a seminary, naturally for reasons of accredited study?...we would have a foothold in Canada and leave Cincinnati free for minor seminarians.....Think about it. It's an idea, I think, that would be a point for PR, for vocations and for other advantages."[10] The decision fell to building the new wing. Accorsi reported in May, 1956, that construction was going slowly, but it would be ready for the new school year.

By 1960, however, the year Busetti was named the minor seminary's rector, recruitment was becoming more difficult, and competition between religious societies and diocesan recruiters increased. In the East, Busetti found new restrictions. Many dioceses would only allow recruiters in schools assigned by the diocesan director of vocations. They could not speak about their own congregation, only of vocations in general. They could not enter into correspondence with boys in the schools, though every possibility for student contact with diocesan recruiters was permitted. Societies that had their own schools, like the Salesians and the Jesuits, had an immediate source of vocations, but those that did not, like the Comboni Missionaries, found recruiting difficult. What made it even harder in the East was what Father Innocent Simoni reported when he settled at Montclair, "No one in the area has ever heard of Comboni Missionaries."[11] However, after Busetti's appointment as rector, the number of students increased to well over 100, and 1963 would mark the pinnacle of enrollment at Forestville.[12]

THE MONROE NOVITIATE

Even while the number of new recruits was increasing at the minor seminary, attrition took its toll on those who returned. But when greater numbers enrolled, greater numbers could be expected to persist, graduate, and go on to Monroe as postulants. Even then, Italian novices were needed to form a meaningful community, and Accorsi had asked again for some in 1953. But getting novices into the United States had met new difficulties. Neither Accorsi nor Todesco understood what was preventing the American Consulate in Italy from approving their immigration papers.[13] They discovered that it was because the novitiate was not an accredited college.

Foreign students could only study in America at an accredited institution. The solution came in 1953 when Monroe Catholic Central received this accreditation. Comboni novices from overseas could enter the U.S. if they enrolled in one of its classes. Italian as well as Filipino novices then began arriving in the United States.

Ministry began to expand when Archbishop Mooney asked for a chaplain to serve at Monroe's Mercy Hospital. Father Paolucci, then the novitiate's treasurer, added this to other duties. In a short time, Comboni priests were assisting at ten parishes, some on a daily basis. The people greatly appreciated these services, and offered them their enthusiastic support. Besides the Verona Mission Club and the Knights of Columbus, individuals came forward with a pool table for a recreation room and hundreds of Russian Olive and Tamarind trees to landscape the buildings. Mr. Troglio, owner of a shoe repair shop, set up machinery at the novitiate, and until he taught a novice to operate it, he made weekly visits to repair the community's shoes. Two marble statues of Mary, the Blessed Mother, were donated by local people, and at Christmas, a woman paid for delivery of seven tons of foodstuffs to the door of the Comboni community. Beyond individual gifts of labor and love was the collective gift from the Sisters, Servants, of the Immaculate Heart of Mary Convent in Monroe, who sent food from their farms on a regular basis.

The novitiate tried to be self-sufficient. Firewood was cut to save on fuel. Rabbits were raised as a source of food. A novice learned to repair shoes. Another did the laundry. When a recalcitrant water pump refused to cooperate, a bucket and rope operation was installed. For years, the driveway went unpaved due to the stringent frugality of the community, thus leading to the frequent need to push automobiles out of snow or mud. Michigan winters were severe, especially when the "lake effect" blew Arctic winds and snow from Canada. In summer there were constant attacks of mosquitoes that thrived in the swampy environs. It was to clear the swamps that, in 1955, the scholastics at Cincinnati went to Monroe. Living separately in a little house, but joining the novices in the chapel and refectory, many then students now remember the sounds of robust and youthful voices vibrating throughout the small chapel as a young novice played on a harmonium.[14]

Based on increasing numbers of students, a drive was launched to gain accreditation for Monroe as a college. Father Ongaro, who was teaching as well as serving in ministry, was asked to build a library for this purpose. He began driving back and forth to Detroit several times a week to obtain a master's degree in library science. Ten new postulants arrived in Monroe in the fall of 1956, and Father Chiodi was happy with both their number and quality. He believed the fruits of work in America were becoming visible.[15] By 1957, there were twenty novices, and the staff numbered six priests and a lay brother. Now there was a need for more space and, after a visit to Monroe, Accorsi reported to Todesco, "I had a good impression of the novitiate...and I can ...see our spirit as I had not seen in previous years... Father Chiodi is serious about building. I told him he could use the funds that he is able to collect. I think he can take care of himself."

In late 1957, Accorsi wrote his Superior again about Monroe, "...Seems to me we are on the right track, and for this I am thankful to God. We have nineteen student novices including three Italians and one postulant brother." Todesco sent a jubilant reply, "I rejoice with you...I feel so much spiritual satisfaction for the good spirit that you say is now found in the novitiate. May the Heart of Christ reign in that cenacle that prepares future hopes for the society...."[16]

By March, 1958, Chiodi received permission from the Archdiocese of Detroit to preach mission appeals in eleven parishes in Monroe County. Funds raised from these were understood to be for the novitiate's expansion. After his first vacation in eleven years, Chiodi returned to the U. S. to work on building plans. A contract with a Monroe company was signed, and in the spring, Mr. Penker, so much a part of building Comboni houses in Cincinnati, came to oversee construction.[17]

THE ELUSIVE SCHOLASTICATE

It is difficult to follow Accorsi's thinking about a new scholasticate without concluding that there was more to his search than finding larger accommodations for students and an accredited school for them to attend. Perhaps he was really searching for that serendipitous conjunction of attributes found at Cincinnati and Monroe: a diocese that welcomed his society; a significant and supportive Catholic population; property and/or a building with enough acreage for the religious formation and study required of Comboni Missionary students; and a seminary nearby equipped to teach philosophy and theology. Recalling the difficulties Comboni Missionaries encountered before acceptance into the Cincinnati and Detroit archdioceses, if this was his hope, it seems Utopian.

The first opportunity for relocating the scholasticate came in 1954 when a house with 100 acres of land in El Cajon near San Diego was for sale. Accorsi had Bishop Buddy's permission to open a seminary, but Buddy offered an alternative. Comboni Missionaries could have five acres on the campus of the University of San Diego then under construction. Todesco gave Accorsi permission to purchase the El Cajon property since it was then several years before the University of San Diego seminary was expected to open.[18]

In Philadelphia, Accorsi had a strong following of lay people, and the diocese had a large concentration of Catholics. That location would also provide access to the highly populated East Coast. In 1955, Accorsi told Todesco he had an appointment with Philadelphia's Archbishop O'Hara, but he met with a refusal. He told Todesco, "To my request to the Bishop of Philadelphia to accept a scholasticate, and permit our students to attend the Diocesan seminary, the answer is negative. He has so many exempt societies and does not want to multiply them, to avoid putting [his] exemption in jeopardy..."[19]

Two other Comboni priests in the American province also felt urgency about a new scholasticate. The first was superior of the scholastics, Father John Battelli; the second, Father Alexander Medeghini, pastor of the chapel at Washington, Georgia. Medeghini scouted the South for opportunities. He found a villa in Lakemont, Georgia, and an invitation from the Abbot of St. Bernard Abbey in Alabama. A letter to Accorsi from the Benedictine Father Bede Luibel, Abbot of St. Bernard Abbey, spoke of Medeghini's visit, and extended an invitation to Accorsi. His Chapter would have no difficulty with deeding over ten to fifteen acres for the use of Comboni Missionaries, he said, but he would be glad to look for other properties. Accorsi accepted the invitation, and Medeghini took him from the Atlanta airport to the Georgia and Alabama sites.[20] After the visit, Accorsi wrote a cordial and appreciative letter to Luibel, thanking him for his "delicate hospitality," telling him that the private property he inspected near the abbey did not seem acceptable to his counselors, but he would wait until his Superior General arrived in the States to consider further the Abbot's generous offer.

In his letter to Todesco, however, it is obvious that Accorsi had already made up his mind, "I stopped by to see Father Medeghini. The projects and the proposals of which Father Battelli wrote to you about were taken into consideration and eliminated. A house that is inadequate with five acres for $22,000 did not merit consideration....the abbot of St. Bernard, Alabama was, and is, ready to give us the use of 25 acres on the college campus....But we would always be attached to the abbey with the impossibility of supporting ourselves financially, and in an area with very few Catholics." The villa in Georgia was "more appetizing, on the lake, among pine trees, with a nice motor boat..." But it "was not wise to tie up $20,000" for the purchase price."[21]

A more likely reason for Accorsi's lack of interest in the Georgia or Alabama sites was that he was never interested in the South. It was the East or Midwest he had targeted. Less than a month after his letter to Abbot Luibel, Accorsi was writing to Prior Hugh Wilt of St. Vincent Archabbey in Latrobe, Pennsylvania, about his "friendly conversation" with Bishop Lamb of the Greensburg Diocese. Lamb had not been encouraging, but he had not closed the door, "If I were... not successful in the places he suggested, [he told me] to go back to him, and he would not leave us cold..." Accorsi asked if "the good Benedictine Fathers" could also find it "not impossible to squeeze our few students in the class rooms of their school..." Father Wilt agreed to accept Comboni students, but only if Bishop Lamb gave his written approval.[22]

By early 1956, Accorsi admitted that "Greensburg is unapproachable." The situation was so bleak that Accorsi asked the Comboni Missionaries' contact with the Holy See, Father Bevilacqua, to approach Cardinal Fumasoni-Biondi of Propaganda Fide. Perhaps the Cardinal would know of a "worthy diocese" to approach about a scholasticate.[23] An exasperated Accorsi told Todesco, "I take the liberty to remind you, Father, that if the Lord were to inspire a change in the regional superior here, I think that many would be very happy, and I with them..."[24]

In May, Abbot Bede Luibel made Accorsi another offer. A Sisters' convent on his campus, now vacated, had a chapel, office, private bedroom and bath, a dormitory, a study room, showers as well as other facilities. It could accommodate ten to twelve people. Luibel was willing to put this house at Accorsi's disposal until other arrangements could be made. The abbot admitted that twelve additional philosophy students in his program would help him gain full accreditation from the Southern Association of Colleges Board of Examiners who would visit that fall. Accorsi replied he was "deeply grateful," but with 18 philosophy and theology students, the convent did not appear to be adequate. Accorsi's response sounded genuine, but only a few days later he lamented to Todesco, "We are still up in the air on the scholasticate. Our efforts have done no good. We will have to continue to try."[25]

Accorsi was so intent on the Greensburg diocese that he continued to seek a strategy through which to enter it. Auxiliary Bishop Hyland of Atlanta knew Lamb from Philadelphia, which was where Hyland was born and studied for the priesthood. He wrote a letter of commendation for Accorsi to the Greensburg bishop. It began, "I can testify to the excellent religious spirit of the Verona Fathers and to their zeal for and their interest in the home missions of the United States. Indeed, it is in a sense of deep gratitude to the Verona Fathers that I write to you in their behalf." Hyland offered some description of the Comboni Missionaries, and told Lamb he would never regret a decision in Accorsi's favor for in doing so, Lamb would be giving "a notable contribution to the cause of the home missions in the United States for years to come."

Todesco had deep reservations about Greensburg; but he told Accorsi that the Apostolic Delegate of the United States expected Lamb to accept the Comboni Missionaries. Accorsi had only to present his case positively, tell Lamb that everything was in place, a house located, and the Benedictines at Latrobe ready to accept Accorsi's scholastics. But Lamb turned down Accorsi, and Bishop Hyland may have identified the reason. Hyland told Accorsi he was sorry but not surprised to learn of Lamb's reaction. He also said, "...it occurs to me that you would never be too happy in the Diocese of Greensburg without the wholehearted approval of the Bishop. Then, too, I am told that the relations between Bishop Lamb and the Benedictines are not too cordial."[26] A bishop that had less than cordial relations with one religious community was not likely to accept another.

By early October, 1956, Accorsi wrote to Father Bevilacqua in Italy,"If I were to tell you the number of dioceses I tried with regard to the scholasticate, you would have the impression of reading a church directory. In many dioceses there is no major seminary...and the others don't want us for one reason or another." He had followed Todesco's suggestion to investigate St. Louis because of the large percentage of Catholics and an enlarged major seminary. But there, non-resident students were not admitted...."

Concurrently with communicating to Bevilacqua, Accorsi commiserated by letter to Todesco, "The scholasticate begins to be a problem. O quanto sa di sale...[How much it tastes like salt...]! You know how complicated our case is because we need a seminary for philosophy and theology. Most seminaries have the two areas of study separate." About Todesco's suggestion regarding Canada, Accorsi said, "the bishops would like to have Italian Institutes for the immigrants. Does this interest you?" Todesco declined because "At this moment, we have absolutely no personnel. We have too much meat on the fire."[27]

Accorsi now had more than a few rejections. Besides Greensburg, Philadelphia and St. Louis there were refusals from the Cleveland diocese; and in the Diocese of Greenbay, Wisconsin, there was a refusal from the

Abbot of the seminary school; in Stratford, Wisconsin, someone wanted to donate to a seminary, but the Capuchin theological school was too far away. A ray of hope appeared when Bishop Martin D. McNamara, of the diocese of Joliet, Illinois, seemed willing to accept a scholasticate if it were located in a certain area where there were no Catholics. This would place the students twenty miles from the city of Lisle, and a Benedictine Abbey willing to accept students if their number did not exceed twenty.[28]

While he walked through the labyrinth of church bureaucracies for a scholasticate, Accorsi was also attending to the replacement of personnel on vacation and in study; attempting to placate confreres who did not want to change posts; overseeing construction at Sacred Heart Seminary; opening new communities in both Montclair, New Jersey, and Los Angeles; and making his annual visits to all the "houses." Thus, it is understandable that even Todesco, carrying the burden as Father General, offered Accorsi frequent condolences, in 1956 writing, "Thanks and many thanks [for your] trips, refusals, poor receptions and everything...Surely the Lord will find the right place." He encouraged Accorsi about the Joliet possibility even if Bishop McNamara's restrictions appeared stringent. "I would not be at all sorry if you would buy a piece of land and build on it at different times according to our economic possibilities."

Todesco articulated a strong desire for Americans and all "foreign" theology students to go to Italy for study. There were those who resisted this in the American Province including the superior of the scholastics, Father Battelli, and others who believed that students going to Italy too early in their training could lose their vocations. They held that those students who were struggling with their studies would be overwhelmed with a new language and culture. Todesco disagreed, "...you know how much I really want [that all scholastics come], and so far, everyone has come, from Portugal, England, and the U.S. I gave orders that even those from Mexico [should] come to Italy, and I would be unhappy to break that tradition... " Todesco quoted a scholastic from Providence, Rhode Island as saying, "Father, send them all to Italy. Here we learn to suffer and to understand what it means to give oneself to the Lord in missionary life!"[29]

YORKVILLE: A LAST OPTION

After a painfully slow search for a scholasticate, there was some movement in late 1957. On the eve of the new year, Accorsi saw a real estate man about property in the Joliet diocese. Having paid cash for the house at

Montclair, he could obtain a bank loan totaling $200,000 for both the land and a scholasticate building. Todesco restated his support, but wanted to know if the bishop had approved. Six months later, Accorsi could report nothing new except that Father Busetti was talking to a real estate man, and Bishop McNamara had made new restrictions.[30] That summer, long letters passed between Accorsi and Todesco regarding a pending donation of a ranch that had become complicated as the owners negotiated over months, even years, on the details. This situation called on all Accorsi's diplomatic skills. Hearing so much about this case, Todesco may have wondered what was happening in Joliet. Accorsi wrote him that he knew, "someone [in the American province] is in a hurry and talks about me as not interested...But...we cannot rush. The salesman takes his time, and I don't think that even he can work miracles... and if the land is not for sale, we cannot steal it. I am waiting to hear from you." Todesco replied, "For the future scholasticate, what do you want me to say? I know that there are those who push, and naturally they...wish to see this particular project implemented. If we were able to reach this goal soon, there is no doubt that you too would be more satisfied."[31] Three months later, Todesco prodded Accorsi again, "What about the scholasticate? I would be sorry if, even for the year 1958-1959, this community were still without its own residence. See that the bishop, misinterpreting our lack of decision, does not find the need to respond affirmatively to other institutions, and then close the door on us."

There is no record of a response from Accorsi, and Todesco asked again in November, "Any news from Joliet?"

Accorsi responded, "As for the scholasticate, we still have nothing, but I hope that before Christmas we may have an acceptable proposal." Then he outlined the questions about construction at Joliet. If American scholastics continued to grow, there would be no need to bring more Italian scholastics to the U.S. and if those American scholastics who were studying theology [the four years before ordination] went to Italy, then only scholastics in the second year of college and philosophy would be left in the States. These questions all had an impact on the size of the house to be built. He added, "Here, everyone is in agreement...that we have school in-house for all the scholastics." It would be more convenient, eliminate many moral dangers from external contacts, and save money since tuition at Mt. St. Mary's in Cincinnati was costing $5,000 annually, and the tuition at Joliet would be even higher. He asked, "What do you think of school in-house for the scholastics as soon as possible? If this had been a previous decision, we would have had an easier time finding a place [since] given the fact that the greatest problem was finding a seminary offering both philosophy and theology..."[32]

In December, 1957, Bishop McNamara accepted the Comboni Missionaries on the condition they establish their scholasticate in Kendall County. Accorsi put a down-payment on a farm of over two hundred acres in Yorkville, Illinois, and reported to Todesco, "I don't think it's ideal, but having seen the pressure from Verona and by other interested parties here, I have decided in favor of what Father Battelli, Father De Grandis, and Father Di Francesco have opted for."

The farm was 40 miles from Chicago, and about 18 miles from Lisle where the scholastics would go to school. It was 2-1/2 miles from Oswego where a chapel had the possibility of becoming a parish. The property had a little house, fifty acres in woods, a great deal of farm land, a creek that never ran dry, and enough sand and gravel to last them for several years. Total cost, $85,000. Accorsi was planning on a two-story building with a basement, half of which would be elevated above the flat ground.[33]

When Accorsi returned from Monroe in early January, 1958, he found a letter from Todesco. The letter, not available, can only be deduced from Accorsi's response to it. Speaking of the scholasticate, he wrote, "...it seems to me rather difficult to think of something concrete....Our finances don't allow it....How can we engage in bids when we do not know if we are going to...implement them?...I still don't have a...plan with regard to the scholasticate...I was hoping the Chapter would shed some light, that...superiors [would be concerned] that all the American scholastics study their theology in Italy..." He added that if only others in the province were, "more cooperative and not in such a hurry, many difficulties would vanish. I understand perfectly well that we would need an ideal situation. But since we cannot always latch on to the *ideal*, we have to do the best we can."[Emphasis added] Todesco responded, "I read your letter to the Consulta....Everyone has agreed to continue for another year yet as we have done so far, given the scarcity of personnel and the need to send missionaries to the missions...As for construction, please send to Verona at least a sketch on how you intend to proceed..."[34]

In 1958, there is a seven month hiatus in available correspondence between Accorsi and Todesco. Father Chiodi was then on vacation, and Accorsi had to press the architect to complete plans for the Monroe addition, and at Sacred Heart Seminary, the young men had become unruly. Father Ongaro had to be called from Pala Mission to restore order there. Accorsi also had to decide whether or not to accept another West End parish in Cincinnati, and one of his priests decided to incardinate in the Denver diocese.

THE GIUFFRÈ AFFAIR

In 1958, a new obstacle to the scholasticate arose. Accorsi complained to Todesco, "the financial situation is becoming complicated...with the Giuffrè case. After repeated insistence on the part of Father Rizzi, we deposited $75,000 with the assurance that we would receive high interest, and now? If we should lose not only the interest, but also the capital, how are we going to make it?... the Giuffrè case [has us all] in fear and trembling..."[35]

To thousands of citizens in the Romagna region around Bologna, Italy, Giambattista Giuffrè was a selfless benefactor whose savings he increased and whose towns he rebuilt. To the Roman Catholic priests and friars he aided, Giuffrè was, in the words of Monsignor Antonio Bergamaschi, Bishop of Montelfeltro, "a generous soul open to any welfare initiative." A onetime bank clerk, in 1949, Giuffrè began offering the banks' customers 25-30% interest on their money, more than double paid by their banks. He eventually paid 100% interest to customers. For a time, he repaid the loans and interest promptly. But in early 1957, the Vatican's Sacred Congregation of the Council advised Italian bishops to warn their clergy against, "any shadowy financial dealings even under the best possible conditions." Some religious societies and institutions began suffering great losses, which together with other creditors of Giuffrè, amounted to $18 million.[36]

It appears the $75,000 that Accorsi mentioned to Todesco may have been the only loss to the American province, but it paid quite a bit more for other losses in Italy. That this would distress Accorsi, so fiscally conservative, is to be expected. The scandal was similar to the one that ruined many Americans during the junk bond scandals of the 1980s. Giuffrè losses would make money tighter for Accorsi and his successor. But it did not bring plans for Yorkville to a halt. In the same letter that Giuffrè is mentioned, Accorsi said he would ask permission to have a Comboni priest live at the small Yorkville house and to exercise ministry in Oswego, 2-1/2 miles away.

In December, 1958, Accorsi called a meeting of all the local superiors. Agreement was reached on the construction at Monroe that cost close to a quarter of a million dollars. Someone asked Accorsi if plans couldn't be made for the scholasticate so that construction could begin there. Accorsi wanted to wait for the General Chapter. To Todesco he wrote, "even our financial situation would not allow us to consider to build at this time unless the

Giuffrè affair...be resolved satisfactorily...I need for you to tell me your thought as to whether to start the building of the scholasticate at the present moment." Then he described an "explosion" that took place at the December meeting. It began with an accusation from a confrere that even Father Todesco did not know why Accorsi delayed building the scholasticate. Someone at this meeting said, "Everyone knows that Father Accorsi does not care about the scholasticate." In reporting this to Todesco, Accorsi reminded him that he, Todesco, had been quoted directly and indirectly, and asked him, "Please have the kindness to let me know your opinion on this subject of the building of the scholasticate at the present moment."

No further correspondence from Todesco to Accorsi is available. From Accorsi there is only the one in which he reported that a unanimous decision was taken by "everyone," that the scholastics in philosophy should study in-house because, "The atmosphere in the seminary [Mt. St. Mary's] doesn't seem too encouraging for our students....We have young people of good will, but who would not succeed [intellectually] and perhaps would be rejected....All things considered, the fathers ask you to allow that school be done in-house."[37]

AT THE 1959 CHAPTER

On June 5, the feast of the Sacred Heart was celebrated with many good friends including Monsignor Reardon of St. Williams in Price Hill and Father Hageman of Immaculate Heart of Mary in Forestville. Accorsi gave a farewell speech to the group, and shortly thereafter left for Venegono, Italy for the General Chapter. He went there as the outgoing provincial of the province, and Father John Battelli went as the delegate of the province.

Accorsi's report to the Chapter was as candid and prickly as its author. The fifty-five year old pioneer of the American foundation said, "It is not a secret that not a few confreres (and also some superiors) had a certain sense of doubtful reservation regarding the region of the United States..." They had feared that "the characteristic spirit of the congregation would be derailed in the vortex of American life." But those who actually visited their confreres in America, he said, could testify that, "although we live in America, our religious life is not affected by 'Americanism.'" Five American students had been ordained as well as Italian scholastics who, after ordination, left America for the missions. There were five Americans studying theology at Venegono; nine in philosophy in Cincinnati; sixteen novices; and fifty minor seminarians. The ratio of personnel to the work in America had worsened. In

1958, the number of Comboni priests rose by 40%; in 1959 they rose by only 20%. This was at a time when total communities increased by at least 50%, total minor seminarians by 300%, novices by 142%, and scholastics by 70%.

The major issues concerning the scholasticate were reported, how it was difficult to find both a bishop who welcomed the society and a seminary with philosophy and theology that would accept its students. Accorsi reported that although, "...America is still the land of great opportunity...we must work in order to find it....economic life in the United States is much more expensive than elsewhere....whatever we are spending for our minor seminary, we would be able to support two houses of similar proportions in Italy...." He said, "[After] the Chapter of '53...the province took over...a debt of almost $200,000...for the construction of the seminary chapel..."[3] This debt was paid. The new wing at the minor seminary cost $175,000, and the purchase price of the house in Montclair was $28,750. Yorkville's cost of $80,000 was already reduced by a third, and the province was in the process of paying the $300,000 for the construction of the new wing of the novitiate.

Accorsi then turned to a subject many may have wished he had ignored, "I could then be silent about...the fact that upon insistent suggestions from Verona, we sent $75,000 for the big pot of Giuffré...and it looks like we have lost it all to the last penny...The only consolation we have is that beyond an act of trust in the superiors, our amount saved many of our communities from the obligation of refunding the Propagation of the Faith...For further information, ask the superiors!" [ellipses not added] All in all, he said, the American Province had been at the service of every province of Africa and South America, and it had given something that could not be calculated in dollars: the education of the scholastics, "Though they are limited in number, the scholastics and young fathers have obtained academic degrees in non-Comboni colleges and universities. Not a few have their B.A. and some also the M.A." In conclusion, Accorsi believed that the future of the American province was bright, and that this would continue if the Comboni missionaries there "lived for His glory" because "the deep Catholic life of the United States admires and helps religious societies that are faithful to the spirit of their vocation."[38]

On August 1, Accorsi wrote Chiodi, "I know you are aware of the results of the elections of the Chapter, therefore I am not going to talk about it. At least, Father Battelli will be able to present our own situation and our own

---

[3] This is $50,000 more than Rizzi reported in 1953.

needs." The elections had surprising outcomes. The former general superior, Father Anthony Todesco, was appointed as the new American provincial. The new Superior General elected was Father Gaetano Briani, known to be unfavorable to the United States. Battelli, who went to the chapter as a delegate, was now a Vicar General. These elections not only produced surprises, they would mark a turning point for the American province.

Accorsi did not return to the United States till September; he had been asked to accompany Cardinal Lercaro on the latter's trip to the U. S. When he did get to Cincinnati, he had to continue the duties of a provincial in Todesco's stead, telling Chiodi, "As I am acting Superior until Fr. T. comes, I am anxious for him to make his appearance as soon as possible, but he seems to be in no hurry."[39]

From 1940 till he stepped down as provincial in 1959, Accorsi's role in the American province was pivotal to its growth. He laid the foundation for the work of all those who followed him. Though dedicated to the African missions and to a rigorous interpretation of his institute's rules and spirituality, he developed a deep appreciation of American culture and the generosity of its people. Accorsi's stewardship of the American foundation earns him the title of "Founder" of the North American Province.

12. A Change of Direction, 1960-1961

Accorsi complained about Todesco's delay in taking over the American provincialate, but he did not consider that someone who had spent twelve years leading the entire congregation through one of its most difficult periods might need a respite. Besides beginning his tenure when Italy was recovering from war, Todesco had witnessed open persecution of missionaries, confiscation of schools in Sudan, and constant danger of expulsion as the new wars against colonialism took place in Africa. Yet the number of Comboni communities was expanding from 66 to 190, the number of members from 663 to 1210, and the number of aspirants from 600 to 1300.[1] Todesco's contribution to the Institute was phenomenal. But his forte was not as an administrator, but as a spiritual director. Under Superior General Anthony Vignato, he had been named novice master in Italy, and those who went through their novitiate with him continued to respect his gifts in this area. Even after election as Superior General in 1947, many still referred to Todesco, as "the novice master."

This description did not take into account his broad vision of his society and his ability to look beyond its initial call to evangelize Africa. When the Vatican urged new missions on his institute, Todesco accepted them with enthusiasm, sending missionaries to the United States, Mexico, Ecuador, Brazil, and new areas in Africa. Although some confreres worried about those who went to the United States in 1947, Todesco was convinced that America was critical to the growth of the Comboni Institute. But he remained strict in the application of the rules the society; quick to denounce criticism of authority, and insistent on the strictest observance of regulations.[2] And like other Italian religious, he had doubts about the spiritual depth of the American Church.

Despite these doubts, on the whole, priestly formation in America before 1960 deviated little from that in Italy. Due to the Vatican's warnings against the threat of "Modernism," seminaries in the United States were often more conservative in principle than those in Europe. The eminent historian of the

American Church, John Tracy Ellis, wrote that, long before Vatican II, diocesan seminaries in America demanded that candidates to the priesthood maintain a degree of remoteness from the world lest they be victimized by its contagion. At the Catholic University of America, for example, priests who were students were expected to perform certain religious exercises in common, including a half-hour of meditation each morning, an examination of conscience before the midday meal, a half-hour spiritual conference before the evening meal, night prayers, and several other spiritual exercises.[3] This regimen was not far from that demanded of a religious society. When Todesco came to the United States in 1960, the distinctions between American seminaries and those of Comboni Missionaries were few, and Todesco had little cause to believe this would ever change.

TAKING CHARGE

As the new provincial of the United States, Todesco faced three immediate issues. The first had to do with the financial impact of the Giuffrè affair. The second was the matter of separating philosophy from theology students, and the number from each group to send to Italy. A third was to establish a new scholasticate. Although Yorkville had been purchased for this purpose, Todesco would not see it as a promising location. As an intermediate solution to the second issue, one of Todesco's first moves was to assume the role of superior of the scholastics. Due to crowded conditions at Sacred Heart Seminary, he sent philosophy students to Monroe for in-house study, and some theology students went to Italy.

Losses from the Giuffrè scandal had put new pressure on financing in the American province. A widely circulated rumor among Comboni missionaries maintains that Todesco was blamed for the losses incurred by Giuffrè investments. The rumor adds that, in no uncertain words, he was put on notice that, as provincial of America, he was expected to redress these losses. When Accorsi referred to the "big pot of Giuffrè" at the 1959 General Chapter in connection to the loan "in favor of the General Administration...." He observed that, "Obviously, the payment of that debt needs to be done from Verona."[4]

Whether this loan was connected to the society's losses is not substantiated in available records, but Todesco's diary offers support that it was. An April 6, 1960, entry refers to the fact that he accompanied Father Remus Catellani, the provincial treasurer, to the bank "to pay for one third of the loan of the Mother House, and the interest of the other two thirds."

Catellani also went to Monroe with Father Victor Turchetti, then Provincial of Mexico, to apply for a loan of $40,000 for the Mexican province (which was later repaid by Turchetti and the Mexican Province). Todesco explains, however, that these loans were obtained only "with some sacrifices from our administration. We will have to cover our debt for the house of Monroe with the Bank. May St. Joseph come to our help before God and men." Money problems made it fairly common for the provincial treasurer to seek out individual communities for their savings to cover these debts, a fact that did not enhance his image with some confreres.[5]

Todesco was a striking contrast to Accorsi. The new provincial preferred consultation with his appointed councilors, but often discarded their advice in favor of that from the General Administration. Accorsi, on the other hand, was more of a "lone wolf" who listened to those whose advice he respected, but often took decisions on his own. Todesco was far more absorbed in the work of formation, making frequent visits to seminaries, and issuing periodic "letters" about deviations he had observed. Accorsi, on the other hand, could be acerbic in criticizing laxity of the rules, but once satisfied that a superior was faithful to his duties, he allowed him more independence in his work. Much more than Todesco, he preferred working with lay people.

Within a month of taking charge at Cincinnati, Todesco decided to transfer Accorsi from the Suire Avenue house in Cincinnati to the Montclair residence. Accorsi's new role was to act as "superior of the [Montclair] house, and to organize every kind of public relations of the Province." Father Catellani, the treasurer, moved to the Suire address, and a Mr. Doran, representing the Community Council Service (CCS) was hired to advise on organizing a fund-raising campaign. At the first meeting, with Fathers Catellani, Branchesi and Battirossi also present, the question of financing a future scholasticate was raised.[6]

ESTABLISHING A SCHOLASTICATE

In early February, 1960, after consulting with Mr. Penker, the Cincinnati contractor about the possibility of building at Yorkville, Todesco left for California to meet Auxiliary Bishop Ackerman of San Diego, a good friend of the Comboni Missionaries. Ackerman expressed "great satisfaction about opening a [Comboni] scholasticate near San Diego."[7] This notation in Todesco's diary is the first indication that Yorkville would not house Comboni scholastics. The momentum now tilted toward San Diego.

In March, 1960, Father Alexander Nardi, pastor at Santa Ysabel Mission, phoned Todesco that twenty acres at Anza, California, was available, and enthusiasm was so high about a seminary on the West Coast that several groups were collecting funds to buy land for it at Jamul. But Todesco had to wait until Superior General Briani came to the U.S. that fall.[8] When Briani arrived in September, Bishop Buddy praised the work of Comboni missionaries at Santa Ysabel and Pala, and offered to allow Comboni scholastics to study at the diocesan seminary. Briani was impressed, and he told Todesco that members of the General Council were convinced that San Diego was the right choice since it was a better location for the Mexican and Brazilian scholastics. After visiting a few sites for the seminary, Briani left to visit other Comboni communities in America, and Father Nardi was put in charge of negotiations for property.[9]

Nardi had to substitute in Irwindale for Father Marigo, disabled by an attack of phlebitis. His replacement as negotiator was thirty-one year old Father Louis Buffoni. Ordained in the United States, Buffoni was an ebullient promoter who coached athletics at Sacred Heart Seminary, and won support for student sports from his confreres and from lay people. In Monroe, he had convinced benefactors to build a gymnasium at the novitiate. But he had less skill at negotiating real estate. When Todesco flew to California to check on his progress, he found prices of the properties exorbitant. A welcome alternative came from Bishop Buddy. Buddy would give Comboni Missionaries a land lease that would allow a scholasticate to be built on the new University of San Diego campus. The lease would be renewable after five years, and stipulate that, if either party wished to discontinue the contract, the diocese could either buy the scholasticate building, or the Comboni Missionaries could purchase the land on which the building stood.[10]

This offer came in January of 1961. Todesco sent a message to Briani in Verona, and continued to look at other properties. Some unofficial and unstated "word" came from Briani, but the General Council still had to be consulted.[11] It apparently declined Buddy's offer, for it was decided to purchase the Quiet Hills Farm in Escondido. When this purchase met obstacles in the form of easements and property restrictions, Todesco asked Buddy if his offer was still open. Buddy replied, "let me hasten to assure you of our willingness to work out a plan for the construction of your Community House on the University Campus." He had seen plans that Buffoni brought him, and he was ready to have a contract drawn up for Todesco's signature.[12] The issue of locating a new scholasticate was at last closed.

REDEFINING YORKVILLE

The decision to build a scholasticate in San Diego put the fate of the Yorkville property in doubt. As an interim measure, Todesco made the second of several major personnel moves. Father Gabriel Chiodi, novice master in America for 12 years, was transferred to Yorkville, and Father Bart Battirossi took his place in Monroe.[13] When Chiodi arrived in Yorkville, the farmhouse on the Comboni property was still occupied. He began work from a motel, and he found a benefactor, Mr. J. Phalen, who paid his first month's expenses. Chiodi spent a week meeting the local priests and Bishop McNamara of Joliet. On November 25, he visited St. Procopius Abbey, once suggested by Accorsi as a seminary for Comboni scholastics. He also visited the Missionaries of the Sacred Heart in Geneva, Illinois. At night, Chiodi worked on speeches and promotion material. When a house was rented, and furniture trucked in from Cincinnati, Father Seraph Meneghello became the second member of the Yorkville community.

Chiodi made several trips to Chicago to visit the Catholic Extension Society's office. He was pleased when the Extension Society sent him a generous shipment of furnishings for a chapel. At the onset of winter, temperatures dipped below zero degrees Fahrenheit, and Arctic winds brought heavy snowfalls. But winter also brought a first request for ministry when a pastor at Morris, Illinois asked Chiodi's assistance at his parish, and the Yorkville community had its first source of income.

In January, 1961, Todesco visited Yorkville and heard that the farm house would soon be vacated. He promised to send two Comboni lay brothers to remodel it. The remodeling proceeded with the help of Brothers Jerry Charbonneau, Victor De Gasperi, and Sebastian Bello'. Even the former owner, Mr. Hudson, occasionally lent a hand. In March, Todesco announced that Yorkville would become a center for lay brother candidates, and in June, an Open House for Kendall County friends was held with fifty visitors attending. Chiodi's diary reported the day was a big success for the community. The Yorkville residence soon received a stream of visitors: boy scout troops, nuns with school girls on outings, and Comboni scholastics.[14]

In July, 1961, Chiodi was transferred to San Diego as superior of the new scholasticate. Father Carillo, formerly pastor of Pala Mission, was appointed to Yorkville. Always one to capitalize on local assets, Carillo spent that September canning vegetables and fruit. In November, he met with Todesco and Brother Charbonneau to plan a future building. Todesco hoped something could be built by the following fall for lay brother candidates.

Classes, he said, could be held at St. Procopius, and shops for training located at Yorkville. Carillo could keep funds from local mission appeals for construction expenses, and he could begin drilling a well and building a camp for boy scouts and future aspirants. As Carillo began another campaign for construction funds, it was no surprise that he took up the challenge with enthusiasm and with his famous spaghetti dinners.[15]

In April, 1962, Todesco examined the Yorkville project and limited its cost to $20,000. He insisted the Yorkville community make every effort to raise this money, and he delayed the opening of the seminary for a year. On June 30, 1962, Bishop McNamara blessed the cornerstone for a building that could house twenty people. But plans to open it for students were again delayed. The delays, Todesco told Carillo, were because permission had not come from Superior General Briani. A report in the provincial newsletter, *Family News*, confirmed this. Carillo recalled later that a number of young men had applied for study, but the continual delays caused them to turn to other religious societies. Years after his work at Yorkville, Carillo discovered that General Briani had never approved a training center for lay brothers at Yorkville.[16] Yorkville's status would be redesigned several times, but its proximity to Chicago would eventually lead to the development of an international scholasticate (see "Working to Survive").

A CANADIAN CONNECTION

In the late 1940s, a young Canadian from Walkerville, Ontario, wrote to Accorsi asking for information about the Comboni Missionaries. Three days later, Jerry Charbonneau heard his doorbell ring. Because his mother was deaf, he answered the door, and standing there before him was Father Accorsi. As a surprised Charbonneau asked the priest to step inside, Accorsi began speaking in sign language to Mrs. Charbonneau. Soon thereafter, her son Jerry accompanied Accorsi to Sacred Heart Seminary to begin a career as a Comboni Missionary.[17] This contact may be the first the American province made with a Canadian aside from Father Rizieri Frizzero's stay there as a prisoner of war during World War II.

When Accorsi was still provincial, Todesco had asked him to consider Canada as a location for the scholasticate. Todesco thought that gaining "a foothold in Canada" had its advantages, and vocations from French-speaking youth would be valuable in French-speaking Africa.[18] Todesco was not the only one enthusiastic about Canada. Father Battelli, Vicar General since 1959, also supported the idea of a Canadian foundation.

On June 26, 1961, Todesco left for Canada with (now) Brother Jerry Charbonneau. General Briani had agreed to open a Canadian foundation, and Todesco carried a letter of introduction from Monsignor Antoniutti, the Nuncio in Spain, ex-Nuncio of Canada. At his first stop in London, Ontario, Todesco was warmly welcomed by Bishop Cody. But at Peterboro, Bishop Webster explained that his diocese had few Catholics, and did not need help. At Toronto, Todesco found no one available to meet him, and after a visit at the Charbonneau family home, he and Charbonneau returned to the States. Todesco's letters to two other Canadian bishops brought more refusals. Bishop Martin of the diocese of Nicolet said his diocese was small and already had four religious communities, and Bishop McCarily of St. Catharine's wrote that his diocese had been in existence for only three years and already had "a number of communities of religious men."[19]

Todesco did receive encouragement from the Most Reverend Bruno Desrochers, Bishop of Sainte Anne de la Pocatiere, who offered teaching appointments at a school at Montmagny. Superior General Briani approved this idea, and arrangements were made to send two fathers from Italy. By November, 1961, Todesco and Catellani met with Bishop Desrochers about specific details. Todesco described these to Battelli. There were day high schools operating at Montmagny and Riviere de Loup'. If two Comboni priests came to teach, they would receive a salary of $2000-$3000 a year and could eventually take over the school, find a residence for their own minor seminarians, and send them to this school. Comboni missionaries would require a bachelor's degree, but five years of teaching experience was considered its equivalent. Todesco expected Father Domenico Ghirotto to come for St. Anne's, and another priest to follow from Italy, since, as he told Battelli, "our Region cannot supply the personnel for Canada. Our personnel is extended to the limit. If one should get sick, we wouldn't know how to substitute for him."[20]

Meanwhile, a request forwarded to Todesco asked for a substitute at a parish in St. Jean sur Richelieu, a suburb of Montreal, and Accorsi went to fill it. Todesco believed that the St. Jean appointment would not be permanent since "the Verona Superiors do not deem opportune to establish [there] a community..." But he gave Battelli a summary of the situation at St. Jean as Accorsi reported it, "The pastor of St. Thomas More [parish] is also the pastor of the only English school in the city, St. Patrick School. This same priest also was in charge of all religious instruction, but he had no other burdens...such as finances, discipline, or scholastic matters. These were the responsibility of a Board of Education."

Accorsi believed the parish to be a good opportunity for vocations. He wrote about St. Jean to Marie Buse in Cincinnati, "I have taken charge of the small 'English-speaking' community...These people have the impression that they 'have been pushed around' on account of the fact that they have had 7 pastors in 5 years. Now they think they have finally found the permanent pastor, and they are rallying around, and are really warming up to me. And yet, I was told not to say that I am here only for a couple of months. And, of course, I try to be active as if I had to stay..."[21]

Todesco gained a different perspective of Canadian opportunities after Father Ghirotto arrived. With Buffoni, Ghirotto proceeded to the Montmagny school, but there found only one priest to speak with them. No one was expecting them, nor could the bishop meet with them. They were told they would need five, not two, priests to teach, that they would have to teach from eight in the morning to six in the evening, and that there were no lodgings available, etc. Ghirotto proceeded to St. Jean to speak with Accorsi. It did not take long to see its advantages. As Todesco reported, "In this diocese, they beg and entreat us to go there, and will allow us the freedom to do all the PR work that we wish...we have a school of 400 students in which to work without the responsibility of teaching and specializations... I see a better reason concerning our goal for vocations than in St. Anne..." He filled another page of his letter to Battelli with reasons why this switch was a favorable one. Nine days later, Battelli sent a telegram:

"ACCEPT ST. JEAN'S IMMEDIATELY."

To Marie and Carl Buse, Accorsi wrote, "...if St. Jean is going to be our first foundation in Canada....It will be the starting point, like dear Holy Trinity was for U.S....Fr. Todesco is due to come...for [a] formal agreement....I did not have much time to go around: actually I wanted to spend as much time here as possible to befriend people, and to prepare the ground for the Fathers to come....I would have been happy here: people were kind and loved me..."[22]

PASTOR OF THE PITS

The Irwindale, California church was surrounded by industry. Huge trucks roared back and forth at sand and gravel pits, and cement factories spewed out clouds of dust into the atmosphere. It is not surprising then that some people began calling Father Marigo the "Pastor of the Pits." By 1959, he and his assistant Father Gino Doniney saw attendance at Sunday Mass increase so dramatically they scheduled four Masses at the church and one in the fields for migrant workers. The camp for Mexican migrants housing anywhere from 300 to 700 workers was near the church, and when the missionaries showed a Mexican film on Sunday evenings, half the camp came to view it. By 1960, Marigo and Doniney raised enough funds to free their congregation from debt and save $3000 for a new rectory. They were also doing all the work normally hired out, becoming accustomed to pots and pans, brooms and dish water, and picks, shovels, hammers and paint brushes.[23] When Todesco and Catellani first visited Marigo and Doniney, they found them in living conditions inadequate even for Comboni Missionaries. To ease their situation, Todesco gave them permission to buy a house that would belong to the province and be used as a future center.

Despite their hard work, the two priests' communication with the chancery was often puzzling "as though archdiocesan officials were thinking along lines they were not disclosing." One reason for this was a lack of a telephone, a luxury the missionaries could not afford. When someone reported this to the chancery offices, things began to improve. Another issue was that a third party had been remiss in communicating the missionaries' needs to the chancery. Auxiliary Bishop Alden J. Bell had asked a local pastor to look for a house or property for the two priests, but the pastor continued to report that nothing was reasonably priced.[24] Meanwhile, the number of people attending Sunday Mass at the little stone chapel exploded, and a sixth Mass on Sunday was planned. Confessions were numerous, partly because Marigo and Doniney were the only priests in the vicinity who spoke Spanish. In December, 1960, Bishop Manning confirmed fifty children, and he announced publicly that he had never been so warmly welcomed in his entire fifteen years as bishop in Los Angeles. The little church in Irwindale continued to have a surprising number of people from other parishes. Marigo commented, "Having begun with only one Mass....In 1964 we were obliged to have eight Masses. The spiritual work intensified.... Confessions were heard in English, Spanish, and Italian. This attracted people from all over the San Gabriel Valley."[25]

Support from parishioners allowed more improvements. The chapel was painted inside and out. The alter was rebuilt. A monument to Our Lady of Guadalupe erected, and a reproduction of the apparition of the Blessed Mother to Juan Diego was placed in the front of the church. Bishop Manning wrote to pastors of surrounding parishes about relocating their parish boundaries to create a new parish.[26] On May 1, 1964, the Los Angeles Chancery announced that "His Eminence, with the concurrence of His Board of Consultors at the meeting held on April 28th, 1964, has decreed the official erection of Our Lady of Guadalupe Parish in Irwindale." Ground-breaking for the new church was delayed till 1965, but when construction began, the church was completed in seven months thanks to Charles Smith, the contractor; Barker and Ott, the Architects, and the generosity of all parishioners. Dedicated on October 17, 1965, it was a culmination of the work and invincible spirit of Marigo and his Comboni associates and of the faith of their parishioners. [27]

GEORGIA

WASHINGTON, ELBERTON, HARTWELL, THOMSON.

In 1956, Father Paolucci, took over as pastor at Washington, Georgia. He described his parish territory as an equilateral triangle, with 100 miles on each side that covered the seven counties of Wilkes, Taliaferro, McDuffy, Columbia, Green, Elbert, and Hart. The total population was approximately 100,000. There were only 300 Catholics, and fifty percent of these had migrated from the North. One Comboni missionary served Washington, Sharon, and Thomson in the south, and the other served Hartwell and Elberton in the north. Together they covered 50,000 miles a year, most over secondary roads some of which were rough and unpaved. Father Paolucci remembered that such travel made it hard to stay awake on a long trip.

The rural South has a history of entrenched prejudice against Catholics. Nurtured through the centuries, a tradition of mutual hatred and suspicion developed. Comboni missionaries heard that local ministers castigated Catholics as people driven by the Devil. They denounced the pope as the Anti-Christ, and claimed that priests grew horns on their head, ate the flesh of babies at their ceremonies, etc., etc. Cooperation and good will, however, eventually broke through these prejudices. In 1957, eighty-four-year old Pat Darden, the sole person to know its whereabouts, led Paolucci to Locust Grove Cemetery, a deserted and vastly overgrown Catholic grave site. Paolucci began to clear and clean it, then seeing the difficulty he was having, three men of the parish joined him with pickaxes and chain saws. They fought tangled vines, weeds, and cleared underbrush from old graves, then put them back into good repair.

On another occasion, Paolucci received a notice from the Diocesan Tribunal of Atlanta to procure an affidavit from a man living in his parish. The man's son was a soldier stationed in Germany who wanted to marry a German woman who was Catholic. The father's address took Paolucci's car through the sparse woods and over the rolling hills of Georgia's back country.

After hours of traveling its red clay roads, Paolucci came to a dead end, his car facing a ditch. High on the hill before him sat an old log cabin. When the priest began climbing the hill, a pack of barking dogs rushed toward him, and an elderly but rugged looking man appeared on the cabin's porch, a rifle by his side. Paolucci continued climbing, and, within earshot of the man, called out, "Sir, could I speak with you?"

The man picked up his rifle and pointed it at the priest, "Start talking!" "Call your dogs back, and let's talk man to man," Paolucci said, edging closer. The rifle was lowered, and Paolucci moved slowly toward the cabin, all the while describing his mission to its owner. He was a Catholic priest. The man's son in Germany wanted to marry a Catholic girl. He needed the man's sworn testimony that his son was legally free to marry. The man gasped a surprised, "Whhhat? Well pardon me sir. I've always been told that Catholic preachers wear horns. Now I know it ain't true." Paolucci retorted, "Well, maybe you haven't seen enough of them." Both men broke into laughter. Paolucci was invited into the cabin for a meal of grits and black-eyed peas cooking over a wood fire. When all the business and dinner were concluded, the lone widower told the priest, "Y'all come back, understand?"

It was this kind of personal contact, coupled with genuine southern hospitality, that built a modicum of trust between the people of Georgia and Comboni missionaries.[28] But they faced yet another obstacle, one that came from within their own ranks. Some confreres believed that the Georgia missions had little value, and they were quite blunt about expressing this opinion. Even though the missions in Georgia had converts, and "lost' Catholics were returning to the Church, Georgia was seen by the General Administration as a diversion of personnel from Africa. There was also the preconception rooted in the minds of many post-World War II Europeans that the United States was a land of plenty and, therefore, did not qualify as a mission country. Others held the view that, if there were any missionary work in America, it could only be found among non-white populations.[29]

By the time Todesco arrived in America, Comboni missionaries toiling in Washington and surrounding counties of Georgia had become catalysts in the growth of the Catholic faith in their area. They helped build a chapel at Hartwell, baptized the first two groups of black Catholics at Thomson, restored the church at Sharon, brought about the first white converts at Hartwell, saw that the sacristy at Sharon was repaired, and rehabilitated many places of worship. All this was accomplished through the cooperation of the people, and a very generous bishop.

TOCCOA.

Accepted two years after the other Georgia counties, the Toccoa mission area included the northeastern corner of Georgia bordering the states of North and South Carolina. It extended 90 miles from north to south, and 35 miles from east to west. It was frequented by tourists who enjoyed the rolling hills, pine trees, lakes, and healthy climate. Except for these visitors, the population distribution was similar to the other counties in Georgia served by Comboni Missionaries. Catholics made up less than three percent, and most of these were from the North where they represented the leading edge of a growing trend by industry to move to the South where lower wages and taxes prevailed. Racially, the people were twenty-five percent African-American, descendants of slaves who had worked the cotton plantations a century earlier. In the 1950s and 1960s, segregation was fully accepted by the white majority in the South, and Blacks appeared to acquiesce, primarily due to fear of reprisals. A truism among all missionaries serving the area was that black men or women asked to join the Church believed it was hard enough being a Negro without adding the onus of being a *Catholic* Negro.

Bishop Hyland funded construction for a house in Toccoa, and the pastor, Father Turchetti, helped build it. Turchetti had three volunteers for catechetical instruction in the elementary and high schools. Except for this, he was largely alone. He still managed to build a vacation camp in a pine woods at Lake Burton for Comboni scholastics, for which they were forever grateful. It was for them the first counterpart to the summer resorts available to students in Italy.[30] When Turchetti was appointed as provincial of the Mexican Province, Father Peter Tarquini replaced him. Like others who served in Georgia, Turchetti loved his mission despite the hardships. When he left it, he wrote Hyland, "I still miss very much Toccoa with all my good people: I can truly say that the three years I spent in Georgia were the happiest of my priestly life, and I will be always grateful to Your Excellency and the fine clergy of the Diocese of Atlanta for the genuine spirit of fraternal charity with which I was always treated."[31]

A CLERICAL FINESSE

Superior General Briani brought to the Institute a more rigid perception of mission in America. Todesco had favored developing ministry in America both for its financial support and potential for vocations. Briani failed to understand why any ministry in America was necessary. He even opposed it. If his vision was not as broad as Todesco's, he was still a man of strong opinions. The Georgia missions would be the first focus of Briani's desire to move Comboni Missionaries out of America. In April, 1960, Todesco was forced to raise the topic of leaving Georgia to Bishop Hyland. Hyland followed with an attachment to his letter, "Without meaning to influence in any way any future decisions on your part, I am taking the liberty of sending you herewith a petition I have received from some of our Catholic men...a well deserved tribute to the [Comboni Fathers]."[32]

Todesco thanked the bishop, and adroitly side-stepped its intent, saying that he would come to Georgia at the end of April to pay the bishop his respects. The following October, General Briani met with Bishop Hyland. There is no record of what passed between the bishop and the general, but Father Gino Doniney, then pastor at Toccoa, recalled the visit, "When Father General came for a visit, his mind was in Africa, not in Georgia. And he didn't show too much appreciation for what we were doing. After he was there a day, or two, he saw that we were doing everything - the cleaning, cooking, teaching - and he said to us, 'this is real mission, I like the way you act - it's a very, very good example to everybody else. It is real mission.'"[33]

The following year, Bishop Francis E. Hyland retired. As the first Bishop of the Atlanta Diocese, he had spoken out on social and moral issues and condemned racial bias. To Comboni missionaries, he was always kind and generous. His successor, Bishop Paul J. Hallinan, proved to be equally considerate. It was to Hallinan that a Comboni missionary gave a warning that Todesco was about to close the Georgia missions. This missionary later recalled, "Our provincial, Father Anthony Todesco...told us that he was coming to notify the bishop that the province had decided to leave...the diocese....When Bishop Hallinan arrived [at Washington]....I told him the reason my provincial had come. He thanked me, and said he would take care of the matter... .When the time came for the bishop to talk, ninety percent of the sermon was a eulogy to Comboni Missionaries...what a blessing it was to have them...how grateful he was to our Provincial for these dedicated men in such a poor area....The sermon ended with an applause by the people. Later, when I asked Father Todesco if he talked to the bishop about us leaving Georgia, he said, 'How could I after what he said?'"[34]

The subject of Comboni Missionaries in Georgia counties arose again in 1962. On May 22, Todesco's diary reports a visit paid to Hallinan informing him of the "intentions of the Superiors to withdraw the fathers from the Georgia missions." The diary continues with, "There was a strong reaction. The archbishop says he hopes the decision will not be serious, because otherwise he would feel obliged to have recourse to the Holy See..." By mid-

June, Hallinan sent a letter to General Briani restating his warning, the work of the two Comboni fathers...was "truly outstanding." Their work was not easy as there "were few Catholics, but the number is increasing and the future is full of promise." He mentioned that the Apostolic Delegate, Egidio Vagnozzi, was especially concerned about the Church in the Southern States and "He never fails to ask me how the work is progressing, and he has given me the assurance that his concern is but a reflection of the Holy Father's paternal solicitude...Perhaps the number of Catholics [Comboni missionaries] serve seems small. The important thing is...the slow but sure planting of the seed of faith in a region largely Protestant. He added "I have been particularly concerned that the tragic mistake of two generations ago not be repeated [when] scores of people of Italian descent [were] lost to the faith because there were not priests.... We are doing our best to reach these unfortunate lapsed Catholics, but the original loss cuts very deep....It is essential...that the work of the [Comboni Fathers] continue and be increased. We have only 34 diocesan priests to care for 70 counties, and the work of the Church would be paralyzed without the great and generous help of religious orders like yours....it would be impossible to agree to any withdrawal of priests. In conscience, I could not close these missions without recourse to the Holy See. Instead, I proposed that...we might consider obtaining the service of more of your priests in order to open up new missions in this area...."[35]

Hallinan copied this letter to Todesco and to the two Comboni missionaries at Washington and at Toccoa. A letter accompanying a copy to Todesco thanked him for his "cooperation" and said it had been most encouraging. Todesco replied that he hoped General Briani would be able to "cooperate with Your Excellency in this matter." Not long after, a letter came from Briani. He was deeply appreciative of Hallinan's kind words, and wrote, "I agree with you that our Priests should continue to take care of the parishes of Washington and Toccoa... However, I do not think it will be possible to send more Priests in the future, because of much need of personnel in the mission-fields entrusted to us by the Sacred Congregation 'De Propaganda Fide.' Moreover, the same Congregation has recently given us instructions not to scatter our forces here and there, but to concentrate our efforts in the above mentioned mission-territories."[36]

The Archbishop of Atlanta had won the battle, but not the war.

13. Seminary Growth/Leadership Change

1962-1964

Todesco's fundamental concern with vocations had led to a deep commitment to expanding Comboni seminaries in North America. That the hour for this work was growing late was understood by few, and the zeal with which Todesco pursued his goals should be understood in this light. While he concentrated on seminary growth, change was rapidly transforming the milieu in which Todesco worked. He was eventually forced to the decisions necessary to keep the province running despite decreasing numbers of missionaries. In 1961, however, anticipation was high among the Comboni scholastics preparing to go to the new seminary in San Diego.

SAN DIEGO'S CHALLENGE

On the morning of August 29, 1961, twenty-six Comboni students left Cincinnati for San Diego. With four cars and a truck, the caravan of students was on its own. The trip took them through Missouri, Oklahoma, Texas, New Mexico, the Grand Canyon (not on the official itinerary), and Arizona on their way to California. Generous hospitality was extended wherever they stopped. At St. Louis they had supper with the family of the seminarian David Baltz, and slept at the Jesuit novitiate. At Tulsa, they stayed with members of the Augustinian order. At Amarillo, they lodged with the Brothers of Christian Schools. At Albuquerque, a Franciscan Orphanage offered them shelter. At Flagstaff, they bedded down in a Catholic school's hallway. Finally, at Phoenix, Arizona, a Franciscan Indian Mission took them in. One who was on this trip recalls talking with schoolchildren and sleeping on bare gymnasium floors. Night temperatures ranged from 32°F at Flagstaff, 6900 feet above sea level, to 105°F at Phoenix, 1100 feet above sea level. It was so cold at Flagstaff, that the travelers sat up all night playing cards to keep from freezing. At dawn everyone piled into the cars and truck to cross the Yuma desert before, as one said, "the sun got hot and exploded our tires."[1]

Arriving earlier in San Diego, Todesco and Chiodi signed a five-year lease for the scholasticate property. With this business concluded, they drove to Santa Ysabel where they found the students tired, but glad to have seen the prairies, mountains, and deserts of the western United States. On September 9, Todesco received the perpetual vows of four scholastics and the renewal of temporary vows of sixteen others. It was the first time in the history of the society that an entire scholasticate professed vows at a mission field chapel.

When classes began, the scholasticate building was still under construction. Todesco noted in his diary, "Only the dormitories can be used. They [the students] lack everything...They pray in the Campus Chapel, study in the University library, and eat in the diocesan seminary..."[2] Former students remember that there was no running water in the partially completed seminary. To brush their teeth, they had to leave their premises at 5:30 a.m. and walk a block to the University library's bathroom. Showers were taken at the lay students' dormitories.

As superior of the scholastics, Father Gabriel Chiodi was in an entirely different atmosphere from Monroe. Those who were novices under him in Monroe, and were among the first to go to San Diego, still hold him in high regard.[3] He was, they say, a responsible superior and a methodic man who impressed a Jesuit sense of order and schedule. He could be severe with anyone who challenged his authority; but as novice master, he never criticized a student in public, and he defended his students against criticism from inside and outside the novitiate. He knew how to balance discipline with recreation. When things grew tense, he would announce, "Boys, today it's time to go out." Then everyone piled into cars for a picnic, a visit to an historical landmark, or a short pilgrimage to a shrine. At San Diego with the scholastics, Chiodi even tolerated good-humored impertinence. If at mealtime, a student was reading from a book the others considered outdated, certain passages would bring forth roars of laughter. To this, Chiodi would merely rap on the table and say, "It's not _that_ funny!" Then there would be another round of laughter. One former student recalled, "There was a certain amount of good will. We had a tremendous choir. A student from New York was the director, and he knew how to play the drums. Two could play piano, but Father Joe Bragotti was the best. We had one piece we sang in six voices.... Performances were given on feast days, for benefactors, and to regale one of our own on his birthday."[4]

Missing was the summer camp in Georgia, a vacation away from the rigors of seminary life. But the university campus did have a gymnasium and a basketball court. At that time its football and soccer field were used by the

San Diego Chargers. Father Raymond Pax recalled how, while tossing
football passes to another student, "There was this boy who wanted to toss
passes to us. We agreed he could. He turned out to be the son of Sid Gilmore,
then coach for the San Diego Chargers. I happened to catch one of his passes
behind my back. He was pretty amazed, but to tell the truth, so was I."[5]

This anecdote illustrates a new challenge Chiodi faced. Although the
University of San Diego was a Catholic institution, its campus attracted
people from all walks of life. No longer could he depend on the surrounding
community to shield his students who were studying on a cosmopolitan and
co-educational university campus. These circumstances were apparently
appreciated by diocesan officials as well. Soon after classes at San Diego
began, they decided to move both their philosophy and theology students from
the University's classes to the diocesan seminary on campus. As a result,
Comboni philosophy students were refused access to classes at the University.
Without such access, they could not obtain the academic credits required for
a bachelor's degree. When Todesco found out, he noted in his diary, "It is a
real disappointment...rather a betrayal."

Students wanted Chiodi to challenge this policy, but he refused. Dealing
directly with the diocesan authorities of the campus seminary could have put
him in an awkward position between the seminary's rector and his own
students. He was, as he recalled, between "the sword and the wall." It was
really an issue for Todesco, and the students wrote directly to him. A former
student described the result, "...the provincial [Todesco] came out, went
straight to the bishop and said, 'I want these [students] to go to the university
even though they'll be the only ones wearing the cassock...' So the bishop
said, 'If that's what you want, father...' The five of us were the only
seminarians to go to the university in the second semester, and the university
did flip flops to make sure we graduated with our degrees..."[6]

Whether or not Todesco met personally with Buddy, he did write the
Bishop a letter, "...We are informed that this year our students could not, or
were advised not to, attend the Philosophy courses at the University and
receive degrees....From the very first contacts that we had with Your
Excellency, we were encouraged to avail ourselves of the opportunity afforded
to us by the University. This is the only way we have to prepare our future
teachers and professors [for] teaching in our mission seminaries and schools
and in the houses of formation in the Society itself...."

Buddy responded favorably to Todesco's concern. He wrote, "You will
be pleased to know that arrangements have been completed with Father
Cadden, Dean of the College for Men, to admit your students for the second

semester...it was a misunderstanding that they did not continue because we never intended to exclude your students from the College courses..."

The move to San Diego seemed justified when, in May of 1962, ten Mexican scholastics arrived. They contributed to a cultural exchange that later expanded when a few African Americans joined the community. Todesco, however, had not forsaken the idea of building a permanent scholasticate in California; he continued to look for property, and he also concentrated on raising funds for his seminary objectives including construction at Monroe and Cincinnati. But his work load caught up with him. In June, a kidney ailment, his first recorded illness as provincial, forced him to curtail duties.[7]

FURTHER CHALLENGES

That summer, Todesco wrote, "Great difficulties are encountered in this period to cover for one another in the different houses and commitments. The movement of fathers continues in order to fill the various holes." To add to his troubles, in late August, Todesco received news that two scholastics from San Diego and two from Monroe were leaving the society. Two weeks later, he heard that two American scholastics in Italy were also leaving the Comboni Missionaries. The year was a challenging one, and Todesco sought support from the General Administration. On October 9, 1962, he left for Italy to discuss with Briani "the needs and development of the Region." He stayed in Rome two weeks visiting other confreres in Italy in order to "study for ten days points of programs to be developed in the U.S.A." But ten days stretched into two months. When he returned to America, he came with permission to expand American seminaries in three directions. He could complete construction at Sacred Heart Seminary; he could transform the Monroe novitiate into a fully accredited college; and he could build another minor seminary on the East Coast.[8] The American Provincial had reason to be encouraged.

At Christmas, 1962, Todesco circulated a letter with a brief reference to the results of his trip, "The time I spent in Italy afforded me the opportunity to deal with the Very Reverend Major Superiors. The needs of our growing Region were discussed at length....The agreements reached with the Major Superiors will certainly bear good fruits in the not too distant future..." No details were given about these agreements. Most of the letter contained admonitions and directives about exactness and punctuality in their daily schedule, the wearing their cassocks, faithfulness in observing days of recollection, and promptness in making quarterly Mass reports.[9]

Todesco's visit to Rome paralleled the preparation period for the Second Vatican Council. He had spoken to Comboni Missionary bishops who were in Rome specifically for that Council. Yet nothing in Todesco's letter spoke of these historically remarkable events. As the former general of his society, it might be expected that he would give some thought to this historical gathering, one that was declared the greatest intellectual and spiritual ferment in the Church since the Protestant Reformation. Perhaps his preoccupation with plans for his province interfered with this. But the tone of his letter to his superiors in America is striking in this respect, that it totally avoided any mention of the "opening of windows" by Pope John XXIII, the Second Vatican Council, and the soul-searching energy this was generating.

VOCATION EXPECTATIONS

Although he lost some priests to foreign missions and a few scholastics were leaving the society, Todesco's drive to expand seminaries in North America was at first supported by solid statistics. The summer vocation camp drew 145 boys in 1961 and 200 in 1962. The number of freshmen at Sacred Heart Seminary rose from 30 in 1961 to 58 in 1963. The total number of minor seminarians rose from 63 in 1961 to 91 in 1962.[10]

In addition to Father Busetti's success as a recruiter, credit also belongs to Father Angelo Biancalana and those assisting him. In 1960, Biancalana began full-time work with Busetti in vocation promotion covering East Chicago, St. Louis, and other areas of the Midwest. A young priest himself, his exuberance and lively personality were valuable assets in recruiting new candidates. In 1962, he was named Assistant Vocation Director, and correspondence at his Forestville office increased to the point that he was given a part-time secretary. Over the next years, he was the chief recruiter with full-time assistance from Fathers Joseph Bragotti, Robert Bosse, Kenneth Gerth, and Benedict Paletti. The primary method of attracting young men to the Comboni Institute was through personal contacts. This included invitations to an Open House at Cincinnati where candidates and their parents attended Mass, shared a lunch, and heard a talk on missions and the religious vocation. In the early 1960s, it proved an extremely successful method and Todesco's plans to expand seminaries seemed a reasonable and praiseworthy objective.[11]

In 1963, property near Escondido in Southern California was purchased for a seminary. Todesco had advised Bishop Buddy on this, "Time flies and the five-year lease that we have with Your Excellency will soon expire. It is our hope that we will be able to move by that date. The property is part of the Bernardo Winery estate, situated in Green Valley. Father Chiodi...will give you more details..." Chancellor James T. Booth acknowledged Todesco's letter, and reported that Buddy had some concerns "due to the great expense involved," but no impediments were raised.[12] After this purchase, Todesco visited nearby institutes with minor seminaries to see "if they would accept some of our aspirants while we are waiting to build our own minor seminary."[13] This entry leaves in doubt whether Todesco had decided to build a minor instead of a major seminary, or whether he was simply exploring possibilities. The fact that Mexican students were going to the San Diego scholasticate, and Hispanic populations were growing in the region may have put these matters in doubt.

Expansion in the Midwest meant construction of a new wing at Sacred Heart Seminary. Father Charles Walter later described this as, "probably the most necessary thing that should have been built years earlier." The priests, he said, had been living in "subhuman conditions" for years; their living quarters measuring about 7' x 10' including office and bedroom. This last construction, he said, finally gave them some breathing space, though it was still cement block construction which astonished many of the missionaries from overseas with its sobriety and austerity.[14]

Although the number of graduates from Sacred Heart Seminary did not increase in the early 1960s, virtually 100% of them entered the novitiate, thus maintaining a steady number of novices. Figures from the summer of 1962 indicate that Monroe was housing twenty novices and three lay brother students. Archbishop Dearden had approved plans to transform Monroe into a college. But before accreditation could take place, a college-level library and science laboratory had to be in place. Father Ongaro, in charge of both tasks, was studying for another master's degree, this time in library science. Both he and Father Battirossi, the novice master, began a fund-raising campaign for the college. A public relations firm in Detroit was hired, but raising money was largely due to personal contacts made by the priests: Battirossi, Ongaro, and their confreres at Monroe. Local people showed great interest in a college, and fund-raising went forward. Books were donated, and provisions for storing them acquired. Brother Valentino Fabris, a master carpenter, constructed four twenty-foot-long library tables, each supported by two pedestal legs, and all in solid maple. By March, 1963, the college library had the 35,000 volumes required by Michigan's Department of Education. The room could accommodate sixty-four people at its tables. For the science lab, Ongaro found a college that was willing to sell first-rate laboratory tables and equipment at a nominal price. This was fortunate since, despite benefactors' generosity, funds for developing college level status did not come easily. With requests for funds to expand the society outside the province, the treasurer, Father Catellani, was forced to draw on individual communities' savings, including those at Monroe.[15]

In June, 1963, Todesco launched a property search for a minor seminary in the East. It began in the New Jersey diocese of Paterson. By the end of the month Accorsi, then at Montclair, reported that the property targeted for acquisition was probably available, but a change of bishops earlier in the year could lead to the Comboni Institute being denied permission to open in that diocese. The next day Accorsi confirmed that Bishop James J. Navagh had refused his consent. Todesco and his treasurer, Catellani, then went on a property-hunting excursion in the Trenton diocese of New Jersey. Here, things went smoothly. A site was located, and Bishop George W. Ahr gave the purchase his approval.

Todesco was not the only head of a society expanding seminaries in 1963. On the day the land deal in the Trenton diocese was scheduled to close, Bishop Ahr sent him a letter asking him if he was serious about the purchase. If he was not, another Institute was making the same request. Todesco noted, "It seems that this Institute [even] wanted to buy the same property we intended to buy."[16]

Todesco had moved quickly to implement objectives supported by his General Administration. The expansion of Sacred Heart Seminary, the upgrading of the Monroe novitiate to the status of college, and the purchase of property for a seminary on the East Coast, were all achieved within a year of his 1962 visit to Italy. Besides these three initiatives, property for a possible permanent seminary on the West Coast was purchased. In a relatively short time, Todesco had achieved many of his seminary objectives in North America.

LEADERSHIP CHANGES

ACCORSI CALLED AWAY.

After he was sent to Montclair in 1960, there are few references to Father Accorsi in Todesco's letters, diary, or even *Family News* ,the internal newsletter of the American province. If it were not for those who then knew him when he was at Montclair, there would be little or no record that Accorsi was still in the province. The "lone wolf" may even have preferred it that way.

Father Remus Catellani recalls how Accorsi came to his assistance at the time the Columbia property was purchased. Catellani was treasurer, but, as he remembers, "...I didn't have enough money. Father Accorsi was...at Montclair and had been saving money. He said to me, 'You give me fifty thousand dollars, and I'll put the other hundred to it.' And we paid a hundred and fifty thousand dollars in cash. He told me later, 'This breaks my back, and you must be grateful to the people who helped us.' And to this day, people there remember the man... He spent very little on himself, but when it came to the cause, he went all out."[17]

Accorsi was now in his sixties, and not the same man confreres remembered from earlier years. The removal of responsibilities as major superior left him a little warmer in communications. Father Denis Wilkinson recalls that at Columbia, Accorsi cooked meals for him, and on one occasion, Accorsi said, with surprising emotion, "You are a good friend, Denis." His companion was amazed to see tears in his superior's eyes.[18] Father Joseph Bragotti, after his ordination in 1962, went to Montclair to take a pre-med course and work in vocation promotion. At first, he saw only the old Accorsi, a man who went days without speaking, who lived on iced tea and lettuce, who came in late at night tired from his appointments, and went silently up to his room. But when the young priest came to him for the usual permissions, Accorsi told him to forget "that sort of thing. "Here's money. You have to eat. There is a supermarket, and here is a kitchen. You don't have to live the way I do." When the old car Bragotti was using blew its engine, he called Accorsi for advice. He was told, "You are there. You make the judgement." The aging car would have cost $400 to repair, so Bragotti decided to take its junk value, $55. Returning to Montclair by bus, Accorsi asked him, "How did you get here?" "By bus," Bragotti replied. "Oh. Where is the car?"
"I sold it for $55." "Ah."

A few days later, Accorsi bought Bragotti a blue Falcon for his work. Then he introduced him to friends of the Comboni Missionaries. Few of these were Italian, and many had national reputations, e.g., a publisher of a leading woman's magazine; another publisher, this time of a respected religious journal. Before taking his young charge to meet one of these benefactors, Accorsi phoned the family and told someone on the other end of the line, "I am coming over to introduce you to a baby priest." When the two priests arrived at the house, children ran to the door, and began climbing all over the older missionary. He told them his mission stories and showed them a watch that rang on the hour. Bragotti recalled, "They loved him, but back in the house, he could still be an ogre. If I went downstairs in the morning, and he was already saying prayers in the chapel, he'd say, 'You've been three minutes late for the past week. Can't you set your clock right so we can start prayers together?"[19]

On October 25, 1963, Accorsi left on vacation to Italy. He wrote to Marie and Carl Buse in Cincinnati, "I reported to Verona and was told to 'go home and stay until called,' a very easy obedience!...I am really basking in the warm affection of Laura and my 5 brothers and their families." Later, he wrote Marie Buse that he had been expecting to return to America, but, "You know, the Superiors are unpredictable, and could hold me until they please....I do not know what will be in store for me after I return...." When Accorsi returned to the United States in May, he was assigned to Monroe for public relations work.[20] Two letters came to Accorsi at Monroe. The first, brief and to the point, was from Superior General Briani, "I inform you with great pleasure that the Consulta has appointed you Regional Superior of Verona. More than an honor, it's a big burden which is imposed on your shoulders, but the Heart of Jesus will help you to carry it well for his greater glory and for the good of the Society..."

The second, from Accorsi's Regional Superior, Todesco, was a bit longer. It confirmed the notification of Accorsi's appointment as Superior of Verona and conveyed congratulations. Todesco said he felt, "rather sad that you have to leave our region which owes so much to your zeal and great spirit of sacrifice. I am certain that not only the benefactors and friends, but all of our confreres will feel strongly your departure from the region." He reminded Accorsi to "...take care of the applications for mission appeals in the different dioceses so that the one who is taking over from you will not find it difficult..." Then he added, "...during this time, you will have set aside...some funds. I would ask you to let me see your financial account with the Mass intentions....Let me know if...we have to provide you with a ticket, reservations, etc. from here."[21]

Accorsi's letter to Briani is dated a day later than the one he received from Todesco. He began, "...A note from Fr. Todesco has struck like lightning from out of the blue. I have not yet settled down here from Montclair than I am told with your note to return to Italy....The conclusion is, in conscience, I cannot accept. I have always felt inadequate for positions of similar responsibility. Now I am more convinced than ever. I am not even going to try to enumerate the serious reasons that force me to say this. Some reasons are well-known. Many, perhaps, are not. It is exactly in order to avoid damage to the society that I beg you...to exempt me from this post which is definitely above my strength....Apart from personal reasons, how could I absolve satisfactorily a duty on which the life of our future community depends since we are talking about the formation of our young students....I have no experience in formation....Even when I was forced to be Regional Superior, I kept for myself the...activity that was external, as Father Battelli could testify....Most Reverend Father, I write this letter after discernment and prayer. Even the confreres to whom I have told of this thing are puzzled. They...think that if my work could be at all useful, it would be better here than in Italy...at my age and with my aches! For the good of the Society that I have always loved, I beg you Father and I implore you again not to force me to accept this post. If I am allowed according to the Rule to refuse, I would ask you to interpret the present note in that sense... I pray that the Lord may enlighten you to discern the good of the Society."[22]

No light of that sort changed Briani's intentions; he responded: "...I understand that responsibility is a burden, and we all would much rather do without it, also, because our deficiencies are always considerable. But we should confide in the Heart of Jesus who chooses the instruments which are less apt so that we may remain in our humility, and he is the only one who does the work and carries out His will....I expressed your desire also to the other two counselors, but their advice is that we should not rescind the decision taken....try to be here by the middle of this month or soon thereafter."[23]

On August 20, Accorsi left for Italy. With the shortage of personnel, and the extraordinary experience Accorsi had in public relations, such an important personnel change would certainly have required consultation between the American provincial and his superior, Briani. In February, when Accorsi was still in Italy, Briani detoured to the United States on his way to Mexico, but stopped at Montclair for a day, and in Cincinnati for several days.[24] It can be assumed he had some urgent business to discuss, possibly the effects of persecution in Sudan from which news would soon break that hundreds of Comboni Missionary were expelled.[25] However, while these expulsions were published in *Family News*, Briani's visit was not. Therefore, the General's visit was not only unofficial, it was intended to be private, and perhaps then Accorsi's transfer was discussed.

SAN DIEGO: AN ERA ENDS.

In September, 1963, Bishop Charles Francis Buddy, the first bishop of the San Diego Diocese officially retired. His poor health and heavy responsibilities in a rapidly growing diocese had led to the appointment of

Bishop Francis James Furey as Coadjutor and Apostolic Administrator only months before. Stories circulated that Buddy was forced to retire due to the diocese' heavy indebtedness. But these rumors ignore several facts. First, Buddy was 76 years old at retirement, and he had been in poor health for some time having been treated for glaucoma, a cataract, sciatica, and spinal arthritis. Secondly, Dun and Bradstreet had issued a report in 1963 attesting to the high credit of the diocese. It reported that Bishop Buddy's administration had been "run in a highly capable and successful manner."

On March 6, 1966, Buddy was on a confirmation trip to a northern outpost of his diocese. While at a motel room at Banning, California, he told his chauffeur that he felt ill. Later he was found unconscious, apparently a victim of a heart attack. He was taken by ambulance to Pass Memorial Hospital, and pronounced dead at 9:43 a.m.[26]

PASTORAL CHANGES

SANTA YSABEL.

From 1961 to 1969, Fathers Didoni, Nardi, Tarquini and Pazzaglia successively served as pastors at Santa Ysabel, and its many outlying chapels. In 1961, Catholic lay people from Los Angeles and San Diego took an interest in the development of Santa Ysabel, and founded an organization called the Santa Ysabel Reconstruction Group (SYRG). SYRG drilled a new well to alleviate a critical water shortage for local Indians. It funded excavation of the original mission buildings constructed in 1818. A Comboni college student from Khartoum excavated the area and uncovered some original mission ovens. Stephen Berardi, a young artist and graduate of the Art Institute of Chicago, made a scale model of a museum to display these and other artifacts found near Santa Ysabel. Members of SYRG built this museum, doing much of the work themselves with donations from benefactors. Original carvings of Berardi titled "The Madonna of the Indians" and "The Angel of the Lost Bells" were put on display and drew more visitors to fund-raising events. Press releases about Santa Ysabel were published in the Los Angeles and San Diego newspapers. In 1964, Comboni Father Peter Tarquini's *The Story of Santa Ysabel Mission* was published and this also increased publicity for the mission.[27]

PALA MISSION.

The Pala Mission School grew from 101 children in 1961 to 156 in 1963. By 1965, the kindergarten had to be discontinued to make room for the increased numbers of older children. By the end of the decade, over two hundred students were enrolled. Father Dino De Grandis succeeded Father Carillo, and he was replaced by Father Gino Doniney in 1965. Under Doniney, new school rooms were built to accommodate growth, but expenses for the school continued to rise. In 1963, costs were amounting to $17,000 a year. The children's parents were asked to donate only a small part of this. While the Corpus Christi Fiesta raised some of the remaining funds, the school still depended on benefactors to keep it operating.

In the mid-nineteen-sixties, another fund-raising idea developed. The children themselves helped earn money by drawing sketches about the first Christmas with a distinctive touch of Native American culture. These sketches were put on 5-1/2" x 8" Christmas cards. Father Victor Turchetti, at Pala after returning from Mexico, recalls that, "It was a big project. Father Didoni started these silkscreened, homemade Christmas cards. When I arrived, I found that a group of ladies, one from San Diego, one from Escondido, and another from Delmar were helping the project. We sold the cards for twenty-five cents each. The [children's designs] were processed and adapted by a local artist from San Diego who did everything for free. One winter, there were about 4000 or 5000 cards printed. Later, there were 100,000. We had a large mailing list from people who visited the mission. It made us famous all over Southern California."[28]

CINCINNATI: ST. ANTHONY'S.

In 1960, St. Anthony's Church was doomed to the wrecking ball even though its school was experiencing the highest student enrollment in fifty years, a total of 195 youngsters. Only 75 of these were Catholic, but again, even those not Catholic attended daily Mass. At the parish Centennial in 1960, Archbishop Karl Alter celebrated the Pontifical Mass, and commented that he was very pleased with the Comboni Missionaries' work in his archdiocese.[29]

Father Paolucci was called from Georgia to close St. Anthony's, a church that could seat one thousand people, its Gothic arches sixty feet in height. The City of Cincinnati offered $360,000 for it because it was in good condition. The offer was accepted by the Archdiocese, and Paolucci was given the task of inventorying and distributing all the contents of the church, convent, school, and rectory that were not "hinged or nailed down." A book of over 2000 objects was put together consisting of such items as fourteen Stations of the Cross carved from wood by German craftsmen; a central chandelier twenty feet in diameter; a monumental organ built in Baden Baden, Germany;

dozens of statues of saints; a life-size scene of Calvary; and much more. Paolucci first celebrated mass at St. Anthony on August 27, 1961. He last celebrated it there on November 4, 1962.[30]

Before St. Anthony's closed, Todesco wrote to Cincinnati's Auxiliary Bishop, Paul F. Leibold, about taking over St. Michael's Church in the Price Hill area of Cincinnati. In a previous communication, Todesco must have had the impression that Leibold was making another short-term ministry. He wrote Leibold, "I mentioned that our priests might be somewhat discouraged to undertake again a job which would be short-lived. I was pleased to learn that my impressions were incorrect."[31] In September, 1962, Archbishop Alter sent the official offer of St. Michael's to Todesco. It was addressed to General Briani since at issue was the fact that St. Michael's was a white parish being exchanged for a black one. Alter was aware that the Comboni Missionaries' General Administration might find this exchange unacceptable. He wrote,"...I am...inviting the Fathers to accept the care of another parish [that is] a neighboring parish to St. Anthony's. While it is not a Negro parish, it is a missionary parish inasmuch as many of the residents...have moved in from the southern part of the United States and are not Catholics..."

In October, when Todesco went to Italy, he met with Briani about this offer and other matters. With Briani averse to opening new ministries in North America, convincing him to accept St. Michael's must have required great diplomacy. But Briani agreed to the exchange, and he wrote Alter that he was doing so simply on the fact that it was accepted by the Regional Superior of the United States, i.e., Todesco.[32]

Having closed St. Anthony's, Paolucci transferred to St. Michael's on the other side of the Mill Creek, a waterway that carried tons of industrial waste to the Ohio River. St. Michael's in Lower Price Hill was not far from the West End, but it was in a neighborhood largely made up of Appalachian migrants, a new ethnic group for the Comboni missionaries to serve. St. Michael's buildings included a commodious rectory, a three-story school house on the west side of the church, a duplicate of this building on the east side, and a large well-preserved school building. The church was relatively small, but its physical plant was in fair condition, and there was an ample savings account for remodeling projects. The first was a new senior citizens' and bingo center. Then the west side building was remodeled to provide office space for Comboni promotion and vocation staff members and the provincial treasurer. These offices now made up the Secretariat for Mission Promotion of the North American Province, and by 1964, only the provincial's office remained in the old house on the Forestville grounds.[33]

TOCCOA.

On May 11, 1964, Todesco flew to Atlanta and met Archbishop Hallinan now sick in the hospital. There are those who believe that this was the only condition under which Todesco could wring a concession from the archbishop. The fact remains, however, that Hallinan agreed to take back the Toccoa mission by the middle of July. A dearth of personnel in the American province had forced Father Doniney to be alone at Toccoa for most of the year, a circumstance in which his predecessor, Father Turchetti, had also found himself.[34]

What made a lack of new personnel more painful was that a turning point had come regarding minor seminarians. The number of young men attending the summer camps dropped from 250 in 1963 to 170 in 1964. The number of new students entering Sacred Heart Seminary dropped from 58 in 1963 to 24 in 1964. At least some of these losses could be attributed to the growing scarcity of personnel in the American province. While Accorsi was on vacation in 1963-64, Biancalana, the only full-time recruiter, had to substitute for him. Then when Accorsi was called to Italy as its provincial, the province lost a preeminent promoter. Todesco noted the loss of new students, but put an optimistic face on it, "Defections are many, but perhaps providential." Though the number of seminarians was down to 70 in 1964 from 100 in 1963, he believed that, "There were defections in number, but we trust in better quality."[35] Fewer vocations, however, were not the only losses the province would experience.

A TURNING POINT

The years 1962, 1963, and 1964 were watershed years for more than the Comboni Missionary Institute and its American Province. In Rome, events of great moment both to the Catholic Church and the world were taking place. The four Sessions of the Second Vatican II Council were in progress. In 1963, Pope John XXIII died, and the American president, John F. Kennedy, was assassinated. Recalling these years, Father Paolucci remembers them as a time when "the rise and fall of new ideologies caused ripples that are still disturbing men's minds....On the wake of Pope John's death, controversy arose about which 'windows' should be opened...and if we should even do away with windows altogether."

In August of 1963, returning from a vacation in Italy, Paolucci found that, among his confreres, schedules were deviating from their former cohesiveness, and community members were more likely to go their own way. There were new amenities such as television sets, pool tables, and stereos, signifying a considerable relaxation from earlier days. An effort was made to bring back unity to community life. Confreres at St. Michael's agreed to meet twice daily for prayers, to take meals together, and to enjoy recreation in common. Some of the older confreres, including Paolucci, hoped the new relaxations and concessions "would last a small eternity." But change had opened doors and, Paolucci's journal notes, "beyond were open spaces."[36]

14. Seminaries in Transition, 1965-1966

The years 1965 and 1966 brought changes both in the Church and in America that created conflict in the social structure of each. In the United States, the Civil Rights movement and Vietnam War protests pointed to a deeply felt sense of injustice and of outrage at leaders who tolerated it. In the Church, the initial euphoria of Vatican II began to fade, and reactions polarized. Some were impatient for change, some afraid of it, and some were adamantly opposed to it. These events affected the North American province as well as other segments of American society. In Europe, a similar social ferment surfaced.

REFLECTIONS ON MISSION

On May 23, 1965, Archbishop Alter celebrated the twenty-fifth anniversary of the Comboni Missionaries in North America. Father Julius Rizzi came as General Briani's representative, and Bishop Angelo Barbisotti, the former Pala Mission pastor, came from Esmeraldas, Ecuador. The following evening, one hundred diocesan clergy were entertained at dinner, and Auxiliary Bishop Leibold brought words of congratulations.[1]

A common theme of the Silver Jubilee was the contribution the American Province made to the rest of the Institute. Archbishop Alter observed that Comboni Missionaries in America had provided "a fruitful source of support for the 'Verona Fathers' missions in other lands." Father Briani's letter claimed that the "tremendous growth of our Society [had received the] "steadfast support of the clergy and of countless benefactors [in America]." and that this had "probably been the main factor" in the society's growth. Todesco's open letter to friends and benefactors carried the same theme, but revised a bit of history regarding the society's mission in America. He claimed that the "...progress of our African Missions and the sad plight of the ever-pressing spiritual needs of Latin America *were the deciding factors which brought the Verona Fathers to the U.S.A. in 1940....*Our missionaries could now look...to the United States not only to consolidate their gains made in Africa but also to salvage what was left of the once prosperous Church in South America."[2] [Emphasis added.]

Todesco's version of the Comboni Institute's mission in America differs markedly from Father Vignato's reported motive for going there, i.e., to do "useful work among the Negroes...." It contrasts with the private instructions Vignato gave Mason in 1939 that the United States was a place in which to find English-speaking vocations. Todesco even diverged from his own statement in 1955 at which time he declared that his society's work in America was not only to support foreign missions, but to dedicate themselves "to the Apostolate among the Blacks and other comparable groups..."[3]

In the difficult days of the 1940s, it was acknowledged that the United States province was not only supplying the needs of confreres abroad, but was ministering to "the poor and abandoned" in America. But on the Jubilee anniversary of the province, Todesco's Open Letter portrayed his institute's reason for being in America as a kind of in-house Marshall Plan. By 1965, this idea of mission in North America was undoubtedly viewed by many confreres with a certain measure of disdain. The strong sense of purpose shared by of those who first came to the United States was being challenged, and the role of the province within the congregation questioned. These perceptions, primarily of those not working in North America, would converge with strong currents of change in the Church and society to present new challenges for the province.

SEMINARIES IN TRANSITION

Two days after the Jubilee celebration, Todesco left for Italy. He returned with Father Briani's consent to increase the number of American seminaries. Confirmed was the opening of a minor seminary in the East, a college-level residence in Canada, and a minor seminary on the West Coast if feasible. Even a Comboni scholasticate independent of the University of San Diego could be built. Due to the General Administration's lessening of personnel support, and Briani's insistence on sending newly ordained American priests to the missions, these plans appear Quixotic. Perhaps, along with many other heads of seminaries, Comboni superiors believed the dip in vocations was a temporary phenomenon. However, events in Italy should have put this in doubt. On his departure from Italy, Todesco also brought back three American theology students who had been studying at Milan: Damien Graziano, William Jansen, and Jacob Perna. They returned at a time when the situation at Venegono was, to put it mildly, precarious. Reactions to the Second Vatican Council were as alive in the Comboni Missionary Institute as they were in other religious societies, and confusion was most critical in the European seminaries.

IN ITALY.

During the 1960s, a seminary crisis of some magnitude developed in Italy, its source was an increasing challenge by students to superiors' authority. Open questioning by students combined with the eagerness of young professors to discuss new ideas emerging from the Second Vatican Council. Its decrees on ministry, the life of priests, and renewal of religious life gave rise to energetic exchanges. Since the final draft and publication of these documents were delayed, they were open to interpretation, thus fueling an impatience with the status quo. Superiors tended to resist what they believed were hasty changes. The growing demand for change led to a counter direction, that is, toward a stricter interpretation of the rules. Thus the gulf between superiors and their younger charges widened, and open rebellion erupted. It met with strong resistance from Superior General Briani. Remaining faithful to the principles he believed contributed to the growth of his society, he reacted by "applying the brakes with both hands."[4]

At Venegono the student discontent was at its highest, and some classrooms of younger faculty monitored. At one point in the scholasticates' rebellion, talking in corridors was forbidden; letters withheld; some mail censored; and all entertainment discontinued. The revolt against authority and its attempted suppression took the American students at Venegono by surprise, particularly when exposed to opinions that the "American way of life" was uniquely sinful. "What were we Americans supposed to think about this?" a Comboni missionary told the author. To have one's country singled out for censure seemed to militate against community. Ironically, despite the alleged perception by superiors that America was a land of temptations, when Todesco left Italy in July, 1965, one of the three students to be brought back believes Todesco brought them home to save their vocations. And, indeed, all three of these students were eventually ordained as Comboni Missionary priests.

IN THE UNITED STATES.

The Civil Rights movement in the U.S. was in full force in 1965, and protests against the war in Vietnam gained momentum. Young people crossed color barriers to protest injustice, and some were threatened, beaten, and even murdered. On television, Americans watched police officers turn fire hoses on African Americans as they marched peacefully for their rights. Viewers were horrified to see throngs of hostile white crowds scream racial epithets at the marchers while police stood with dogs trained to attack any demonstrator who returned the violence. Public outrage eventually forced President Kennedy to send federal troops to protect those working within the law against injustice. But the Benedictine monk, Cyprian Davis, wrote, "By and large Catholics, either black or white, were not in the forefront of the Civil Rights movement or among the leadership of the protest organizations....The real change in Catholic attitudes came with the clarion call by Martin Luther King, Jr., to all of the nation's clergy to come to Selma, Alabama, in March 1965. The response of white Catholic priests and sisters was enormous, despite the disapproval of the bishop of Mobile-Birmingham [Alabama]."[5]

When Father Todesco brought the three scholastics back to America, the country was in the throes of social turmoil. But nowhere in his diary does the American provincial mention this and seldom does any of it appear in provincial publications.

FRUSTRATION MOUNTS

Father Mario Ongaro, a formation superior during these critical years, described the process in the Comboni seminaries of North America, "The transition was not...anticipated. It simply imposed itself on the educational system as a spontaneous blossoming of student rights...This new breed of students did not reject the faith, just the manner in which it was expressed. The individual person...was well on his way to becoming his own measure of any political, religious or economic system... I, myself, traveled the gamut as an educator from demanding strict discipline to slowly developing a more permissive system of cooperating with students in their own formation."[6]

At the Comboni novitiate in Monroe, tension was increasing and some believe it carried over into the San Diego scholasticate. Former students say that "a return to the formation of the 1930s" was taking place. It was attributed to various superiors. Some credited it to the naturally restrained style of the novice master, Father Battirossi. Others saw Todesco's long experience as novice master as the source. Still others look to the older confreres who were, as one Comboni priest said, "wanting to tighten things up." But it would seem that these superiors were simply following Briani's sense that something was going wrong in formation that had to be suppressed with vigilance.

Todesco, however, was not only the closest to Briani in authority, he had an overwhelming, even primary, interest in formation. Under him, rules that had been dismissed by either Battirossi or Chiodi as irrelevant to America in the twentieth century, now were put forth with some seriousness. Passages from old spiritual guides that once provided students with a few laughs, now were translated with earnestness, e.g., the rule about not speaking to women washing clothes at public fountains, and the admonition to disrobe at night in bed for modesty's sake. When novices worked outdoors in the hot humid summers of Monroe, they had previously been allowed to shower afterward. Now permission was required for more than two showers a week. Frustration and tension at the novitiate translated into attrition. When Todesco went to Monroe for his annual visitation in March of 1966, he found the community, "'meager, meager,' and," he wrote, "the small number is discouraging to the members of the community. The continued defections bring bewilderment."[7]

San Diego had frustrations of another kind. As superior of scholastics at San Diego, Chiodi seldom had more than one other Comboni missionary with him, and like himself, that missionary also had teaching duties. No longer in Monroe's relatively homogenous population: white, middle class, and substantially Catholic, Chiodi's students now lived among one that was Anglo, Black, Hispanic, Native American, and Asian. Establishing a funding base in San Diego was quite a different matter than doing so in Monroe. A Portuguese fishing community gave him support, but the kind of financial support he had in Monroe never materialized. At the same time, Todesco was demanding that all communities be self-supporting, putting an even greater burden on Chiodi and his students. A Comboni priest then a student at San Diego recalls, "It seemed that the province was unwilling to spend extra money for the scholasticate....We held spaghetti dinners and performed for benefactors in order to pay for our people going to the university... life was a struggle. It was a very difficult thing for him [Chiodi]."

That Chiodi labored to accommodate to the changing nature of seminary life is recognized by those who were his students in the early years at San Diego. They say, that within limits, he allowed a measure of freedom to students. They could travel about campus freely during appropriate hours, and Chiodi tried, not always successfully, to duplicate the outings for which he was famous in Monroe. What was especially appreciated were their first true missionary experiences. Collecting food, medicine, and clothing, Chiodi would take them to Tijuana and Baja California to distribute these to the poor. One of these students later explained that, prior to this, his formation had been devoid of missionary experiences, "The pity of [our monastic preparation] was that once you arrived in the foreign missions, rigid schedules and many pietistic practices were pretty much left behind."[8]

As year followed year, the solidarity of community life in the San Diego weakened. Ethnic diversity often led to conflicting viewpoints. In the novitiate, there had been a   multi-cultural mix of Italian and American students with a few African Americans or Filipinos. But in San Diego, a good proportion of the scholastics were now Hispanic. This gave rise to differences in views of religious practice, and a double-edged isolation for the one or two African Americans. Misunderstandings could be expected, but how to handle these was another question. Even superiors with far less heterogeneity and far more resources than Chiodi were having difficulty. Losses at the scholasticate as well as the novitiate began to mount. Although 40% of Comboni novices persisted to ordination during the period of 1950 to 1960, only 23% persisted to ordination from 1960 to 1964. Perhaps a better way to describe what was happening is to look at absolute numbers. In the six school years from 1954-55 to 1959-60, 28 Comboni students were ordained. In the six years from 1960-61 to 1965-66, only 13 were ordained, a 46% drop in the number of students persisting to ordination. Two-thirds of these were Americans.[9]

AUTHORITY IN QUESTION

Confronted with a sense of loss and confusion, Todesco's messages continued to reflect the views of his superior, Briani. In 1966, he addressed an open letter to all "Father Superiors and Confreres" reiterating the rules about wearing the cassock and prohibitions against regular attendance at public theaters or movie houses. Radios in private rooms were denied, and the Great Silence was to be kept. Retirement should always be at 10 p.m. Those with permission to drink coffee during the day should not stop in the kitchen if a lady were there. In this case, going to the kitchen required permission. All were also to avoid the "spirit of criticism."

These directives completely overlooked what religious writers were advising. The Sulpician priest, Frank Norris, for example, wrote, "...so must the seminary of the age of Vatican II be expressive of the broader and enhanced vision which the Church has given of her own nature... it is a question of seeking honestly the answer to some very important questions... What should be the purpose of the seminary today ...How is the seminary to educate men...How can the modern seminary ...make candidates for the priesthood first of all truly *human persons*? What is the real nature of authority in the Church?"[10] [emphasis not added]

In avoiding such questions, Todesco was not alone. As Ongaro later observed, "Superiors were not only taken by surprise by the times, they didn't know what to make of them. They felt, instead, an even greater personal responsibility to mold the future missionaries in the strict discipline of the rules and regulations. This resulted in misunderstandings, recriminations, even open defiance and expulsion/defection."

These outcomes were not isolated to Comboni Missionaries. In 1965, Vincentian Father Stafford Poole observed, "There is a good deal of ferment in seminaries today...No matter what the institution, the problems seem largely the same. A new generation with new problems has descended on us, and many persons in authority feel both confused and vaguely apprehensive."[11]

Leaders of the American province shared this apprehension. Criticism of superiors was particularly unnerving because it undermined authority, and this challenge was not taken lightly. Superiors had not grasped that respect for unquestioned authority was fading, eroded by changes in society and in the Church. Whether priest, student, or lay person, responses to this fact depended on the individual. Some clung to concepts of undisputed authority, some waited hoping matters would reach equilibrium, and some welcomed change as a liberating experience. Many more were caught between these alternatives, hoping to fulfill their obligations to superiors, but unable to control the circumstances this obligation demanded. An example of this occurred when a scholastic at San Diego was accused of challenging his superiors' authority. Letters between Todesco and Chiodi illustrate the misunderstanding this could precipitate.

Around July 7, 1967, Chiodi sent Todesco forms and applications for the renewal of several students' vows. Either before or after this, Todesco and his Council decided to withhold their permission for one of these students to renew vows. Sometime before July 15, Chiodi phoned Todesco and asked that this decision be modified, and that instead, the student be suspended from studies at San Diego and be allowed to take vows for a trial year somewhere other than San Diego.[12] The exact date of this phone call is unknown, but a letter from Todesco on July 15 gave Chiodi authority to offer this alternative to the student. A partial record of Chiodi's reply on July 23 is available in a letter Todesco then sent Chiodi. In it, Todesco questioned the decision to even accept this student as a scholastic. He questioned why this student was allowed to leave for Baja California while his status was being debated. Todesco quoted Chiodi as asserting that Todesco's letters had arrived too late to take action, and when the student returned from Baja, it would be time for the annual retreat. "It is a mess," Chiodi is reported to have said, "I don't know whether it will be advisable to give him the red light right at the end." To this, Todesco snapped back, "Is this your answer? You consider it a mistake not to admit him? Is it the first time that we ask someone to leave just a few days before the vows?" Todesco then launched a series of accusations laying all blame for the "mess" on Chiodi. Himself he exonerated by reporting, "You understand that we were not able to eliminate him before his departure from Cincinnati because we did not have any serious or positive information on his account...I would have appreciated a note from you suggesting that he be stopped until you were able to send a detailed report about him."[13]

Why Todesco held Chiodi responsible for evaluating this student is not clear. Chiodi had been superior of the scholasticate since 1961, and not the student's novice master. More important is that an issue between a student and the superior of the scholasticate had escalated into an issue between a superior and his provincial. The experienced and spiritually solid Father Chiodi had written a letter in which he, himself, described the situation as a "mess." Today, this admission would be recognized more as a need for consultation than a reprimand. Tradition perhaps gave a superior this "right," but it was a failed means of recourse during that critical period. Chiodi had seen one of his own assistants leave the priesthood. He had watched as student after student left the scholasticate, some willing to accept menial work to remaining in the seminary. Confronted with these disturbing events, Chiodi, 2200 miles away from provincial headquarters, was virtually isolated. Todesco's lack of understanding did not improve the situation in San Diego or staunch the losses in the scholasticate, and these losses were eventually laid at his door.

From the viewpoint of Comboni students, much of the rebellion Comboni superiors witnessed in the 1960s had more to do with culture than dogma or rules. Some say the tension between students and superiors was created by the "Euro-centeredness" of older Italian superiors. They did not have, as one of the younger priests believed, "the right categories for judging the people they were educating...They took what was acceptable behavior in religious life in Italy in the 1930s and believed it acceptable for the United States in 1960. Formation practices in Verona decades earlier were brought here without the realization that much of it was cultural baggage."[14]

But if "Euro-centeredness" was the only cause of confusion and student losses in Comboni seminaries of North America, it does not explain why, in Italy, defections also continued, and   as *Family News* reported, other institutions were suffering similar losses. Statistics gathered later show that, from 1966 to 1968, minor seminary, college, and theology student enrollment in both religious and diocesan institutions of the United States dropped by approximately 26%, and by 1971, it dropped by another 25%. Statistics of minor seminarians at Forestville are scarce during these years. The number of new students entering are reported, but not the total. For example, it is reported that 17 new students entered in 1967, but no total is given. In 1968, a total of 35 is reported, a figure approximately one third that of the seminary's all-time high.[15] But before any drop of this magnitude was reached, religious leaders tended to believe that dips in the numbers of candidates entering their seminaries was a temporary phenomenon.

DEVELOPING VOCATIONS IN CANADA

In December of 1962, thirty-nine-year old Father Andrea De Malde' joined Fathers Ghirotto and De Berti at St. Thomas More parish in St. Jean's, Canada. He was to promote the society's work and recruit vocations. After three-months of acclimatization, De Malde' began visiting the maritime provinces of Newfoundland, Nova Scotia, and New Brunswick, as well as Quebec, Ontario and Manitoba. For three and a half years, he traveled the vast expanse of these Canadian provinces introducing bishops and diocesan directors to his society which, in most cases, was totally unknown to them. In time, De Malde' was permitted to make mission appeals.

Though few Comboni missionaries expelled from Southern Sudan were sent to North America, one who did come was thirty-six year old Father Adelmo Spagnolo. Assigned to St. Jean's, he later described how he began, "I didn't know French, but since I had to learn English the hard way...in Monroe, I learned French the same way, in a parish in Montreal." After three months learning the language, Spagnolo began receiving speaking engagements. "[When] I went to Quebec...because I was expelled from Sudan, I created quite a stir. Wherever I went, I presented myself to the bishop as 'one of those who were expelled,' and I began then to visit schools and have mission appeals." Spagnolo could only visit eight of thirty high schools in the Archdiocese of Quebec each month since they had as many as thirty-five classrooms.[16]

With the foundation work laid by Fathers Ghirotto, De Malde', and Spagnolo, Todesco was ready to begin to lay the groundwork for vocations. In September, 1965, Todesco traveled to Ottawa, Canada, to meet Archbishop Pignedoli, the Apostolic Delegate. His reception was courteous and encouraging, and the Delegate saw no hindrances to expanding in Canada. The next day, the Vicar General of the Diocese of St. Jean urged Todesco to settle in the fast growing town of Brossard, across the St. Lawrence River from Montreal. Todesco found property prices high. But Ghirotto was put in touch with an Italian engineer, a Mr. Santorelli, who sold the Comboni Missionaries two acres of land in Brossard for a future center and residence. In December, Todesco and Catellani signed contracts for the property. When they found "concrete evidence of major difficulties looming ahead because of recently enacted governmental legislation on school and education," Todesco appealed to the General Administration for advice. He asked Vicar General John Battelli to fly to Canada for consultation. Father Briani was away from the Generalate at that time, but Battelli assured Todesco that Briani had approved making a $150,000 loan for a Brossard residence because he had heard Spagnolo was optimistic about Canadian vocations.[17] Battelli flew to Montreal on January 20, 1966, to meet with Fathers Todesco, Ghirotto, De Malde, and Valente. Discussions centered on school problems, construction at Brossard, the possibility of a future seminary, and the College at Cap Rouge. A visit was paid to the Regional Superior of the Consolata Fathers to learn about communitarian organizations of religious, and whether or not the Comboni Missionaries could join the one operated by the Consolatas. Battelli left for Italy optimistic about the society's future in Canada.[18]

After consulting with Briani, Battelli wrote Todesco that "the news is good." The General supported a residence at Brossard. The Consolata Fathers had informed him they would accept Comboni Missionary students at their seminary in Oka (near Montreal). Briani was not concerned that Comboni seminarians would mingle with seminarians of other religious societies at Oka, and he had consented to send a Comboni priest to join its teaching staff. A second priest would come to study for a teaching certificate at Laval University in Cap Rouge near Quebec. Here, the Comboni Missionaries would use a new approach to the novitiate, asking those applying to the society to first attend the communitarian college at Cap Rouge. Briani also agreed to send a third priest to assist Valente at St. Thomas More parish at St. Jean's. In conclusion, Battelli wrote, "I can assure you that the Superior General, also the others, are favorable to our work in Canada [but the General is] rather concerned that the fathers who are coming should not be employed in work other than the purpose for which they come..."

In early March, 1966, Todesco wrote Battelli that he was grateful for his news with the "wonderful promises it carries... I see that you have been able to get practically everything that we were wishing for in order to give a good start to our presence in Canada." What was missing, he said, were the student candidates to join these new ventures. Hopefully, Father Spagnolo would recruit some by September. As a precaution, he asked Battelli to try again to send Italian candidates reminding him that, "It's a question of great urgency and serious consequences for our existence in that country [Canada]."[19]

But Battelli had been too optimistic about his superior's support for Canada. Todesco received a letter from Briani that included the remark,"... it seems to me that all the information [about Canada] given by Father Battelli pertains to personnel. I will do my best'" About Briani's offhandedness Todesco lamented, "Worse than this, it cannot get! I am under the impression that the Superior General has not understood the problem, and thinks that on our part we are only over-concerned with personnel."

Battelli, Todesco said, should tell the General that personnel was only part of the problem, and that the priest he intended to send to Canada was not qualified. Todesco informed Battelli that in his own reply to Briani he had said, "that the Canadian problem did not admit of makeshift decisions about personnel, but that we were in need of qualified people, such as would be a credit to the Institute. At this moment, the Institute is too much in the public eye, and we cannot make use of just anybody." Not only that, Todesco continued, the Consolata Fathers were waiting for two French-speaking Comboni priests to join their seminary community, and they had scheduled them for twenty hours of classes. If qualified personnel could not be sent, it would be better, "to withdraw and not expect vocations from Canada.... It is really a new province; therefore, we should be prepared to make some sacrifices about personnel so as to begin properly."[20]

Todesco and Battelli won the concessions needed from Briani. On May 22, 1966, there was a ground-breaking ceremony for a future residence at Brossard. Unfortunately, the Bank of Canada refused the loan for it, and Catellani had to find the money among friends at Cincinnati banks. In July, the three priests sent to new positions in Canada arrived. They were Fathers Giulio Mariani, Lino Negrato, and Giovanni Nobili. Mariani went to Laval University at Cap Rouge to become certified to teach at the communitarian college in that city. Students there belonged to at least fifteen separate religious communities, each with its own residence. Mariani would live with three graduates of Sacred Heart Seminary at the Marianhill Fathers' house. Father Nobili was assigned to the Consolata Fathers' seminary in Oka to teach and assist fifteen high school students. Father Negrato was assigned to the Comboni center at Brossard.

Todesco spent part of June and early July making arrangements for all this to happen. He spoke to Father Mangiano, Provincial of the Consolata Fathers, regarding minor seminarians he was sending to their high school. He arranged with the Superior of the Marianhill Fathers to board Mariani and the students with him. And he presented to the President of the Cap Rouge College the documents required to admit the Comboni Institute to the Confederation of Religious of Cap Rouge. In his diary he reports, "This first phase of adjustment is going to be difficult, and may bring surprises in the dispersion of personnel. May St. Joseph help us."[21]

By January, 1967, Todesco's plans were in operation. Mariani was registered at Laval University and Nobili was teaching at Oka. Father Battirossi moved from Monroe to St. Thomas More parish in St. Jean, and Father Valente replaced him as novice master. Father Erbisti took over Ghirotto's duties at Chambly, and Ghirotto went to Brossard as superior with Fathers Spagnolo and Negrato, the latter as a recruiter. Finally, Brother Giacomelli assisted the priests in the house and offices, meanwhile learning French. The first issue of *Baobab* was launched, a French edition of the Italian magazine for boys,"Piccolo Missionario."[22]

COLUMBIA

The property for the seminary in the East was on the northwest side of New Jersey, 60 miles west of the Comboni residence at Montclair. In the fall of 1965, Father Branchesi sent a brochure to the Vicar General of the Newark Diocese describing Comboni Missionaries' work in eleven countries of Africa and in Latin America as well as in North America. These missions required more priests and brothers, and New Jersey was cited as an ideal place to build a seminary since it was the center of Catholic population in America, young men had already inquired about the society, and Bishop Ahr had given permission to open a seminary. The financing was outlined. The land had been paid by benefactors who knew Father Accorsi. Lay brothers' and students' work would save $75,000, and donations already amounted to $95,000. A bank loan of $100,000 was needed to start construction, and projected funds were available to pay off the loan in three years. Total cost: approximately one million dollars.[23]

Such a costly venture in 1965 now seems risky, but as late as 1967, when seminary enrollments were beginning to drop, lay people were still supporting the project. Seven high-ranking businessmen from Essex County formed a fund-raising group. Among these were presidents, vice presidents, and directors of local companies. Sargent Shriver, head of the Peace Corps, and brother-in-law to the late President John F. Kennedy, wrote a letter of support, comparing the Comboni Missionaries' work to that of his Peace Corps, an agency that sent volunteers to Third World countries, "This mission seminary will train young Americans who are devoted to hard work and poverty. It will prepare them to build mutual understanding and respect among all the peoples of the world under God. Through their work they will contribute to the cause of peace."[24] Enthusiasm for the seminary rode a strong wave of altruism in America, one that powered Shriver's Peace Corps, the Civil Rights Movement, and President Johnson's War on Poverty. In December, 1967, a Montclair seminary committee chose an architect, and news came that a potential benefactor was ready to donate the $100,000 required to begin construction.

Todesco had misgivings about the project. *Family News* reported: "In view of the Vocation crisis and an antagonistic tendency [among clerical educators] toward Minor Seminaries, we have been rather hesitant and slow in regard to the construction of this new Seminary. However....those interested in building the Seminary have assured us that one of their members is ready to furnish the amount needed for completion of the project." On July 4, when ground was broken for the seminary, 500 people joined Todesco at the construction site and watched him dig the first dirt for the new "center." It is not surprising that the American provincial found it difficult to resist their enthusiasm.[25] But the American provincial had taken on an obligation he would not be able to fulfill.

Debts and Who Paid Them

The generosity showed Comboni Missionaries in the East was duplicated in many cities. In Philadelphia, it was the Sons of the Sacred Heart Mission League. In Cincinnati, it was the Mission Apostolate of the Sacred Heart (MASH) and the Sacred Heart Seminary Guild, the last still managing a thriving bargain shop in the Over the Rhine area of Cincinnati for which Brother Victor De Gasperi picked up and delivered items. The Cincinnati Festival Committee, operating since 1947, was in the 1960s steered by prominent business men: Mr. Charles Curro of the Central Trust Bank, Mr. Peter Palazollo, who owned a spaghetti factory, and Mr. Stephen LaPille, owner of a restaurant chain. These men were loyal to Comboni Missionaries and to Father Catellani who worked with them. The communities of Irwindale, Monroe, Montclair, and Yorkville, also had devoted workers

194

Defining Mission

among lay friends, and in the new communities in Canada, Father Spagnolo saw individuals come forward to help.

Despite these benefactors' generosity, finding money to further expansion plans proved difficult. The yearly obligation to the General Administration was always five to ten thousand dollars more than the required $25,000. Then there were the gifts to other provinces for their projects. There were the visitors who came to the U.S. for their customary mission appeals including Bishop Ferrara, once pastor of old Holy Trinity Church, and Bishop Barbisotti from Ecuador. These old friends were always warmly welcomed. But others Todesco only heard about when he received a phone call asking, "Do you know a Father____who is here representing Comboni Missionaries in____,and asking for funds?" Confreres who made no previous arrangements with diocesan authorities, put Todesco and his society in an embarrassing situation. They left the impression that the society lacked an organized plan for funding requests, and worse, that Comboni missionaries were actively competing with one another for funds. This became particularly painful because Todesco and his province were in heavy debt. Todesco was even considering a possible sale of the Yorkville property.[26] However, on Briani's visit to America, the support Yorkville was receiving so impressed him that the property was not sold. Back in Italy, the Superior General sent word to Todesco to assume the loan obligation of $135,000 for the Brossard construction, and that, "By order of the Superior General," Todesco should send $35,000 to Father Baj for the novitiate in Spain as well as a similar amount to alleviate "the critical financial situation of our London Province." Under his superior's orders, Todesco was forced to withdraw $70,000 from the Columbia, New Jersey, seminary fund to meet these obligations.

Unscheduled diversions of funds left many in the province frustrated. Plans for the province were often interrupted, and the resulting sacrifices in time and energy ignored. Yet there were many confreres in other provinces that thought Combonis in North America were not doing enough for foreign missions. What was accomplished by Todesco's province was eventually reported to the 1969 General Chapter: all buildings in the United States and Canada financed without subsidy, between thirty and forty thousand dollars sent annually to the General Administration each year, and all revenues from mission appeals sent to foreign missions primarily in South America.[27]

Sometime during the years 1965-1966, Todesco arrived at a critical milestone: the apogee of progress in his provincialate. No one could point to the exact moment at which this point was reached. But, while Todesco had put forth an heroic effort to expand seminaries and contribute with largess to the rest of his congregation, the means to do so were slowly dissipating. Fewer vocations and fewer able-bodied men in the province were enough to slow success. But an incredible number of circumstances developed over the next two years, some of which Todesco could not control, others he failed to maneuver successfully, that combined to undermine his accomplishments.

15. Years of Crisis, 1967-1969

In January of 1967, Todesco saw Father Bart Battirossi off to Italy for a well-earned vacation. In two years, Todesco would also leave for Italy. He clearly stated his feelings about this to the Vicar General, John Battelli, "I am tired, and I long to be free as soon as possible from any responsibility. Even my health is not doing too well. We must be patient and go on... for Him..."[1] But before he could lay aside responsibilities in North America, Todesco would be sorely tested.

CANADA

On June 16, 1967 the new Comboni center in Brossard was dedicated, Bishop Gerald Coderre of St. Jean's diocese, blessed it, and four hundred French and English friends attended. Even this strong support did not make the foundation in Canada an easy one. Brossard was now the focal point of Canadian work, but as work there increased, it took a toll on Father Ghirotto. He was experiencing general exhaustion and lack of sleep. Todesco asked Battelli for an "outstanding father" so Ghirotto could go to Georgia where climate and less responsibility would allow him to recuperate. But his substitute had to be fluent in French and proficient in English. Battelli's response reflected Father Briani's thoughts on the matter: Why not replace Ghirotto with Father Busetti, and have Father Ongaro take over Busetti's duties as rector? If this arrangement were acceptable, the General would allow Ghirotto to remain in the United States.[2]

Todesco needed another substitute in Canada. Brother Giacomelli had worked hard at Brossard. But the Canadian immigration office told him his medical records from Rome showed "a sickness in the lungs;" therefore, he had to leave the country.[3] Then news came from the Consolata Fathers that their preparatory seminary at Oka would close at the end of the school year due to "financial, scholastic, and vocational motives." This meant disbanding the small group of Comboni Missionary aspirants attending that school.

Finally, the Comboni priest assigned at the Cap Rouge college had been asked to teach Marxism, and he quit the college and made independent arrangements to join the faculty at the Petit Seminare in Shawingan, Quebec.

Back in the United States, Father Francis Didoni, once superior of the minor seminary, said his doctor would no longer allow him to work as director of public relations and editor of *Frontier Call*. Changes going on in the church had so deeply affected him that he wanted to go to Rome for a renewal course. He hoped this would help him, "to see if all my ideas have been wrong."[4] In one month's time, events unfolded that threatened Todesco's efforts to establish a Canadian foundation and his key missionary in charge of promotion was resigning.

When Briani seemed to oppose replacing Ghirotto and Giacomelli, Todesco's next letter to Battelli reflected real desperation, "Father, I don't have one person more than what is strictly needed. I see the need to prepare personnel for the future, but I don't know who to send. I see the urgent need to organize public relations work for vocations...and I don't find people who can do it....This year, I have lost Fathers Endrizzi, Conti, Cereda, De Grandis, Marigo, Bragotti, and now Father Didoni. Three new ones are coming, naturally still green, immature, while the rest of the personnel are what they are. Believe me, Father, I am really tired and discouraged...."

Battelli sympathized with Todesco, but he said, "I am not able to choose someone from the personnel present in Italy because assignments were given before the departure of the Superior General...it is difficult to move one without moving many others. You can easily imagine how many letters I receive from various provincials with regard to personnel...I cannot do much, or rather, I do very little for the reasons I state above...difficulties are not lacking." He then described these, "Today, Father Accorsi [then provincial in Italy] will be at Verona to talk about personnel, and I anticipate some difficulty, some vacant spots, etc....You may know that [two American scholastics] have left us and now even the Ethiopian scholastic... and others are going to leave the society. They say that this is the result of the historical moment in which we find ourselves."[5]

Todesco replied that he would do his best., "I will go to Canada before winter, but that foundation is not settled....the impression of those that...had occasion to pass through there [is that] the personnel is not united...they do not understand why they were sent to Canada..." An exception was Father Spagnolo, who was substituting for Ghirotto and working hard.

Todesco had not yet visited Canada when, on December 19, the telephone brought news that a raffle at Brossard had failed, and the losses had to be covered. After Christmas, Catellani, went to study the situation. Not available is a letter of December 28, 1967, that Todesco sent to Battelli describing Catellani's report, and Battelli responded again with sympathy, "I'm really sorry things are not going well. You know how much that foundation [Canada] means to me..."

Together, they decided on a course to restore a sense of community in Canada. One missionary would return to Italy, and if necessary, Todesco would send Ghirotto back to Brossard. Todesco would still need a replacement for the one going to Italy, and it was imperative to choose "priests who understand they are in Canada to develop a new foundation..." In spring, 1968, Battelli sent Father Angelo Grande, young and ordained only two years. He had studied language in France, and was a good writer capable of taking over the recruiting magazine Spagnolo initiated (*Baobab*).[6] Now other matters demanded Todesco's attention.

A CRITICAL QUESTION: A DESPERATE DECISION

Todesco's visit to San Diego in January, 1968, was motivated by more than an inspection of the scholasticate. Rumors had circulated that the diocesan theologate was moving to Los Angeles. Todesco consulted with Father Bernardo Becchio, Provincial of Mexico, who also had students at San Diego. Father Valente, the master of novices, flew in from Monroe to join discussions with Todesco and Chiodi. Todesco reported results to Battelli, "I think that, with the multiplication of the dioceses in California, they [diocesan authorities in California] intend to form at least two important regional seminaries, one in Los Angeles and the other one in San Francisco."

The magnitude of this decision on the scholasticate was greater than Todesco anticipated. On April 6, 1968, he received notice that the diocesan seminary of San Diego would be transferred not to Los Angeles, but to San Francisco, and this would take place the following September. Four days after this shock, Todesco collected his thoughts on paper for Father Chiodi. Briani and Battelli had cautioned him to move slowly, he wrote, and not take a hasty decision about the scholasticate, "According to them, even if for two or three years [the scholastics] were to occupy a temporary place, it would not be too bad, knowing how different institutions are looking into the organization of communitarian schools....Unfortunately, the Superior General will be away in Africa three more months, and so everything will remain in suspense..."[7]

The idea of a joint scholasticate among missionaries began during Accorsi's provincialate, and in March, 1968, Father Lawrence Chiesa of the

Pontifical Institute for Foreign Missions (P.I.M.E.) wrote Todesco thanking him for his visit and for clarifying his position on a communitarian theologate. Chiesa cited reasons for such a theologate: problems stemming from being foreigners; being relatively small institutions with increasingly vacant facilities; and the resulting loss of contact with benefactors. He said his institute and the Consolata Fathers would try to help one another "in order to survive," and he understood that the impending General Chapter in 1969 made it difficult for Todesco to commit to a decision.[8]

Chiesa's letter held little comfort for Todesco. After all, as he wrote Chiodi on April 19, "In this last period, we have lost about ten scholastics..." Confronted with this and the demise of the San Diego seminary, Todesco turned again to Battelli for advice. "In these days, he wrote, "we held a meeting with the fathers to deal with the problem of the scholasticate. For theology, everybody was in agreement...that the scholastics should join another institute with the Verbites [Divine Word Missionaries] in Techny, Illinois or with the Jesuits of Aurora, Illinois. But they would not suggest either Sacred Heart Seminary in Cincinnati or the Josephinum. The scholastics in theology are few, seven or eight, and if I cannot come to some agreement with these institutes, I would... break up the group, two prefects at SHS, three at Brossard with the Jesuits at Montreal, and the others to Italy....For the college, the fathers were not in agreement. The majority were against...a college in Monroe. They would [prefer] one on a university campus or with other institutions....Naturally, the fathers in Monroe were unhappy and reacted strongly." This was largely due to the money spent on the college library and laboratory for a college, and they did not want to present Monroe as a junior college when only a small group of novices were present for they anticipated the number of novices would decrease. The alternative, Todesco believed, was to leave the college where it was, on the San Diego campus at the School of Philosophy. He asked Battelli, "What do you think? I think that for the time being, we could go on as we are...."

While waiting for Battelli's response, Todesco scouted the alternatives mentioned. The Yorkville Center in Illinois was not far away from the Divine Word Missionaries who were willing to combine Comboni scholastics with theirs. About the Jesuits at Aurora, Todesco remarked, "They require many conditions, above all a high academic record..."[9]

Battelli's letter was prompt. He promised to speak to others at the Comboni Administration about sending American scholastics to Italy. He knew that four Mexican scholastics, presumably affected by the San Diego seminary closing, were also going to Italy. Admitting the difficulties involved, and that he viewed the situation from a distance, he wrote, "I will tell you what has crossed my mind a few times...." He suggested bringing both the novitiate and the college to Cincinnati, and sending them to St. Gregory's or Mount St. Mary's, "I don't think it would be impossible to keep the novices separate in the large building at Forestville (especially now that we are [doubting] the wisdom of keeping the novices too separate from the professed)." He advised moving the minor seminary in Cincinnati to Monroe, and sending these students to Monroe Central High School, run by the Holy Cross Fathers, or even to the public school. He wrote, "In time, establish the theologate near Chicago at Yorkville, sending scholastics either to the Jesuit school in Aurora or elsewhere." In San Diego and Columbia, he saw the possibility of opening minor seminaries. In concluding, he warned Todesco, "As I told you, this could be a crazy idea, but at least, *it will resolve your problem of the teaching personnel.*" [emphasis added]

An American Comboni priest, who attended the meeting at which the issues Battelli addressed were discussed, claims the group asked for more time, but not long after, they found Todesco had already made a decision. They were told it was a closed matter. Battelli's caveats about his advice did not prevent Todesco from taking it. In describing problems with students in San Diego, Chiodi had written to Todesco "Nowadays, we can expect anything!"[10] Many in the province at that time might have agreed this comment applied equally to the wholesale shift of seminaries.

THE BIG SWITCH

On May 14, 1968, Todesco visited Monroe and San Diego to prepare for the transfers. By May 26, his diary notes, "We decide, also at the suggestion of Father Battelli, to unite College, Theology, and Novitiate at our Sacred Heart Seminary....The students will attend classes at St. Gregory's and Mt. St. Mary's....Our high school of Cincinnati will be transferred to Monroe. At San Diego, we will start a high school for the West..." For Todesco, there was only one real obstacle to these plans, Auxiliary Bishop Quinn of San Diego had asked for the scholasticate house for his own college students. In late May, Todesco met with Quinn who repeated his request. When Todesco presented his own plan for a minor seminary, Quinn agreed to his wishes.

In a letter to Bishop Francis J. Furey of San Diego, Todesco officially announced the return of his scholastics to Cincinnati and conveyed the gratitude and appreciation of his priests and students leaving the diocese. He added, "The plans of our Superiors are not completely clear as yet...in our house of San Diego...two or three priests. [who] will continue their usual help in ministry in the Diocese, and at the same time... try to organize a vocational program in the Dioceses of California. Our hope is that... by September 1969, in San Diego, we will initiate a preparatory Seminary for our Society. If the Good Lord will favor us with a good number of vocations, we may even [build] on the grounds...purchased in Rancho Bernardo..."[11]

Furey returned compliments, but added a caveat, "Naturally we are...grateful for the many good things you did...during your years here...[Nonetheless] as a member of the Bishops' Committee on Priestly Formation, [I must say] the Committee is drastically opposed to the multiplication of seminaries....there are already far too many seminaries, and [amalgamation] is more desirable than expansion. In your case there may be some good reasons to the contrary...."[12]

Furey's objections were addressed as early as 1965 by Professor James Michael Lee of Notre Dame University. Lee claimed a consensus among American educators was that, to provide an educational program of minimum quality, a four year school needed an enrollment of at least 400 students. This was substantiated by research on the quality of the faculty, on whether or not its members were spread thinly across departments; on the depth of courses available; on resources such as libraries, laboratories, visiting lecturers, sports, etc; and on the tendency of small institutions toward insularity which limited valuable experience. On the issue of seminary size, Todesco was not culpable as Furey thought. He was not planning in-house study for scholastics, but hoped to send them to the large seminaries of St. Gregory's and Mt. St. Mary's in Cincinnati. He did not mention this to Furey since, on the day he was writing to Furey, he was also writing to Archbishop Alter for the necessary permission to do this, which he would receive.[13]

Plans for what the Comboni magazine called "The Big Switch" were carried out in the summer and fall of 1968. Thirty-five minor seminarians in Cincinnati were sent to Monroe where the Superior was Father Erbisti, a capable faculty member of Sacred Heart Seminary for years. His assistants were Fathers David Baltz, Kenneth Dahlen, Peter Premarini, and Louis Perna. Because of the small number of students, all but freshmen were sent to Catholic Central High School.[14]

On June 1, 1968, the last graduation ceremonies were held for Comboni scholastics at the University of San Diego. The next day, students belonging to the North American province packed for Cincinnati. By the end of the month, the expensive scholasticate, designed in the elaborate Spanish Renaissance style of the campus, was virtually empty. Only Fathers Busetti and Nardi took up residence in the building to begin a vocation and promotion center. Fourteen scholastics had moved to the first floor of Sacred Heart Seminary (three Americans were in Italy). They were joined by eighteen novices from Monroe on the second floor. Father Valente, who had been novice master, was now superior to both communities, and Father Ongaro acted as spiritual director of scholastics. A new American priest, Father Dennis Conway, was appointed vice superior. As Battelli had predicted, this arrangement alleviated the personnel shortage since the Comboni priests in charge of the combined community now performed double duty. But uprooting every one of the formation houses was hardly conducive to a sense of community; rather it was probably the most de-stabilizing alternative.

A priest then at the Forestville seminary later recalled, "It was a bit of an awkward situation having scholastics and novices in the same house, but in separate communities. They weren't allowed to speak to or deal with each other. Yet many...had been pals in high school. It was awkward....Later, when there were only seven scholastics...living together was a matter of survival ...there was no place to hide. Our superior then [Valente] was not one who was a strict disciplinarian, and there was also some confusion between what he wanted and what other superiors wanted."[15] But advantages of the arrangement were outlined in *Family News*, "The Superior - Novice Master will [be able to] form according to his method of formation even after the novitiate is over, and [he] will be able to perfect...over a long period of time a single formative imprint to novices and scholastics alike..." This process was contrary to those recommended by Professor Lee's research (see above), e.g., that seminaries broaden the contacts and increase the time and number of faculty for scholastics.

While all three formation houses were moving, Todesco confessed to his diary, "A severe crisis has taken place this year in our scholasticate, as in many other Institutes. We have lost more than half of our scholastics. We cannot pinpoint all the reasons...The period we go through is difficult and delicate for the whole Church and all institutions; and our scholastics were influenced by the times. I do not exclude the rather free atmosphere of San Diego, neither do I deny a certain misunderstanding on our part.... This year [1967-1968] we gave a period of self analysis to the scholastics who work in our parishes...with the desire that the trial would help them...The trial was not successful, and the three returned to their families."[16]

Comboni priests who knew those who left the scholasticate during this period claim they were among the brightest and best candidates for ordination, and Todesco's phrase "returned to their families" was a euphemism. Some who left the Comboni seminaries did not abandon their goal of becoming a priest. They simply transferred to diocesan seminaries.

"POINTS OF DISCUSSION"

Shortly after the "Big Switch," letters went out to all native-born Americans both in the province and in foreign missions. This brought seven American Comboni priests together at Columbia, New Jersey, to voice concerns about their province and their priorities for its renewal. The results were recorded in the document, "Points of Discussion." The seven at the meeting hoped their confreres, particularly Italians who were American citizens, would understand their need to speak out from a purely American viewpoint before the General Chapter. If superiors chose to view the initiative as disobedience, this risk was taken since in the past, "individuals have been...chastised for being too free in the expression of their ideas." Topics ranged widely, but comments in "Points of Discussion" fit easily into several categories: 1) competency of personnel, 2) administrative decision-making, 3) the practice of internationality, 4) updating of formation, 5) the question of sending young priests to foreign missions and their ability to choose a field of work, 6) and the flight of students from the scholasticate.

The Americans wanted more competent personnel, and they wanted more Americans appointed to leadership. Some confreres, they believed, were not qualified to fill any posts. The group wanted this reported to Rome (not realizing that the General Administration was largely responsible for who was sent to the province). Judging competency, they said, was difficult since, as one remarked, "many of the Italians have a totally different idea of what 'competent' means." A list of candidates who would capably represent them as delegate to the General Chapter included Fathers Remus Catellani, Sergio Contran, Archie Fornasari, and Alvin Ruhe. It was also decided to work to assure that Father Fornasari would remain in Rome as a "*peritus.*"[4]

The relocation of seminaries was cited as a prime example of poor administrative and financial judgement. It was recalled that, "There were consultations with the priests, the scholastics, and even with the novices [in America] to get their opinion, [but]...a decision came out which absolutely

---

[4] The word *peritus*, is commonly translated as "expert." After Vatican Council II, its usage was modified when members of the hierarchy brought with them non-voting experts in theology, biblical studies, etc., who came to be known in the plural form as *periti*.

nobody expected, completely different than all the proposals...made." The Croziers' method was cited. Before moving anyone, the individual was consulted ."Sometimes in our congregation," it was said, "notification of a change comes from outside sources." Related to this was "the idea of the permanent pastorate abolished [everywhere else] except in our Congregation" which prevented younger, experienced priests from taking charge.[17]

The group wanted financial reports published semi-annually, increased use of professional advisors, and more input on financial decisions. The "$300,000 debt that Fr. Todesco contracted while Superior General" was discussed in a meeting with him. He is reported as saying the money to pay the debt was initially "borrowed" from the U.S. province, then he "was asked from Italy to forget $100,000 of this debt." Later, he was asked to forgive another $15,000. But the remaining $185,000 was paid back by permitting the American province to send Mass intentions to Rome without the accompanying donations. Inequalities in the financial support of American missionaries was mentioned since those who did not receive financial help from benefactors back home received nothing. Inequalities on vacation money were also cited. In Europe national boundaries dictated the frequency of vacations, with those living outside of Italy limited to vacations every other year whereas Italians had vacations every year. However, in the U.S. the policy based on national boundaries did not hold. Americans studying in San Diego had not been allowed to go home every year.[18]

Although some Comboni missionaries have denied the Columbia meeting was about "Italians vs. Americans," Italian hegemony in the society was an issue at Columbia. The group went so far as to declare that any potential "amalgamation which would mean the formation of a National Italian Missionary Institute," would lead to "withdrawal on our part." Furthermore, they asked why some members of the society, which was claimed to be an international body, did not act as if it were. Todesco, for example, was quoted as saying he thought it too much to expect an American to be elected a delegate to the General Chapter since, if that happened, then the Portuguese, Spaniards, Mexicans, and the others would want one too. No one believed an actual "class distinction" existed between Italian and non-Italian-speaking Americans, they said, but a common lack of courtesy could be witnessed on "those occasions when Italian is spoken even though there is someone present who does not understand it."[19]

The group discussed whether a young priest sent to a foreign mission for six years could readjust to life at home again. The practice of sending someone to the missions immediately after ordination was currently in question. Instead, religious societies were first giving their newly ordained one or two years in their home province working under expert guidance.[20] Recommendations from the American scholastics about formation were quite specific: 1) introduce a trained equipé, 2) invite outside professors to lecture, 3) move away from internal schools, 4) offer more preparation for mission work, 5) involve students in apostolic work, and 6) allow scholastics to earn money during summer vacation for a foreign mission experience.

The most serious discussion centered on the impending defection of scholastics. The report claimed "The mood of the students was discussed, and...if something's not done soon, we will not...expect them to stay with us..." When this was reported to Father Todesco, he insisted official permission had to come from Rome, and this could only come at the General Chapter. He was told that those in close contact with the scholastics knew the issue could not wait. If it did, "many of our best scholastics would be lost" because they had been keeping up "with the progress in formation in other congregations..." which they believed were more aware of the issues.[21]

After two days, the meeting, and discussions with Todesco, were over. The group narrowed its choice of delegates for the General Chapter to Fathers Sergio Contran and Alvin Ruhe. Criticism of the meeting would later arise about it even though it was relatively polite in tone. Some believed the meeting was instigated by older confreres, and little attention was paid to its recommendations. This proved unfortunate, for with consultation and support, those native-born Americans who were lost might have provided the very catalyst for renewal the province needed.

RETRENCHMENT

It would be perhaps unfair to accuse Father Briani of asking for only the youngest, strongest, and most experienced Comboni Missionaries from North America, and sending back only the tired, recalcitrant, or inexperienced as replacements. But in Todesco's view, that appeared to be the case. In 1967, he lost Marigo to Mexico, Bragotti to Uganda, and Brothers Miller and Charbonneau to Esmeraldas and Uganda respectively. Then five more young priests were called to foreign missions. These nine amounted to a loss of twenty percent of Comboni Missionaries in the North American province. When Todesco pleaded shortages, the response was that shortages were common everywhere. This was partly true, but in comparing numbers of those in England, Portugal, and Spain with those in the United States and Canada, the proportion of missionaries to the size of the countries was completely out of balance. As a result, those who remained in North America had to stretch themselves to fit the work in the province, and health issues were increasing. Father Samuel Baiani, then working n Louisville, was near collapse and was moved to Columbia for rest. In January, 1968, Todesco heard that a priest at Montclair had lost blood due to a perforated ulcer. At the same time, Father Benedict Paletti, doing vocation work in the East, was undergoing treatments for leukemia without success. In Georgia, a priest was admitted to the hospital with a bleeding ulcer. Another, doing outstanding work in ministry, suffered a severe nervous break-down. By early 1969, a lay brother was admitted to the hospital with problems associated with arteriosclerosis. In February, Father Paolucci underwent gastric surgery, continued to lose blood, and his condition was so critical he received the "last sacraments."[22]

In addition to those who were ill, Todesco had missionaries who, for one reason or another, could never accommodate to working in North America. Todesco told Battelli, "The personnel is not united, and they do not understand why they were sent... " At a recent meeting, one of these priests had stood up and "read a declaration of no confidence toward the society and the major superiors" announcing that he was leaving the institute. Todesco replied that he had "no idea of what the confrere was thinking about..." and he could not understand his bitterness.[23]

Faced with this kind of behavior, and receiving personnel too old for strenuous work, Todesco became less willing to comply with requests for his missionaries. When in April, 1968, Battelli asked for a young American priest, Todesco made a counter-offer of an older one. It was refused.[24] That fall, Battelli asked for Father Raymond Pax, a young American in charge of the Irwindale church after another confrere's health collapsed. Todesco gave Battelli an overview of his situation, "Father, as I am experiencing...the difficulties of dealing with and finding the right places for the personnel that is often riddled with deficiencies, I can imagine what difficulties the Superior General [has] in handling the personnel on a chess board so vast....That is why I am not objecting too strongly with regard to the personnel the Superior General is sending me....If sometimes I express...discouragement, it is because I see that the number of strange and deficient personality cases is increasing, and I find it difficult to keep the work going in an efficient way, and the communities at peace." Then Todesco referred to the request for Pax, "The departure of Father Pax from the parish would mean first, an upset for the parish itself, a fully functioning and organized parish, and only [this way] for a few months. Secondly, I have no one else to send there to substitute for him....Father, believe me, now the personnel is just starting in their new assignments, and it is strictly sufficient for the needs..."

That same month, a beleaguered Todesco heard that forty-seven-year old Father Didoni had died due to a faulty gas connection at his family's home in Italy. Didoni was the one so troubled by changes in the Church and society that he asked to go to Italy for a renewal course.[25] News of his death was compounded by news that Father Louis Buffoni had suffered cardiac arrest and died at 40 years of age. His death came only months after his return to the province from Sudan. Todesco had been told that Buffoni might be a good substitute for Ghirotto in Canada. But discovering Buffoni's health was not the best, and that he intended to enroll at the University of Fordham, he wrote Battelli, "Father, if he [Buffoni] doesn't come willingly...You can keep him in Italy, and he can study at the Gregorian or at Propaganda. He was offered to me by the Superior General to do PR work..." Later it was found that when Buffoni left Africa, medical tests in Italy indicated that his heart was enlarged. The prognosis was rest and a special diet."[26] One must wonder if Briani had read this medical report before sending Buffoni as a replacement for Ghirotto in Canada even though that work had repeatedly tried the health of Ghirotto, another seasoned missionary.

Buffoni's case illustrates the attitude about health matters in those years. Stoicism was the rule; unless a confrere dropped in his tracks, he was assumed well enough to work. Such a policy naturally led to more serious illnesses and even deaths. Rather than being considered valuable resources whose health was vital to the work of the society, a mystique of the "suffering servant" led superiors as well as individuals to ignore symptoms of serious illness.. The consequences went beyond health issues. What cannot be documented is that this lack of concern certainly contributed to personnel losses in an era when the society could least afford them. Because this loss paralleled a swift drop in vocations, after this the North American Province would never fully recoup the momentum of the early 1960s.

PREPARING FOR THE FUTURE

In these years of crisis, a source of hope was the Tenth General Chapter. The Holy See had directed all religious societies to thoroughly review Second Vatican Council documents, particularly those on mission and the life of the religious and priestly life. Every society had to apply the directives in these documents to determine its identity, its reason for being, and its rules, then revise its rules and procedures accordingly. It was a momentous undertaking.

When on March 28, 1967, the forty priests, lay brothers, and scholastics of the North American province met to prepare for this process, they had little time to do it. Nine committees were formed, and for four days, work continued in morning and afternoon sessions.[27]

In accordance with directives from Rome, on July 10, 1967, Todesco appointed a Regional Committee whose members were Father Alfred Paolucci, Chairman; Father William Jansen, Secretary; and Fathers Januarius Carillo; Remus Catellani; Peter Tarquini; Joseph Valente; and Brother Victor De Gasperi. A questionnaire from Rome was translated into English. Another committee distributed the survey and issued guidelines to facilitate a good rate of response. The questionnaire was composed of seventeen documents totaling 200 pages. It was sent to each member of the province including all students in vows. More paperwork followed.[28] Due to a shortage of people, the committees had difficulty maintaining schedules. But tabulation of the questionnaire began by early 1968. Father Archie Fornasari, who helped formulate the survey, was called to Rome as a member of the Central Commission to draft General Chapter documents. Fornasari's work toward his doctoral degree at the Catholic University of America had been interrupted by work on the questionnaire. Now, as he completed his dissertation, he barely had time to defend it before leaving for Italy. It is said he prepared his doctoral defense on the train to Baltimore.

In November, 1968, there was the first election process for chapter delegates. On December 12, thirty priests and lay brothers gathered to prepare for the Chapter. Photographs taken for the provincial magazine captured the intensity of those gathered around tables. Listening attentively, taking notes, standing to speak, gesturing to make a point, were many of the pioneers of the province: Brothers Dall' Alda and De Gasperi, Fathers Branchesi, Catellani, Carillo, Mondini, Ongaro, Paolucci, Spagnolo, and others including a last photo of Father Louis Buffoni a few months before his death.[29]

When ballots were counted on January 27, 1969, Fathers Fornasari and Branchesi were elected to represent the Comboni priests from North America. Brother John Volpato was elected to represent all lay brothers on the entire American continent.[30] On March, 1969, Todesco prepared to leave America for Italy and the General Chapter. He did not leave it in the relatively peaceful state it enjoyed when Accorsi stepped down. The crises of 1968, his illness in December, and the death of his protégé, Buffoni, left him neither time nor energy to prepare a provincial report. Before his departure, he named Father Busetti his representative until a new provincial was elected. His last diary entry reads: "Father Todesco leaves the Region definitely, and goes to Italy.

He asks forgiveness from everybody for his faults in the government of the Region, and prays that his successor will correct and perfect [the situation], and bring the Region to great success of holiness and progress."

Todesco's last years as the North American Provincial contrast sharply with his first. The energy he put into expanding seminaries and opening in Canada was exhausted. Euphoria about vocations was over. A tight personnel situation in 1960 had deteriorated due to health problems and fewer young confreres. A province in 1960 with little debt, was now described by its treasurer as, "so heavily burdened with ...debts that many times [in order] to pay one bank we had to borrow from another."[31] By 1969, new initiatives in Canada and the East Coast Seminary were struggling. At Columbia, objections about construction surfaced as younger confreres in North America saw it as a waste of resources and another strain on personnel. Determining to what degree Todesco was responsible for these disturbing changes is not easy. On one hand, he had little control over the closing of the San Diego seminary and the downward trend of vocations. The lack of personnel derived largely, if not entirely, from General Briani's preoccupation with Africa. The debt was partly due to requests from the General Administration and other provinces. On the other hand, Todesco's decision-making primarily depended on advice from a few superiors, and it largely ignored the signs of the times.

Todesco never understood American or Canadian cultures. American English, it is said, was difficult for him and, unlike Father Hamlet Accorsi, he did not seek contact with lay people. Many years after leaving America, he told a young confrere in Africa, Father Joe Bragotti, "I was in the States for ten years, but I never knew what was going on." On his return to Italy, he had been troubled by what he saw. He wrote to Busetti,"...Father what a painful situation! Just think that both in Florence and in Gozzano the two Masters of novices have run away, in the impossibility of continuing their work! At Venegono, there is a group of 'hippies.'...The Minor Seminaries are in dissolution, the attitude of the young fathers is one of rebellion..."

From San Diego, Busetti wrote back, "The news you sent is not very consoling. [Here] Everything is calm. At least until the election of the new provincial..."[32]

16. Renewal and Choice

Father Todesco was not the only religious superior who failed to understand the changes going on in the Church during the 1960s. Thousands of Catholic leaders, feeling the fault lines of cultural earthquakes under their feet, clung relentlessly to the shaking pillars of tradition. When on January 25, 1959, Pope John XXIII summoned an ecumenical council of the Roman Catholic Church, his action had been both historic and unexpected. No one was prepared for the radical outcome of this call. Theologically, the Second Vatican Council brought a fundamental shift in church thinking. At a time when it was considered virtually unchanging, there re-emerged at the Council an ancient symbol of the Church as "a tent of the pilgrim people of God, pitched in the desert and shaken by all the storms of history, [and] laboriously seeking its way into the future...striving over and over again to make sure of its faith..."[1]

It was as a result of a mandate from the Second Vatican Council that the Comboni Missionaries Tenth General Chapter was a chapter of renewal.

FROM THE FOUNDER TO VATICAN II

Daniel Comboni, founder of the Comboni Missionary Institute, set down guidelines in 1869 that were typical of his forthright nature. His *"Regolamento Pei Missonari Degli Instituti dei Neri in Egitto"* contained no attempt at theological or scriptural underpinnings. He clearly excluded religious profession, but he expected unconditional obedience, apostolic poverty, formation of a common community, and an intense prayer life. Evangelization, and the preparation for it, was Comboni's vision for his followers. Before he died, these rules were restated in two other documents, and one was temporarily approved by Bishop Luigi di Canossa of Verona in 1871, A second edition of this rule was issued in 1872.[2]

After Comboni's death, the Jesuits developed a new set of rules for the congregation, changing its name from "The Institute for the African

Missions" to "Congregation of the Sons of the Sacred Heart of Jesus" (FSCJ). Rome approved these rules in 1895. They were assigned the laborious title of "Constitutions and Rules of the Society of the Sons of the Sacred Heart of Jesus, Missionaries for Central Africa." From the start, there was disagreement about whether the society was primarily mission oriented or primarily concerned with living the life of a religious.[3]

The 1895 Rule received permanent approval in 1910, and remained substantially unchanged even when the Institute separated into two congregations in 1923. The largely German congregation became "The Missionary Sons of the Sacred Heart" (MFSC), and the largely Italian congregation became "Sons of the Sacred Heart of Jesus" (FSCJ). In 1930, a *"Breve Regolamento per le Missioni"* was published to reconcile certain aspects that conflicted with the needs of religious members in a mission field. Two other revisions in 1953 and 1958 integrated certain missionary elements and incorporated guidelines on priestly formation advised by the Holy See. In 1963, a Directory, or practical guide to the rules, was published as a companion to the Constitution.[4]

In 1965, Pope Paul VI published an apostolic letter calling for implementation of the Council decree *Perfectae Caritatis*. This set into motion a renewal process for all religious societies. The Pope directed that a general chapter (or convocation) of renewal be held within three years of the decree, and he gave permission for this chapter to alter a society's constitution on an experimental basis. The publication of *Perfectae Caritatis* constituted another major break with the past. It forced religious societies to examine their history, the original inspiration of their founder, and to re-write much, if not all, of their constitution. For the Comboni Missionaries, *Perfectae Caritatis* gave added impetus to the study of Daniel Comboni, their founder. Already, thousands of his letters had been widely read by members of the Institute. Through a survey distributed throughout the society, every member was asked to contribute to the preparation for the Tenth General Chapter which would respond to the questionnaire. The entire volume of information, over 600 pages, represented the content to be debated at the chapter, and this debate would determine the Institute's future.

THE CHAPTER BEGINS

On May 16, 1969, the General Chapter opened in Rome with sixty-nine delegates including, for the first time, lay brothers. A decision was made to invite members of the separated German congregation as observers, and it was also judged appropriate to extend invitations to one observer from each nationality not already represented by elected delegates. Thus, an African, an American, and a Spanish Comboni Missionary were invited as observers. Twenty-nine year old Father Charles Walter was selected to represent native-born Americans.[5]

On May 21, 1969, Superior General Briani gave an overview of his ten-year administration. He reported that minor seminaries had increased from 17 to 22, and students had increased from 1203 to 1637. Among these were 566 Italians, 347 Portuguese, 212 Brazilians, 210 Mexicans, 110 Spaniards, 81 Ethiopians, 77 English, and 34 Americans. Novitiates had increased from 6 to 7, novices from 165 to 185, and scholastics from 212 to 222. There had been 422 priests ordained as Comboni Missionaries, bringing the total to 993. But 46, or over 10%, had left the society. Regarding lay brothers, 131 had joined the society in the preceding 10 years, and 75 had left. As for expansion, Comboni Missionaries had returned to Ethiopia, had opened new missions in Uganda and one each in the R.C.A. (Republic of Central Africa), Togo, and Burundi. Priests were also sent to two dioceses in Mozambique. The previous ten years witnessed the opening of 107 new houses throughout the society: 82 in Africa and 25 in Latin America. At the same time, 61 houses were closed: 47 in Southern Sudan (due to forced expulsion), and 6 in Latin America. (No mention was made of those closed in North America.)

Positive initiatives regarding a future reunion with the German congregation of Comboni Missionaries had been taken. The German confreres were ready to reunite, Briani said, but they wanted a separate German province so their members would not be isolated from their mission. Briani admitted that at the beginning of his tenure, the society had been in financial "difficulties," but he maintained things began to improve "thanks to Divine Providence." Other major accomplishments were the building of the General Curia and International Theologate in Rome, the Novitiate at Moncada in Spain, and purchase of the house where Daniel Comboni was born.[6]

The stark contrast between the number of students in the minor seminary of North America (34) and those of other countries or regions, often two to sixteen times greater, raises questions about how this disparity came about. To be sure, vocation recruitment had plummeted in all Western countries, but a greater congruency might be expected to exist between the number of students in England (77) and those in North America.

TODESCO'S REPORT

On June 10-11, Father Anthony Todesco gave his report. North America, at that point in time, he said, had 45 priests, 6 lay brothers, 17 scholastics, 16 first and second year novices, and 4 lay brothers. There were 15 communities including 8 parishes or missions, 5 promotion centers, and 2 houses of formation. Three new communities were begun in the U.S. (The scholasticate in San Diego, Yorkville, and Columbia), and two in Canada (St. Thomas More in St. Jean, and Brossard). Three communities had been closed (St. Michael's in Louisville, Toccoa in Georgia, and the Suire Avenue residence in Cincinnati). The two new junior seminaries planned in the East and the West were now an impossibility as new concepts about formation were making junior seminaries obsolete. Todesco explained his reasons for moving the scholasticate to San Diego, citing academic degrees, the availability of apostolic work, and its availability for Mexican scholastics.

Todesco believed combining scholastics and novices at Sacred Heart brought about "greater contact with teachers, [and a] more evident spirit of community." He admitted some negative outcomes: "novices [are now] in an atmosphere that can lead them astray; they may feel less disposed to develop self-control; Father Master [Valente] may have difficulty in guiding two different communities..." About finances, Todesco maintained that, while U.S. and Canadian communities were "self-supporting," they were not rich. They had only a "comfortable balance between debts and credits." The North American province had fulfilled obligations in provincial construction projects, faithfully met their quota of contributions to the General Administration, and provided hundreds of thousands of dollars to Comboni missionaries outside the province.

During the questioning period, Todesco was asked, "How is it you had so many members (students) who left the society?" He replied, "The loss of 25 scholastics in ten years is high. Before passing judgement on this, however, we must consider the new problems, various circumstances, and unforeseen happenings...We also had to go through [a] crisis...first in the novitiate and later in the scholasticate...At this moment we cannot say that we really have critical situations in our seminaries; the superiors are doing their best to avoid such cases." He quoted an unnamed confrere as agreeing that the vocational program in the United States was disorganized due to too few recruiters for the size of the country.

Two other questions were put to Todesco. One was whether the society was working enough among "Negroes," and why black parishes were being exchanged for white ones, as when St. Anthony's was exchanged for St. Michael's in Cincinnati. Todesco told the delegates he was pleased to hear expansion of black ministry now met with favor, but he reminded them that "Now the attitude of the bishops and the clergy towards the religious and the possibility of giving them [black] parishes is totally changed to an unfavorable manner...they are trying hard to gradually totally eliminate the difference between black churches and white churches..."

Someone asked whether it was true that "our American confreres are ready to leave the Society if we do not intend to work for the Negroes in the USA. What does this mean?" Todesco said, "They understand better than we do the [need to assist] the American Negroes. However, another Capitular [delegate] said we must not stress too much in our publicity and recruiting efforts that we are for Home Missions since we still are primarily for the foreign missions..."[7] Indeed, there was confusion about the possibility of working in "home missions." For years, the magazine *Frontier Call* had listed all parishes and missions in North America as "missions," and until the end of the 1950s, it described the "Verona Fathers" on its editorial page as "a Religious Society of priests and brothers, devoted exclusively to Missionary work at *home* and abroad..." [Emphasis added] As a result, some seminarians believed they could serve only in the United States, and a significant number left the Comboni Institute to incardinate in American dioceses and serve a growing number of their country's poor.

QUESTIONS RAISED; ANSWERS DEBATED

The focus of the questionnaire distributed among Comboni Missionaries prior to the chapter was adapted to the format of the society's constitution which had five divisions including: the nature and purpose of the congregation, its government, formation of its members, the minor seminaries, lay brothers, missionary life, and temporal goods. A close look at the questionnaire reveals that scientific method did not interfere with the methodology employed to report results. First, most of the survey's questions were open-ended, and a confrere could respond in his own words. Given the complexity of the questions, e.g., which methods of formation were considered most effective, this design could produce such a variety of responses that exact quantification of results would be impossible. Secondly, the responses were interpreted and categorized by many confreres, from many cultures, with many viewpoints. Thus, any initial variability in responses was multiplied exponentially. Thirdly, the return rate of approximately 50% in the

North American province, if reflected in other provinces, raises the question of the motivations and thinking of those who did not respond. Under these conditions, it would be hard to view the survey as statistically verifiable.

Despite this, the survey served its purpose. It was a means for crystallizing issues, opening debate, and forcing internal dialogue. This was exactly the goal Father Fornasari and his colleagues intended.[8] For days, weeks, months, hundreds of Comboni Missionaries discussed, argued, made a case for or against new and old ideas, formation methods, structures, the definition of mission, the way communities should pray. They were prodded into thinking about the true purpose of the society, their commitment to Daniel Comboni, his charism, his missionary spirituality, and what that meant in the last half of the twentieth century. Until this renewal chapter, only the superiors were presumed to have all the answers. Now, the survey was asking every individual confrere to contribute them. The dialogue thus provoked led to rethinking every facet of the society's life.

On June 17, 1969, discussion began on "The Nature and Purpose of the Congregation and the Missions." Perhaps the most important of these issues was the Purpose of Mission. Delegates were to be guided by two main principles: the need to return to the evangelical and Combonian origins, and the need to respond to the Church at large. A debate centered on which of two historical events took precedence. Was it the fact that the congregation had been founded with a strictly missionary goal? Or was it the fact that it had been transformed into a religious congregation? Father Capovilla, a prominent and well-respected Comboni missionary, held that Daniel Comboni founded the institute as an association of secular priests and laymen, and that the rules he drew up left no doubt about this fact. Then the testimony of two contemporaries of Comboni to Propaganda Fide in 1894 was examined. They had maintained that Comboni had the goal of consolidating his mission work into a congregation with simple vows, and that he would have agreed to the form given it by Italian Jesuits.

Conflicts about the primary purpose of the society divided Comboni missionaries into two camps: those who felt the spiritual practices and development were primary, and those who believed they were but springboards to a total dedication to mission. One might see this as a duel between the contemplative and the active life, but it was far more complicated. Comboni had been deeply dedicated to the Church, the missions, and the evangelization of Africa in that order. In true apostolic style, he prayed, suffered, and worked unsparingly of himself to attain this goal. But his vision had been somewhat obscured by the Jesuit's view of asceticism, and this view had taken deep root in the Comboni Institute. It made the issues surrounding the debate difficult to resolve.

On June 17, the Tenth General Chapter agreed that Daniel Comboni gave the institute a strictly missionary purpose as he was impelled toward Africa. Yet this choice was seen in the circumstances of his time, i.e., the abandonment of Africans, the signs of the times, e.g., widespread slave trade, and a faithfulness to the Church. It was declared that the Comboni Congregation was "a totally missionary family, whose members are united as brothers in the Spirit of Christ by the common missionary charism lived in the religious life, and who set out to evangelize and found the Church in the midst of those groups of human beings to whom the Father destines them."

While chapter delegates discussed the "Purpose of Mission Activity," several observations were made relating to the North American Province. In Africa, a whole tribe might be baptized when the tribal leader received baptism, and conversions could run into the hundreds. In the United States, Comboni missionaries in black parishes might produce only ten to twenty conversions a year, and they were often made to feel this was inadequate. But the Second Vatican Council decree, *Ad Gentes*, proclaimed that if the Church is really rooted in a group of people, she must be a sign and instrument of salvation, and appear to the eyes of all as the family of God. Visible signs of the Church, such as preaching the Gospel, administering the Sacraments, and having its hierarchy, only had a value, the decree said, if they expressed the real and intimate reality of the Church, e.g., brotherliness united in the Holy Spirit. This depth of evangelization could not be accomplished with mass baptisms. Understanding this, the delegates agreed to a last paragraph in the "Purpose of Missionary Activity" section that read, "The sign [of true evangelization] is effective and clear if it is understandable, and its form is not in the order of quantity, but rather in that of quality. As a consequence, a small flock really nourished by the Spirit of Christ is more of an instrument than a large shapeless group of Christians who are so only in name."[9]

There were many "interventions" by delegates concerning this section. When a vote was taken on it, the last paragraph about the "little flock" was left out and moved to a future discussion. But the principle found its way into the final Constitutions of the Comboni Institute in the section on Missionary Activity: "A well-enlightened missionary activity will seek quality more than quantity, the influence that the baptized may have on society, rather than their number. A 'little flock' that is truly inspired by Christ's spirit is more of a sign and an instrument of salvation - and consequently more of a church - than an amorphous mass that is only nominally Christian."[10]

Also related to the North American Province was the debate on "Mission Field." Daniel Comboni's rules were dedicated to "the conversion of Africa" and "especially the Negroes who still lie in darkness and the shadow of death..." But after Vatican II, the Institute had to consider the "signs of the times" and the missions it had accepted from Propaganda Fide (including North America.). Therefore, the Institute's duty to the Church was not limited to bringing the Church to Africans. Chapter delegates concluded that, while Africa remained central to the Institute's mission, those missions entrusted to it by Propaganda Fide were also true missions. The first was the field of work; the second was a true mission responsibility. The Institute would use the following criteria to determine "true mission": 1) to accept those among the poorest and most abandoned, 2) to give prudent attention to the "signs of the times," 3) to respond to the call of the Church regarding mission.[11] This debate was among the most hotly disputed of the chapter, and the conclusion was that all three conditions had to be fulfilled before accepting a mission. But the debate continues to this day.

DEMOCRATIC ELECTIONS

Before the first session of the Open Chapter ended on July 25, 1969, a new superior general and his councilors were elected. Father Tarcisio Agostoni was elected as Superior General. At 48 years of age, he had extensive teaching experience as well as administrative and organizational skills. His work in communications and as founder of *Leadership* (a Catholic magazine of general interest), was greatly respected in Uganda and throughout the society. A precedent was set when two Americans, Fathers Robert Bosse and Archie Fornasari, were elected as two of the four assistants to Agostoni. Bosse was the first graduate of Sacred Heart Seminary to become a priest when he was ordained in 1963, and the first and only non-European born priest to serve as assistant to the superior general since the congregation was founded. Fornasari was one of the first Italians students to go to the United States, arriving in 1948. He had been deeply involved in preparations for the Tenth General Chapter.[12]

The second session of the Tenth Chapter opened on September 3, 1969. In a written report, Father Remus Catellani put forth the finances of the North American Province. He said that some confreres outside the province believed the American province had "done very little for the Missions and for the General Administration" in terms of money. The facts were that not only did the province begin with no subsidy, but there were "times when we were obliged to negotiate loans for the General Administration, and not just small loans. We were also requested to pay our yearly assessments in advance, and to give special aid to good causes in Italy or Africa without public disclosure...If there was any lack of enthusiasm on our part, it stemmed from the fact that the American province was deeply in debt because of the many loans with banks to pay for our buildings in Cincinnati, Monroe, San Diego, Brossard, and Yorkville. This did not include the purchase of land and buildings, notably Columbia, Yorkville, and San Diego."

Catellani mentioned that the revenues that paid for the province's debts came from loans from priests and lay people in the Cincinnati archdiocese, an annuity program instituted in 1950, and real estate the province owned, some donated, and some greatly increased in value. The financial success of the province, he wrote, was also due to the individual confreres in the province, to generous benefactors, (both priests and lay people), and to Divine Providence. Complaints had come, Catellani noted, from those who had to be "turned down from time to time, or who were referred to the General Administration of Rome or Verona" as Father Briani had told him to do.[13]

On December 6, 1969, the General Chapter closed. Superior General Agostoni told the delegates, "We have reached in these days a broad, substantial unanimity. I am convinced that this unanimity is not simply a silent acceptance of a compromise, but the fruit of mature reflection...It was a fine exercise in dialogue, sincerity, and search for the truth...I would like to ask that this exercise continue among yourselves and with the General Council..." Later, Pope Paul VI addressed the capitulars, giving them the Apostolic Benediction and speaking with superiors and members from various countries.[14]

Before the chapter closed, certain directives on planning were published to be initiated before the next chapter. Of significance to North America were several paragraphs that stated, "In carrying out this plan, only authentically missionary fields of work may be opened, with precedence to Africa. The Society, in force of its African vocation, recognizes [it has] an obligation of evangelization also towards the Negroes of the Untied States of America, though within the limits of its actual possibilities and the other purposes of the U.S. Province..."[15] This statement, except for the clause "its actual possibilities," largely ignored Todesco's report that the situation concerning African Americans had radically changed. Nor did it seem to recognize that even black priests, seminarians, and nuns in the United States were criticizing their church for being paternalistic and Euro-centric. Only a year before the Tenth General Chapter opened, fifty-eight black priests met in Detroit,

Michigan, and organized the Black Catholic Clergy Caucus, declaring that "the Catholic Church in the United States [is] a white racist institution..."[16]

Despite the lack of understanding of racial foment in the United States, the principles laid down in the Planning addendum of the Tenth Chapter gave every province a genuine guideline from which to work for renewal. This work would proceed in North America where, as the Chapter's work was ending, the first "free" election process of an American province was taking place.

17. Expanding Black Ministry

On a summer day in 1957, the young priests at the Comboni community in Brescia, Italy were finishing dinner. The Vicar General, Father Gaetano Briani, joined them. After a few casual remarks, he asked one of them, "Do you want to go to Africa?" "Yes." was the response. He turned to Father Sergio Contran and said, " Do you want to go to the States?" "Surely," said Contran. Briani repeated this questioning in the tone of a good-natured test of obedience. Everyone laughed and resumed their discussions. The following December, Contran received a call from Briani. "Why aren't you going to Genoa?" he asked.

"What for?" Contran replied.

"To go to the American Consulate!" Briani retorted. Contran thought a mistake had been made. But when he visited his Superior General, (then) Father Todesco, he was told, "Your mission is in the States." Once there, Contran developed a proficiency in the English language, then taught philosophy at the Monroe novitiate. He was transferred to Sacred Heart Seminary as Professor of Latin and History, and he took a Master's Degree in Education at Xavier University. Later he was assigned to the Columbia Mission Center.[1] Contran was at Columbia when the meeting of American-born priests took place, its outcome summarized in the paper "Points of Discussion" (see "Years of Crisis"). When the Americans wanted to select candidates for the General Chapter, Contran was one of several they agreed upon after much discussion. Though it was suggested by some that Contran initiated the Columbia meeting, younger priests interviewed by the author repudiated this.

ELECTING A NEW PROVINCIAL

On January 26, 1970, when votes for an American provincial were counted, Father Busetti received 11 votes, Father Catellani 16, and Father Contran 26.[2] The new provincial was not only the first elected provincial of

North America, he was twenty years younger than any of his predecessors. The four provincial councilors elected were: Fathers Catellani (provincial treasurer under Todesco); Aldo Cescatti (pastor of Our Lady of Guadalupe); Caesar Mazzolari (spiritual director at Sacred Heart Seminary); and Robert Meyer (rector of Sacred Heart Seminary). In a joint letter, the new Provincial Council named its theme, "There will be an extensive amount of work for all of us to do...to implement the marvelous work of our recent Chapter... it will require work, willingness to adjust and unselfish cooperation. It will not be painless..." Indeed, it would not be pain-free. Not since the beginning of the foundation would so much be expected of so few.

A burning issue at the Comboni Missionaries' 1969 General Chapter had been determining what mission fields were true to their charism, and the question of how to distinguish between what was, and what was not, an authentic mission persisted. New criteria were offered. One said authenticity was present in "groups that were completely alien to the Church." An example given was the Negroes of the United States. Another sign was mission work directed to "groups where the Church had taken root, but undergone radical changes," as in Latin America.[3] This still left the matter open to interpretation. Contran and his Council would be responsible for this interpretation as it pertained to expanding black ministry in North America. The difficulty of this assignment could only be understood within the context of the Civil Rights movement.

KING'S DREAM VS. "BLACK POWER"

On August 11, 1965, two police officers near the Watts area of Los Angeles arrested a Negro youth whose dangerous driving was reported by another Negro. An altercation between the youth's family and an officer drew a crowd of bystanders. One of the officers believed he was spat upon, and he started to arrest the woman he suspected. She was wearing a white apron and the crowd thought she was pregnant. Violence broke out, and she was arrested only with the aid of the Los Angeles' Sheriff's Department. In a matter of hours, a minor civil disturbance exploded into virtual war. A mob flooded the streets, looted stores, hauled white motorists from cars, burned their cars, and set fire to buildings. The shout "Burn, baby, burn" echoed throughout the nights as barricades were thrown up, snipers shot at police, and firemen were unable to respond to fires without National Guard escorts. The violence began outside the Watts area, but it spread quickly to the Watts business district where it destroyed many buildings. When it ended, 34 people were dead and 1,032 wounded. Property damage amounted to $40 million, and close to 4000 people were arrested. It shocked the nation and set a precedent for the three years of riots that followed, largely in northern cities. In 1966, riots broke out in Chicago, Cleveland, Dayton, Milwaukee, and San Francisco with damage amounting to $5 million. In 1967, 150 riots included 40 that were recorded as serious. Violence in Boston, Buffalo, Cincinnati, New Haven, Providence, Wilmington, and a hundred other cities, found unprecedented numbers of African Americans involved, many throwing Molotov cocktails, looting and burning stores, and firing upon police.[4]

The California Governor's Commission, (the McCone Report) claimed that rioters in Los Angeles were marginally related to the community, that they were unemployed or school dropouts.[5] But two independent researchers, David O. Sears and John B. McConahay, claimed that the "new ghetto man" was not a marginal citizen. They wrote "Most blacks perceived the [Watts] riot as (1) a purposeful symbolic protest (2) against legitimate grievances, (3) designed to call attention to blacks' problems..."[6]

Some cited President Johnson's actions at the 1964 Democratic Party's convention when he denied the Mississippi Freedom Democratic Party's (MFDP's) request to replace the all-white, Mississippi delegation with members of the MFDP which had managed to enroll 60,000 Blacks and elect delegates despite obstacles. Afraid of losing the southern whites' votes,.Johnson seated only two MFDP delegates. Martin Luther King, who agreed to this compromise, was later criticized, and at a speech he gave at Watts, he was heckled. Militant black leaders gained influence, and Malcolm X, a leader of the Nation of Islam, proclaimed, "We *need* a Mau Mau. If they don't want to deal with the Mississippi Freedom Democratic Party..." [Emphasis not added.] When Whitney Young, head of the National Urban League, called for a "domestic Marshall Plan" to close the economic gap between Blacks and Whites, it was too late. Historian Harvard Sitkoff wrote, "Early in 1966, [President] Johnson admitted, 'Because of Vietnam, we cannot do all that we should...do.' Drastic cuts in the domestic budget followed, and the war on poverty and government efforts to achieve racial equality ground to a halt."[7] It was to the Watts area that Comboni Missionaries would soon be called.

HOLY CROSS PARISH

Bishop Thomas J. Conaty of Los Angeles established Holy Cross parish in 1906. Six lots at the corner of Main and 47th Streets were purchased, and a temporary wooden church opened for services. South Main Street was then a dirt road in the middle of farm country. Sixty years later, Holy Cross had changed from a pioneer to an inner-city parish of Blacks and Hispanics. Holy Cross was only a block away from where rioters were looting and burning in 1965. By 1970, at least four successive pastors had served the parish: Fathers Doherty, Pierce, Gualberon, and Rucker, and its parish plant required costly repairs and requirements.[8]

When the Vicar General of the Los Angeles archdiocese, Monsignor Benjamin Hawkes, offered Comboni Missionaries the parish in 1969, Todesco was due to leave the province, and the offer was not accepted. In 1970, Father Cescatti, pastor at Our Lady of Guadalupe, spoke with Hawkes about Holy Cross, and the subject was referred to the Provincial Council. The parish was accepted.[9] Fifty-eight year old Father Alexander Nardi began as pastor in 1970. His associate was Father Xavier Colleoni.[10] Nardi had been pastor of Holy Trinity in Cincinnati, and was involved in ministry in the Indian missions. He had used a vacation to learn Spanish in the Comboni mission in Ecuador. Father Colleoni came to the U.S. as a student in 1948, was ordained in 1952, taught at Sacred Heart Seminary, and assisted at Cincinnati parishes.

Nardi was frustrated with the empty talk he heard from government and other official groups. He saw how the elderly and poor were refused their food stamps and other services, how they were turned away with, "Sorry, you're too late. We cannot do anything for you." He began devising a plan to open a center to respond to people's needs. But he needed help. When he tried to enlist the principal of Holy Cross School, her Mother Superior refused to release her for extra work. One day, as he was driving to Pala Mission to visit confreres, he had a strong urge to go back. It was a crazy thing to do, he thought, but he turned around and went back to Holy Cross. When he arrived at the office, the phone was ringing. It was the Mother Superior telling him she now had a nun for the center. When Sister Regina Quilter, C.S.J. arrived, she, Nardi, Colleoni, and Vickie Callan, a staff member, began work.[11]

It took one year to open the new center in two rooms at the rear of the parish rectory. Fifteen dedicated volunteers offered their services. St. Martin de Porres Center mushroomed into an organization offering counseling, food, clothing, housing, jobs, and a dozen other services to the community. Those who were helped by the center then began to volunteer. "One day," Sister Regina told a reporter, "We were down to our last bag of food when the high school students from Thousand Oaks arrived with a load of groceries." Other schools sent help, she said, including St. Catherine's School in Laguna Beach,

St. Mary's Academy and St. Jerome's in Los Angeles. The Verona Mission League in Irwindale parish also contributed to the center.[12]

A grant from the Campaign for Human Development Archdiocesan Committee supplied a 24 hour telephone to respond to anyone in need: drug addicts, alcoholics, immigrants, the poor, the unemployed. Volunteers arranged job interviews, transported the elderly and sick to doctors and hospitals, helped foreigners make out immigration papers, and generally offered counsel and support. News about St. Martin de Porres spread through the diocese. Archbishop Timothy Manning, recently raised to the rank of a Cardinal, paid a visit to Holy Cross for Confirmation ceremonies. Thereafter in Rome to receive the cardinal's red hat, Manning spoke about the center at the North American College. Excerpts of this talk were heard over the radio, and calls came from as far away as New York and Cleveland asking for information. Its success outgrew its facilities, two other parishes joined in the work, and it was later moved to larger quarters.[13]

In 1976, when Nardi was transferred, Colleoni was appointed pastor of Holy Cross. A visitor gave a description of the neighborhood: "A Latino family sits on the steps of a deteriorating apartment complex. Several dented automobiles rumble down a pot-holed street. Children play tag beneath a rusting billboard advertising Coca-Cola in Spanish. A neon sign glows in the window of a liquor store, its walls covered with graffiti. Far off in the distance, rising through brownish-grey smog, are the steel and glass towers of downtown Los Angeles."[14]

When first arriving at Holy Cross, Colleoni found only a few Catholics, perhaps 500 in all, mainly African Americans. As he began making home visits, he found as many as twenty to thirty families in one building, each with only one bedroom and a kitchen at their disposal. Such crowding resulted from the high rental costs even when quarters were less than desirable. A family moving into an apartment renting for $400-500 would invite others in to share the cost. From seven people to an apartment, the numbers could grow to fifteen or twenty. One building, Colleoni said, was 40 by 70 feet. It was divided by a long hallway, on either side of which lived seven families.

The Newton Division of the Los Angeles Police Department covered the 9.2 square miles and 84,584 people in Holy Cross parish. Over the previous year, the area had witnessed 59 homicides, 137 rapes, 1,465 assaults, and 1,165 robberies. Liquor stores proliferated and "storefront" churches matched them in number. These small churches housed a growing number of Jehovah Witnesses, Mormons, and other churches not Catholic. With violence a daily event, people were too afraid to walk the five or six blocks to Sunday Mass.

Colleoni knew this and he began saying mass in their apartments, often packed with people. He organized small Christian communities and trained catechists to make home visits. He instituted home meetings to which a family would invite Catholics and non-Catholics for nightly prayers. He started marriage encounter groups, supported athletic competitions for youth groups, and made possible a senior citizens' group that met weekly to knit or play bingo. None of this was accomplished without help. One of Colleoni's assistants, Father Enzo Tavano, alone visited over 800 families of Latinos, which, by the late 1970s were the largest ethnic group in the parish.

Contrasts between the populations of African Americans and Latinos were many. African Americans were largely Creoles from Louisiana with education, citizenship, and the stability of home ownership. Latinos were often young women with children, nearly homeless, with no citizenship, and few prospects. Latino families could have six to fourteen members and were highly migratory. These factors did not make them the best neighbors for the older, more settled African Americans.[15] The key to what held this all together, a visitor in 1979 decided, was Colleoni, a man who won the love of hundreds of people in this troubled community. Although he had a graduate degree in Philosophy, and was able to speak four languages, he reached out to people in small and homely ways. In one case he acted as an occasional fishing companion to an elderly and deaf black gentleman. In another, he paid for a young boy's school tuition out of his own pocket. The rectory was opened to derelicts, a room found for a family living on the streets, or a phone call or knock on the door answered in the middle of the night. When Colleoni once described the family as the living Church, he was asked what roles members of this family played. He said, "You put in your part without expecting to measure success with a yardstick. You work as a tool of God. If the tool is well-fitted, you produce..."[16] In 1982, Colleoni left Holy Cross for other work, but he would return.

NEIGHBORHOODS CHANGE IN CINCINNATI

South Cumminsville lies in Cincinnati's Mill Creek Valley just north of the West End. It was a neighborhood of Irish and German immigrants in the late nineteenth century, and it was for this population that, on October 13, 1910, Archbishop Moeller asked Father John Berning to organize the parish of St. Pius. Berning not only organized it, he built it, paid for it, and continued to repair it for over half a century. His brother, Father Louis Berning, assisted him in his work. In mid-century, it was John Berning's fate to watch his parish neighborhood change from a white and relatively prosperous community to one inhabited by those forced from West End urban development. A Cincinnati Chancery memo from July of 1956 notes: "There has been a new housing project in the Cumminsville area called <u>Millvale</u> - it is [a] low cost hosing (sic) project for NEGROES who have been evacuated from West End.... [emphasis not added] West End pastors say Fr. Bernings are at best indiff (sic) to these people - they will take children in school [only] if the parents go to church ....Many of these children have weak parents and need Cathl (sic) school to save them."[17]

A few months later, Father John Berning reported that the Millvale project would house "between 500 and 600 colored families." He asked the Chancellor what to do. The Chancellor wrote back, "I have heard a lot of Pastors worry about changing neighborhoods - but I have never seen any go bankrupt; so my humble advice is not to wrooy (sic) about it....I feel very little saying this to a fine old Pastor, for I appreciate what the change means to you, but what we cannot alter, we might as well adjust to."[18] In March, 1967, death took the pastor of St. Pius, Father John Berning. A diocesan priest, Father Lawrence R. Krusling, was appointed pastor in his place.

CINCINNATI RIOTS.

It was also in 1967, that riots broke out in Cincinnati. Reverend Martin Luther King shared a platform with prominent religious leaders from Cincinnati: Father Frank M. Oppenheim, S.J. of Xavier University, Rabbi Albert Goldman from the Jewish community, and Reverend Richard D. Isler, Executive Secretary of the Council of Churches. King warned the Negro community that "we can't win freedom through violence." But King's and the other clergymen's urging was ignored. Two nights of burning and looting followed. At the request of Mayor Walter Bachrach, Governor James Rhodes called out the National Guard.[19]

Local clergymen called for responsibility on both sides. Father James E. Shappelle, Chairman of the Archdiocesan Human Relations Commission, said, "Those persons who....have not even troubled themselves to learn about sub-standard housing in Cincinnati or about job opportunities in neighborhoods closed to Negroes can hardly be called innocent." In Northern Kentucky, the Board of Commissioners reaffirmed passage of a fair housing ordinance, but metropolitan newspapers were publishing large advertisements sponsored by the Kenton-Boone (Covington) Board of Realtors attacking this ordinance. Reverend Fred Shuttlesworth, president of the Southern Conference Educational Fund and pastor of a Baptist church in Cincinnati said, "...In Cincinnati, the white power structure wasn't able to differentiate between violence and non-violence. They seem to look on non-violent leaders as just as troublesome as the violent ones..."[20]

Cincinnati's citizens, among the most conservative in the nation, were more likely to respond to the riots with a call for "law and order." But Archbishop Karl J. Alter called for public support of government programs for Blacks "which will give a great share of participation to Negroes in every aspect of our community life.....To talk about love is all well and good, but indifference rather than hatred is the issue. What is wanted and needed is the kind of love...which results in action."[21] The Archdiocese of Cincinnati's Catholic Commission on Human Relations designed a broad program to implement Alter's pastoral letter. It called for new action on building code violations in substandard housing, establishment of credit unions, Negro representation on parish councils and boards of education, and invitation of Negroes into all-white neighborhoods. But when Father Hilaire Valiquette, assistant at St. Martin's parish in Cincinnati, preached racial justice at Sunday Mass, a woman stood up and accused him of speaking on a political issue. She said she hadn't come to church to hear such talk, and twenty white parishioners followed her out.[22]

Such deep-seated intransigence prompted the Archdiocese to launch a human rights program named Project Commitment. It was supported by leaders in the Interracial Councils of Dayton and Cincinnati, the Catholic Commission on Human Relations, the Poverty Commission, and the social action committee of the Councils of Catholic Men and Women. The program began in 1968, and the Cincinnati Archdiocese committed $1.25 million over five years to racial and poverty problems. Paul F. Leibold succeeded Alter after he retired in 1969, and in early 1970, he called for a united effort by churches to root out both "personal racism" and "institutional racism."[23]

ST PIUS CHANGES HANDS.

In 1969, two years after Father Krusling took over St. Pius, it had a debt of $30,000, and he was denied any subsidy. Instead he was told to wait until Monsignor Asplan, treasurer of the archdiocese, raised money for inner-city schools. Meanwhile Krusling should find funds by "stepping up bingo, getting commitments from suburban parishes, or other ways."

In late 1970, Archbishop Leibold wrote to Father Catellani, a Council member well-known in the archdiocese. Recognizing that St. Henry's parish would soon close, Leibold asked if Comboni Missionaries would take over St. Pius. "There is a real need for the black apostolate in that area," he wrote,

"Father Krusling the present Pastor is full time at Moeller High and really cannot do justice to the parish..."[24] Contran and his Council met with Krusling, and a plan was conceived to allow profits from St. Henry's bingo go to St. Pius. Contran told the archbishop this plan appeared acceptable, but if needed, the archdiocese had to provide enough subsidy so that "our Fathers at St. Pius [not be] put in a financial situation which required them to spend their time begging for help, to the detriment of their missionary work."[25]

Father Peter Premarini, then stationed at St. Henry's, learned that all nearby residents would leave within a year since the area was destined for light industries. When Leibold received Permarini's report on this, he commented sadly, "Again I see the City passing us by in their renewal plans, and we end up with another St. Edward, De Porres...useless building[s]..."[5] But he thought students at St. Henry's could be absorbed into the St. Joseph and St. Augustine schools which were still open in the West End." Once that happened, St. Henry's bingo profits could be sent to St. Pius. Poverty was now rampant in the Millvale Housing Development. Welfare statistics ranked it in the top 5% of tracts of those on Aid for Dependent Children. Obviously, financial support would be necessary if St. Pius were to serve the Development's residents. Meanwhile, a local priest had proposed a partial merger for the parish. But Leibold told the proposal's author he believed, "the Verona Fathers can do a good job at St. Pius, and...have dedicated men ready to go to the people and serve them. Some of our priests talk a good game, but really do not act...with any persistence when they do have a chance."[26]

Premarini took over St. Pius in February, 1971, but financial problems persisted. A memo to Monsignor Ralph A. Asplan from Leibold carried a tone of gentle criticism. "I received a most appealing call from Fr. Peter of St. Pius pleading begging (sic) for support of St. Pius School....He has a wonderful faculty lined up....four sisters and four lay teachers....If the school is lost there, everything is lost etc. etc. etc. I said what about...Mons. Asplan. He said he did but you were very very pessimistic and he got the message that he would have to sloe (sic) up. Then he went into the matter of when we have to close schools how bad it will look that we just close the poor ones and leave those with money open etc. etc..."A rather contrite reply from Asplan was written on the archbishop's memo sent back to Leibold: "I guess I am the one who got him all upset - I was really trying to convey to him the

---

[5] Leibold was referring to a black parish and high school in the West End served by diocesan priests that had also been closed.

idea that people like him must get their oar in to try to prevent the decision being to close those schools which can't afford to make it on their own - since I believe we should operate less grades at all parishes rather than full grades [in] some places and nothing in other places..."[27]

A note that then went to Asplan from Premarini said, "we can hardly meet the church's ordinary expenses...we are entirely dependent upon the chancery's aid...the school is playing a most important role in the So. (sic) Cumminsville and Milvale (sic) areas....at least 90% of families having children in our school will not be able to afford the $100 tuition per chil, we are planning [a] voucher system..." The Assistant Treasurer of the Archdiocese, Reverend Robert W. Schaefer, sent Premarini a note that was hardly conciliatory: "We realize very well that there is a need for the school in that neighborhood. At the present time...we cannot make any firm guarantee of a specific amount of help."[28] But help did arrive. A grant came from the Stockelman Fund, named after a priest who had long worked to provide means for students from poor families. The parish also began raising funds for the school with festivals, picnics, and other parish activities.

In the fall of 1971, Leibold visited St. Pius. A plaque hung in the school hall in memory of Father Alfred Stockelman. The classrooms and cafeteria were remodeled. Better lighting, fresh paint, indoor lavatories, new playground facilities, and a Public Address system were installed. New media equipment gave the nuns and lay teachers facilities for the quality education unavailable to the children of the neighborhood.[29]

In June, 1972, at the age of fifty-nine, Archbishop Paul F. Leibold died of a stroke. Appointed as the new Archbishop of Cincinnati was Bishop Joseph Bernardin of Atlanta. Bernardin knew the Comboni Missionaries' work from the Atlanta Archdiocese, and he supported their work at St. Pius. Premarini, assisted by then Deacon Thomas Vermiglio and Father Damien Graziano, revitalized St. Pius parish to a new life in the local Church.[30]

LOUISVILLE AND IHM: 1961-1971

After Father Alfio Mondini was transferred from Immaculate Heart of Mary (IHM) parish in 1953, three Comboni missionaries succeeded him: Fathers Dominic Pazzaglia in 1961, Victor Turchetti in 1964, and Januarius Carillo in 1966. Costs associated with the IHM school mounted as it had to replace teaching sisters with lay teachers. The physical plant, built at minimum cost in 1953, required replacement of the heating plant, roof, and other repairs. Turchetti had already written Archbishop Floersh in early 1965,

"The financial worry and the effort to raise enough money to pay our bills take too much of the precious time that we would like to dedicate to the direct apostolate so necessary in this mission parish..."

The parish was in good financial condition compared to the other West End parishes, but in the year 1968-1969, it still was $11,000 short of meeting its budget that included only "the bare essentials."[31]

LOUISVILLE AND CIVIL RIGHTS.

Father Clyde Crews, historian of the Archdiocese of Louisville, contrasted the beginning and end of the 1960s as a transformation from "a bull market on hope, expectation and national consensus to disarray, polarization, and lowered morale." Contributing to this drastic change in the national mood, Crews believed, were the assassinations of President Kennedy, his brother Robert, and Martin Luther King. There was also the sense that the civil rights movement had failed to bring full equality to African Americans.[32]

Archbishop Floersh and his clergy supported civil rights issues. In 1965, after a Protestant minister was beaten to death during a civil rights march in Selma, Alabama, one hundred and forty Louisville priests and nuns marched in support of Selma demonstrators. In September, 1966, Monsignor Alfred F. Horrigan, Chairman of the Louisville and Jefferson County Human Relations Commission, urged passage of an Open Housing ordinance which was not popular with Louisville Catholics. A *Catholic Record* survey had found that 60% of respondents did not believe open housing was a moral issue, and 72% did not think priests and nuns should demonstrate for it. But in early 1967, over 125 Catholic clergy and nuns did take part in an open housing procession. One priest was bodily evicted from the aldermanic chambers for his sit-in support of the ordinance; another spent a night in jail. The latter, Father Timothy Hogan, along with his brother, were arrested, fingerprinted, and confined overnight to jail. Hogan said he learned what it was "to face a life of not being listened to, of not being treated as a person, of not having basic rights honored." Fathers Carillo and Baiani, his assistant, were among those priests supporting the ordinance.[33]

Archbishop Thomas Joseph McDonough succeeded Floersh, and historian Crews described him as "the quintessential 'Vatican Two' Bishop, moderately progressive, cautious, but open to measured change." At age 35, he was Auxiliary Bishop of St. Augustine, Florida; in 1957 named auxiliary in Savannah; and in 1960 named its bishop. As such, he attended the Second Vatican Council sessions. McDonough was a frequent visitor in parishes and at ecumenical gatherings. He did not wait for riots in his archdiocese before letting his views on racial justice known. On Good Friday, April 4, 1968, when Martin Luther King, Jr. was killed in Memphis, Tennessee, McDonough, other ecumenical leaders, and the Mayor of Louisville, headed a memorial march through downtown Louisville. During the riots in the city's West End, priests and religious were conspicuous at police headquarters as they provided counsel and a cooling presence in the midst of flaring tempers.[34]

THE WEST END COMMUNITY COUNCIL AND IHM.

One factor behind the involvement of Louisville's priests' in civil rights was that a number of them had attended St. Meinrad's Benedictine Abbey in Indiana. There, during the 1940s and 1950s, they were taught an awareness of social justice and a sense that activism and demonstrations were appropriate ways to give Christian witness. Some had also grown up in Louisville's West End when it was still broadly integrated. They had lived with black neighbors whose Catholic roots were as deep as their own. But the 1960s saw the flight of white inhabitants. West End parishes struggled to remain viable as school enrollments dropped. In 1955, the West End Catholic school enrollment was at a high of 5,848 students. But by 1965, it fell to 3,745, and by 1970, it fell again to 2,078. From 1950 to 1970, Flaget High School dropped from 1,100 to 375 students.[35]

A former student of St. Meinrad Seminary, Father Anthony Heitzman headed a community action commission designed to train and find jobs for West End citizens. The archdiocese granted the commission $2,500 to train women in secretarial skills. Not afraid to go to bars or taverns to recruit people, Heitzman soon placed or signed up 20 of 96 people who had applied for jobs. He joined a team ministry with three other priests, and McDonough gave them the dual mission of presenting "the gospel as realistically as possible," and establishing interrelationships with suburban areas.

It was at this time that Father Heitzman met with Father Carillo to analyze work at Immaculate Heart of Mary. Carillo wrote McDonough, "We all feel that much good is being accomplished here, but...it is imperative to strengthen and expand the services....However we encounter serious difficulties..." These difficulties were due to the cost of hiring lay teachers due to the shortage of nuns. McDonough promised to assist IHM with $1,000 a month from the new $100,000 Archdiocesan Development Fund.[36]

In the midst of these efforts, McDonough heard that Carillo would not be able to stay in Louisville. His letter to Father Todesco (in Rome for the General Chapter) was barely restrained: "At this time...I am requesting that you consider allowing Father Carillo to [remain at] Immaculate Heart of Mary for at least one more year....Father Carillo's capacity for his work in Louisville has been growing year by year...he is readily accepted by the priests, by the people, and by the agencies....there have been too many changes at the Immaculate Heart of Mary Parish....with each change the people become more discouraged and less cooperative. Father Carillo...has excellent rapport. He knows the problems, and he has certainly grown to understand them....Personally I am deeply concerned that he is being transferred at this time." McDonough wanted Carillo for another year until, "we will be able to evaluate better the situation. His transfer at this time would be a cause of a slowing up in the work and an embarrassment to the people."[37] McDonough was granted his request.

By early January, 1970, Heitzman was named chairman of a Louisville Archdiocesan Social Action Commission. A number of outstanding Catholics served on it including Newton McCravey, Director of the Louisville and Jefferson County Community Action Commission, and Sister Rose Colley, Executive Secretary of the Senate of Lay Religious. The Commission was to "carry out the 'social encyclicals' of the Church by teaching and distributing information." A new organization, the West End Community Council (W.E.C.C.), was formed to oversee the financial needs of West End churches.[38] The W.E.C.C. attracted highly visible black lay Catholics. Among them were Merv Aubespin, a writer for the *Louisville Courier-Journal* and Nat Green who later published a history of black Catholics in Kentucky, *The Silent Believers*. When St. Augustine Church, Louisville's oldest black parish, was renovated, paintings by black artists Houston and Kinshasha Conwill were featured.[6] In 1970, the W.E.C.C. published a major study of its work under the title *Sent to Serve*. It emphasized black pride and consciousness and the need for new forms of worship, particularly in areas of liturgical music.

In early December, 1970, Carillo wrote Archbishop McDonough that his application to the W.E.C.C. for the monthly grant of $1000 had received strong criticism. Some W.E.C.C. members believed that special consideration for IHM was not justified. Carillo said his parishioners believed the best way to fight poverty was through education, and they were working hard to support the school. Could they count on financial support? Then in February,

---

[6] Houston Conwill is the brother of two former Comboni seminarians, Giles and William Conwill.

1971, Carillo asked McDonough for a private audience "to inform you of the progress and problems of our Parish...." Whatever was discussed at this meeting, a major change took place some months later. On June 18, 1971, Auxiliary Bishop Maloney spoke to Father Contran by telephone. Maloney said that, due to budget problem in the West End, and the possible closing of one of its parishes, the archdiocese wanted to make some changes. Since Immaculate Heart of Mary parish was not on a paying basis, the archdiocese wanted to take it over, close an older parish, and place the two priests serving there at IHM. Contran asked how much time he had for a decision. Maloney said he would like a response in the next few days.[39]

The next day, Contran agreed to Maloney's request and offered a schedule that would leave the Comboni Missionaries at IHM for the parish festival in early July. On July 4, the new pastor, Father Heitzman, would be announced. And on July 17, he would assume the parish. The society would leave IHM on Sunday, July 18, 1971. Maloney agreed, and he and Carillo began work on the announcement. It recognized the eighteen years that Comboni Missionaries served at Immaculate Heart of Mary, and said they regretted leaving the people, but with diocesan priests available, it was the right step to take.[40] This was all true, but it left much unsaid. A letter from Maloney to Contran filled in the void, "The Archdiocese of Louisville owes a debt to your Community which it can never really pay. Your priests...had their share of problems, but they have surely also had an overflowing measure of success." He said he had spoken at the farewell ceremony about Father Mondini's "Intense zeal in establishing the Parish..." as well as of the devoted work of pastors who followed him. "...in this last Pastor, "Maloney wrote, " we have had the benefit of the very compassionate and understanding energy and zeal of Father Januarius Carillo to crown the accomplishments of the Pastors and many [over 10] dedicated Associate Pastors, as well as the work of Father Frank DiFrancesco...at Saint Michael Church."[41]

Archbishop McDonough's letter thanked Contran for "the courtesy you accorded us...in transferring the Immaculate Heart of Mary Parish to diocesan priests." and the "selfless dedication in the Archdiocese of Louisville." Contran wrote back that the Archbishop's letter would put to ease the mind of his superiors in Rome. "From far away, things take up a different connotation, and they were not happy [or] convinced with the reasons given for the sudden change...if we would have had a little more time...we might have been more prepared for this decision...." McDonough then wrote that he wanted Contran's Superior to know "...The decision requesting the Verona Fathers to leave Immaculate Heart of Mary Parish in Louisville was a difficult one...there are always many uncertainties as to whether the right decision is being made....I hope the People of God [at IHM] will accept this change in the spirit of the Gospel....When you next contact your Superior in Rome... put his mind at ease and assure him that it was purely an administrative decision, and in no way evoked dissatisfaction with the Comboni Missionaries..."

In September, Monsignor Charles C. Boldrick sent Carillo the substance of a resolution passed at the Louisville Priests' Senate. It expressed appreciation and regret at the departure of Comboni Missionaries, and recognized "with fraternal admiration and grateful appreciation the work done over the years by the Verona Fathers in developing and promoting I.H.M. Parish in Louisville..."[42]

From the beginning of 1970 to the middle of 1971, attempts to expand a black apostolate in North America were mixed. Holy Cross parish, once a black parish, was becoming increasingly Hispanic. St. Pius, a black parish, was merely a replacement for St. Henry's, razed for urban renewal. Immaculate Heart of Mary, also black, went back to the archdiocese partly due to Todesco's transfer policies and partly to the availability of Louisville priests. By the end of 1971, attempts to increase black ministry may have seemed a Sisyphean task for each black parish gained was matched by a loss.

In 1973, Contran asked Monsignor John A. Rawden to exchange the Los Angeles parish of Our Lady of Guadalupe, now largely white, for one that was African American. But the request was shelved.[43] It was the next provincial who would succeed in this exchange. For Contran and his administration there were other hurdles to leap as they urged their confreres through the process of renewal.

18. Formation: Hope and Despair

Even as Father Sergio Contran and his Provincial Council worked to expand black ministry, they were also approving radically new approaches to formation and provincial structures. A provincial directory for the North American Province had to be written, and major functions of the province organized into secretariats that had direct contact with the General Administration. Finally, a court of appeals would be established to arbitrate issues arising among confreres and their superiors.[1]

A priority on the Council's calendar were documents having to do with formation, the developmental process of molding young men into mature missionaries of a religious society. This process was reformulated by the Second Vatican Council and promulgated through its documents. The Comboni Institute, like other religious societies, was called to adjust its practices accordingly. As happens whenever theoretical constructs meet the test of reality, discovering what works and what does not takes time and patience.

RENEWAL AND FORMATION

"We used to have 'the long black line, in cassock and biretta....And we went into classrooms and offices thus attired. We had a host of evident symbols...of a common life....Those evident symbols are gone now...We shall have to use a lot of imagination to find new symbols and realities which can nourish the bonds of our companionship."[2]

This reflection by a Jesuit priest on changes wrought during the 1960s and 1970s hints at the culture shock religious societies experienced from demands of renewal as well as the concomitant loss of vocations. By the spring of 1970, the number of students in Comboni formation houses were at a new low: twelve scholastics were enrolled at Mt. St. Mary's Seminary or Xavier University; eleven novices were housed with scholastics at Sacred

Heart Seminary; forty-three students at Monroe were divided between those studying in-house and those going to Catholic Central High School.

The Second Vatican Council recommended postponing the novitiate until after college in order to assure a greater maturity in religious societies' candidates. This was believed to guarantee greater stability and persistence in vocation choice. Vatican Council documents also decreed: "Before seminarians commenced their specifically ecclesiastical studies, they should already have received that literary and scientific education which is the prerequisite to higher studies in their country." Positioning the novitiate after college, therefore, served two purposes. Upon graduating from college, a candidate would not only be more mature, he would be ready for "higher studies."

At its first meeting, the Provincial Council decided that, with fewer or no candidates, the novitiate would be temporarily closed. How to accommodate current novices and high school graduates wanting to enter the novitiate was left to the judgement of the rector of the minor seminary.[3] Acting on the Provincial Council's directives, a Formation Committee announced that educators should be trained to work in equipes (teams), with smaller groups of students each having its own leader. This was intended to increase the attention students received and enhance their personal development. In a partial reversal of past practices, a more active cooperation with the student's parents and family was advised, and the role of students as participators in decision-making stressed. Before entering the novitiate, a student would be encouraged to earn money in order to better understand "the many expenses involved in [his] formation" and to develop "a more practical sense of what poverty entailed."[4] Scholastics were to be exposed to missionary-pastoral experiences and actively participate in pastoral, charitable, and educational initiatives. This would be followed by a period of study and analysis.[5] Earlier attempts were made to engage scholastics in mission work, but now scholastics planned and executed their own work in apostolic ministry.

Switching gears from traditional formation practices was not an easy or even operation. It was launched without those skilled in the new methods to explain them. However it was recognized that at least someone familiar with the rationale behind the new methods should be in charge. The priest selected was Father Mario Ongaro who moved from his post as Counselor of Studies to that of Formation Secretary. With his long tenure in seminary education, and a master's degree in psychology, he was singularly qualified for the task, particularly since psychological testing was now widely required of entering students.

In early 1970, enthusiasm for the new guidelines ran high, and members of the Formation Committee met quarterly. A first decision was to bring Monroe high school graduates to Sacred Heart Seminary where they could pursue undergraduate study at local colleges or universities. There was little concern about combining high school graduates with theology students. Rather, the benefits of a larger community was emphasized, e.g., the savings in space, staff, and money.[6]

Involving scholastics in apostolic ministry proved a major success. Four students worked in New Orleans on the Witness '70 project. Two others were on projects in the Hispanic parish of Our Lady of Guadalupe. A deacon and eight novices conducted a Day Camp at Forestville for Cincinnati's black youth from the inner-city. At St. Henry's Church there were two other scholastics working in summer activities for children with financial help from the Archdiocese of Cincinnati and the Cincinnati Recreation Commission. This program was begun by the young American Father Raymond Pax as a work-week program of games, crafts, music lessons, and trips around the city organized by program supervisor, Joan Moeller. Assisting her were young West End area adults and college students many of whom had been members of the West End parishes headed by Comboni missionaries. At Sacred Heart Seminary, students ran a Day Camp for youngsters from Lower Price Hill referred to as a "meeting with nature," sponsored by the Bible Center associated with St. Michael's Church, and the Santa Maria Neighborhood House. Over a five-week period, hundreds of youngsters participated at no cost. With the help of their students, Comboni missionaries at St. Michael's and St. Henry's parish also created the Riverside Baseball League, an integrated league that functioned the entire summer teaching good sportsmanship as well as providing recreation.[7]

ADJUSTING TO THE EQUIPE

The equipe system, designed to provide students with greater access to role models, was also intended to help its leaders develop and assess students. In reality, the new system tested both the leaders and the students and led to frustration for both parties. In the first place, such development and assessment had previously been accomplished within a strong hierarchical structure with a vice rector and spiritual director who played the respective roles of disciplinarian and encourager. Theology students were used as prefects to supervise minor seminarians. As prefects they had no authority to make or change rules, or even advise students on studies or spiritual matters.

His task was to report student difficulties or infractions to the vice rector as well as act as a model for younger students.[8] With the equipe system, the old hierarchical model of three people collapsed into a horizontal model of a single priest who, himself, had never experienced such an arrangement. It was a radical departure from his own formation. Secondly, since the goals of the new formation methods were outlined in broad brush strokes, each team leader had a different interpretation of how to achieve them. Thirdly, team leaders, although carrying the roles of three confreres, now had few of their prerogatives. All these factors added up to an abrupt switch in modes of communication..

One who remembers this adjustment is Father David Baltz. As rector of the Monroe seminary when these changes were introduced, he had with him two co-educators.[9] Baltz, from the St. Louis area, had been ordained only four years earlier. When in Venegono as a student, he had followed the progress of the Second Vatican Council, but even with this exposure, on returning to America in 1967, he was shocked by changes at the minor seminary. From over a hundred students when he left for Italy, the student population had dropped to no more than fifty. Then in 1968, the radical transfer of minor seminarians from Cincinnati to Monroe had taken place. Baltz said, "We were taking them to a setting that really better suited our vision for a novitiate: a quiet place, out in the woods. Buried in the cemetery there were our men who had died in this province. It felt a bit like we were invading a sacred place...."

Thrust into these changes Baltz felt very young taking over as rector, "We had to reorganize the whole program...do away with [old] authority structures...develop a family type atmosphere of peers with more emphasis on community as a formative agent....The young men had their own rooms, and I had a room like their's just down the hall. There were two or three groups like this, each with ten or twelve students. Building a team approach took a lot of dialogue between the fellows and myself. They no longer related to me as the vice-rector in charge of discipline. I was more like an elder brother."[10]

In 1971, Ongaro began a series of meetings called "Conferences on Education." Intended to coordinate formation from the recruitment stage through post-ordination training, they brought together the four educators from the high school and college seminaries, two pastors, the vocation director, a lay brother, and two student representatives. Ongaro reported the results of these meetings to the Provincial Council:"formation remains considerably more difficult than it has ever been, largely because, having been forced to discard the authority-obedience model, it is faced with the necessity of carving a new path through dialogue. [It is] a very slow process demanding more time, a large dose of patience, not only from those in formation, but from all confreres."[11]

At a Conference on Education meeting in late 1971, a college student criticized the vocation director's criteria for selecting recruits,. He thought the director expected too much from high school freshmen. This exchange launched a long discussion and two points of view emerged. One held that the seminary would die unless it took in as many students as possible with the goal of at least making them good Christians. The other held that the purpose of the seminary was to develop priests, becoming a good Christian was a prerequisite for the seminary, and contemporary youth were underestimated. Arguments flew back and forth, some maintaining that the gradual process of traditional formation made long -term commitment possible, others claiming that, as the seminary was then structured, it was a ghetto restricted to a few who preached charity that they did not practice in community. In the midst of this clamor, a practical question was asked: If one assumed that the seminary structure should be retained, what could improve it? Responses came from all directions including new recruiting criteria. The present ones, it was said, were better suited to the profile of a reformatory inmate. A list of competencies required of educators included leadership skills, missionary experience, increased initiative, and a closer rapport with students. A suggestion came to open the minor seminary as a retreat house so young men could experience a more intensive Christian life on a trial basis. In the end, students conceded that the present seminary system could turn out "professional" priests, but not Christians concerned about people. The meeting turned out to be a true dialogue between the generations.

Months later, in a confidential report, Ongaro said he believed all educators were showing goodwill, despite the fact that they had limited or no formal preparation. Second, he was mainly concerned that educators were spending too much time in outside activities that left them physically or psychologically inadequate to the demands of the equipe. When he was asked whether or not he considered group formation valid, he replied, "I would never go back to the old system."[12]

In June, 1972, evaluations of both the Monroe and the Cincinnati seminary programs were reported. At Monroe, the evaluation was conducted by a member of the formation committee who interviewed individual students, individual educators, and students along with their educators. Questions concentrated on views of the traditional system versus group-system formation. Twenty-two of the twenty-five students interviewed favored the group system. But they felt the educators were not sufficiently available to them due to involvement with outside ministry. Outside the classroom, students said, contact with educators was limited to reprimands or advice on grades, and the educators' attitudes in these conferences were less than tactful. Students wanted more responsibility, more open dialogue with educators, more group activities, and the bans on smoking eliminated. The educators understood that students wanted more structure, and one admitted he had avoided it for fear of stifling group development. Team leaders agreed they may have accepted too many extra-curricular commitments, and they even admitted that this was partly due to ministry being more rewarding. But beyond these admissions, there was the sense that the educators were poorly prepared for their task, and that the group system at Monroe was deemed an encouraging experiment, not to be judged a failure after only one year.

In Cincinnati, combining college and theology students at Sacred Heart Seminary was not as beneficial as had been hoped. As a result, the Council's request to send American theology students abroad was granted. Three went to Italy and one to Spain. The General Administration urged the North American province to open an international scholasticate, but the Provincial Council responded that it lacked trained personnel to do so. Now the equipe system continued at Sacred Heart Seminary with only college students.[13] These equipes were evaluated in 1972, and the evaluator was not as conciliatory as the one sent to Monroe. He admitted that he was intentionally critical, and justified this on the basis that prior evaluations had accentuated only positive points. He reported considerable differences in the educators' personalities that affected the students, and that there was a "deplorable lack of concern with the care of the house," as well as a "selfish attitude of many students." The only positive feature he found was the prayer life.

The spiritual director of the Cincinnati seminary had not yet seen this report. Admitting some defensiveness, he claimed that any evaluation at the end of the school year was bound to be flawed since everyone was tired. The year had certainly been a trying one, and he was still in the process of learning his role in shared responsibility. When educators found themselves facing demands for which they were not professionally prepared, he said, they had little recourse lest they "lay themselves open for...rejection."

This candid admission evoked both admiration and impatience. One confrere called for better leadership. Another decried the educator's lack of organization or initiative. Again, the question of outside ministry and associations was raised as well as how important it was to have compatibility between student groups and their priest team-leaders. What was left unanswered was: what were the characteristics that made a good educator or team leader?[14] The truth few wanted to ponder was that prepared personnel were not only in short supply, but the shortage of vocations had taken its toll on the educators' morale. The enormous changes that tended to emphasize the development and autonomy of the individual student, and the unraveling of the hierarchical model, were having its effects on community life.

Almost two decades later, Father Albert Dilanni wrote about how these attempts to provide more freedom and "fraternity/intimacy/community" in the post-Vatican II era led to an "era of the divided heart." It was a time, he believed, "not entirely past, in which many of us, all of us to some degree, were *sidetracked*, distracted, not completely present to the task, unhappy."[15] [Emphasis not added] Certainly the confusion and discontent witnessed both among students and their educators at the Comboni seminaries reflected this state of affairs.

REOPENING THE NOVITIATE

A novitiate could not be evaluated since, from 1970 till 1974, it did not exist. In fact, by 1973, the North American Province had no students in vows at all. At its September meeting that year, the Provincial Council announced that a novitiate would open in 1974 at Yorkville. By spring, 1974, candidates for the post of novice master were narrowed to Father Joseph Forlani, who had come to America in 1950, was ordained in 1958, and served in the missions of Ethiopia from 1963 to 1973. By telephone, Father Agostoni agreed to send him by late summer. Council members feared this allowed too little time for preparation, but the General Administration overruled their fears, and plans began for settling the novices in Yorkville. It was a relatively private location, yet close to urban centers with opportunities for an apostolate among African Americans and the poor. It had great potential as a vocation promotion center due to its large Catholic population. Father Charles Walter, just returned to his home province, joined Forlani at Yorkville as superior of the small community.[16]

In accordance with the Vatican document "On the Renewal of Religious Life," the novitiate program was divided into discrete periods. The first six months would be an initial "desert' period." While not a total withdrawal from public activities, it would be a separation from family and friends as a new discipline. By Easter of 1975, the novices would spend a week with their families, then go for an apostolic experience with Comboni novices in Mexico. From the end of the summer until Christmas, they would experience community at a local Comboni parish or house. Another desert experience would complete their preparation for taking vows in May of 1976.[17]

When Contran was elected provincial, his confreres were still running vocation camps, hosting vocation weekends, and planning other vocation programs. Earlier, this would have produced a substantial number of candidates for the minor seminary. But in 1970, scouting for vocations demanded more time and more personnel. A vocation director was needed to organize this work that extended over the Midwest and the East and West Coasts. In early 1970, the Council asked Contran to "fight for three missionaries" as vocation workers, but no positive response came from the General Administration.

When the 1970-1971 classes opened, Council members were relieved to see that the drop in student enrollment had leveled off. There were forty-seven high school students at Monroe, and twenty-six college students and two deacons at Cincinnati. Two lay brother candidates were studying at a trade school in Northern Kentucky. That fall, two students took their first vows.[18]

On the East Coast, a vocation recruitment meeting drew virtually all the pioneers of the province: Accorsi (now returned from Italy, Oliver Branchesi (in charge of promotion work at Montclair), Charles Busetti (stationed in the San Diego area), and Remus Catellani (provincial finances). Joining them were Father Caesar Mazzolari and several other Comboni priests. Optimism ran high at this meeting with a unanimous call for a strong vocation plan in the East. The only deterrent to its development was the already heavy schedules these priests carried, and the health of others, e.g. an ailing Accorsi. On the West Coast, the vocation center at the former scholasticate in San Diego was closed. A new board of trustees at the University of San Diego wanted the building returned, and after difficult negotiations with diocesan authorities (see "Renewal and Reaction), it was decided to relinquish it to the University. The Council considered alternatives, including building on property the province owned in Rancho Bernardo, renting a house in San Diego, or combining recruitment and promotion in Los Angeles. The third alternative proved the most attractive since the Los Angeles Archdiocesan authorities were willing to accept Comboni students in their seminary.

When Father Agostoni visited the province in November, 1970, he asked that everyone "at work in the care of souls [pastor] should do his very best to assist in ... recruiting among the people they serve." The students themselves should be offered the opportunity of working in the field of recruiting.[19] But he did not offer additional missionaries for this work, although one priest was allowed to return to North America. A former vocation director in the province, Father Angelo Biancalana came back from Uganda.

Biancalana had spent five years among the Karamoja people. After learning the difficult dialect, he taught English at the Gulu minor seminary. Before returning to the U.S., he was at a primitive parish along the Ugandan border. Arriving in the United States after living in the African bush was a traumatic experience. Biancalana recalled, "I came back in 1970 having missed practically everything, Vatican II and all its consequences, the lack of vocations, and the steep decline of students in seminaries. Yes, also the social upheaval, the change, especially in the youth scene around the country." It was a struggle, he admitted, to even reenter this altered American society.

Other Comboni missionaries recalled the psychological and physical effects of moving from an intensely personal, physically demanding life, in a traditional and often isolated village of Africa, to the relatively competitive and psychologically demanding Western lifestyle. From living in a simple hut and traveling to distant missions by motorcycle, a missionary is then exposed to a highly technological society of the U.S. that moves at breakneck speeds. The simple rhythms of the bush are exchanged for ringing telephones, routine meetings, and endless demands for communication. African missions might pose dangers to life and present obstacles to travel, but the positive feedback from the people made such trials bearable. These contrasts often led missionaries to prefer their work in Africa to that in North America.

Biancalana negotiated his cultural transfer more easily by immersing himself in the Better World course given in Rome. It derived from a movement begun by Jesuit Father Lombardi.[20] In the summer of 1971, Biancalana took up responsibilities as vocation director, and by August, he had sent applications to twenty-two dioceses in the Midwest and sixteen in the East requesting permission to recruit vocations. Results were good. Comboni Missionaries could now recruit at 140 schools not counting those in the Archdiocese of Cincinnati. But intensive vocation promotion through the school year of 1971 and 1972 produced only five new students, with the total number at Monroe now down to twenty-seven, a drop of over 50% from the previous year. That fall, Biancalana, assisted by Fathers Busetti, Catellani, Tarquini, and a student, began work in Ohio, Indiana, Illinois, Kentucky and Wisconsin. They spoke at schools, organized vocation weekends, and hosted open houses at Monroe and Cincinnati.[21]

The Provincial Council repeatedly requested vocation personnel from the General Administration, citing the need as "the most urgent in the province." When few of these requests were granted, adjustments to vocation promotion had to be made. Plans for a new promotion center on the West Coast were abandoned. With fewer students at the Monroe seminary, Father John Taneburgo was transferred from Monroe to the vocation department at St. Michael's in Cincinnati. "Stealing from Peter to pay Paul" was the only option open to the province for securing vocation recruiters.

By the summer of 1972, there was an upward trend in attendance at recruiting programs. Sixty young men came to two sessions of summer vocation camp, double the number in 1971. No numbers are available for that fall's enrollment, but Biancalana and Taneburgo again worked the vocation routes with Father Bragotti helping on a part-time basis. They covered the Archdioceses of Cincinnati, Chicago, Philadelphia, Newark, Trenton, Detroit, and gave youth retreats in the Toledo diocese. Carillo worked on the East Coast.[22]

After meeting with confreres on the West Coast in early 1973, Father Agostoni told the Provincial Council that an independent vocation and promotion center in Los Angeles looked promising. He agreed to send someone to run it. The vocation work could, he said, at least initially develop in the manner of the "diaspora," with candidates followed while they remained at home. Council minutes noted that the support of all the confreres on the West Coast was necessary for such a plan to succeed. Biancalana and Taneburgo continued working through the winter and spring of 1973, and young men from the Midwest went to Monroe for vocation weekends and to open houses in Monroe and Cincinnati. The Archdiocesan Vocation Day held at Sacred Heart Seminary drew over 140 people, mostly teenagers. It seemed that young people still earnestly sought to know God's will in their lives.[23]

In May, 1973, the Comboni Vicar General, Ottorino Sina, visited the province. Formation work in the high school, he said, was going in the proper direction. He realized there was an "urgent need of more personnel" for recruiting and formation, particularly in Cincinnati. No new personnel had been allocated to the North American Province since the arrival of Biancalana two years earlier. When Sina mentioned friction in the vocation department, council members defended those involved, saying that when people were utterly frustrated, it was not fair to ask them to continue their work. At this meeting, a letter from Biancalana was read asking to be relieved as vocation director. Having followed all the avenues that normally led to seminary recruitment, and having done this with only one full-time partner, Biancalana wanted to return to Africa.[24]

Ongaro later described the situation in the 1970s, "The recruiters were very exasperated because they worked a great deal and had little or nothing to show for it. Students would indicate interest, but before long, would drop out and apply to several orders, then choose none." This was happening in other societies as well as diocesan seminaries. Although the number of Catholics was increasing, age, defections from the priesthood, and fewer people entering the seminaries meant priests were disappearing by the hundreds. Ongaro added, "In the 1950s, we had one vocation director for the entire United States, and he brought in about 25 to 30 students a year. Later, even three or four vocation directors brought in very, very few students...vocation directors burned out fast....If they were on the job for more than a few years, they became totally disaffected." Ongaro also experienced the pitfalls of burnout. In late 1973, he, too, tendered his resignation as Formation Secretary to the Provincial Council, but he was persuaded to continue for another year.[25]

Whether intentional or not, one offshoot of this rather desperate period in vocation recruiting was a blurring of the Institute's rules regarding choice of mission field. In 1971, an entire issue of the *Verona Fathers Mission* magazine was devoted to vocations. It gave several examples that tended to mislead readers about the amount of freedom a Comboni Missionary had in choosing a mission field. One article described what was available to those entering Comboni seminaries: "Off the fence, walking among the people. And what do I see? A suffering child in black Africa...behind the barbed wire of ignorance, hunger....A Latin American family only surviving, no water, cattle dying, children covered with sores....An African with hands outstretched, but with no hands... Two boys - no four boys... hoping for what they cannot have because they are tied to a system of poverty in *an American city*.... " [Emphasis added] Further on, under "Your Mission Field," was the following: "After ordination, you will be sent to the field of missionary activity which you will chose (sic). If you have selected the African continent, you may be working in Egypt or the Sudan...or in Uganda, Burundi, the Congo....If you have chosen the Americas, you may find yourself in Mexico, Brasil, Ecuador or Peru; *or you may be working with minority groups (Blacks, Indians) of the United States or Canada.*"[26] [Emphasis added]

Though perhaps unintentional, inferring that North America was a territory in which an American could exclusively serve was disingenuous. The 1969 General Chapter clearly determined that Comboni Missionaries were expected to leave their own country and serve in foreign missions for a large portion of their careers. Ambiguous references to the contrary as cited above troubled the province later when, after a brief experience in a foreign mission, an American missionary expected to return to his homeland. It is now conceded by some that promotion literature may have strayed from the rules when beleaguered vocation workers were severely tried by poor results. Unfortunately, this may have unwittingly contributed to the number of American scholastics, as well as ordained priests, leaving the Institute to incardinate in an American diocese or enroll in a diocesan seminary.

Biancalana returned to his Uganda mission, and Taneburgo was appointed vocation director. The 1973 summer vocation camps were well attended, and eighteen new students enrolled at the minor seminary. But with only seven returning, the number of students did not rise. Taneburgo's letter in *Family News* spoke eloquently of his dedication to his task. Quoting Pope Paul VI, he wrote, "God, who reserves for Himself the right to call those whom He chooses, asks, nevertheless, for the collaboration of His ministers so that youth may be helped to understand the action of heavenly grace...to bring to maturity the divine germ which has been planted in their souls." He asked the communities to pray for the goodwill of both the youth and their parents, and requested permission to bring young people into Comboni Missionary communities to learn about the society and his confreres' way of life. Avoiding the criticism some clergy lodged against materialism, parental resistance, and society in general, he put a positive focus on what could be accomplished.[27]

In the spring of 1974, Taneburgo reported how he and others had covered many dioceses and cities, including huge metropolitan centers like Chicago, and that over fifty young men had attended the vocation camp. But the number of students enrolling at the minor seminary that fall was reported as "indeed low." Continuing failure to increase enrollment at the minor seminary affected all stages of formation. Father Baltz at Monroe had to contend not only with restructuring his relationship to students, but with the fact of fewer students. He recalled that, "Each year we were losing them...from fifty to forty, to thirty-five, to thirty, and whatever it was when I left [1974], maybe about twenty-five....we could no longer keep up our internal program of education. We closed our in-house teaching program, and made use of the high school...run by the Holy Cross Fathers...I began to teach math there..."

At the Council meeting in October, 1974, the subject of Taneburgo's request to go to the foreign missions was presented. His reason was the excessive stress resulting from responsibilities as vocation director, responsibilities he had carried with no full-time collaborator for over a year. At the Council's request, Taneburgo agreed to continue his work till the end of the 1974-1975 school year, then he would be granted a mission assignment.[28] Taneburgo had refused to blame outside forces as he worked to recruit candidates, but the influences being blamed by others such as fewer large families, and lack of discipline among the young, were perhaps symptoms of greater forces at work. These forces were thought to be linked to the widespread lack of commitment by individuals to any long term relationship, whether a religious vocation or a marriage.

In 1981, Father John Staudenmaier, S.J., professor of history at Detroit University, introduced a theory of why commitment became more difficult. He believed that the erosion of commitment to religious vocations, or to married life, is best understood as a reaction to a set of technologically related events. He saw these events as having a "cumulative effect on young people" that "cast their interior lives into an area dominated by a single tension," and he named the elements of this tension that shaped young people and produced a despair that could be massive, overwhelming, and debilitating. They were: 1) World War II; 2) the proliferation of nuclear weapons; 3) the exploration of space; and 4) recent evidence that our energy intensive technological systems put pressure on global resources. World War II proved how technology could take the form of the demonic, how sophisticated engineering could lead to the death camps of Nazis Germany and how the atomic bomb could put an end to all life on our planet. In addressing formation leaders, Staudenmaier said, "Once it is possible for me to think that a...weapon system can destroy the planet rather than a city, my imagination will never be the same again about the planet." Space travel, he said, and photos of the earth, showed how exquisite, yet how small and vulnerable our planet is. And a growing awareness of the limits to our natural resources forces attention to technology's effects beyond a national scale to a planetary one.[29]

Staudenmaier believed these four events provided the mature person with reason both to hope and despair. Those in religious life had to understand that young people were now from a culture dominated by global forces. To be born under their influence, he suggests, affects the ability to believe in an enduring reality or that a single individual can impact society. This makes it difficult to believe anything is related to the past. Helping a young religious toward commitment, Staudenmaier believed, was related to having reverence for the story of his or her life. This "story," or ability to relate life events as connected, leads to connections between the spiritual and public life that allows a person to make a commitment. And only through this process can young people develop hope that their future matters.[30]

For years, those in religious and diocesan seminaries believed they were wrestling with certain symptomatic losses: of religious conformity, of respect for authority, of stable community life, of a generous stream of vocations. Staudenmaier suggested that it is much more complicated, i.e., a total reorientation of individuals to a world driven by technological forces they cannot control. If he is right, then the value of caring human communication, whether in a religious society or among lay people, may be the critical means to building and maintaining Christian hope and commitment.

19. Renewal and Reaction

Besides the frustration associated with formation and vocation work, the Provincial Council had to deal with difficult administrative issues. These included reformulation of provincial guidelines, resolving differences over personnel and mission with the General Administration, and, in 1970, a disappointing outcome of negotiations with the Diocese of San Diego.

A CONTRACT IN DISPUTE

In 1961, the Comboni Missionaries signed the contract that allowed them to build a scholasticate on the University of San Diego's campus. In 1966, after Bishop Furey succeeded Bishop Buddy, this contract was renewed for another five years. In 1970, a year before the contract was due to expire, Bishop Maher, Furey's successor, disagreed with Father Contran on the interpretations of the contract's terms.

The 1961 contract had permitted Comboni Missionaries to sell to a third party both the scholasticate building they constructed as well as the land on which it stood. If, however, the diocese wanted the property returned, it agreed to pay Comboni Missionaries $110,000 less one fortieth that amount for each year that elapsed since the "improvement," or scholasticate building, was completed. Bishop Furey had told his attorney, "According to...the termination of the Lease to the Sons of the Sacred Heart [the missionaries legal name] the latter have the option to purchase the ground on which their *domus formata* stands. This is one element of the proposed arrangement to which I do not agree..." Furey's point was legitimate. His wish was honored, and he approved a new contract with Comboni Missionaries extending their lease another five years. The new agreement revoked the Comboni Missionaries right to sell or purchase the property on which the scholasticate was built. It also revoked their right to be reimbursed for the "improvements" they built on the property. In the inscrutable language of lawyers, however, it added a clause that seemed to reinstate the missionaries right to compensation. If the University of San Diego terminated the contract at any time during the five-year extension period, it had to pay the missionaries a sum equal to the cost of improvements ($110,000) less one fortieth of this sum for every year that elapsed since the completion of the improvements.

In 1970, after Bishop Maher succeeded Furey, an argument was put forward on whether or not the Diocese of San Diego owed the Comboni Missionaries anything at all past the contract's expiration date in 1971. On the other hand, if Comboni Missionaries chose to vacate their building before this expiration date, it would pay them $20,000 (less than a quarter of what the above formula provided). At stake was a large building constructed in the elaborate Spanish Renaissance architectural style required for campus buildings. In comparison to the cement block, connect-the-boxes style that Comboni Missionaries built elsewhere in North America, the scholasticate building was palatial.

Father Contran, found himself in a "Catch-22" situation. If he waited until 1971, he would receive no money for the scholasticate building. If he accepted the diocese's offer, he would receive only a fraction of its cost. Furthermore, he was disquieted when he discovered a discrepancy between the contract that Cincinnati lawyers had prepared for Father Todesco in 1966, and the one that the San Diego Diocese quoted from, or, indeed, the one Contran found in his own files. Contran relayed his concerns to Bishop Maher, pointing out that "Two drafts of a new contract were prepared by our lawyers, one in Cincinnati and one in San Diego. But...the copy signed was strictly the one prepared under directives from Bishop Furey, and neither lawyer [of ours] had a chance to see it." Secondly, there should not be any impediment to Comboni Missionaries renewing the contract for another five years, since "it was understood in the first contract, and there is nothing in the second [that] seems to contradict it."

Contran was inferring that, if the depreciation rate was set at one fortieth of the repayment amount, this meant that the right to renew the lease should extend over a forty year period. He expected, therefore, that an impartial hearing of his interpretation in the courts would prevail.[1] An attorney in San Diego agreed with him. In a letter to the diocesan attorney, he wrote, "It is clear as a matter of law that if these parties did not have the special relationship of Bishop and Priest, and the matter was subject to litigation or arbitration, the contract would be reformed according to the intention of the parties, and the bishop or University would be required to pay a fair consideration for the building." He added, however, that the missionaries had no desire to litigate the matter...but instead wanted him to re-consider it.[2] He appealed to Maher for a sense of justice. Maher stood fast. The diocesan attorney maintained that, not only were the Comboni Missionaries not being forced out of their building by the diocese or the University ahead of the contract's expiration, but "the University has little, if any, use for the improvements placed on the property by the Sons of the Sacred Heart..."[3]

This last claim lacks credibility when, at that time, student enrollment was crowding college and university buildings all over the United States. In 1968, Bishop Quinn had already asked for the scholasticate building, but Todesco wanted to keep it for a potential minor seminary. Additional evidence points to the fact that the scholasticate building was indeed thought to be an asset by University and diocesan officials. In December, 1969, the University of San Diego President, Monsignor John E. Baer, wrote to Bishop Maher that he had read the 1966 lease and had determined that: "...if the diocese terminated the contract between now and March 31, 1970, the payment required [of the diocese] would be $88,400 according to my calculations. Also, if such termination were planned, we should probably consult our attorney, as I am predicating my conclusion solely on my own reading of the document."

Baer added that after a conversation with another priest on campus, "we have both agreed that there are decided advantages in a proposal to move the seminary from De Sales Hall to the area now occupied by the Verona Fathers [Comboni Missionaries]. The construction of residential quarters for the seminarians would be a necessity. But the seminary would realize at least two major advantages: a complex actually designed for and functional as a seminary; and continuance of proximity to the University and the Library without constant undesirable interruption of the seminary community life.

"The advantages to the University are even greater: use of the most centrally located campus building for administration and office space; and temporary use of rooms for resident students (pending construction of new campus housing) that could generate close to $50,000 annual income in room fees..."[4]

Not having this information, the Comboni Missionaries had little alternative but to vacate the building before 1971. They received $20,000 for this large and elaborate structure. On the diocese's part, it had acted according to the letter of the law, but not the spirit. On the Comboni Missionaries' part, Father Todesco had apparently lacked prudence in 1966 when he signed, or had signed, a contract that his own attorneys had not drawn up. The outcome of this disagreement between the Comboni Missionaries and the Diocese of

San Diego on the interpretation of a legal document illustrates the vulnerability of religious societies serving under diocesan jurisdiction.

A DOCUMENT AS A TARGET

In early 1972, Contran was re-elected to a second term as provincial. He was joined by four new Provincial Council members, Fathers Baltz, Mazzolari, Ongaro, and Saoncella. In a letter to his confreres, Contran set out his objectives for his second term: the continued study of renewal documents with emphasis on communal prayer, and open communication and cooperation. To his Council, he presented other initiatives. Besides establishing a U.S. novitiate (which, as noted above, would take place two years later), and preparing for the Pan American Conference in January of 1973, a provincial directory would be written. A committee of three was charged with preparing it: Fathers Januarius Carillo, Kenneth Dahlen, and Mario Ongaro.[5]

When the Comboni Institute's revised Constitution, *The Rule of Life*, was eventually published, it explained the purpose and parameters of the provincial directory. But in 1972, it was not yet available. As a result, there were as many expectations of what a directory should do as there were members of the province. It was a daunting task, but the priests in charge of it produced a draft in three months. It was forwarded to members of the province for discussion at the Easter assembly.[6] The eighteen page document included ten sections: Preface, Introduction, Community Life, Pastoral Activity, Mission Promotion, Vocation Promotion, Mission Secretariat, Missionary Formation, Administration of Province, and the Economics of the Province. The reception it met at the Easter meeting was less than cordial.

The "Preface," someone claimed, had "failed miserably. It was nothing more than "empty words," and it was "too cold and legislative." Another said, "The Introduction should make clear the main goal of the U.S. It is sad to hear every day that our Society is not doing its real work in the U.S... It's very frustrating for some confreres." Others attacked the phrase, "little effort is made to justify the norms, [presented] because their justification is found in the Chapter Documents, which they interpret." They pointed out that some justification was warranted, since "interpretation" of the Chapter Documents admits of other interpretations. The section on "Pastoral Life" touched an even deeper nerve, that of mission in the United States. It stated, "The apostolic activity of the U.S. Province embraces primarily the Blacks, then the Indians and the poor; no other apostolate should be accepted or retained permanently....black parishes will be sought after, not merely accepted when offered." Though this statement reflected both the Chapter Documents and the views of the Father General, many faulted it. One confrere believed it compromised the Institute's "true" mission to Africa. Another said only "Third World" countries constituted opportunities for a true Comboni Missionary apostolate. A third asked, "Do Blacks like having white missionaries? How prepared are we to deal with 'Black Power?'"

Criticism of the directory draft went to the heart of troubles in the province. Founded in the turmoil of war, unscathed by the war's bloodletting and destruction in Europe, situated in the relatively (then) wealthy nation of the United States, the province undoubtedly received its share of both gratitude and disdain from many in the Comboni Institute. Such ambivalence reflected not only differences with the North American province, but deep reservations about the United States itself. Its mores, pluralism, and often overbearing international presence made it a country that even many of its own "loved to hate." Could such a nation warrant the precious personnel of the Comboni Missionary Institute? Many thought not. But was sending personnel to the province the same as contributing it to a nation some, fairly or not, held culpable? This was the distinction that was not, or could not, be made. Within this context fits the double standard to which the North American province was held: on the one hand, undeserving of personnel because its mission status was in question; on the other, pushed to expand its promotional work and expected (and willing) to raise large sums of money for the society's work.

But even this last contribution was often held in disdain. Commenting on the directory, a confrere lashed out at what he believed was a waste of personnel in the United States where, according to him, there were communities "that are exclusively money making...people in parishes or work financially profitable, but practically foreign to our missionary commitment..." At almost the opposite end of this view was one from a confrere who worked many years in Africa as well as in the States, "Is this chapter [on pastoral work] the shortest because it is less important...or because we do not know what to say....?" Thirty years of pastoral experience with Blacks and Indians in the States, he said, should have produced some words of advice. "There are plenty of guidelines for pastoral work in Africa; let us make ours for America."

The directory draft was not only a scapegoat for disagreement on the mission of the province, it became a target for all the frustration, discontent, and sense of drift felt by its members. Those looking for new inspiration and motivation chafed at words like "efficiency" and "uniformity." For younger confreres, anything was still possible, more seminaries, better and more publications, and more vocations among Americans. Some wanted a stronger community spirit, yet called for greater freedom. For all who wanted to leave the American province behind, there were those who wanted the society to truly "insert itself into American culture." Older members felt their hard work for the congregation in the 1940s, 1950s, and 1960s was now overlooked and undervalued. In summary, the provincial directory was expected to solve every difficulty, heal every wound, mend all divisions, and "fire up" its readers to greater achievements than even its strongest critics had attained.[7]

In *Out of Chaos*, Gerald Arbuckle aptly describes the state of frustration that exploded over the directory draft. Postulating several stages that religious societies passed through on their way to "refounding," he described how the stages that are marked by confusion and disorientation, may be followed by the renewal chapter. But this chapter will not necessarily bring new tranquility. On the contrary, it can bring, he said, utter chaos, and this chaos would continue until true discernment was completed and irrelevancies put aside.[8] In the spring of 1973, Comboni Missionaries in North America were at an early stage of this discernment process, and they could not agree which issues were relevant and which were not.

At the Easter, 1973, Provincial Assembly, the directory draft was rejected and a new committee elected. This time not three confreres, but five were to produce a directory draft: Fathers Bragotti, Branchesi, Dahlen, Della Rocco, and Mazzolari.[9]

OPPOSING VIEWS

If there was disagreement among members of the North American province, so was there disagreement between the Province and the General Council. On his first visit in 1970, Superior General Agostoni told a gathering of confreres that the main purpose of their work in the United States and Canada was promotion and vocations. It was, he said, the "greatest contribution they could make to the "missionary character of our Society and its missions..." No one could miss the point of his excluding pastoral work. If they did, his intentions were underscored at a Provincial Council meeting where he recommended removing two of the four priests then serving the California Indian Missions.[10] This request would have returned the Indian missions to its status under the Franciscans before 1948, even then known as inadequate.

In 1970, the General also suggested that the Council review its policy of publishing the kind of full-fledged magazine that other missionary societies in America circulated. He believed a newsletter would suffice, with more information about vocation centers. To whom this newsletter would go, and how it would attract, at the same time, both adult benefactors and vocation candidates in the United States was not addressed. Lacking familiarity with the enormous diversity in religious, racial, and cultural values, Agostoni's advisors could not have understood what was successful in the United States. It is also possible that, given the hegemony of an "African imperative" in the society, the General Administration was not so much expressing a rejection of work in America, as suggesting it was out of step with mainstream opinion in the society. After discussing the matter, members of the Provincial Council came to a decision. "During his visit [in November]," they noted, "Fr. General suggested we review our position in the missions of Pala and Santa Ysabel...the Council is of the opinion that, for the time being, and unless things change drastically in the personnel situation, it is better to let things stay as they are."[11] Publication of the magazine continued.

The year 1972 was not an easy one for the American province. It had received no new personnel since 1970, and it had lost at least two capable missionaries, Father Grande, called from Canada to the missions, and Brother Denis Wilkinson, who left for Rome to study for the priesthood. Three members of the province were seriously ill, Fathers Della Rocco, Paolucci, and Pazzaglia. Even Contran suffered a bout with kidney stones. When in February of 1973, Agostoni attended a Provincial Council meeting, he was asked to express what the feeling of the confreres at large was about the U.S. Province. While he acknowledged things were difficult everywhere, he said the impression of the province in terms of productivity and type of apostolate was rather poor. He quickly added that this was partly due to insufficient information about the province, but he believed this image would not improve unless work among the Blacks in the U.S. was intensified. Pastoral work in well-formed parishes would not enhance the image of the Comboni presence in the U.S. Furthermore, the General Curia expected the province to establish vocation centers on the East and West Coast, and proceed firmly toward establishing both a novitiate and an international scholasticate.[12] Fewer members in the province had increased financial support for the congregation in the 1970s, and they had moved forward in formation renewal as well as other areas. Given this, Agostoni's assessment appears rather severe.

The Canadian foundation was another point of divergence. In 1970, the Provincial Council wanted "the Superior General to clear our relation[ship] with Canada, namely their status in relation to the U.S. province [and] appoint an observer to study the present Canadian situation, its functioning and general goals."[13] With Agostoni present, the difficulties concerning the French language and culture, lack of precise directives from the General Administration, and the need for better programs and increased initiative were raised. It was later agreed that the General Council would spell out its expectations, and a councillor from Canada would be a spokesman to the U. S. Council. But a confidential memo noted that not only Spagnolo, but also Father Grande, would soon leave for Africa. Upon their departure, only one priest, Father Confalonieri, would remain as religious superior at the Brossard community.[14]

In 1971, the parish of Good Shepherd had been formed for the English-speaking people of Brossard (then 20% of the population), and the chapel of the Comboni center opened to the parishioners. Father Ghirotto, who had pioneered the Brossard community, returned to America apparently restored to good health, was assigned pastor of the new parish. Ghirotto's tenure there was brief, however, for the assessment of his health had been optimistic. After a few months, acting alone as pastor of the new parish took its toll, and Father Alfonse Rossi, who had been in the Sudanese missions, replaced him. Ghirotto was sent to work at the General Secretariat in Rome.[15]

A note from the Provincial Council in 1972 reported, "After the departure of Fr. Grande, every effort to replace him has failed. The situation in Brossard is rather strained, and it needs clarification and help." When Agostoni visited the following winter, he advised that instead of "pushing forward" with more personnel or more communities, thought should be given to "consolidation" and working through a system of the "diaspora" by following seminary candidates at home until the end of college. Then they would complete a period of postulancy before entering the novitiate. Greater vocational appeal, Agostoni directed, should come from increased "vocational dimension," although what that phrase meant was not defined.[16]

When the Vicar General, Ottorino Sina, attended a Provincial Council meeting in May, 1973, it was decided to suspend circulation of the recruiting magazine "Baobab" for young Canadians, but publication of "Echo Missionaire" would be continued. Rossi remained as pastor at Good Shepherd, but two more missionaries in Canada would be sent to the foreign missions. Some of Sina's remarks about the North American province were conciliatory, others less so. He felt that the hard-working confreres in California needed updating courses; and he also offered to send someone from Europe to give them retreats. When asked for his observations about the province, Sina first admitted the urgent personnel needs for recruiting and formation, then asked Council members whether they believed work in black parishes and among Indians was indeed valid for Comboni Missionaries. He had heard the views expressed on the provincial directory draft, i.e., that the Comboni presence was not needed in the United States. Council members assured him that such work was definitely in keeping with the society's purpose. Sina further observed that "materially life in the U.S. is a rather comfortable life, or at least in a comfortable style." Council members replied that "while it may appear to be a comfortable life, psychologically the work brought tension and constant strain..." It would seem that the many missionaries forced to leave the province due to stress and ill health should have made this fact evident.

When Sina expressed concern about the existence of one-man communities in the province, it is not clear that he made a connection between the shortage of personnel that led to one-man communities, and its outcome: that these communities became, de facto, unable to participate in family councils and community prayer.[17] Although both Agostoni and Sina offered valid points about the province, some of their comments lacked understanding of the United States, its size, diversity, and culture. But if Todesco had to admit that he, after ten years in the country, never understood it, perhaps it was unrealistic to expect Agostoni and Sina to do so.

VIEW FROM THE TOP

Agostoni's perceptions and opinions about the North American Province may seem harsh but, in truth, the province would prove to be the least of his concerns. If Contran, in 1969, was elected provincial of a province undergoing major crises, Agostoni took over the entire Comboni Institute when crises were virtually endemic on several continents. Not yet fifty years old when elected Superior General, he was recognized as a missionary of superior talent and accomplishments. He served during one of the most unstable periods in both Church and secular history, and the renewal Chapter had essentially written the agenda for many of his obligations. He was to oversee the new structures of life and government throughout the Institute including developing secretariats, international scholasticates, and initiating meetings with other religious Institutes. This work would unfold on four continents: Africa, Latin America, North America and Western Europe. Even as vocations in Western provinces diminished, new formation methods had to be developed. About these changes, Agostoni later noted, "The past was

258

Defining Mission

characterized by the maximum demand, even to the extent of belittling the needs of the person. During this period [1969-1979] instead, maximum respect prevailed, belittling the necessary demands."[18]

In the early 1970s, Agostoni had to deal with serious threats to African missions. Beginning in 1972, Idi Amin, president of Uganda, began denying entry permits to Comboni missionaries. Expulsion of those already in the country was imminent, and before Agostoni left office, Uganda would claim five Comboni martyrs. In Mozambique, guerilla warfare was being waged against the Portuguese controlled government. When Comboni missionaries denounced the injustices of the Colonial government, and asked for recognition of the liberation movements and rights of Mozambique people to independence, the Comboni regional superior and twelve confreres were deported. In Burundi, Comboni missionaries contended with the government over the massacre of 250,000 Hutu people in 1972. This led to deportation of all Comboni missionaries.

Due to events in Uganda, and the need to pull Comboni missionaries out of that country, commitments were made to a Kenya diocese in 1971. Over three years, these commitments grew to sixteen communities with forty confreres. Then the sad state of the Indios in Southern Mexico was recognized, and missionaries from Baja California were sent to work with them. In accordance with the 1969 Chapter, small groups of missionaries in Zaire, Togo, Central African Republic, and Ethiopia were reinforced with missionaries and raised to the status of autonomous regions. The purpose of doing this was to have missions in nations of similar languages close to one another so that if missionaries were expelled from one, they could easily move to the other.[19]

Besides overseeing progress in the Institute's renewal, dealing with the post-Colonial struggle for power in African missions, and managing personnel in times of great instability, Agostoni was involved in reuniting the two branches of Comboni Missionaries, the Italian with the German. In the summer of 1973, the German branch held a General Chapter that confirmed the desirability of reunion. Agostoni then sent a letter to members of the Italian congregation reinforcing commitment to reunion, and declaring that active commitment to it was a must for all Comboni missionaries. A complicated order of events would unfold to effect this reunion, and Agostoni would follow it to its conclusion.[20] This short summary only touches on the complexity of Agostoni's position as Superior General of the Comboni Missionaries. But it offers reasons why, with a plethora of issues facing him, the Superior General may not have held the needs of the North American Province among his highest priorities.

CITING THE EVIDENCE

As 1973 progressed, five of the most experienced young priests were called to the foreign missions while only three were promised to return. In late summer, another relatively young American, who had been ailing, died of a heart attack. Forty-four year old Father Vincent Della Rocco had been in the United States Air Force and served in Korea and the Philippines before entering the Comboni Missionaries' novitiate. Ordained in 1960, he spent ten years in Uganda both as pastor and teacher. In 1965, he was in charge of the United States Relief Services for Uganda, and six years later, he was assigned to vocation work in the United States. He began organizing a Mission Secretariat, which he was forced to abandon when heart problems surfaced.[21] The depletion of personnel in North America became chronic.

By the end of 1973, Contran and his Council decided to act. If Agostoni, as he had suggested, needed more information on the province, they would provide it. In a document titled "The Province of the United States - the Last Four Years, 1970-1973," a series of requests denied were listed:: "March 10, 1970, The Provincial is charged with asking Rome for personnel for vocations and formation;" "April 12, 1971, We ask to [be allowed to] send the [theology] students to Rome for lack of personnel;" "October 5, 1971, We are waiting for the nomination of a master of novices [by the General Administration];" " February 28, 1972, The Council...states that our need for personnel should be presented to Rome...so that they may become aware of our needs for vocations and formation...;" "May 21, 1973, [Assistant General] Fr. Sina himself... acknowledges the urgent need for more personnel for vocations and formation."

Scarcity of personnel, it said, had slowed down the growth of promotion centers and made such plans "a dead letter." Yorkville, where the possibility for vocations and promotion was excellent, was cited as such a loss. In 1970, seminaries in the East and West were abandoned for lack of personnel. Despite this, the General Administration had still called for an Eastern and Western center. It also expected more personnel to work among Blacks, and the opening of both a novitiate and an international scholasticate.

The report listed the missionaries called from the province after January, 1970: (Vittorio) Agostini, Cometto, Baiani, Turchetti, Ghirotto, Grande, Valente, Catellani, Pax, Paolucci, Gerth, Erbisti, Spagnolo, Jansen, Conway,

Noventa, and Bellezze. Neither Fathers Todesco or Fornasari returned to the province after the 1969 General Chapter. Two confreres, Paletti and Della Rocco, had died. Six others had asked for exclaustration. This brought the number of priests who no longer worked in the province to twenty-seven. Added to this were seven newly ordained priests who were called to the missions. Only four replacements had come to replace those lost, and among those was Father Angelo Biancalana now due to return to the missions. At the time of this report, thirty-two priests were working in the province at an average age of forty-eight years. They served sixteen communities including seven parishes, two seminaries (not including the proposed novitiate), two sets of administrative offices, and five promotion centers.

It was pointed out that rotation was necessary "for the ones who have worked and increased the strength of the province," and a good inculturation in the Anglo-Saxon world was required of new people. Finally, the report concluded with, "It may sound like a trite recurring theme. But the only need that the province has at the present is a reinforcement of personnel. As long as this is not done, it would be unfair to expect greater results."[22]

Even though this report sent to Father Agostoni in late 1973 did not refer to expulsions, wars, or massacres, it did speak of something vital to the Institute. The U.S. province was in the midst of a crisis in morale that could lead to a potential loss not only of its future development, but of its ability to function as a province with strength or energy.

TOWARD RECONCILIATION

When Agostoni visited the province in January, 1974, he brought with him a note of cordiality and understanding. The Superior General was more supportive of his confreres and their situation. He reminded Council members that the need for personnel was shared by many provinces of the Society, and he brought with him a clarification of mission work in the United States, the tone of which reflected a broader understanding of the province. Work in the black apostolate was still valid, he said, and this was understood to be true even though the "environment and circumstances are different from those of other mission areas." Furthermore he pointed out that, "The criterion for any choice is that missionary work be needed wherever we accept apostolate... we should look also for the likelihood of being able to make the local church more aware of some special need of the people of God..."[23]

When he was told that the second committee elected to draft a directory had not started "any practical course of action." Agostoni explained that the directory should provide "specific directives," serve as the "by-laws" for a province, contain a clear and brief statement of goals, and define policies. It should describe the provincial secretariats and specify points necessary for community life in the States. Following these comments, the Council appointed Father Caesar Mazzolari to draft another directory, "using all the help he deems necessary [and] following the suggestions of Father General..."[24]

It seems some attempt was made by Agostoni and Contran to reconcile differences. On his part, Contran addressed a letter to members of the province highlighting Pope Paul IV's call for a year of reconciliation. He quoted the Major Superiors of Religious' admonition to bend extra effort toward a "unity of minds and hearts."[25] However, this did not mitigate the fact that, besides losing personnel to the missions, before the end of 1975, students and priests were completely lost to the society: a theology student asked for dispensation of vows, two priests asked for laicization, and another incardinated in a U.S. diocese. There was also the sudden death of a beloved confrere who spent many years in the African missions, then many more years in the American province. On July 3, 1975, Father Innocent Simoni, on his way to Italy for a vacation, suffered a massive stroke while waiting for his flight at Kennedy Airport.[26]

TAKING STOCK

In the fall of 1974, Father Charles Walter, then serving as superior of the newly opened novitiate at Yorkville, was elected a Delegate to the General Chapter. By early 1975, the Provincial Directory finally reached a draft stage as a set of "Renewal Documents" thanks to Father Mazzolari.[27] A "Report to the General Chapter" included the achievements, disappointments, requirements, and contributions of the province from 1970 to 1975. It even gave the size of the United States (5,000,000 square miles), its population (212 million), and the fact, that unlike a number of countries in Europe, poverty existed in socially depressed areas of the U.S. due to its highly competitive economics and "a fast and often ruthless pace of life."The civil rights movement and the Vietnam War protests had deeply divided the whole nation, and the financial crises of the mid-seventies led to higher unemployment which had "shaken the sense of security and self-reliance of the people."

The number of students were said to be ten at the minor seminary, nine in the college community, and two candidates at the novitiate opened the year before. Five theology students from the U.S. were studying in Rome, Uganda, and Spain. In formation, the Conference on Education meetings may have been unorthodox by Chapter Documents standards, but they had served to bring together members and kept educators from developing a ghetto mentality.

Some background was given about the origins of parish work: how the Indian missions were accepted to start the work of the Comboni Missionaries in North America and to support missions in Baja California; how Our Lady of Guadalupe had been a Mexican migrants' church that led to entrance into the Los Angeles archdiocese; how, in Cincinnati, the black parish of St. Anthony's was exchanged for a white parish, St. Michael's, only when black churches in the West End were closing. Similar explanations were given about Canadian parishes. With some dissembling, Georgia was said to have been closed in 1970 because "work among the Blacks was almost non-existent."

A financial report showed contributions to the General Administration just short of half a million dollars, not including over one million dollars sent to the missions, most of which went to Sudan ($414,630) and Uganda ($98,444).

Regarding vows, new interpretations of obedience had produced a keener sense of responsibility for some; for others, it had lessened a sense of accountability. Perceiving chastity as a means of dedication to people, without preference or exception, had slowly gained ground, and self-discipline recognized as favoring emotional freedom and the capacity to love everyone. This led to "greater spontaneity and openness in interpersonal relationships with the resulting risks." A search for new meaning to poverty ...in the North American Province was described as "service, sharing, siding with the oppressed in their fight for justice, availability, and work."

The report emphasized hope and optimism in a province, and added that a proposal for an international scholasticate would be presented to the General Administration and the General Chapter. It noted that, "Cooperation with the general administration and the missions had been significant though painful. It was significant not only in contributions, but especially with the nineteen members who left the province without replacement. It was painful because the decrease of one third in personnel has hurt the province...."[28]

Father Sergio Contran, and Provincial Council members could leave their posts with some satisfaction. Elected after a decade of crises in their province, they had been questioned about its legitimacy both by those within it and those without. Yet they continued to work with diligence and perseverance.

The seeds of renewal they planted would take time to grow, and some would lie cold in the soil of time. But a semblance of order would appear in the next decade, though not, perhaps, as it had appeared in earlier years. Those years belonged to a different age, a different time in the history of religious life and of the province.

20. Working to Survive

December, 1975, would bring a new provincial. Father Sergio Contran had left behind a strong legacy of renewal in formation and in the structure of the province. A sense of empowerment of the individual was found in the yearly assemblies and meetings. But there was also an undercurrent of rebellion, in part resulting from years of suppressed frustration.

At a special meeting before the provincial election, Fathers Archie Fornasari and Charles Walter outlined the effect that renewal documents had on the election. Fornasari spoke of the progress made in renewal. Walter addressed two other issues. The first was the change in the interpretation of the word "mission." Before the Second Vatican Council and the Chapter of renewal, mission territories were entrusted by the Holy See to the Congregation, and no matter where he was sent, when a confrere left his native land he was presumed to be going to "mission." In 1969, the Vatican determined that all mission territories were to be recognized as local churches. What defined "mission" now was whether the mission of the Church was fulfilled. Walter wanted to lay to rest any ambivalence about ministry in the United States; Comboni missionaries who had served the mission of the Church had served as true missionaries.

The second issue Walter addressed was related to the first. With the changed meaning of mission came a new relationship between the Comboni General Administration and its provinces. To maintain its specific missionary identity, it was now more important for the society's members to follow the main thrust of the congregation. Otherwise they, or their province, could become isolated from the congregation's charism. Therefore, the autonomy of Comboni Missionary provinces did not function like that of religious orders, e.g., the Dominicans or Franciscans. Comboni provinces were more fluid in practice, but they were not independent entities. Instead they had a relationship of co-responsibility with the General Administration.[1]

On December 29, 1975, ballots for a provincial were counted. Thirty-six of the thirty-eight of those returned went to Fathers Charles Busetti and Mario

Ongaro, with Busetti leading Ongaro by two votes. In January, Fornasari and Ongaro were elected as provincial councilors, and according to custom, two other councilors were appointed by the provincial and the elected councilors. They were Father Joe Bragotti and Brother Bernie Pratt.[2]

In the three years that Father Busetti headed the province, progress would be made on several fronts. An International Scholasticate would be opened in Chicago; the goals of pastoral work would be clarified; and American-born Comboni missionaries would assume more positions of authority. But the struggle for renewed purpose was slow in developing. What stimulated it perhaps more than any other was the resurrection of a scholasticate in North America.

THE INTERNATIONAL SCHOLASTICATE OF CHICAGO

FOUNDING CATHOLIC THEOLOGICAL UNION.
In the early 1960s, the "Decree on the Training of Priests" presented a more humane and enlightened approach to the preparation of priests for ministry. It outlined general principles, with each country developing a program of priestly formation adapted to its special needs and spirit. In the United States this document energized leaders of religious societies, for it offered an incentive to improve the education of future priests and to move toward a new form of training them. This was critical since, in some seminaries, deficiencies had developed. One area in need of remedy was the fact of relatively small numbers of students in some theology schools, often in rural rather than urban areas. In 1965-66, for example, there were 169 Roman Catholic theologates, most with fewer than fifty students. These seminaries often had such a small faculty that its members carried heavy teaching loads. Course selections offered few if any electives, and the size of the student body allowed little interaction with a more diverse group.

In his history of the Catholic Theological Union, Paul Bechtold, C.P., pointed out that perhaps the most critical issue for seminary training at the theology level was, "By and large the Catholic seminaries were not accredited [and this] did not help the self image of the student. Nor did the seminary have the external validation that motivates education excellence." He added that lack of accreditation also caused "many difficulties when a seminarian or priest tried to enroll in a college or university for graduate work, or to teach in a college or secondary school." Bechtold wrote that most significantly, "until 1966, no Catholic seminary was a member of the American Association of Theological Schools...." the officially recognized accrediting agency for theological schools and seminaries. This lack of Catholic membership was not due to bias, but to the fact that the seminaries had not applied.[3]

Aware of these deficiencies, informed educators began to look at how collaboration might maximize educational resources. They wanted to locate near a university (possibly near a Protestant seminary for ecumenical reasons), and in an urban setting where field experience was available. They also wanted to assure that both their students and programs would qualify for professional and regional accreditation.

Meetings to explore how their objectives for theology training could be met included Benedictine, Franciscan, Passionist, and Servite representatives. A dynamic group, it attracted like-thinking leaders of men's religious congregations that focussed on a combined seminary institute in the vicinity of the University of Chicago. By January, 1965, Cardinal Albert Meyer, Archbishop of Chicago was told about this initiative, but it was under his successor, Archbishop Cody, that it was able to open. Bechtold recalled that even, in the summer of 1967, when the school was still on the drawing board, the Provincials and some of their consultors began to function as trustees. These trustees represented the Servites of Mary, the Franciscans, and the Passionists. A *Memorandum of Agreement* was drawn up to pool their resources, and the new seminary was named Catholic Theological Union at Chicago (CTU). Classes began with 105 students on October 1, 1968. The following year, the Divine Word Missionaries joined the CTU.[4]

COMBONI MISSIONARIES AND CTU.

Father Peter Tarquini, Superior at the Yorkville community in 1970, was one of the first Comboni missionaries to contact Catholic Theological Union. He and a student visited CTU and were impressed with what they saw. Tarquini later returned with Father Contran, then provincial, and Father Fornasari, then Assistant General of the society.

Father Charles Walter's interest in CTU began when he was stationed at a Comboni mission in South Africa. There he met Father Carroll Stuhlmueller, C.P., a biblical scholar from CTU. Stuhlmueller was in South Africa teaching a course for missionaries, and Walter took him on a tour of the Comboni missions. In 1974, when Walter returned to the U. S. as superior at Yorkville, he arranged for the novices to take a course in biblical studies at Chicago's Archdiocesan Center for Continuing Education. There he again met Stuhlmueller who was giving the lectures; he later took Walter on a tour of CTU. Back at Yorkville, Walter discussed with Father Forlani the idea of initiating a new scholasticate in the province by joining CTU. A proposal about this could be sent to the upcoming General Chapter. After consulting with (then) president of Catholic Theological Union, Paul Bechtold, Walter drafted this proposal which the Provincial Council approved. When Walter was elected a representative to the General Chapter, he took with him his confreres' enthusiasm for the new scholasticate. At the Chapter he was elected Assistant General, and in that capacity he saw the proposal through to its conclusion. On November 5, 1975, the General Council of the Comboni Missionaries approved the opening of an international theologate in the U.S. with Catholic Theological Union of Chicago as the school its students would attend. Contran, as outgoing provincial, notified CTU that Comboni students would enroll the following school year.[5]

A building at 5512 Hyde Park Drive, within walking distance of CTU, became available. It was purchased by the Comboni Missionaries of North America, and in September of 1976, fourteen students, from Italy, Portugal, Spain, Mexico, and the U.S., began their studies at CTU. With them were Fathers Archie Fornasari and Mario Casella as their directors. Fornasari would maintain a long association with CTU as one of its professors.[6] Three years after its founding, the Comboni International Scholasticate at Chicago developed into a thriving community, engaged not only in study, but in an active apostolate with Blacks and Latinos in seven parishes and two social organizations. Due to their location in Chicago, they were exposed to a diversity of religious personalities not available to earlier scholastics in the U.S. In 1979 alone, Monsignor Raymond Caesar, S.V.D., a native of Eunice, Louisiana, and Bishop of Gonoka Diocese of Papua, New Guinea would ordain three Comboni students. Kabanga Songssonga, Archbishop of Lumubashi, Zaire, visited, celebrated Mass, and dined with them. When Pope John Paul II visited Chicago, Comboni scholastics would be present at the ceremonies.[7]

FORMATION: QUESTIONS WITHOUT ANSWERS

Formation secretaries serving in the late 1970s included Fathers Ongaro, Gasparini, Fornasari, and Conway. These priests would probably say today that this service was one of the most exasperating experiences of their lives.

In April, 1976, when Father Ongaro was secretary, he reported a number of issues that educators had identified through a questionnaire. Among these were: 1) there was not a continuity of development through all stages of formation; rather a distinct break occurred in student development between the college postulancy period and the novitiate. 2) a possible reason for this break was that postulants had little sense of what it meant to be a Comboni missionary. 3) there was a "lukewarm interest of several Fathers towards the students" which made identification with Comboni missionaries difficult. Added to this was the absence of English translations of society documents. 4) confusion existed among students about what "vocational choice" prior to entering the novitiate really meant. But they could accept the idea that the choice after postulancy corresponded to "engagement," and the vows at the end of the novitiate to "marriage." 5) preparation of qualified educators was neglected, but not for lack of concern over this issue, rather for lack of personnel. The result was "low self-confidence of the educators" in their work, and this was thought to be a concern for the whole society. 6) regarding the recruiting and formation of lay brothers, although four out of ten college students were following a vocational program at the university that led to becoming a lay brother, none lasted beyond a few years. This was thought due to a lack of clear thinking on that vocation, and lack of commitment on the part of students who might be hedging their options in case they decided to leave.

At the September, 1976, Formation Assembly meeting, Father Louis Gasparini was now rector at Monroe. He reported only nine students at the high school, and he said there would be no high school graduates joining the postulancy students that year. He explained that the guiding principles for high school formation was to allow "the student to be what he is - a teenager, and within bounds, allow[ing] him to make his own mistakes." This view was founded on the belief that growth through experience was more permanent and valuable to an individual's development than earlier modes of formation.

At Cincinnati, where Father Serra directed college students, there were only six postulants; Serra reported on the college students' prayer life which included morning and evening prayers, daily mass, and a weekly liturgy emphasizing shared reflections and prayers. To increase identification with Comboni Missionaries, confreres from the missions were asked to share their experiences with the students, but the great distances between Comboni communities, he said, seriously interfered with providing role models for students, and a dearth of literature in English certainly added to the problem of identification with the institute or its founder, Daniel Comboni.

Father Forlani, the novice master, reported only five novices, and he acknowledged that the first "desert" experience in the novitiate needed restructuring. It was too highly structured and its expectations were too high. The small number of those in the novitiate, and the isolation of the house appeared to contribute to a "pressure cooker" atmosphere not amenable to student persistence.

Father Fornasari, at the Chicago scholasticate, reported that there would be sixteen scholastics from various provinces at the new international scholasticate.[8]

The atmosphere at this Formation Assembly meeting was one of frustration. Too many issues were left unanswered, and conflicts erupted about formation approaches. Finally, it was admitted that "progress [in] formation must bend somewhat according to the personality of the student..."[9] At the meeting, Fornasari was elected Secretary of Formation.

The fact of a death of English texts on the society or its founder continued to be a serious impediment in formation. In 1978, as the Secretary for Mission Promotion, Father William Jansen would make a concerted effort to correct this by searching for translators. His attempts failed when translators actually did a "transliteration" that was unreadable in English. This happened to the "Charter for Mission Promotion or Animation," a highly regarded document prepared by the General Secretariat of Animation. Jansen looked in vain for an American theologian who would be expert in Italian. Finally, Father Contran assumed the task of translating the "Charter..." document. Jansen did find someone to prepare a book about Daniel Comboni using available English resources. By October, 1979, a copy of this biography, written by Betsy Wones, was distributed at the Provincial Mission Promotion.[10]

Difficulties were also encountered with mission films. Films authorized by Italian Comboni missionaries were not only rendered in Italian, but often were not appropriate for American audiences. When the mission promotion secretary asked for the films' master negatives to edit for viewing in America, authorities in Italy refused the request. There was also "a strong sense of frustration" at the Mission Promotion Assembly about the lack of news and articles from the Generalate in Rome. Letters about these gaps in communication were to be sent to members of the General Council.[11]

In 1978, Father Gasparini was elected Formation Secretary, and he listed the priorities of the Monroe community that included Fathers Crozzoletto and Wilkinson. They were: 1. the formation of the seven resident seminarians; 2. "Live-in Weekend" experiences for prospective seminarians; 3. organizing, and staffing weekend mission-oriented retreats for young men; 4. Marriage Encounters, weekend retreats for young adults sponsored by the Detroit Archdiocese, and priests' retreat groups.[12] However, despite experiments in formation, students' perseverance beyond high school did not increase.

Gasparini's report indicated the obvious; Monroe was becoming more a retreat house than a seminary.

When the Formation Secretariat gave its next report to the annual Provincial Assembly, it was greeted with criticism. There was a call to study causes for student attrition, give more attention to lay brothers, and put greater stress on linking student development to concrete models of Comboni missionaries. In other words, it was recognized that little progress had been made in these areas. Wilkinson, once a lay brother himself, sparked a lively discussion about accepting the lay brother as a part of "ministry." This cause was carried forward at a subsequent Provincial Council meeting when Father Conway noted that a large number of young men in the United States contacting the Comboni Missionaries were interested in the lay brotherhood. His remark was picked up by the General Council in Rome, and Fornasari, perhaps in response to its interest, reported that Catholic Theological Union was developing a theology-ministry program for non-priest ministers which could well serve student-Brothers.[13]

In mid-1976, Busetti and his Council received a report from vocation directors and Father Contran, the latter working with them on day-to-day operations. The report offered guidelines on the various duties and responsibilities of recruiters. As of July 9, 1976, a Mission Center West had been officially constituted at which Fathers Branchesi and Durigon and Brother Pratt were stationed. Fathers Carillo, Erbisti, and Nardi were at the eastern Center at Montclair.[14] In 1978, Father Dennis Conway was vocation director, but his vocation team had fewer recruiters. Summer camps were still functioning, special vocation weekends were increasing, and a monthly newsletter was launched to keep in touch with young men attending these events. Communication was maintained with the students in college since that period was critical to vocation identification. Still, vocation recruiters' efforts met little success, and a re-tooling of strategies and guidelines continued.

However, newly ordained American-born Combonis were now allowed to work in their home province before going to mission. In the late 1970s, Americans also began returning from overseas' study or assignments. Among these were Ken Gerth in 1976, Dennis Conway and Brian Quigley in 1977, William Jansen in 1978, Paul Donohue, Paul Ewers, Jon Jensen, Joe Rankin, Tom Vermiglio, Jerry Charbonneau, and Bernie Pratt in 1979. The return of these Americans brought new energy and possibilities to recruitment. There was also talk of bringing Comboni missionaries from Mexico to do vocation work in the Los Angeles area since the number of Latinos in the United States was growing.[15] Still, by 1979, the work of vocation recruiters brought few new students to Comboni seminaries.

A QUESTION OF IDENTITY

The late 1970s found Comboni Missionaries in United States and Canada in a rush of name-changing. By 1978, the phrase "North American Province" supplanted "United States Province" both in general references and under the provincial newsletter's title. It is said that the Canadian missionary, Brother Jerry Charbonneau, suggested the new name as a more adequate description of the province. North American Province was quickly condensed to NAP in common parlance. The mission promotion secretariat also advised changing, albeit slowly, the titles "Verona Fathers" or "Verona Missionaries" to "Comboni Missionaries." Although it was admitted that the society in North America had limited recognition, the risk of losing what had been gained was put aside in order to identify more closely with Daniel Comboni whose beatification was now steadfastly promoted in Rome.[16]

In another attempt to create a unified identity, the society's centers all shared the title: "Comboni Mission Center." They adopted an identical logo and organized their advertising to focus on specific locations. A linkage with the Comboni Missionary Sisters in Richmond, Virginia through Sister Claudia began when she collaborated on articles for the magazine which changed twice, once to Verona Missions, then to Comboni Mission Magazine. It was published bi-monthly, and began receiving twice the amount of mail and many more request for reprint rights. Father Jansen, after returning from his foreign mission assignment in 1978, took over as editor and built on the efforts of previous editors, primarily Father Bragotti. Catholic Press Association awards followed.[17]

Not only names, but places changed in appearance and purpose. The old farm house had long since disappeared. Father Ongaro recalled how, after the exodus of scholastics to San Diego in 1961, it was largely unused. Then "Like a tired old giant, this cradle of the Comboni Missionaries in the U.S. that had sheltered many young students...was sitting on the lawn waiting to collapse...For a few more years it served as headquarters of the provincial superior, but its deterioration became unmanageable, and it was decided to burn it down during a fire department practice. On a September morning in 1967, it went spectacularly up in flames, inexpensively helpful to the last."[18]

Drastic reductions in the property around Sacred Heart Seminary began. On January 15, 1979, a meeting took place with developers who wanted to lease some of the seminary's property. Father Contran later explained the motivation for doing this. A benefactor had said to him, "You're asking us to help you. Why don't you do something about what you have?" The man was referring to the fifty-six acres on which the seminary stood. Supporting this view were Comboni missionaries who believed that, in the spirit of poverty, the land should not be held for its own sake, but used to support the purpose of the society. Others in the province were against a wholesale disposal of the property, not only because of its historical value, but also for its potential financial assets of leased instead of sold.[19]

Sacred Heart Seminary was now Comboni Mission Center. Father Ongaro returned from working with five other missionaries (One Austrian, one American, two Germans, and one Italian), on a draft of a Constitution for the reunited German and Italian branches of Comboni Missionaries. Almost immediately he was appointed manager of the center in Cincinnati. Now the former seminary functioned as a mission center and a facility for retreats.[20]

At Monroe, a different set of circumstances changed the building. On Holy Saturday, 1979, while students were on Easter Holiday, a woman mopping the chapel floor heard glass shattering and realized there was a fire in the building. She ran for help. Meanwhile, Fathers Gasparini and Crozzoletto were also in the building when the alarm went off but they escaped without injury. The fire spread from the kitchen to the gymnasium and the library. By the time firemen arrived, black smoke poured through the back of the building, and flames rolled out of the dining room and kitchen. Gasparini, Crozzoletto, and Wilkinson, the last returning from town, all helped fight the fire. But even four fire departments had difficulty bringing it under control. There was only one fire hydrant on the grounds. Because it was at the end of the water line, it had low water pressure. The firemen had to truck in water and pump it from a nearby pond. It took an hour before the fire was extinguished. By that time, a third of the complex was lost. The rest sustained serious smoke damage.

The City of Monroe rallied around the Comboni Missionaries. Verona Mission Club members vowed the July festival would not be canceled since now the missionaries' need for funds was greater than ever. The club's auxiliary set up a temporary office and meeting room for the priests, and letters of support poured in. The Youth Outreach Office of the Detroit Archdiocese wrote, "Everyone who shared in our experiences [at the facility] speaks of the home-like atmosphere....As is evidenced by the festival and by the constant use on weekends, the people of this diocese recognize the Verona [Comboni] seminary as one of the better places to be. If it were taken away by a fire or for any other reason, the people of this diocese will be without a friend..."

Hundreds of volunteers helped with the cleanup, and thirty-six truckloads of rubble were hauled away. Dozens of women worked an entire day removing soot from the chapel, and workers painted and replaced ceiling tiles, rewired electrical circuits, and repaired plumbing, but money for re-building was not forthcoming. The building had been woefully underinsured, and Comboni Missionaries were apparently not informed of this fact. Despite this, the Provincial Council decided to rebuild, and to negotiate with the insurance company over the discrepancy involved.[21]

ADJUSTING THE "PASTORAL PRESENCE"

At the end of 1975, Busetti and his Council, in conjunction with the Superior General, published a Statement of Policy announcing the conditions necessary to bring the "pastoral presence" in the province in line with the renewal documents of 1969 and 1975. These conditions included, 1) working with subcultural groups that needed to be fully evangelized, 2) personnel devoted to such work in proportion to personnel in other areas of service, 3) a style of work that was missionary in practice and not that of an already established parish, 4) this policy to be reviewed and, during the interim, commitments kept to "Blacks, the Indians in California, and the Appalachians of St. Michael as long as they conformed to the above stated principles," 5) Comboni Missionaries should not work in a vacuum, but establish close links with the local Church, government, and social organizations.[22] Father Hugo Riva's experience at St. Albert the Great closely fit the criteria of this policy.

ST. ALBERT THE GREAT.
Through much of his provincialate, Contran had tried to exchange Our Lady of Guadalupe parish in the Los Angeles Archdiocese for one that was African American. After his election as provincial, Busetti met with Cardinal Manning, and within months, Monsignor John A. Rawden, Chancellor of Los Angeles, wrote Busetti that St. Albert the Great, in the Compton area, would be available on July 1, 1977. In June, Rawden notified John Cardinal Wright at the Sacred Congregation of Clergy in Rome that the Verona Fathers (Comboni Missionaries) would be taking over this parish from the previous religious society. Busetti appointed Father Hugo Riva pastor of St. Albert's.[23]

Riva had come to the United States in 1947. After his ordination in 1950, he went immediately to the mission of Mupoi in Southern Sudan where he worked under a former Comboni pioneer to America, Monsignor Dominic Ferrara. Eight years later, the Sudanese government found Riva guilty of "criminal intimidation" for threatening God's punishment to a man running an immoral dance show. Along with 120 other Comboni missionaries, he was expelled and sent back to the United States. Before his appointment to St. Albert's, Riva worked at both the Santa Ysabel and Pala mission chapels. He was incensed when he understood how the California Indians had had their lands looted, their people massacred, and even in contemporary society, were subjected to neglect. He told the author, "After taking away all their lands, then we teach in the schools that they are the savages?" It was shocking, he said, to find in a country of such wealth as the United States that many Native Americans still lived without a roof over their heads and without electricity, food, or water in San Diego County.

At St. Albert's Riva found a different set of circumstances. The parish population was approximately one third Hispanic and two thirds African American, and its school served 500 students, the majority of whom were black. Riva's arrival at St. Albert's was more than a decade after the 1965 Watts Riots. Cardinal Timothy Manning had been Archbishop of Los Angeles for seven years, but Riva's new parishioners were still upset about what they believed was a denial of money under Manning's predecessor, Cardinal McIntyre.

Riva found St. Albert's deeply in debt, and he informed the chancery that if his society had been aware of this, it would never have accepted the parish. In actuality, the Comboni Missionary policy about parish debt was more a guideline than a firm policy. But Riva's dismay at discovering a substantial debt as well as other difficulties, may have determined the intensity of his message. The Comboni priest found a ready ally in Rt. Rev. Monsignor Benjamin G. Hawkes. Hawkes told him, "Don't worry. Don't worry. Make a list of all the debts and I'll send you the check." The archdiocese' treasurer kept his word, and he later told Riva, "Father, when you need money, there's a telephone on your desk. Just call me." This offer was tested when, at Christmas, funds to pay the teachers' salaries were insufficient. Riva went to Hawkes and was asked, "How much do you need?" Riva said, "Send me $50,000. And the check arrived promptly. On another occasion, Hawkes heard that there were Mexican children who wanted a Catholic education but could not afford it. Again he came to the rescue.

Riva's work at St. Albert's and other parishes convinced him that America had great missionary potential, and that work in the U.S. could be even more difficult than some in Africa, albeit in different ways. Missionaries in Africa, he said, had more control of their time and were generally freer of stress. In America, one was a slave to the telephone, forced to work with numerous bureaucracies, always short of money for neglected minorities, and deprived of sufficient personnel.[24]

MINISTRY VERSUS VOCATIONS IN CANADA.

When Father John Battelli returned to the United States in 1975, the General Administration had asked him to study the potential of the Comboni presence in Canada. The Brossard community had been founded for recruiting French-speaking vocations, but permission to do this was given by the Bishop of St. John's Diocese only if a Comboni priest also worked with the English-speaking population in a parish or school. Good Shepherd parish had grown under Comboni stewardship to two thousand people of various ethnic origins. By July, 1976, Battelli offered his observations about Brossard at a Provincial Council Meeting. A five year contract to care for the parish was up for renewal, and he believed the situation still had great potential for vocations.

At Good Shepherd, Battelli was assisted by Father Confalonieri who helped with weekly mission appeals, published a quarterly newsletter in three languages (circulation 20,000), and contacted agencies that sponsored mission projects. Promised more personnel, Confalonieri had kept *Baobab* alive. It was the only mission magazine for young French Canadians, and it was well received. When it dropped in circulation for lack of a distribution campaign, and the personnel promised failed to arrive, Battelli and Confalonieri regretfully discontinued it. The Provincial Council again called for two missionaries from the General Administration to do vocation work and resume publication of *Baobab* so critical to successful recruitment. Battelli and Confalonieri advised that it now appeared that the Canadian province of Ontario had even better vocation and financial potential, and several religious communities had already decided to move there. But the idea was tabled for lack of personnel.[25]

That same year, Father Robert Erbisti, who had earlier served in Canada, returned to the U.S. Province from the Ethiopian missions. He was on a mission appeal in Ontario when a priest at St. Mary's parish asked him about bringing Comboni Missionaries to Cambridge. In 1978, this possibility arose at a luncheon meeting between Father Busetti and Bishop Paul Francis Reding of the Diocese of Hamilton, Ontario. The bishop agreed to let Comboni Missionaries open a mission center. A permanent one was established at Cambridge when a small house and ten acres of land was purchased. Half the population of Canada was located within a hundred mile radius of this house, and there were no restrictions on vocation promotion. The two priests at the center received a friendly reception from local clergy and the numerous Catholics in the area.[26] By now, after five years on the market, the Columbia, New Jersey, property had been sold, and the pews from its former chapel were loaded on a rented truck and taken to Cambridge.

Adjusting the "parish presence" did not end in Los Angeles and Canada. Bringing the province into balance with the Comboni Missionary charism continued to occupy the next administration. But before the election of a new administration, Busetti, the American provincial, was called away. At the General Chapter of 1979, he was appointed Treasurer of the Comboni Missionary Institute. Some in the province believe that leaving America was too much for him. Within months of his appointment, Busetti suffered a massive heart attack. He was sent to recuperate in Limone, Italy, the birthplace of Daniel Comboni, located on the shores of Lake Garda. But in January, 1980, he suffered another attack and died at the age of 59.[27]

PASSING THE TORCH

By 1979, Americans were experiencing a distinct sense of loss: of idealism, of economic security, of integrity in government. A sense of something lost had also overtaken Comboni missionaries of North America. Not only had many of the gains made early in its history been lost, but even those who made that history had died or were called away.

The missionary who was the symbol of early success in the province had returned to the province in 1970. Hamlet Accorsi was then 67 years old and not in good health. In 1975, he celebrated his Golden Jubilee at Sacred Heart Seminary with old friends from the Mission Apostolate and the Sacred Heart Seminary Guild. He had continued his correspondence with the Buse family, and after Carl Buse died, he wrote to Marie. A letter to her in 1976 reveals that Accorsi still maintained a formidable work pace:

"I just came back last night (it was 1:30 a.m.) from Altoona, Pa., where I have preached a Mission Appeal. Last Sunday I preached 9 Masses. This to prove to you that I am alright (sic), and thanks to the Lord - still able to work..." His next letter to Mrs. Buse found her in a rest home. Accorsi was still preaching and recalling his early years in Cincinnati, "How can I forget those first years at Holy Trinity, and your kindness to me..." Then his tone turned more somber: "Now we are approaching the GOAL (I am close behind you) and our main interest has to be to prepare for IT: the Lord's call will not be far away. This is not supposed to be a <u>sad</u> thought, but a comforting one, because THER (sic) we will be out of all the personal miseries and the awful things of the world of today, and we will be reunited with all those we have loved here, and who have preceded us in God's kingdom."[28]

On August 15, 1977, Accorsi was ordered to absolute rest. In his Last Will and Testament he asked God, "If I am not too bold, I pray you let me have my purgatory before I die...Grant that my last act of love on this earth be followed by an act of love in Heaven." Months of suffering followed due to a severe kidney dysfunction and other ailments. Early on January 12, 1978, Father Hamlet Accorsi, founder of the American province, died with serenity.[29] The deaths of Accorsi and Busetti marked the passing of charismatic leaders of the province. There were still some in their generation distinguishing themselves, among them Fathers Bart Battirossi, Januarius Carillo, Frank Di Francesco, and Alfred Paolucci. Those students who first came to America now represented a valuable bridge to more youthful members of the province as advisors and in posts requiring experience. But they were less likely to be chosen for leadership roles. Now American-born Comboni missionaries had an unwritten mandate to assume these positions.

21. Setting Priorities: Ministry and Vocations

With Father Busetti gone to Rome as General Treasurer, the office of provincial was open. North American members could either choose someone to either fill the remaining term or fill that period plus the three year term that followed. They chose the longer period and gave this privilege (or tribulation) to an American-born Comboni missionary, Father Charles Walter. Walter began his provincialate after four years on the General Council. He was part of the administration that reunified the German and Italian branches of Comboni Missionaries. He was also one of the six missionaries who wrote the new constitutions published as the *Rule of Life* (ROL), and unanimously approved at the XIII General Chapter in 1979. A guide for renewal of the Comboni missionaries, the ROL reflected the spirit of the Second Vatican Council and the founder of the Congregation, Daniel Comboni.[1] By March, 1980, Council members Brother Jerry Charbonneau and Fathers Xavier Colleoni, Dennis Conway, and Mario Ongaro joined Walter. Conway, vice provincial under Busetti, was again elected to that office.

Key issues for the Council were: a continuing shortage of personnel, one and two-men communities no longer serving their original purpose, vocations declining or nonexistent, and the need to incorporate the ROL into a new provincial directory. Added to these were Assistant General Francesco Pierli's comments when visiting the NAP. He praised the province for the "large amount of work shouldered in missionary, vocational and funding activity," and added, "I don't want to neglect that many...missionaries and local churches owe a great deal to the brotherly understanding and sympathy of the NAP." But the time had come for genuine renewal. In pastoral work, he specified areas to be addressed: a) commitment to missionary and pastoral service to Blacks; b) a reexamination and possible severing of commitments to Appalachians and Indians; c) since vocations were more numerous among the poor "where families are numerous and youth more accustomed to sacrifice," vocation promotion among Latinos would be a "step in the right direction."[2] Pierli's views would be reflected in the new Provincial Council's decisions, and those about pastoral work possibly affected the province more than any of the others. Pierli's point about developing Latino vocations found support in a serendipitous combination of events when a newly ordained American-born priest was assigned to Holy Cross parish in Los Angeles..

CASA COMBONI

Father Jon Jensen, from St. Charles, Illinois, was ordained in 1979. As a novice, he worked in Mexico, and in theology, he studied at the Jesuit-run Pontifical University in Granada, Spain. There he worked with the "Jesus Abandoned" center run by lay volunteers who searched for the poor and homeless among prostitutes, alcoholics, and the destitute living on Granada's streets. Jensen described this experience as one that helped him connect his theology with reality. After his ordination, Jensen was assigned to Holy Cross parish as assistant to Father Xavier Colleoni who introduced him to the parish. Jensen met Father Mike Kwiatkowski, another American Comboni working in vocation recruiting. The two discussed the potential for Hispanic vocations and agreed that the young men they were discussing did not speak English, did not have the required education, and did not have economic resources. They would normally not be able to enter missionary life or be qualified for formal religious training. But if vocations among them could be found, a place to house them was needed. [3]

Jensen sent a proposal to the Provincial Council to assist such candidates. It included teaching them the English language and helping them complete a G.E.D (General High School Equivalency Diploma). After this, they could go to a community college. Those who persisted could join the pre-postulancy house at St. Michael's in Cincinnati. Meanwhile, the young men could help with expenses by working part-time and getting involved with apostolate work at Holy Cross. In December, 1980, the Provincial Council reviewed Jensen's proposal and sent it to all vocation directors for recommendations. In February, 1981, approval was given to purchase a house in Los Angeles for Hispanic candidates. By spring, Jensen was named administrator of what was now called Casa Comboni. The building was in terrible shape, but Jensen and youth groups from Holy Cross began scraping, patching, and painting walls to make it habitable. By fall, Casa Comboni was not only filled to capacity, it had a waiting list. Now the Council established a scholarship fund for Casa Comboni students. [4]

In the spring of 1982, Jensen received a phone call from the Archdiocesan office. Bishop Arzube asked him to come to the chancery the following morning. The Comboni priest wondered what had triggered this summons. Had he run awry of some diocesan rules? What Arzube actually wanted to know was whether he would accept an offer to work as Associate Director of the Spanish-Speaking Apostolate. Although surprised, Jensen understood that the position would open up new opportunities to work with Spanish-speaking youth, and he would be better able to make chancery officials aware of their needs. When the archdiocese sent the Provincial Council a request for Jensen's services, the Council thought Jensen could combine the work with that at Casa Comboni, but it was concerned that Jensen could undertake too much and harm his health.[5] This concern was valid, for as Jensen's work for the archdiocese was noticed by Cardinal Manning, the Archdiocese increased his responsibilities. When another Comboni priest took Colleoni's place at Holy Cross, he joined Jensen at Casa Comboni and helped manage the house.

Casa Comboni was a good start, but a houseful of students, a stream of visitors, and a wild schedule of students coming and going, all lent a sense of chaos about it. Council members wanted someone there who could set schedules, instill a sense of order, and bring a sense of serenity to the lives of its inhabitants. After his term as vice provincial, Father Mario Ongaro went to Casa Comboni as Superior and Educator. Ongaro, with fifteen years in formation work, was an admitted disciplinarian who believed a community should have structure. He also had advanced degrees and experience in counseling and psychology which gave him a broad understanding of developmental issues. It was expected he would have a different perspective than Jensen, and one of these was about language. Although he understood Spanish, Ongaro was determined not to speak it at Casa Comboni except in extraordinary circumstances. He was convinced that the students, virtually all from Latin America, would not succeed in the United States without English. This opinion was not shared by Jensen, but neither of the priests allowed their disagreement to become a community issue.[6]

An in-house evaluation of Casa Comboni in 1984, mandated as part of the National Survey of Seminary Education, pointed to two fundamental characteristics in the Hispanic society from which students came. One was the prevalence of popular religious devotions, primarily to Mary as Our Lady of Guadalupe. The other was oppression due to poverty, the lack of decent jobs, a sense of being racial outcasts, and a lack of control over government. Young Hispanics at Casa Comboni were dependable workers, had good will, were respectful, made few demands about food and lodging, but they had limited opportunity for academic or religious studies. For these students, Casa

Comboni became a door through which they could embark on a missionary career, and for Comboni Missionaries the students were a source of vocations.

The report noted the enormous burden then shouldered by Jon Jensen, the "Vocation Director." He was described as "literally strangled by...work... going on every hour of the day and much of the night, meeting all classes of Hispanics...groups, couples, individuals who need counseling, co-workers, retreat planning, encounters [groups], religious [celebrations], and ministry." It eventually strained his health and led Jensen to ask the Provincial Council to choose between full time work at Casa Comboni or full time work with the archdiocese. The Council decided he should remain with the archdiocese, and soon thereafter, Jensen was no longer active at Casa Comboni.[7]

The evaluation also reported on the work of the "Educator," Ongaro, who had main responsibility for the students. By 1984, three hours of study were required; students were prepared for the G.E.D. by other students; and a retired Sister of Providence taught them English. That year, six of seven students passed a G.E.D. given in Spanish. Of the four who passed and began courses at college, three later left college and Casa Comboni. Learning English was the main difficulty. Students enrolled in summer college courses were taking them in English, but with what success remained to be seen. Study was difficult due to crowding, interruptions from visitors, and street noises. External teachers reported students were too tired from activities in ministry, running constantly to classes, and other distractions.

Casa Comboni operated on a relatively low annual budget of fifty thousand dollars. This included Jensen's salary from the archdiocese, ministry (most of which came in the form of mass intentions from the provincial), student wages; and donations. The province contributed more over the years, and future plans were to move Casa Comboni to a house that could also serve as a vocation center, and could offer fewer distractions. The length of stay at Casa Comboni was short compared to other formation phases, but the work expected of students was quite complex. Initiating a young man into community life and prayer after years away from studies demanded much of him, and when he completed a course of studies at Casa Comboni, even at a low level of formation, he was considered a "graduate."[8]

In 1987, six years later, on behalf of Bishop John Marshall, Representative of the Holy See for the Study of Seminaries in the United States, Reverend Charles E. Miller, C.M., and Reverend Jeremiah McCarthy would visit Casa Comboni. Their report then declared the purpose of Casa Comboni to be an excellent as well as a difficult one due to its focus on young men who could find American culture alien and even hostile. Casa Comboni residents seemed, they wrote, "overwhelmed by the idea of having a 'Papal Visitation,'" but cooperation and eager assistance was clearly visible. The team judged that the "house is doing an adequate job of preparing these young men for late formation which could be truly termed 'priestly'."

By then, Father Miguel Angel Villegas had taken Jon Jensen's place as co-director with Ongaro. The spirit of the house was found to be good, and relationships between the students amiable. The province provided Casa Comboni with 20% of its income, and the report added that educators were tightening admissions policies which had been rather lax. Now entrants required some knowledge of English, had to have completed high school requirements, and had to be no older than 25 years of age. The team supported this and added that plans to move to larger facilities were also recommended. A yearly and written evaluation of all students indicating their strengths and areas for growth was advised, and a structured program on the value of celibacy was recommended. The visitors believed Apostolic work on "skid row" was an excellent experience and well supervised. Availability of psychological counseling was seen as commendable.[9] By this time, Casa Comboni had not added many students to the list of Comboni Missionaries. But it won the gratitude of young Hispanics who found friends, deepened their Catholic faith, and grew in their ability to integrate and succeed in the North American environment. By the early 1990s, it was estimated that at least six young men from Casa Comboni made a lasting commitment to Comboni Missionaries.

MINISTRY IN TRANSITION

During Walter's provincialate both Good Shepherd parish in Canada and Santa Ysabel Mission in California would be returned to their respective dioceses, and the San Diego diocese would be informed that Pala Mission would be given back as personnel decreased. Besides St. Vitus parish in Chicago, the four parishes still under the care of Comboni Missionaries were St. Michael's and St. Pius in Cincinnati, and St Albert's and Holy Cross in Los Angeles. Of these four, only one, St. Michael's, was under serious review for return to the Cincinnati archdiocese.

ST. MICHAEL'S.

In 1980, Father Louis Gasparini was transferred from the Monroe high school seminary to St. Michael's parish as pastor.[10] St. Michael's also housed six Comboni students with Father Dennis Conway as their "educator."

Gasparini described the parish in Lower Price Hill as "one of the poorest neighborhoods in a wealthy city in the world's richest country." Ninety percent of its people lived on some form of government support. Most were migrants from the mountain states of Kentucky and Tennessee, where isolated communities offered few educational or job opportunities. Coming from such isolated and thinly populated regions, they were suspicious of strangers and fiercely independent. Catholicism was held suspect, and Catholic clergy even demonized. As these "poor whites" arrived in the North looking for jobs, their lack of appropriate dress, mainstream speech, and experience in a "nine-to-five" work day raised further barriers to their acceptance. A vicious cycle of hopelessness and alcoholism could develop. If the strong clan ties that held the mountain families together began to fray, the next generation became part of a downward cycle, with children dropping out of school and the parents unable to support them. As Gasparini pointed out, "They [Appalachian migrants] are now a forgotten minority...with a history of being abandoned.[11]

Gasparini found a dedicated, if small, group of Catholics at St. Michael's. His predecessor, Father Saoncella, had developed this faithful cadre of workers, often from outside parish boundaries. They led the choir, ran the bingo, and managed other parish affairs. Although many came from a distance, they shared a sense of community with one another, but not necessarily with the Appalachians. While not always in favor of annual festivals, Gasparini thought one in this parish might bring people together. But it had to be geared more to people than to raising money. His idea found support. Parish buildings were crowded together on a hillside with little open space; therefore, a park was rented and festival equipment moved to it. Everyone's ideas were solicited. When the festival opened, those without transportation were bused to it. The main theme, Gasparini said, was that "everybody worked shoulder to shoulder... Catholics, non-Catholics, and nobody took a penny home [for this]."[12] Surprisingly, the festival made fifteen thousand dollars. After bills were paid, Gasparini used some remaining funds for a dinner for the workers to celebrate their success. He gave them a full accounting of festival finances, and the result was a greater sense of inclusiveness among parishioners.

Steps were taken not only to bring people together, but to address the situation of poverty among Appalachians. This included the Neighborhood Community Corporation of which Gasparini was a founder. Its goal was the renovation of housing so the poor could obtain affordable housing. The non-profit organization, Habitat for Humanity, was contracted to build it. A second step was to make space at St. Michael's for a learning center so those without a high school education could study for the high school equivalency test and receive a General Educational Diploma (G.E.D.). Gasparini and members of the parish staff sat on local boards where decisions affecting Lower Price Hill were made. They were members of the Urban Appalachian Council and the Santa Maria Neighborhood Council in order to bring an increasing awareness of Lower Price Hill needs. Such contacts led to positive outcomes such as when a K-Mart store sold 300 laundry baskets below cost that were then filled by friends and volunteers of the Santa Maria Neighborhood House. They gave not only their money, goods, time, and energy, but also their laughter."[13]

Perhaps the most valuable initiative, one that gave spiritual balance to his "community action" agenda, was the evangelization program that reached out on a door-to-door basis. After meeting on Thursday evenings for prayer, teams of two knocked on every door of streets designated for visits. The purpose was to make contact with people whether or not they belonged to a religious denomination, to tell them that there were people who cared about them, and that St. Michael's was a community they could turn to for help. After several years, these teams wanted to preach the Gospel. A group of sixteen people, including Gasparini and Sister Janice (then assisting at the parish), prepared themselves for more than three months. They used a manual on preaching the Gospel that told them how to get past the initial greeting so they could begin sharing Jesus' story. It was an amazing process that attracted even the elderly, the shy, and those who had never before left their homes at night. When they began knocking on doors, they were usually invited in. Later they would write notes of thanks to all those they visited, and would share with one another the incredible receptions they received. Gasparini recalled, "We marveled at how we were often meeting Christ, who somehow got there before we did. And the Jesus [in each one of us met] the Jesus in the other."[14]

By 1986, St. Michael's was involved with the Archdiocese of Cincinnati's "For the Harvest" program that planned to cluster parishes with similar problems close to one another. Its goal was to share resources, including priests now that a shortfall of vocations was evidenced. Despite Gasparini's enthusiasm and the re-invigorating atmosphere he generated at St. Michael's, the need to decrease commitments led the province to return St. Michael's to the diocese. The CARA study had indicated this parish was likely to be returned. It had been rather an embarrassment to North American provincials because it served a white population. Its acceptance in exchange for St. Anthony's in the West End was never really understood or condoned by a General Administration that believed serving any white population in the U.S. was inconsistent with the Comboni charism for the "poorest and most abandoned." After thirty years of service, Comboni Missionaries would leave St. Michael's in 1992.

ST. PIUS PARISH.

In 1976, Father Caesar Mazzolari succeeded Father Premarini at St. Pius in Cincinnati. Mazzolari had been a Provincial Council member, a spiritual director at Sacred Heart Seminary, and Coordinator at St. Michael's Bible Center. At the last, he directed Saturday Bible classes for children and distributed food vouchers, clothing, and care to the poor living in Lower Price Hill. He also developed visual aids for the school that introduced Appalachian children to children all over the world, giving them a broader understanding of the plight of children in other lands. Mazzolari had a gift for reaching those who were alienated from mainstream society.[15]

At St. Pius with Mazzolari was Father Ken Dahlen as associate pastor. Dahlen, a native of Amsterdam, New York, served in World War II as a navy photographer. He had a bachelor's degree before joining the Comboni Missionaries, and after his ordination in 1954, he taught science and biology at Comboni seminaries and was associate pastor at both St. Henry's and St. Anthony's parishes. Dahlen not only welcomed the renewal the Second Vatican Council initiated, it was said that "if there was ever a person for whom Vatican II was a new Pentecost, it was Father Ken...who could get to the heart of a matter through his simplicity and forthrightness."[16]

With great hope and trust, Mazzolari and Dahlen launched a project to develop warmth, openness, and a "family" atmosphere in the parish. They began remodeling the rectory basement into two large rooms for parish meetings. Teenagers, skilled workers from the neighborhood, even the school principal, Sister André, joined them, and a parish center took shape. The center led to new groups springing up: a youth group, a St. Vincent de Paul Society chapter, and a prayer group, the *Anawin* ("little people of God"). Under the charismatic leadership of Father Dahlen, the Anawin prayer group met regularly in St. Martin de Porres Chapel which parishioners built in the church sanctuary. The St. Vincent de Paul chapter was unique in that, instead of an all-male membership, it was composed of four couples in the community who served the community's needs for food, clothing, partial payment of rent, and essential furniture.

Sister André, a gifted and dynamic principal, directed the children's "Gospel Choir," and at Sunday Mass, children performed a prayerful "liturgical dance." They were called "Children of Joy," and their number soon grew to eighteen. In 1980, they witnessed their faith in the neighborhood streets with an hour long program of Gospel songs, dances, and the reenactment of Gospel scenes called "Good News on Wheels" that gained wide recognition in the community.

A major issue at St. Pius was the growing gap between income and expenses for the school. Despite archdiocesan support and a tuition of $50 per year, its future remained uncertain. Mazzolari established a school board to determine how to keep it open. The diocese was encouraging St. Pius to merge (along with two other parishes) with St. Boniface, a largely white school. This was after the Civil Rights movement when many Blacks believed that a school where children could discover their own black heritage was critical to their developing their heritage as African Americans. Blacks in Cincinnati remembered their loss of solidarity when urban renewal forced whole neighborhoods of black families out of the West End. The archdiocese, therefore, allowed the parish to conduct a self-study to see if a merger could be avoided. Under the supervision of Miss Marie Rose Obert and the Archdiocesan Office supervision of Sister Mary Ann Drerup, a team of researchers went to work. The outcome of their efforts was acknowledged as one of the finest self-studies of that time.

Meanwhile, Mazzolari was pondering ways to keep the school solvent when a woman came to him with an envelope containing fifty dollars she had saved for over a year. She said she was planting a seed to claim God's promise that bread cast on the waters would be rewarded many times over. Mazzolari was not to open the envelope until its contents were "pressed down, shaken together and running over." Impressed with the woman's faith, Mazzolari asked Archbishop Bernardin for permission to keep St. Pius School open. Then he went to his own society for a one-time contribution that could be made "in the faith, that the Lord would show more ways in which the school could be supported?" The answer was affirmative. Over a four month period, Comboni Missionaries contributed $40,000 to St. Pius. Another religious order and private donors brought the total to $52,000, even more than was predicted. This "loaves and fishes" miracle, together with the parish self-study, convinced parents to raise tuition so the school could survive.

Another miracle was the flowering of community at St. Pius. It produced a strong spirit of evangelization among the people, a capable parish council, new ministers of the Eucharist, hospital ministries, and a housing advocacy made up of professional people who redressed wrongs resulting from landlord neglect of property and tenants' rights. This eventually evolved into the South

Cumminsville Christians United for Better Housing. St. Pius had a solid mix of people serving the parish and school staff that included the Sisters of Oldenburg, at St. Pius School since 1912; and the Sisters of St. Joseph of Medaille who joined ranks with St. Pius through prayer, financial support; and the pastoral ministry of Sister Evelyn LaGory. Volunteers included Comboni seminarians.[17]

Prior to his appointment to St. Pius, Dahlen had developed a series of physical disabilities that severely limited his activities. He had doubted his ability to serve in ministry. When Father Walter named him associate pastor at St. Pius, Dahlen wrote him, "Praise God! I have often wanted to work with my brothers and sisters of the black community, but wanted some confirmation as to whether my desire was of God or myself....."[18] Dahlen had learned to accept his limitations, and the people understood this. He had developed a capacity to empathize and respect anyone no matter who they were or what difficulties they had. As his health deteriorated, Dahlen sometimes had to use crutches at the alter or resort to a cane. One time he had to sit down in order to give his sermon. When Mazzolari became concerned that the work was too much for him, he spoke to his associate about this. Dahlen misconstrued his confrere's intentions and offered to retire. But Mazzolari told him, "You are one of your own greatest apostolates here at St. Pius [with your example] of suffering you give each day."

In late 1980, Dahlen suffered a serious viral infection and was hospitalized. He recovered in time for Christmas and the celebration of his sixty-sixth birthday on the first day of January. A week later, he was found to have peacefully died in his bed, still in his familiar gesture of praise. The following year, Mazzolari was transferred to the Sudanese missions. The life and spirit of the parish remained, but the partnership between the young and charismatic Mazzolari and the ailing yet lively intellect and spirit of Dahlen had ended. Many new initiatives were launched, but the parish felt this loss.[19]

Unfortunately, St. Pius, for all its spirit and cooperation, would be buffeted by additional losses, ones neither the Church nor Comboni Missionaries could control. Younger Comboni priests stationed at St. Pius went into "crisis," a euphemism for doubting their vocation as a priest and/or seeking laicization. The first to do so was the one who followed Mazzolari. Following him were, consecutively, Fathers Valentino Saoncella and Hugo Riva, both in their sixties. Saoncella, with the help of a capable principal at St. Pius school, kept the school financially stable with bingo. But bingos were losing their popularity and the school was eventually merged with St. Boniface. After Riva was transferred to Monroe, the vocation crisis again took its toll. In a relatively short time, two Comboni priests at St. Pius defected from the priesthood. These losses dealt heavy blows to the solidarity of St. Pius as well as to the Comboni Missionaries.

PROGRESS AT ST ALBERT THE GREAT.

In 1977, Father Hugo Riva was the first Comboni priest to serve at St. Albert's. By 1981, the Black Sisters of the Holy Family taught 534 students at its school, and that number remained fairly constant for years. St. Albert's was now a well organized parish complete with an annual carnival organized by both Black and Spanish parishioners. One year it netted $10,000, proving that collaboration between the two ethnic groups was possible.[20] Parish members were active in the South Central Organizing Committee (SCOC) which represented 6500 members of churches and community organizations.[21] After the Watts' riots, it had become a vehicle for those who wanted to improve the quality of life in their neighborhoods.

St. Albert's celebrated Black History month with special liturgies and programs at its grade school and at Regina Coeli High School. It was said that "Blacks truly find a home at St. Albert -- a home that recognizes the value of their culture and attracts converts to the Church."[22] Similarly, Hispanic culture was recognized. The Feast of Our Lady of Guadalupe celebrated each year began early in the morning with *Las Mañanitas*, and culminated in the evening with a solemn procession and a mass with *Mariachi*, a multitude of flowers, and elaborate decorations. The crowds were so great at these ceremonies that the church could not hold all the people.

On September 25, 1983, St. Albert's joined confreres from Holy Cross and Casa Comboni in a farewell liturgy for Father Riva and a welcome for Father Bart Battirossi. At the school, special classes in computer training were added to the curriculum, and similar classes for adults were oversubscribed. Battirossi worked hard to introduce the "Christ Renews His Parish," or "Renew," program, and his efforts were rewarded. Fund-raisers at St. Albert's were successful. The church choir's barbecue netted $3000 for a new piano, and its concert in December made enough money to update the church's public address system. The ushers raised money for new carpeting for the church.[23] When parishioners heard about a gas explosion in Mexico City, and the tragedy of famine in Ethiopia, it collected $1,139 that was divided between the Comboni bishop in Ethiopia and the Comboni provincial in Mexico. Although St. Albert's parishioners were not among the economically thriving middle class, neither were they among the most destitute. Because of this, questions began to arise about the appropriateness of Comboni ministry at St. Albert due to its relatively stable situation.

HOLY CROSS IN THE 1980S.
On May 2, 1982, songs were sung and tears shed at the Sunday Mass at Holy Cross. The reason: its pastor of twelve years, Father Xavier Colleoni, was leaving the parish. Father Sergio Contran took his place and formed a pastoral team with Fathers Gino Doniney, Michael Kwiatkowski, and Ramon Esteban Garcia Reyes.[24] That year, Contran went to Mexico to study Spanish. Meanwhile, his provincial, Father Walter, needed an experienced treasurer and pleaded for one from the General Administration. Skilled treasurers were apparently in short supply, and Walter decided to draft Contran back into the treasurer's job. In 1983, Father William Jansen was appointed pastor of Holy Cross, where, to complicate matters for the new pastor, the newly opened novitiate was to be located.[25]

The situation at Holy Cross in 1983 may be accurately gauged by a report in the provincial newsletter: "We are overwhelmed by the number of people...on the borderline of disaster, exploited in every possible way: rape, gang violence, racial prejudice, job exploitation, etc...we hope to help at least a few of them. The parish rents a store front directly across the street from the church and staffs it with volunteers. ERC (Equal Rights Congress), a civil-rights organization, and the area director of the CYO share space which is donated by the parish at great sacrifice.....A lot of organizational matters have arisen...with the novitiate in the rectory....On December 11, we celebrated the Feast of Our Lady of Guadalupe...and hope to develop the feast into a major parish celebration---a religious, social, and fund raising event. Our goal is to bring the English and Spanish- speaking together and help them to appreciate each other's cultural background...."[26]

This appeared in the Christmas issue, and was written by one well prepared for his task. Jansen had taken courses in Hispanic culture and had studied Spanish in Cuernavaca. When he arrived at Holy Cross, it was during a dramatic increase of Mexican immigrants in Los Angeles. Most Blacks in the parish were elderly, and their children had already moved from the neighborhood. Hispanics were renting or purchasing houses once owned or lived in by African Americans. To illustrate the dramatic population shift taking place at Holy Cross, when Jansen first arrived in 1982, two English and two Spanish masses were said on Sunday. By the time he left in 1991, only one English mass was said with fifty people attending, and six Spanish masses had from 500 to 600 in attendance. A complete change in neighborhood demographics was taking place, not only from Black to Hispanic, but also from the elderly to the very young.

Enormous racial tension resulted. Black parishioners, largely Catholics from Creole sections of the South, saw Hispanics as foreigners invading their neighborhood. At parish meetings, the first few Hispanics attending were ostracized. It posed a challenge to the new pastor since he and his associate, Father Bob Kleiner, were called racists when they tended to Hispanics' needs.[27] It was classic situation played out in America as new immigrants took over neighborhoods from those who came before them. A century before, it was the Irish moving into Anglo and German neighborhoods, then Italians moving into Irish neighborhoods, then Blacks into Jewish and Italian neighborhoods, and at Holy Cross, Hispanics into black neighborhoods. These transitions could trigger a culture clash if significant numbers of the previous group remained in the area.

As the numbers of Mexican and Latin American immigrants grew to a majority, and younger and middle-aged Blacks moved away, the situation eased, but not before violence erupted. At Holy Cross, church assistance programs were disrupted. In one instance, a steelworkers' union brought hot food to the parish hall for distribution to the needy at lunchtime, and it was served largely by Hispanic volunteers. But when confrontations with Blacks broke out, and the police had to be called, Jansen ended the program. The food was free, but armed guards, he said, were expensive.

Before Jansen's arrival, Contran had begun some renovation of the drastically deteriorated parish plant. At this time, the diocese subsidized remodeling costs, but not parish operations. Jansen contacted Monsignor Hawkes, the archdiocesan treasurer, about funding professional personnel (a janitor and secretary) as well as continuing the remodeling. Jansen also contacted government agencies for free cheese, milk, and other foodstuffs to distribute to the poor. He tried distributing this at the rectory door, but when this also led to fights, he rented a building across the street. A number of volunteers worked at the new center, then Jansen was able to hire a nun, Sister Sue Snider, who had previous experience managing a similar center in Pacoima. It was agreed that the center should be integrated with parish life.

Holy Cross had also joined SCOC (South Central Organizing Committee). One of the organization's victories stemmed from community discontent with the proliferation of liquor stores then numbering 1,000 in South Central Los Angeles. There were more liquor stores in this one neighborhood of Los Angeles than in the entire State of Pennsylvania, and some were suspected of harboring drug operations. A campaign was launched by SCOC to ban new liquor stores, and a resulting law barred the opening of any new liquor store without a public use permit. In another SCOC initiative, Jansen organized members of his parish and others in SCOC to stop a building project that would destroy dozens of residences. Success in revoking this plan brought SCOC churches new respect from local politicians. SCOC also sponsored an amnesty program, and Holy Cross was a government-designated registry center for processing immigrants. It would process close to 20,000 people, but only a small number of these actually received amnesty since, to qualify, they had to have come to the United States before 1986.[28]

Even as Jansen worked to improve the social situation of his parishioners, he also developed leadership for their spiritual life. Lay ministers were trained, and lay people sent to courses provided by the archdiocese. New programs were possible after the Los Angeles Archdiocese began subsidizing poor parishes with money, often as much as six million dollars a year. Jansen believed that, at that time, no other diocese was more generous than Los Angeles. Monsignor Hawkes had a reputation of being a hard administrator to deal with, but Jansen said that while Hawkes was "tough up front, if you were tough right back, you would get the money you needed." In making remodeling decisions, Jansen described how Hawkes operated: "Driving himself, Hawkes went around on Saturdays with construction people to see what had to be done. Then one day, you'd be sitting in your office, and a crew of workmen would show up to start some project."

Jansen was named head of a Deanery of the diocese. He worked on a campaign to raise eight million dollars for poor parishes; he was on the archdiocesan committee that developed the first assembly of priests in ministry; he was a member of the Priests' Senate and one of forty priests involved in personnel issues. Jansen was among the first to see the advantages of amalgamating smaller parishes in SCOC to better serve parishioners, an idea that took place long after he left Holy Cross. It is not surprising that Jansen, like Jensen, was asked by the archdiocese to remain in Los Angeles, but he chose to remain a Comboni missionary. By joining compassion for people with a pragmatic sense of the possible, he managed to sort out difficult racial and financial issues at Holy Cross, and bring significant improvements to the people.[29]

OPENING IN CHICAGO.

During Walter's tenure, only one parish was opened. In early 1982, Comboni Missionaries contacted the Archdiocese of Chicago about serving an inner city parish where there were opportunities for Hispanic and Black vocations and apostolic work for scholastics at Catholic Theological Union. With the death of Cardinal Cody in April, 1982, Walter delayed this request. Cody's successor, Archbishop Joseph Bernardin of Cincinnati, was installed as Archbishop of Chicago on August 25. 1982.[30]

Bernardin knew the Comboni missionaries from both the Atlanta and the Cincinnati Archdioceses. He had a personal link to Comboni Father Innocent Simoni whose Fiftieth Anniversary Mass the archbishop concelebrated. Simoni hailed from the same Tyrolean Alps region of Italy from which Bernardin's family had emigrated. At the Centennial Celebration Mass of Bishop Daniel Comboni's death, Bernardin remarked, "On a day such as this, we cannot help but give thanks to God for the example of Daniel Comboni. It was his zeal and insight which began the rebirth of the Church in Africa..."

On December 1, 1982, Walter visited Bernardin with the request for a parish in Chicago. Bernardin expressed happiness at having Comboni missionaries in the archdiocese. He said a diocesan meeting on Hispanic pastoral ministry would be held the following February, and perhaps a decision could be made then. By April, 1983, the Archdiocese of Chicago offered the Comboni Missionaries the Hispanic parish of St. Vitus Church. It had limited potential for promotion, but it offered quarters for formation and vocation work in a poor and urban neighborhood. On June 1, 1983, St. Vitus Parish was assigned to the Comboni Missionaries, and Father Colleoni was appointed its pastor. In 1985, Father Juan Huitrado succeeded him and Colleoni went to the Pala Mission.[31]

22. An American Perspective

Father Walter was well aware that changes in religious life had undermined, even destroyed, many of its structures, and without them, no organization could survive. He was not alone in recognizing this. Seán Sammon, in *Review for Religious*, addressed the problem of losing the old and searching for the new that would allow religious societies to survive. "Twenty-five years ago, men and women religious knew the task they were about: to dismantle the old model of religious life. But what to put in its place "was another matter." Surely it was not, he believed, "to exhaust our energies trying to maintain the status quo."[1]

Walter brought to his new office a keen awareness of the issues Sammon addressed. With considerable experience in the Comboni General Administration, he brought to his province a deep understanding of the society's *Rule of Life* (ROL), and a strong desire to implement it. Doing this was underscored by the Assistant General, Father Pierli, who emphasized the urgency of bringing provincial affairs into agreement with the ROL. After recognizing the NAP's help to the rest of the congregation, he had commented that this recognition did not permit the status quo. "I should repeat quite adamantly that a change of strategy, of deployment of communities, and setting of priorities does not come under question."[2]

THE CARA SURVEY

THE NEED FOR SELF STUDY.

Before the Provincial Council could address points of renewal, it had to revise the Provincial Directory to correspond to the ROL (*Rule of Life*) and the new General Directory. The previous directory was approved in 1975, but only after much controversy. Therefore, the Council wanted a new directory to be an authentic reflection of the ROL as it applied to North America. The four priests who assumed the task of writing this document were: Fathers Louis Gasparini, Todd Riebe, Mario Ongaro, and the provincial, Charles

Walter. They put the initials of their last names together and called their group GROW. To begin with, they wanted a careful study of the realities and culture of North America. They also wanted a clear sense of the state of the province and the opinions of its members. Finally, the survey had to pose questions so that responses could be quantified.[3] Walter heard from contacts in the Conference of Major Superiors of Men (CMSM) that the Center for Applied Research in the Apostolate (CARA) could launch such a study. It specialized in applying scientific methods to issues of the Church, and it was qualified to develop a questionnaire and analyze its results. The questionnaire would focus on points of renewal in the NAP, the need to prepare a new directory, and the need to plan for the future of the province. Using statistical sampling and objective analysis would lend credibility to the results that were lacking in some in-house surveys.

THE PROCESS.

The survey threw a wide net. It would include all members of the province, all American-born confreres overseas, all who worked in the NAP since 1970 but were serving overseas, all who had completed study at the Chicago Scholasticate, and all students and novices then in the province. Respondents remained anonymous, but questionnaires were coded to identify group variables such as age and membership in the province.[4]

In late 1980, Walter entreated his confreres to attend the Provincial Assembly and hear Father Conleth Overman, C.P., from CARA explain the survey process. Attached to his letter was a ten-page document that quoted from a CMSM conference. It observed that religious congregations were living in an age of "stumbling" pilgrims and "muttering" prophets. Walter echoed this in his letter, "...we are all stumbling around, trying to find out what God is asking us to do to fulfill our vocation in the new decade..." Not everyone at the fall provincial assembly agreed that a survey was necessary. For one thing, it was an experimental approach not only for the NAP, but possibly for the entire Congregation. Perhaps reflecting remarks at the meeting, Walter commented in his Christmas letter, "After the Mediterranean calm of four years as a Roman, I really feel as if I have fallen from the frying pan into the fire....it has been a confusing experience..."[5]

The CARA staff included Father Overman, the designated Project Director, and James T. Maguire and Edward M. Sullivan who executed the survey. It was designed to discover: 1) issues on which respondents agreed; 2) those on which they did not; 3) identify the issues on which respondents believed consensus was critical; 4) discover the perceptions respondents had of themselves vis à vis the province, and perceptions respondents had of the province vis à vis the congregation.

In July, 1981, a 479-item questionnaire was sent to 105 confreres in the NAP and overseas. Return envelopes were addressed to CARA. By the end of August, the fifty-eight questionnaires returned were included in the initial analysis. Another five arrived in time to go into the report. The six that came too late were virtually all from outside the United States. The response rate of the study was 66% which the analysts believed was quite acceptable for an international survey."[6]

THE SUBSTANCE.

On issues of agreement and disagreement, respondents were asked to name areas of opportunity or challenge; areas of major differences; and areas requiring consensus. Quantification was indicated by the number of "mentions" given to a topic. The following represents only the most frequently mentioned topics.

Regarding the category of "opportunities and challenges," there were 73 "mentions" of opportunities in which the "Apostolate" appeared 29 times. Great concern for minorities and the poor was expressed, and to some extent, social involvement (justice and peace). Regarding "challenges," "Recruitment" was mentioned 16 times, and it was considered a "matter of life or death."

"Differences of opinion" centered around both the "Apostolate" and "Community" with each mentioned 17 times. "Differences" in the "Apostolate" arose between those who had an "older understanding" of ministry and religious life and those who had "a more recent understanding" of it. Connected to this were the now familiar questions: "Should we have parishes, or should we not have parishes?"; "Are pastors second-class citizens?"; and "Was the Society truly missionary in the U.S. or merely a "mission sending and funds raising group?" "Differences" connected to "Community Life" seemed rooted in a juxtaposition between restriction versus freedom. Disagreement centered on "Administration. Here the focus was on the centralization of the decision-making process.

On the need for consensus, the role of the NAP in the U.S. and Canada, as well as in the Congregation was a top priority. CARA analysts pointed to the significance of this finding. If the "Apostolate" was rated so highly, they said, it followed that questions like "What are our valid ministries?" and "How do we define mission?" were important to answer. This was directly related to how the NAP's role was defined both by its members and the rest of the congregation.

The question about "the individual in relation to the province" was able to distinguish between respondents who felt effective in the province and those who did not. The perception of NAP members was that, as a whole, the congregation did not have a high opinion of their province. It was thought that other provinces viewed the NAP as a source of funds and vocations but not much else. Some "optimistic overtones" came from respondents who believed that the American province was an example of pluralism with great potential and a prophetic message, but even these did not indicate that others in the society shared this view.

Altogether, among the eight greatest concerns, the "Apostolate" rated the most mentions (60). "Community" had 40. "Recruitment" had 30. "The NAP" had 27. Following these were "Formation" with 23, "Administration" with 20, "Vowed Life" with 18, and "Finances" with 15.[7] On relations with the local Church, some spoke of a "ghetto mentality" and said public relations had priority over the society's "prophetic stance." Others mentioned that "ethnic tensions" were still an issue in the NAP, and that the society was "a foreigner society - often afraid to take a prophetic stance;" that there was a lack of understanding and commitment to civil rights." Still others found reasons for this neglect: "Room and need for improvement [in relations with local churches were] made difficult by changes in U.S. Church - not one Church, but many cultural and theological positions in tension [with each other]."

CARA analysts saw these differences reflecting a basic division in how mission was perceived. This was an important issue to probe, they said, since mission was the "basic reason for the Society's existence." Any differences in its perception could be disruptive, and on the basis of their interviews and observations they had found this to be the case in the past. But they did not believe responses indicated division along ethnic lines, specifically Italian versus non-Italian. Divisiveness was more likely derived from prior socialization and formation; therefore, "there was a need for re-socialization, re-training, and above all, tolerance."[8]

Although the report stated that the province faced recruitment problems similar to other institutions due to the steady drop in numbers of 17 to 26 year old group, this fact was not reflected in responses. Instead, respondents believed lower recruitment was due to "The general materialism of people and the secular orientation of youth."[9] They also blamed themselves for "Lack of fervor, prayer and deep commitment..." Still, 83% were willing to volunteer for recruiting, but they believed their efforts were severely hampered by the society's lack of identity in America. Response on the topic "Personnel Administration" was characterized by one person's claim that personnel administration was rife with "Ill-defined goals leading to poor motivation, poor corporate identity as [Comboni Missionaries which led] to poor esprit de corps and individualism." This eventually led to a sense of helplessness. (The report was not targeting the new administration which was only one year in office. Respondents noted this point.) Analysts remarked that it would be easy to pass off these comments on the basis of the scarcity of men available for the work of the province, and then conclude that sacrifices were necessary. But another aspect had to be examined, that of morale and its impact. How could an organization as small as the Province function effectively with 40% of its human resources disaffected?

Despite all the critical responses in many categories, there was an amazing degree of unanimity in respondents' answers regarding their (religious) beliefs. There was a high support for the role of the laity, the lay apostolate, and for lay missionaries; all of the twelve questions on this topic received from 67% to 99% affirmative responses. Confounding the idea of a generation gap, the survey found a very "positive and informed" approach to the aging and the elderly. Ninety-one percent of responders scored in the high (positive attitude) category on these questions." A willingness to take on a heavy burden in the apostolate was evident when "'Production' rates for Pastoral Practices" was calculated. Each "hearing confession" session consumed three man-hours that included travel time, preparation, and ending tasks. Along with other pastoral activities, the report concluded that "the workload of the Province is substantial, and knowing where resources of time and manpower are being spent is the starting place for effective Province manpower planning."[10]

When the CARA survey results were published, the Provincial Council had a wealth of information with which to work. It could never address, much less resolve, all the issues reported, but it could proceed toward the goal for which the report was intended: a provincial directory and planning for the future. GROW prepared the first draft of a directory, and by November 1, 1981, it was sent to members of the province for comments. These were returned for revision that same month. By the following January, a revised draft was ratified by the Provincial Council. Members of GROW were then put in charge of developing leadership workshops for superiors and other means of personal and spiritual development.[11]

When he visited in 1982, Father General Calvia commended Council members. In a later letter, he expressed optimism about the NAP, "...we have every reason to hope for the future of the North American Province. There are many positive indications which strengthen this impression... a greater union between communities... greater union between the communities of Canada and the United States, and greater union and understanding between the communities in the States from the East to the Midwest and West." He was pleased that there was increased interest in "the Negroes and the Hispanics," and he saw less divisiveness between younger and senior members and that the province was becoming more Americanized. He said that "the presence of young and not so young American Comboni Missionaries [taking] up posts of responsibility in our houses...is a sign of hope for the future."[12]

A SHRINKING FINANCIAL BASE

From the very first, members of the Provincial Council realized they were facing a financial crisis as well as a shortage of personnel. In an Intercapitular Chapter report, the personnel issues were summarized: 1) The number of men in the province had stabilized at fifty with an average age of forty-nine; 2) These were spread out in two countries more than twice the size of Western Europe; 3) Fifteen new members promised to the NAP had not replaced those going overseas, those still students, or those on leave; 4) Most NAP members overseas were not yet eligible to return, and only one ordination was expected before 1985. To alleviate the personnel crisis, the General Council was asked if students at the Chicago scholasticate could remain in the NAP after their ordination.[13]

Regarding the financial deficit, the Provincial Council took a pro-active stance. The ROL had determined that "The vow of poverty, in imitation of Christ, entails a life which is poor in reality and in spirit, sober and industrious, and a stranger to earthly riches." Seeing that while income was diminishing, grants to communities were increasing, the Council decided that the budget of provincial offices would be cut by 10%. Grants to some other communities and to the magazine were also cut. When this did not produce the desired results, the Comboni Mission Center at Cincinnati took additional cuts. Communities still receiving grants had to submit quarterly reports. The Institutional Development Council (IDC), which had made a presentation to the previous administration to develop, plan, and run a fund-raising program for the NAP, was hired.[14]

The struggle to bring the budget into balance was a material necessity as well as an exercise in the spirit of poverty. The goal was not to see that the Comboni missionaries in North America live in the wretched poverty of many of their parishioners. Nor was it thought they were living in luxurious circumstances. Rather, the intention was that they live with frugality, which many were already doing. More importantly, it was thought that good financial record-keeping and reporting was part of the vow of obedience. Without this discipline, the practical outcome would be that the province could not make long or short range plans with any assurance. Earlier, when the Comboni pioneers came to America, a certain entrepreneurial bent was required to survive and send money to foreign missions. The need to found the province and financially assist the mother house led to self-imposed stringency as well as a dynamic that attracted many benefactors. But the dynamics were quite different in the 1980s. As Father Charles Walter admitted, people of his generation and later had "yet to discover the secret of being good promoters," and this made his work as provincial more difficult.[15] Eventually, pressure from the Provincial Council had its impact, and in 1984 a balanced budget was reported.[16]

Developing a fiscally responsible budget was more important than even Walter had known. New obligations appeared at every turn. First, Casa Comboni, then other vocation efforts required support. Approximately $50,000 a year was set aside for Casa Comboni alone. Accumulating expenses affected the entire province. In 1981, a comprehensive review of health insurance proved necessary when even three young American confreres already had symptoms of serious illness. An investigation of property and automobiles discovered that a "considerable number" of cars had reached the 100,000 mile mark and were "big gas guzzlers." A policy for fleet-buying coordinated with another religious society was recommended.[17] When Father Biancalana returned to the NAP, he attracted candidates in Chicago, and apartments to house them had to be rented. Chicago was now seen by some as the hub of a future-centered province. Along with a search for a promotion center there, the province increased its stake in CTU by becoming one of its corporate members. Then there was the new emphasis on "Justice and Peace," which led to outlays such as the subsidized construction of a home for the poor in St. Pius parish. All these initiatives cost money that had to be raised, at least in part, by decreasing expenses in other departments. Even requests from foreign missions and the General Council were not always granted in full. But a far more painful initiative than the budget cuts was launching a study to determine the viability of established communities and properties.

MATCHING MEN TO RESOURCES

As the average age of confreres rose, fewer men were available for challenging assignments, and as the CARA Report pointed out, the work load of Comboni missionaries in the NAP was still "substantial." In 1982, the toll this was taking could be gauged by the many articles on stress and burnout printed in *Family News* by Walter, its editor. That summer, he asked NAP members' consent to purchase a lake side cottage in Kentucky. "Who among us," he said, "has not had the misfortune to be on the receiving end of an emotional outburst from someone we usually respect for his/her dedication and overall balanced personality?...One of the more pressing concerns in church and religious life circles today is that of burnout and coping with stress by priests and religious in general...." Walter mentioned the U.S. Catholic Bishops' committee booklet, 'The Priest and Stress" which said that priests and religious people were then living in stressful situations that could lead to serious psychological and even physical harm. Recalling that the Comboni Rule of Life recommended periods of rest and relaxation, he saw the purchase of the cottage as affording his "brothers" the kind of peace and quiet they once found in Georgia as seminarians.[18] The Williamsburg Lake cottage was purchased and, in at least one case, it served its purpose well. The only African American Comboni Missionary, Brother Bernard Pratt (see Epilogue), sought this retreat when very ill. He spent his last night and day there, and before he died, he told his confreres with him at the cottage that he felt better than he had in years.

But the cottage was a short term remedy. Walter needed long range solutions. The match between missionaries and communities in the NAP needed adjustment. To achieve this, the Provincial Council launched a major review of communities to determine which were, and which were not serving their stated purpose. The need to let go of a house and its relationship with the surrounding community would prove trying; and it was determined that each evaluation would be conducted with thoroughness and judiciousness. To facilitate this, an internal renewal of the Provincial Council and governing bodies began. Council members immersed themselves in courses on governing styles, planning, and personal communication techniques. They tried to improve their skills through tests that would help them understand their own strengths and weaknesses. They hoped this preparation would help them lessen the pain of disengagement for those their decisions would affect.[19]

GLENDORA AND YORKVILLE.

After the successful launching of Casa Comboni, many considered the newly acquired promotion center in Glendora too far from the central city, and too middle-class an environment for students. Vocation and mission promotion was moved to Holy Cross, and Glendora was rented until late 1985 when it was sold to the Conventual Franciscans. This decision was not popular with those who saw Glendora as a superior promotion center and future retirement home. But Council members believed the facility would not attract poor Hispanics living on the other side of Los Angeles. Eventually Casa Comboni moved to a house in the Los Angeles suburb of Azusa, and a promotion center opened in the suburb of Covina. Both remain open at this writing. Yorkville's novitiate was suspended in 1980 for lack of novices. Only Father Paolucci was at the Yorkville center, and he was slated to go to the missions in Ecuador. The Yorkville promotion center was transferred to the Chicago Scholasticate. After Paolucci's departure, this contact was expected to be maintained through a newsletter until the return of Biancalana. Closing Yorkville would result in "a temporary drop in the financial support [of] a large number of friends," a fact that Council regretted. But personnel realities left them little alternative.[20]

SANTA YSABEL AND PALA.

Walter's predecessor, Busetti, had already proposed returning to the San Diego Diocese several outlying chapels connected to Santa Ysabel. These chapels were now closer to recently established Catholic parishes than to Santa Ysabel. The differences were often of fifty miles or more. Busetti was willing to have a Comboni priest care for St. Elizabeth Church in Julian, only seven miles from Santa Ysabel as an exchange. Maher replied he would contact the pastors of the parishes to see "if it is feasible for them to carry [out] your suggestion ...." But the people at St. Elizabeth's were happy with their present arrangement.[21]

Pala Mission had a slightly different history. The school built during Father Carillo's pastorate had generous benefactors who had funded and subsidized it for many years. But while the school population grew, the benefactors diminished. To raise money, Comboni missionaries continued to hold the June Fiesta, and Father Turchetti and others printed and sold Christmas cards designed by Indian children. The "Green Stamps" that Father Didoni collected were used to purchase a bus for the school. In 1984, Pastor Gino Doniney sent a brief summary about Pala Mission and its school: "More than once a section of our parish has been made a complete ecclesiastical unit...A Deacon is in charge of the Mission in Anza. Temecula and Rancho California have become [new parishes under the jurisdiction] of the diocese of San Bernardino. Valley Center, too, was formed into a new parish....these changes were possible not only because of the work of our priests [but]...because these areas became more thickly inhabited."[22]

Both Santa Ysabel and Pala Missions had prospered under Comboni Missionaries, but both were now in a different environment than when they were taken over in 1948. The Diocese of San Diego was no longer struggling financially as it had under Bishop Buddy. Its numbers had grown, and its population was more prosperous. The Indian missions needed special care, but the *Rule of Life* recommended that, once a mission was stabilized as a parish, it should be returned to the diocese.

No evidence is available that Busetti received word from Bishop Maher about attaching Santa Ysabel's Indian chapels to local parishes, and it was years after the parishes developed within Pala Mission's territory before they were served by diocesan clergy. In the interim, a long established custom in San Diego of diocesan priests serving Anglos, and missionaries serving Indians continued. It was a custom the Comboni Missionaries had to challenge even if they were not short on personnel. What few there were had to be allocated to vocation work. The Provincial Council asked the San Diego Diocese to "find another solution" to the question of a pastor at Santa Ysabel. It notified the diocese that when the older personnel at Pala Mission could no longer continue, they would not be replaced by Comboni Missionaries. When Walter finally met the chancellor of the San Diego Diocese in August of 1983, the latter found no problem in arranging the transfer of Santa Ysabel. The date was set at August, 1984.[23]

CAMBRIDGE AND BROSSARD.

Decisions about Glendora and Yorkville came before the CARA Report. But once it was available, Council members had a better gauge of their confreres thoughts on individual communities. The survey had asked questions on whether or not certain communities should be closed, and whether or not those same communities were likely to be closed. Opinions on Santa Ysabel mission were evenly divided on both questions. Those on Pala Mission were divided 58% to 42% against closing. Thus, the decisions to give Santa Ysabel back to the diocese and to maintain a Comboni presence at Pala were supported by the split "vote" on Santa Ysabel, and the majority "vote" on Pala. But when these same questions were asked about the

Canadian communities of Cambridge in Ontario and Brossard in Quebec, a majority favored keeping both open.[24]

In 1982, the Cambridge community included Father Dominic Pazzaglia in ministry, Father Brian Quigley touring high schools for vocations, and Brother Jerry Charbonneau working with a diocesan vocation committee and as an extraordinary minister at a parish. Both native-born Canadians, Quigley and Charbonneau were achieving some success. By 1984, Quigley had four Canadians in a pre-postulancy program for whom he needed accommodations. Permanent quarters for the pre-postulants materialized when the Sisters of Notre Dame made their Sacred Heart Convent available to Comboni Missionaries. By then, Father John Fraser was also working in the Mission Office of the diocese. He and those at the promotion center moved to the Kitchener residence, and the Cambridge building was sold.[25]

At the Brossard community things were not going as well. Comboni personnel had difficulty inculturating in the French province, and vocations did not develop. Walter and his Council sought more information on prospects there, and the General Secretary of the Religious Conference in Quebec informed them that they were not good. A Comboni missionary making additional inquiries heard from seven separate heads of religious congregations in Canada that the vocation crisis in Quebec was worse than ever. With vocation work in Canada listed in the 1982 (Intercapitular) Personnel Report as the primary reason for a Comboni presence there, the Provincial Council decided to phase out Brossard. The Diocese of St. Jean Longueuil was informed that the parish of Good Shepherd would be given back in December of 1986.[26]

Closing Brossard was painful since the Comboni Missionaries had long struggled to bring it success. When missionaries familiar with Quebec culture staffed it, it went forward. But too often this was not the case. Quigley's success in attracting vocations at Cambridge, however, cushioned the impact of closing Brossard.

AGONIZING OVER MONROE.

When it came to evaluating the Monroe community, with a thirty year presence and strong diocesan, religious, and lay support, there would be no such cushioning effect. In 1982, Father Joe Rankin reported on discussions he and his confreres in Monroe had about the facility. This led the Council to launch a formal evaluation. It assured NAP members the purpose of the study was not to close the community, and that it would be open-minded and objective. After all, 77% of NAP members responding to the CARA questionnaire thought that neither Monroe nor its high school should be, or would be, closed.[27]

To the Council's credit, the evaluation was not hasty. In 1983, it focussed on two lines of thought: whether or not to keep a high school seminary, and whether or not to keep any community at all. It was understood that moving the high school to Chicago would mean giving up strong friendships and support with no equivalent to balance it. But some believed Chicago could prove a greater source of vocations among Hispanics and Blacks. The decision was in Monroe's favor since it was a well-established community and centrally located in the Midwest where early vocations originated.

By 1984, the Council still searched for specific data on finances, numbers of students, personnel, and job assignments at Monroe. In August, it reached a decision to close the high school after the 1984-1985 school year. In early 1985, with the deficit increasing, the Council pressed Monroe staff for programs and plans that could eliminate its annual deficit and even supply a contribution to the missions. After a meeting of department heads, the Council concluded "there currently is too much work being done by too few people [in the province]. This endangers any successful planning, and [results in] a great many problems with regard to continuity..."[28] The Provincial Treasurer, Father Contran, added that the question of the property and a possible move into smaller quarters required decisive action. There were already valid offers for the house. When the three missionaries from Monroe joined the discussion, a consensus was reached that: 1) the Monroe building was too large and future activities should be transferred to a smaller facility, 2) activities not in keeping with the Comboni Missionary charism should not be justified to cover operating expenses, 3) the community would develop mission promotion and education programs for another year giving priority to vocation promotion at the high school and college level.

With a final decision on Monroe not imminent, all programs continued, but the monthly grant to the community was discontinued. A joint meeting with the Monroe Men's Club and Ladies' Auxiliary with Walter was suggested to assure them of his commitment to Monroe and to seek their advice on activities his missionaries should undertake. But the meeting with benefactors was postponed until Council had more specific plans. Unfortunately, two of the three missionaries then at Monroe were up for reassignment to foreign missions, and transitional personnel would be needed.[29]

By early 1986, momentum developed to sell the property. The Council still talked about conferring with benefactors, but it was now hesitant since a new provincial would soon be elected. The return from Ecuador of Father Paolucci, well-known in Monroe, was expected to again provide a sense of stability in a transition period. The Provincial Treasurer was given permission to proceed with a sale, and serious negotiations began with the Brothers of the Holy Cross. Paolucci was expected to work at whatever facility was still available, and the future of a Comboni presence in Monroe was entirely dependent on whether suitable personnel would be available in the future.[30]

COMBONI MISSION CENTER.

The effort to divest the province of commitments did not end with Monroe. Even the former Sacred Heart Seminary was opened to bidders. This began in 1983 when someone representing a group of investors inquired about the property. The offer was rejected, but later another bidder leased a good deal of the tract on Beechmont Avenue. Interest in the first land holding of Comboni Missionaries in North America reflected a significant change in its neighborhood over thirty-five years. Once a sparsely populated rural area called Forestville, by the early 1980s, development was in high gear, and it was now called Anderson Township. The Comboni property was gradually surrounded by private homes north of it. Retail businesses sprang up along the east-west thoroughfare that fronted it.

By 1985, the Provincial Council found many reasons why the building was a burden, citing it was not cost-effective since fewer people used it. Some wanted to move provincial offices to Chicago and combine them with a promotion center. A sticking point appeared when few, if any, investors wanted to buy the missionaries' building as well as their property. Without an attractive offer from an investor, negotiations began to sell much of it, retaining the leased land and the main building with a few acres around it. Once this was accomplished, the original and founding location of Comboni Missionaries in North America became an island community floating in a sea of residential housing, a post office, child care facilities, and busy retail establishments.[31]

EVALUATIONS

In 1982, Father General Calvia had said, "...we have every reason to hope for the future of the North American Province..." Two years later, his Assistant General, Father Pierli, offered a different perspective. While conceding the province "made good steps forward over the past years..." he added, "Then is the province close to a real take-off? God knows the answer, but at any rate I would suggest a few conditions which would enhance the chances for a sure future." More prayer was his remedy along with "an extraordinary charge of spirituality based on prayer and austerity of life..."[32] [Emphasis not added]. Pierli's critique had to puzzle the Provincial Council since it came after enormous efforts on its part to balance the budget, divest itself of commitments, and launch new vocation initiatives. The opening of Casa Comboni, with its strong vocation response from Latin Americans, had been praised by the General Administration, but such initiatives were not rewarded with more missionaries.

After Pierli's letter, Walter approached Father Calvia and his two Assistants General with a request for personnel. He agreed with Pierli that the NAP was at a turning point, but he said this was due to a steady decrease in manpower. He had only forty-eight missionaries, seven of whom were over sixty-five, four undergoing crises, and three unable to take on full time work. The response to this request was that the NAP needed a "higher spirituality," [Emphasis not added] and that "among the provinces [it is] the most deeply embedded in a secularized society." In a letter from Rome, Walter was told that "The rather numerous crises of vocation occurring over there [North America] saddens all of us, and a certain fear creeps in somebody's mind that we pay a rather high toll for the rejuvenation and reshaping of the province..."[33]

This response from the General Administration was discussed, and an answer from the Provincial Council forwarded to Rome that read, "it is very difficult to assess and make judgements on a culture and society that are very complex realities of which the General Administration has only a limited experience, and the problem of the NAP should be seen in the general context of the Society, where personal crises do not seem to be limited to one nationality or province..." The Council thanked the General Administration for assigning the newly ordained of the province to the NAP, and for the return of Fathers Ghirotto and Catellani. But it emphasized the need for "new blood" with positive mission experience. The NAP then had no one to fill three posts in formation, and if these post were not filled, three promising candidates could not begin their postulancy. Without them, Father Converset, the novice master, would have no novices the following year.[34]

None of these arguments convinced the General Administration. When Fathers Walter and Ongaro visited a new General Council in the summer of 1985, they spoke of the physical illnesses and disabilities increasing in the NAP, and how badly missionaries were needed. They received sympathy but no commitments.[35] When an answer did come, it was that no one was available, and someone should be found "in loco." When the Council received this reply, it held a "brainstorming session," and members agreed to turn their attention to "quality of life" issues. Many in the province were experiencing widespread frustration due to their inability to do justice to commitments. There were also confreres who were in a rut and needed spiritual revival. These factors had all led to health problems.

Disappointment was expressed that the format of the recent General Chapter had not done justice to the inspiration of the Spirit and the work put into it. Directives on how to implement its outcomes were scarce. Then it had also called for a revision of commitments, but North America had already addressed such revisions and was continuing to do so. Thus, this would not spark its members' interest. On the other hand, the Chapter's words about "signs of the Kingdom in our world today" was believed of great importance, and the Council wanted to hear more on how individuals and communities could witness to such signs. Thinking through all this led the Council to the conclusion that the next Provincial Assembly would be more people- oriented than structure-oriented.[36]

Assistant General, Father Otto Fuchs, now special liaison to the NAP, attended the rejuvenated Provincial Assembly and said he hoped future meetings would take the same emphasis. He warned that the next provincial still had to work at reviewing commitments and bring them in line with personnel availability. He complimented Walter for doing a fine job of establishing a system and an atmosphere of trust in the NAP. Fuchs advocated more prominence to community councils, more meals shared, a mission statement for each community. He said all the elements of Comboni Missionary activity were present in the NAP, but working among four minority groups was probably too much. His positive assessments were greatly appreciated. Perhaps coming from the once-separated Germans branch of Comboni Missionaries, Fuchs may have appreciated a certain isolation that a province in an Anglo-Saxon culture might experience. Fuchs praised the province for its support of the International Scholasticate which was leading its newly ordained to choose to work in the NAP. He was pleased with the "strong evangelization commitment in the local church." Above all, he avoided deprecating tones and accusations of materialism and secularism.[37]

Before stepping down as provincial, Father Walter visited Peru where he hoped to go on his next assignment. Borrowing from an address by the Jesuit, Father Montagne, he warned his confreres against stressing work over everything else, and developing a "Conrad-Hilton" mentality where everyone comes and goes without much contact. This was common in North America where telephones, telecasts, computers and other forces emphasized "measurable" productivity. In this milieu, he said, those in service professions, particularly religious and missionaries, could find themselves serving others without respite. Walter's achievements as Provincial of North America offered new structure, stability, and increased hope to a province that was buffeted by change and overtaxed by work. He was undoubtedly taxed physically and spiritually in this undertaking. Some later murmured against the flood of paperwork produced during his tenure. But none denied that Walter made a difference in the province, one that produced more confidence and left a plan for future leaders to follow.

In late 1986, Father Brian Quigley was elected provincial of North America. In his first letter to his "Brothers," he said, "As we approach the end of another year, we glance back to the past in order to recognize our blessings (and give thanks), the greatest of which has come to us in the person of Fr. Charlie. I know I speak for all of you when I say that he will be missed. But Charlie's years of dedicated service to the province, coupled with his keen perception and clear leadership, have launched us into the 21st century."[38]

Epilogue

If *Defining Mission: Comboni Missionaries in North America* provides those who read it a better understanding of the NAP, it will have served its purpose. What the future holds for the province is uncertain. It now has parishes in Los Angeles and Chicago; four mission centers in Chicago, Cincinnati, Los Angeles, and Montclair; and thirty-nine priests and brothers, half of whom are over sixty years of age. Vocations, where they exist, are primarily developing as lay missionaries in Chicago.

In many ways, the NAP's situation is similar to that faced by other congregations in the United States; there are fewer vocations, houses are closing, and there are conflicting views regarding options for renewal. In the NAP's case, however, there are reasons that separate it from other North American congregations, and even from other provinces within its own congregation. One is that, from its beginning, it was primarily identified as an Italian foundation by Americans, but seen as an American one by its confreres in other provinces. The dynamic this created can be traced through three stages from 1939 to the present. During the first, there was rapid growth in the province fueled by strong support from the General Administration. During the second, the General Administration's enthusiasm for the province waned, growth leveled off, and doubts surfaced about its mission. During the third, or last stage, frustration increased and morale ebbed. An already overburdened personnel were increasingly scrutinized by major superiors in Rome regarding their "real mission," and the province itself found little support from the General Administration. The reasons for these dynamics are complex, but in hindsight, a few can be identified.

From 1940 through the 1950s, when growth was rapid, the Comboni missionaries in the U. S. found themselves in a country with a large number of Catholics and a thriving economy. Father Anthony Vignato, understanding how serendipitous this was for his society, wrote to Julius Rizzi in July, 1946, that acceptance by Archbishop McNicholas of Cincinnati was seen by his Council as "a blessing from God." Following Vignato as Superior General, Todesco was also enthusiastic about work in the U.S. for it was a time when Europe was suffering the financial aftermath of World War II. He continued to send Italian priests, brothers, and students to the United States, and funds flowed back to the General Administration and its missions. Morale was high. Productivity was phenomenal. Father Victor Turchetti aptly described this first stage, "There was no real pressure [on us]. It was the enthusiasm we had in the beginning; we were new in the country [and] we saw there was a response. People were very kind, and there were a lot of vocations going to other seminaries. So we said, 'Why not build...a high school [for recruits]?'" The enthusiasm Father Turchetti described created a momentum that continued into the 1960s.

As provincial of North America, Todesco used this momentum for further expansion. But toward the end of the decade, the energy, optimism, and productivity of the province began to falter. Changes going on in society and the Church had their impact, but added to this were a series of crises in the province. First, Todesco's superior, Father Briani, had little interest in North America. He sent fewer missionaries to it, while asking more of them from it. Quite often those he did send to the NAP were not prepared for the work in it. Second, Briani's determination to meet seminary crises with drastic action was echoed in America. Todesco cautioned superiors not to waver from the rules, even those other societies were changing due to documents from the Second Vatican Council. Third, Todesco remained aloof from American culture He appeared oblivious to major events taking place within it, both secular and religious. Not until August, 1968, did he confide to his diary, "A severe crisis has taken place in our scholasticate...We have lost more than half our scholastics...We cannot pinpoint all the reasons..." Yet when American priests and students met with him at Columbia, and told him that even more scholastics were on the brink of leaving, he refused to take action. Finally, he did not see the need for a judicious retreat from expansion when capable personnel became scarce. His proclivity to expand, despite this, undoubtedly contributed to serious health issues in the province and possibly to the death of four young missionaries who were suffering illnesses.

Gerald Arbuckle, author of *Out of Chaos, Refounding Religious Congregations*, describes the difficulties that afflicted religious societies after Vatican II. One of his observations seem apt for the situation in the NAP before and after 1969: "Where memories of abuses by authoritarian superiors of the pre-Vatican hierarchical model remain vividly alive, there is strong resistance to any form of authority, no matter how necessary and well-supported theologically it might be."[7]

Just as a positive momentum fueled the beginning of Todesco's provincialate, the series of crises at its end left behind a vacuum in which frustration led to dissention and to the chaos that Arbuckle predicts in such circumstances. The provincials who followed Todesco felt the need for healing, but their superiors in Rome seemed not to understand the weight of their burden. As a result, ministry in the United States came under fire. Work in the NAP was held deficient when compared to work in other provinces. The spirituality of the province was questioned. Even when Father Charles Walter slashed spending and closed houses to conform to renewal documents and his superiors' requests, the mission and spirituality of the NAP's members were held suspect. As time passed, even the most confident and knowledgeable among those in the province doubted that it would ever be recognized for its mission work or unique contribution to the congregation.

Whatever the future has in store for the province, its ownership of a productive past is undeniable. By 1990, it included 129 vocations among North Americans, thirty-three Comboni priests and three Comboni lay brothers. Father Alfred Paolucci summed up their contributions when he calculated that, in man years, the NAP's native sons served the congregation for 1018 years, 241 of which were in foreign missions. The mandate to serve African Americans was fulfilled. The NAP not only served them in parishes, but at a time when many American bishops and religious societies in the United States refused to accept Blacks in their seminaries, the NAP had close to ten black seminarians. Brother Bernie Pratt was one of these. He served in Uganda from 1969 to 1979, narrowly escaping death during Idi Amin's reign of terror. Ironically, he succumbed to a heart attack in 1984 while in the United States. Two other African Americans, Giles and William Conwill, left the Comboni Missionary Institute as scholastics, but Giles Conwill incardinated in the San Diego Diocese. His brother, William, earned a Ph.D. in clinical psychology at Stanford University. Melvin Grier was a high school seminarian at Sacred Heart Seminary, but he transferred to a diocesan high school, and later enlisted in the Air Force. The author was unable to contact other former black seminarians.

---

[7] Gerald Arbuckle, *Out of Chaos, Refounding Religious Congregations*, New York: Paulist Press, 1988, 113.

Ministry in black parishes was extensive. It included work in Cincinnati, Los Angeles, Louisville, and Chicago for a total of more than 150 years of service. This service is continuing in Los Angeles and Chicago. Although ministry to Indians and to poor or non-Catholic white populations was not highly regarded by some confreres outside the NAP, it was often as challenging as ministry to Blacks. This was particularly true of the 80 years or more of service to Indians in California that began in 1948.

Whether to African Americans, Hispanics, Indians, or Whites, ministry served a dual purpose. It benefited the spiritual and the material welfare of parishioners, and it attracted benefactors who contributed to the province and to the mother house and its missions. Published financial reports before 1980 are scarce, but anecdotal evidence appears throughout the narrative. For example, we find that Father Accorsi was able to send substantial sums to Verona and, by 1946, also save $20,000 for a seminary. When, as Superior General, Todesco asked the province for an annual contribution of $20,000, those who worked on provincial finances told the author that more often as much as $30,000 or more was sent. This did not include substantial "gifts" to Superior Generals. These last donations were not made public for, the author was told, the NAP was ordered not to disclose them.

But the dedication and contribution of the Comboni missionaries in North America is not primarily financial. It is embodied in the daily lives of those who served the province. This narrative touched on many of the leaders and innovators who in extraordinary circumstances did extraordinary deeds. But the author apologizes for the many who do not appear in these pages due to limited space and time. Some of these were at the very heart of the NAP's mission. They were Comboni missionaries such as Father Samuel Baiani, recognized for his work with black youth in Louisville; Father Valentino Saoncella, a caring pastor and superior, Father Aleardo De Berti, who had an important role as spiritual director; and Brother Victor De Gasperi who won many friends for the society as he drove his truck in Cincinnati collecting for the Sacred Heart Guild's thrift shop. Then there was Father Larry Endrizzi, born an American, raised in Italy, he was the first American ordained in the United States. Despite poor health, when he was expelled from Sudan, he went to work in the Georgia missions. Known for his exuberance and spiritual excellence, an automobile accident took his life, but not his spirit. In Thomson, Georgia, there is a parish building called the Larry Endrizzi Hall. Endrizzi and his confreres in North America displayed a deep commitment and dedication that left an indelible mark in the lives and hearts of those they served.

NOTES

Chapter 1. An Urgent Mission

1. General Council Minutes; The minutes read, "We are not against considering the proposal, and we wait for more concrete information;" CMAR.

2. *The World Almanac of World War II: The Complete and Comprehensive Documentary of World War II,* ed. Brigadier Peter Young, 1st rev. ed., New York: World Almanac, An Imprint of Pharos Books, 1981, 33-34.

3. Owen Chadwick, *Britain and the Vatican During the Second World War,* Cambridge: Cambridge University Press, 1986, 24, 47, 57-58.

4. *World Almanac,* 36-37; Oliver Branchesi, in a letter to the author, Feb. 2, 1993; Chadwick, 9, 8, 9-11, 77, 227.

5. Branchesi to author, February 2, 1993; Dennis Conway, *Chronology of the North American Province,* an English translation from the *Bollettino,* 1939-1947, 2.

6. Conway, *Chronology,* 1-2

7. Lorenzo Gaiga, M.C.C.J., "In Pace Christi," *Bulletin #164,* 37-46; also interviews with Comboni contemporaries of Father Mason.

8. Anthony Vignato to "To Whom It May Concern," September 29, 1939, CMAR; The Diary of My Trip to America," Edward Mason, CMAC, 2.

9. Dolores Liptak, *Immigrants and Their Church,* New York: MacMillan Publishing Company, 1989, 177; Cyprian Davis, *The History of Black Catholics in the United States,* New York: Crossroads Publishing Co., 1990, 198, 252

10. Edward Mason, M.C.C.J., "The Diary of My Trip to America," CMAC, 1.

11. Philip Gleason, *Keeping the Faith: American Catholicism Past and Present,* Notre Dame, Indiana: University of Notre Dame Press, 1987, 40.

12. *The Catholic Almanac, 1993,* Our Sunday Visitor Publishing Division, Our Sunday Visitor, Inc.: Huntington, Indiana, 1993, 395; Zane L. Miller, *Boss Cox's Cincinnati.* New York: University Press, 1968, 65; Dolores Liptak, *Immigrants and Their Church,* New York: MacMillan Publishing Company, 1989, 76-77.

13. Gleason, 43; Gerald P. Fogarty, *The Vatican and the American Hierarchy,* Collegeville, Minnesota: A Michael Glazier Book, The Liturgical Press, 1982, 1985, 190-194, 346-347; John B. Sheerin, C.S.P., "American Catholics and Ecumenism," 72-73; Aidan Kavanagh, O.S.B., "Spirituality in the American Church," 209; Louis J. Putz, C.S.C., "Religious Education and Seminary Studies: Some Recent Trends," 241- 242, all in *Contemporary Catholicism in the United States,* ed. Philip Gleason, Notre Dame, Indiana: University of Notre Dame Press, 1969; Anthony E. Gilles, *The People of Hope: The Story Behind the Modern Church,* St. Anthony Messenger Press, 1988, 68-73.

14. Liptak, *Immigrants,* 142; David Steven Cohen, *America the Dream of My Life: Selections from the Federal Writers' Project's New Jersey Ethnic Survey,* New Brunswick, Rutgers University Press, 1990, 67.Leonard Bacigalupo, O.F.M., "Some Aspects Involving the Interaction of the Italian and the Irish," in *Italians and*

Irish in America, 116.

15. Liptak, *Immigrants*, 143; Bacigalupo, 117, "In examining these religious factors..."
16. Mason, 4-5; Henry J. Koren, *The Serpent and the Dove: A History of the Congregation of the Holy Ghost in the United States*, Pittsburgh, Pennsylvania, Spiritus Press, 1985, 194, fn 115.
17. Jay P. Dolan, *The American Catholic Experience: A History from Colonial Times to the Present*, Garden City, New York: Doubleday & Company, Inc. 1985, 367; Liptak, *Immigrant Church*, 179.
18. Mason 5, 6-7; Fogarty, 247, 267. An explanation for the climate of this exchange between Mason and McIntyre may be found in Fogarty, 267, referring to Spellman's appointment of McIntyre as his auxiliary bishop (shortly after Mason's visit), "He [Spellman] needed the expertise of the former Wall Street clerk [McIntyre] especially when he learned that he inherited a debt ridden archdiocese."
19. Pastorelli's Journal notes, "Dec. 3rd, Rev. Edward Mason, F.S.C., from Wau, Equatoria, Anglo Egyptian Sudan Africa, stayed overnight. Confirmation at St. Peter Claver's,"JA; Founded in Mill Hill, England in 1866 as the St. Joseph's Society of the Sacred Heart for Foreign Missions (Mill Hill Fathers), the American Josephites became an independent community in 1893.
20. Stephen J. Ochs, *Desegregating the Altar: The Josephites and the Struggle for Black Priests, 1871-1960*, Baton Rouge, Louisiana: Louisiana State University Press: 1990, 362; Mason, 9.
21. Mason, 9-11.
22. ibid.,12-15.
23. ibid., 15, 17-18.
24. Mason 19-20; Fogarty, 258.
25. ibid., 20-22.
26. Mason 21-23; Cicognani to McNicholas, December 6, 1939, Protocol no. 499/39, HACAC.
27. Steven M. Avella, "John T. McNicholas in the Age of Practical Thomism," from *Records of the American Catholic Historical Society of Philadelphia*, vol 97, March-December, 1986, no 1-4, HACAC, 16-20.
28. The Mother of God Mission opened in 1939. See *The Official Catholic Directory*, New Providence, New Jersey: P.J. Kennedy & Sons, 1940.
29. Mason 24-27; Interview in the *Catholic Telegraph Register*, January 12, 1940; Eugene H. Maly Memorial Library, Athenaeum of Ohio. The article's substance was the Comboni missions in the Vicariate Apostolic of Bahr-el-Ghazal, Africa, where Mason worked; Mason, 27-28.
30. Mason 29-30; Fogarty, 258; Mason, 30.
31. McNicholas to Mason, January 13, 1940, (*Copia*). Mason copied the letterhead of the Church of Our Lady of Pompeii in New York on the information from McNicholas, and sent it to Accorsi; Mason to McNicholas, January 20, 1940, (copy), CMAC.

32. Mason, 31-33.

Chapter 2. The Cornerstone

1.   Conway, Chronology, 13; Mason to Accorsi, January 19, 1940, CMAC; Mason to Accorsi, February 12, 1940, CMAC.
2.   Oliver Branchesi, in interviews with Professor Anselmo and Doctor Luigi Accorsi and other members of the Accorsi family, May, 1993, CMAC.
3.   Hamlet Accorsi's Diary Fragment, CMAC; Letters of Hamlet Accorsi to members of his family from 12/29/28 through 1/12/30, a gift to the Comboni Archives from the Accorsi family in 9/93, CMAC.
4.   Janet Callahan, "African Language, Invented By Priest, Puzzles Censors," interview with Accorsi, *Cincinnati Times-Star*, February 20, 1944, CMAC; Paolucci, *Life Journeys, vol ii*, 196.
5.   Carl Fisher, S.S.J., D.D., "Apostolate to African-Americans," Talk given at the 1990 Comboni Missionary Provincial Assembly in Cincinnati, CMAC.
6.   John T. Gillard, S.S.J., *Colored Catholics in the United States*, Baltimore: The Josephite Press, 1941, 161, 167.
7.   Gillard, *The Catholic Church and the American Negro*, Baltimore: St. Joseph Society Press, 1929, 100; John I. Seaman, "The Cincinnati Plan," *The Colored Harvest*, vol 37, no II, JA, 8-10.
8.   Albert F. Von Hagel to McNicholas, August, 31, 1925, drawer 4, file folder 85, Holy Trinity, HACAC.
9.   Wendell P. Dabney, *Cincinnati's Colored Citizens: Historical, Sociological, and Biographical*, Cincinnati: The Dabney Publishing Company, 1926, 376; reprinted by the Johnson Reprint Corporation, Johnson Reprint Company LTD, New York, 1970 as part of The Basic Afro-American Reprint Library, Books on the history, culture, and social environment of Afro-Americans, Selected by Clarence L. Holte from his collection, Eugene H. Maly Memorial Library, the Athenaeum of Ohio.
10. From *Diamond Jubilee of St. Edward Church and the Annals of St. Ann Mission*, Cincinnati, 1940, St. Edward Parish, drawer 1, file folder 36, HACAC, 5, 7.
11. Madonna High School was the first senior high school for Blacks. It opened in 1927. See John T. Gillard, S.S.J., *The Catholic Church and the American Negro*, Baltimore, St. Joseph's Society Press, 1929, 178-179 insert, JA; *Chimes of Madonna High School*, First Commencement Number, Cincinnati, Ohio: Students of Madonna High School, 1931, HACAC.
12. *Catholic Telegraph*, March 24, 1927, "Great Holy Name Meeting", Eugene H. Maly Memorial Library, Athenaeum of Ohio, Cincinnati, 1; *The Colored Harvest*, vol XV, no 2 (March-April), JA, 12.
13. Archbishop's House Notanda, October 22, 1928, drawer 4, file folder 85, Holy Trinity Parish files, HACAC; Msgr. J. Albers, to Walsh, November 5, 1929, and Walsh to Albers, November 14, 1929, drawer 4, file folder 85, Holy Trinity files, HACAC.

14. See the "Report of the Negro Apostolate Meeting," May 28, 1945, Apostolate of the Negro file, HACAC; To "Your Grace" from F.A.T. [Rev. Frank Thill], August 19, 1937, memo says the pastor, Clarence Schmitt, cashed in his $1700 life insurance policy to "keep things going at St. Ed's," Drawer 3, File Folder 21, St. Edward Correspondence, HACAC.

15. Depots of the Chesapeake and Ohio, the Baltimore and Ohio, the Cincinnati, Columbus, and Cleveland, and the Cincinnati, Dayton, and Hamilton lines converged here.

16. Albert F. Von Hagel to McNicholas, August 31, 1925, drawer 4, file folder 85, Holy Trinity, HACAC; Conway, *Chronology*, CMAC, 8; the narrative reports that Accorsi arrived in Italy from Ethiopia on December 30, 1939, and left for America on January 1, 1940.

17. John Buse, conversation with author, Cincinnati, Ohio, October 1, 1993.

18. Conway, *Chronology*, CMAC, 13; Mason to Accorsi, February 2, 1940, CMAC; Cicognani to McNicholas, December 6, 1939, HACAC.

19. Conway, *Chronology*, CMAC, 14, 15.

20. Mason to Accorsi, June 8, 1940.

21. St. Ann's mission, founded in 1865, was the oldest Negro parish in Cincinnati; see Joseph H. Lackner, S.M., article on its history in *U.S. Catholic Historian*, vol 7, no 2 & 3, spring-summer, 1988, 145-156; See also paper by Lackner, "St. Ann's Colored Church and School, Its foundation, Its Beginning Years, and Its People," HACAC.

22. Heyker to Accorsi, July 30, 1940, CMAC.

23. Cicognani to McNicholas, November 18, 1940, HACAC (Accorsi had written Cicognani for a blessing on his work); McNicholas to Cicognani, November 22, 1940, HACAC; Cicognani to McNicholas and Cicognani to Accorsi, November 26, 1940, HACAC.

24. Vignato to Accorsi, December 12, 1940, CMAR; Dennis Conway, *Chronology*. 18.

25. Letter to Archbishop Michael J. Curley, December 4, 1941, AAB; Gerald P. Fogarty, S.J., *The Vatican and the American Hierarchy From 1870 to 1965*, Wilmington, Delaware: Michael Glazier, Inc. 1985, 238-239, 252-253.

26. Anthony Rhodes, *The Vatican in the Age of the Dictators (1922-1945)*, New York: Holt, Rinehart and Winston, 1973, 261; Fogarty, 273; Rhodes, 262-263, 276.

27. Conway, *Chronology*, 18-20; Dennis Conway, *Interviews*, vol 1, 250-251; Conway, *Chronology*, 23, 24.

28. McNicholas to "the Principals of all High Schools of the Archdiocese of Cincinnati," March 6, 1943, HACAC.

29. McNicholas to Accorsi, June 25, 1943, CMAC; Accorsi to McNicholas, July 25, 1943, Holy Trinity files, HACAC; Accorsi to Marie Buse, July 20, 1943, CMAC.

30. Conway, *Chronology*, 22, "Leaders Sponsor Benefit Musical," *The Catholic Telegraph Register*, no date; a related article appeared on February 10, 1944, in *The Cincinnati Times-Star*, News Clipping Notebook, CMAC.

31. Oliver Branchesi to author, February 2, 1993; McNicholas to Ferrara, February 21, 1942, CMAC; Branchesi, 3.
32. From a one-page memoir by Sister M. Gervase following the April 16th, Golden Jubilee Celebration of the Comboni Missionaries in America, SBS.
33. Branchesi, "Reflections on Early Pastoral Work," February 2, 1993, CMAC, 3.
34. Allen Tarlton, O.S.B., interview with author, April 9, 1994; Conway, *Chronology*, 25.
35. Tarlton to "Very Reverend Father," (presumably Rizzi), June 21, 1952, HACAC.
36. Clarence Rivers, interview with author, July 15, 1993.
37. McNicholas to Accorsi, June 1, 1945, CMAC; Conway, *Chronology*, 24.
38. Denis Mack Smith, *Italy, a Modern History*, Ann Arbor: University of Michigan Press, 1959, 78-486; from *Chronology of War Times in Italy*, CMAC.
39. Branchesi, "From the Apennines: the Beginning of the Story of Oliver," Arco, Trento, unpublished autobiography, Easter, 1993, CMAC, 44-45; Alfred Paolucci, in interviewwith author, June 6, 1992.
40. Vignato to Accorsi, July 29, 1945, CMAR.
41. Accorsi to Vignato, September 17, 1945, CMAR; Negri to McNicholas, October 22, 1945, HACAC; Accorsi to McNicholas, November 15, 1945, HACAC.

Chapter 3. The Architect

1. McNicholas to Accorsi, June 1, 1945, CMAC; *The First Twenty Years of Comboni Missionaries in North America, 1940-1960*, ed Alfred Paolucci, CMAC, 33-34.
2. "Report of the Negro Apostolate Meeting," May 28, 1945, Apostolate of the Negro files, HACAC; Robert B. Fairbanks, *Making Better Citizens: Housing Reform and the Community Development Strategy in Cincinnati, 1890-1960*, Urbana: University of Illinois Press, 1988, 159-178.
3. Reverend Michael H. Hinssen, "History of St. Henry's Church, 1873-1917," St. Henry Parish History file, HACAC, 1; Paolucci, *The First Twenty Years*, 33; See flier "St. Henry Hall, 1057 Flint Street: Information --- Free!!," October, 29, [1946?], drawer 4, file folder 21, St. Henry, Cortland, HACAC.
4. Fairbanks, 131, 157, 156.
5. Paolucci, *My Stars: From Pentagram to Pentecost*, a personal journal, CMAC, 80 34; Vignato to Accorsi, November 10, 1945, CMAR.
6. This portion of the letter from McNicholas to the Cardinal Prefect on January 14, 1945 is copied into a letter to Vignato from Celso Constantini, the Cardinal Prefect's secretary, dated March 25, 1946. It has only a brief introduction and a few lines at the end with the customary expressions of respect; CMAR.
7. Vignato to Accorsi, November, 11, 1945, CMAR; Accorsi to Vignato, February 23, 1946, CMAR; Vignato to Accorsi and Ferrara, March 13, 1946, CMAR.
8. Paolucci, *Life Journey of Comboni Missionaries*, vol iii, (1979-1988), Cincinnati: Comboni Mission Center, 1993, CMAC, 169-171.

9. Oliver Branchesi, in letter to author, May 3, 1993; Bruno Colombina to Dennis Conway, March 15, 1988, CMAC; Rizzi to Vignato, July 5, 1946, CMAR.

10. Most likely the Apostolic Delegate to England, David Mathew.

11. Vignato to Rizzi, July 26, 1946, CMAR; William Labodie, "Former African Missionary is Head of New Seminary," *Catholic Telegraph Register*, February 14, 1947.

12. Branchesi, letter to author, February 2, 1993; Conway, Chronology, CMAC, 26; Branchesi, letter to author, May 3, 1993; Conway, *Chronology*, 27; Rizzi to Vignato, December 27, 1946, CMAR.

13. To Rizzi from Dempsey & Dempsey, December 11, 1946, HACAC; JCD at Dempsey and Dempsey to Michael C. Lacinak (Attorney), January 15, 1947, HACAC.

14. Conway, *Chronology*, 27; Chancellor to Rizzi, January 17, 1947, HACAC; .Dempsey and Dempsey to Rizzi, February 3, 1947, HACAC; promissory note signed by Rizzi as "President" and Accorsi as "Secretary" for $30,000, February 20, 1947, CMAC.

15. "Seminary Will Be Established In Archdiocese," *Catholic Telegraph*, January 24, 1947; "Forestville Tract Acquired As Site For New Seminary," *The Cincinnati Enquirer*, January 26, 1947; "Seminary Planned For City," *The Cincinnati Times-Star, January 25, 1947*; Rizzi to Vignato, January 29, 1947, CMAR.

16. William Labodie, "Former African Missioner Is Head of New Seminary," *The Catholic Telegraph*, February 14, 1947, Eugene H. Maly Memorial Library, Athenaeum of Ohio, Cincinnati.

17. January 25, 1947, Newspaper clipping notebook, 1944-1947, CMAC; "Missionary Seminary Will Be Located In Forestville," *Mt Washington Press*, Undated, 1947, Newspaper clipping notebook, 1944-1947, CMAC; Conway, *Chronology*, 28-29; Branchesi, "Forestville," CMAC.

18. Conway, Chronology, 29; Branchesi to the author, "Forestville," CMAC.

19. "Italy is Hungry is Report Made by Myron Taylor"; "NCWC Mobile Relief Trucks Cheer French"; "German Food Crisis Growing Worse," from the New York Times, December 30, 1946, reprinted in an advertisement by the War Relief Service of the National Catholic Welfare Conference; *The Catholic Telegraph*, January 10, 1947.

20. Conway, *Chronology*, 30.

21. Conway, *Chronology*, 13, 22, 30; "Bishop to Officiate at Chapel Dedication," *Cincinnati Times-Star*, July 30, 1947; McNicholas to Accorsi, January 18, 1947, HACAC; Conway, *Chronology*, 33, 31.

22. Mario Ongaro, interview with author, February, 1993; John Gorley Bunker, *Liberty Ships: The Ugly Ducklings of World War II*, Annapolis, Maryland: Naval Institute Press, 1972, 184.

23. Mario Ongaro, interview with author, February, 1993; John Gorley Bunker, *Liberty Ships: The Ugly Ducklings of World War II*, Annapolis, Maryland: Naval Institute Press, 1972, 184; Ongaro interview with author.

24. Hugo Riva, interview with Dennis Conway, vol ii, 82; Archimedes Fornasari, interview with Dennis Conway, vol I, 258-261; Charles Curro, in interview with author, July 13, 1993; author's conversations with Comboni missionaries who worked with Accorsi.

25. Accorsi to Vignato, January 31, 1947, CMAR; Conway, *Chronology*, 31.

Chapter 4. The Foundation

1. Conway, *Chronology*, 3; Accorsi to Vignato, January 31, 1947, CMAR.

2. Branchesi to author, March 3, 1993.

3. Rizzi to Chancery, December 11, 1947, HACAC; Clarence G. Issenmann to Rizzi, December 23, 1947, CMAC; Rizzi to Issenmann, February 11, 1948, CMAC.

4. Branchesi to author, March 3, 1993.

5. Conway, *Chronology*, 33; Alfred Paolucci, *Life Journeys of Comboni Missionaries*, vol ii, 249, 250; Conway, *Chronology*, 34.

6. From the "First Visit of Superior General Todesco to the Houses of America, April 15, 1948, CMAR; Todesco to Rizzi, July 5, 1948, CMAR.

7. Paolucci, *Life Journey*, 249, 252.

8. Ongaro, interview with author, February, 1993; Conway, *Chronology*, 35; Accorsi to Carl and Marie Buse, August 5, 1948, CMAC; Conway, *Chronology*, 35; Hayes to Rizzi, November 29, 1948, CMAC.

9. Rizzi to Hayes, January 3, 1949, CMAC; Conway, *Chronology*, 36; George L. Leech to Rizzi, February 28, 1949, CMAC; Rizzi to Bano, March 14, 1949, CMAR.

10. Rizzi to Briani, March, 28, 1949, CMAR.

11. Vogelpohl to Rizzi, February 12, 1949, CMAC; Rizzi to McNicholas, April 5, 1949, CMAC; McNicholas to Rizzi, May 12, 1949, CMAC; Issenmann to Rizzi, June 6, 1949, CMAC; Woznicki to Rizzi, July 1, 1949, CMAC.

12. Issenmann to Rizzi, August 10, 1949, CMAC; From Father Timothy McNicholas (the archbishop's nephew) to author, 1994; In-house memo from CGI [Clarence G. Issenmann], August 12, 1949, HACAC; Conway, *Chronology*, 43.

13. Conway, *Chronology*, 45; Sister Mary of St. Hedde to Schulte, August 19, 1949, CMAC; Paul C. Schulte to "Sons of the Sacred Heart, August 20, 1949, CMAC; Conway, *Chronology*, 45, 46.

14. Rizzi to Todesco, December 10, 1948, CMA; Conway, *Chronology*, 39, 41; "Our New Seminary," *Frontier Call*, vol 2, no 5, Sept.-Oct., 1949, 7.

15. Conway, "Interviews with Comboni Missionaries," vol 2, 85-87, and vol 1, 261; Faricy to Issenmann, November 7, 1949; Leibold to Faricy, November 10, 1949; Leibold's memo, November 22, 1949; Leibold to Rizzi, November 25, 1949, HACAC.

16. Conway, *Chronology*, 49; Joint letter of De Bernardi, Fornasari, Gori, and Riva to Mc Nicholas, March 21, 1950, HACAC.

17. Rizzi to Morotti, July 4, 1949; Rizzi to Morotti, September 4, 1949; John A. Donovan to Rizzi, September 13, 1949; Rizzi Personnel File, CMAC.

18. Walter Mattiato to author, Easter, 1993; Rizzi to Mooney, August, 21, 1950, CMAC; Hickey to Rizzi, August 28, 1950, CMAC.

19. Paolucci, *The First Twenty Years, 1940-1960*, Cincinnati: 1993, CMAC, 76; Mattiato to author, Easter, 1993; Mattiato to author; Rizzi to Todesco, June 22, 1951, CMAR.

20. *Frontier Call,* November/December, 1951, 74-75; Conway, *Chronology*, 57, 59, 60, 61, 62, CMAC; Maurer to Sister Andrea, December 29, 1951, SSIHM; Moody to Mother M. Teresa, January 16, 1952, SSIHM; Rabaut to Mother M. Teresa, January 16, 1952, SSIHM; Bruce M. Mohler to A.C. Maurer, March 26, 1952, SSIHM; Mother M. Teresa to Moody, April 2, 1952, SSIHM; Conway, 69, CMAC.

21. *Frontier Call* , November/December, 1951, 75; Marino Perghem to Conway, February 28, 1988, CMAC; Rizzi to Todesco, January 20, 1992, CMAR.

22. Conway, 68, CMAC; Rizzi to Mooney, August 22, 1952, CMAC; Gabriel Chiodi to Conway, March 1, 1988, CMAC.

23. Rizzi to Todesco, June 22, 1951, CMAR; Gillen to Rizzi, September 21, 1952, CMAC; Rizzi to Gillen, October 3, 1952, CMAC; Gillen to Rizzi, November 17, 1953, CMAC; Rizzi to Gillen, December 5, 1952, CMAC; Gillen to Rizzi, April 21, 1953, CMAC; J.B. Tennelly to Rizzi, May 4, 1953, CMAC; Rizzi to Bishop Joseph M. Gilmore to Rizzi, May 20, 1953, CMAC; Rizzi's memorandum about his visit to the Blackfoot Reservation in Browning, Montana dated May 23 to May 26, 1953, CMAC.

24. Rizzi to Todesco, October 4, 1952, CMAR; Branchesi, *Safari for Souls: Life of Bishop Daniel Comboni*, Cincinnati, Verona Fathers, 92-93, CMAC.

25. *Frontier Call,* January/February 1953, 13,14; *Frontier Call,*May/June, 1952, 39, CMAC; Norman Kogan, *A Political History of Postwar Italy*, New York:, Frederick A. Praeger, 1966, 41-45, 65-69; *Catholic Telegraph Register*, January 10, 1947.

Chapter 5. In the California Missions

1. Buddy to Rizzi, May 10, 1948, CMAC; Rizzi to Buddy, May 20, 1948, CMAC; Rizzi to Buddy, May 25, 1948, SDDA.

2. R. Bruce Harley and Catherine Louise LaCoste, CSJ, *Most Rev. Charles Francis Buddy: First Bishop of San Diego, 1936-1966, and a Brief History of the Diocese of San Diego, 1769-1966*, vol xi in *Readings in Diocesan Heritage*, San Diego, University of San Diego Print Shop, 1991, 80, 2-3, 9-11, x, 23-24.

3. Buddy to Rizzi, August 19, 1948, CMAC; Barbisotti to Buddy, October 23, 1948, SDDA; Buddy to Barbisotti, October 26, 1948, CMAC.

4. Buddy to Barbisotti, November 30, 1948, CMAC; Barbisotti to Buddy, December 3, 1948, CMAC.

5. Harley and LaCoste, 2-3.; Buddy to Rizzi, December 7, 1948, CMAC; Rizzi to Buddy, December 9, 1948, CMAC; Rizzi to Buddy [telegram], December 9, 1948, SDDA.

6. Rizzi to Todesco, December 10, 1948, CMAR; Conway, *Interviews*, vol I, 75, 1988; Bartholomew Battirossi to author, March 4, 1993, CMAC.

7. Edward D. Castillo, "The Impact of Euro-American Exploration and Settlement," *Handbook of North American Indians*, vol 8, *California*, gen ed William C. Sturtevant, vol Robert F. Heizer, Washington: Smithsonian Institution, 1978, 99;

Robert F. Heizer, "History of Research," *Handbook. of Indians, 7.*

8. Castillo, "The Impact...", 104-105.
9. William R. Benson, "The Stone and Kelsey Massacre on the Shores of Clear Lake in 1849," *Quarterly of the California Historical Society, 1932, 11 (3), 266-273*, San Francisco, (in Castillo, "Impact"), 107.
10. U.S. Congress, Senate, "Special Report of the Superintendent of Indian Affairs in California; 32d Cong. 2d sess. Senate Document No. 57, (Serial No. 665) Washington: U.S. Government Printing Office, 1853, 9, (In Castillo, "Impact...", 108-109.)
11. Castillo, "Impact...," 116.
12. Florence C. Shipek, "History of Southern California Mission Indians," In *Handbook of North American Indians*, 611.
13. Oblasser to Buddy, March 12, 1945, SDDA.
14. Oblasser to Buddy, July 28, 1948, SDDA; Buddy to Oblasser, October 4, 1948, SDDA; Oblasser to Buddy, October 7, 1948, SDDA..
15. Conway, *Interviews*, vol 1, CMAC, 76.
16. Conway, *Chronology*, 38; Battirossi to author, March 4, 1993.
17. Battirossi to author.
18. Conway, interview with Carillo, 77, 78.
19. Richard R. Daniels to Carillo, September 9, 1949, SDDA; attachment from Carillo to Buddy, September 19, 1949, SDDA.
20. Carillo to Buddy, January 13, 1950, SDDA; Conway, *Chronology*, 50-53; Thomas J. McNamara to Carillo, June 21, 1950, SDDA.
21. Conway, *Chronology*, 58, 59, 61.
22. Carillo to Buddy, June 20, 1952, SDDA; Waterfall to Carillo, June 25, 1952, SDDA; Conway, *Chronology*, 66, 68, 69, CMAC; James H. McCauley, "Does This Solve the Mystery of the Missing Bells of Santa Ysabel?" *Western Treasures*, October, 1966, 60-61; Carillo to Buddy, September 1, 1952, SDDA; Conway, *Chronology*, 74.
23. Carillo to Buddy, September 8, 1952, SDDA; Petition to Buddy, September, 1952, SDDA;
24. Castillo, "Impact," 105; Shipek, 611; J.M. Carillo, *The Story of Mission San Antonio de Pala*, Cincinnati: Comboni Mission Center, 1959, 23-24.
25. Carillo, *San Antonio de Pala*, 9-11, 18-20.
26. Conway, *Chronology*, 42; Buddy to Barbisotti, December 15, 1948, SDDA; Daniels to Barbisott (sic), January 12, 1949, SDDA; Barbisotti to Buddy, February 18, 1949, SDDA; Buddy to Barbisotti, March 9, 1949, SDDA; Barbisotti to Buddy, March 14, 1949, SDDA.
27. Barbisotti to Bernard Cullen, September 20, 1949, SDDA; Conway, *Chronology*, 46, 47.
28. Conway, *Chronology*, 50, 51, CMAC; Rizzi to Todesco, January 25, 1950, CMAR; *Note Lasciate Dal Rev. MOP. Generale - Nella Sua Visita Agli Stati Unite*, January, 1951, CMAR.

29. Conway, *Chronology*, 58, 65, 75, CMAC; Rizzi to Todesco, March 17, 1952, May 3, 1952, and April 15, 1953, CMAR; Conway, *Chronology*, 61, 62, 66, CMAC; Waterfall to Barbisotti, November 9, 1951, SDDA.

30. Barbisotti to Chancery, December 27, 1951, SDDA; Conway, *Chronology*, 74, CMAC.

31. *Diarium Filiorum Sacri Cordi Jesu* (Diary of the Sons of the Sacred Heart of Jesus), Pala, California, October 28, 1952, 166, CMAC.

32. Rizzi to McIntyre, March 14, 1952, CMAC; Rizzi to Todesco, March 17, 1952, CMAR; Castillo, "The Impact of Euro-American Exploration," *Handbook...Indians*, 122.

33. Rizzi to Todesco, May 3, 1952, CMAR; Buddy to Rizzi, July 23, 1952, CMAR.

34. Rizzi to Todesco, July 25, 1952, Rizzi to Todesco, July 26, 1952, October 4, 1952, CMAR.

35. Rizzi to Todesco, July 25, 1952, Rizzi to Todesco, July 26, 1952, Rizzi to Todesco, October 4, 1952, CMAR.

36. Paolucci, *Life Journeys*, vol ii, 1965-1969, Cincinnati, 79, 80, 81.

Chapter 6. Confronting Racism

1. "Charles B. Lobert Exemplified Cause of Catholic Negro," *Catholic Telegraph Register*, February 13, 1948, JA.

2. Paolucci, *My Stars*, 69-76, CMAC; Paolucci, interview with author, June 16, 1992, 3-4; Paolucci, *My Stars*, 80.

3. Paolucci , in interview with author, 5; Paolucci, *My* Stars, 81.

4. Dennis Conway, *Interviews*, vol ii, 54; Paolucci, *My Stars,* 83; Clarence G. Issenmann to Julius Rizzi, September 18, 1947, CMAC; Paolucci, *My Stars*, 84.

5. Paolucci to Clarence G. Issenmann, April 24, 1948, St. Henry files, HACAC; Paolucci to Paul F. Leibold, November 29, 1948, St. Henry files, HACAC; Paolucci to Ralph Asplan, May 13, 1949, St. Henry files, HACAC; Paolucci to Asplan, May 25, 1949, St. Henry files, HACAC.

6. Dennis Conway, *Chronology*, 34; *The Apostolate of the Negro*, vol 4, no 2, HACAC, 4; *The Apostolate of the Negro*, vol 3, no 3, 5. HACAC; Conway, *Chronology*, 43; *The First Twenty Years of Comboni Missionaries in North America, 1940-1960*, ed Alfred Paolucci, Cincinnati: Comboni Mission Center, 1994, CMAC, 36.

7. Paolucci, *The First Twenty Years, "* 48; Paolucci, *My Stars*, 86, 87.

8. Paolucci, interview with author; Dennis Conway, *Interviews*, CMAC, 56; LaVerne Muldrow Summerlin, interview with author, January 17, 1994.

9. Conway, *Chronology*, 50-51.

10. Leibold to Rizzi, August 18, 1950, St. Henry parish files, file 4, drawer 21, HACAC; Paolucci to Leibold, February 21, 1951, St. Henry file, HACAC.

11. Paolucci, *My Stars*, 89-90.

12. ibid., 89-90, 92-93.

13. ibid., 93.

14. Paolucci, 93; Conway, *Chronology*, 74, 75, 77, 81.
15. "Let Negroes Enter, Group Asks Coney in Pastoral Letter" appears copied on the Archdiocese of Cincinnati letterhead together with a typed note about Battirossi's phone call occurring on July 28, 1954, memo signed by pfl (Paul F. Leibold), St. Henry's file, HACAC.

Chapter 7. Holy Trinity, Beginning of a Black Diaspora

1. Giles A. Conwill, "The Word Becomes Flesh: A Program for Reaching the American Black," in *What Christians Can Learn From One Another*, ed Glenn C. Smith, Tyndale House Publishers, Inc., 1988.
2. "Black Catholics in the United States, A Historical Chronology," Ronald L. Sharps, compiled with the assistance of Fr. Peter Hogan, Josephite Archives, Baltimore, Maryland, 1991.
3. Marilyn Wenzke Nickels, *Black Catholic Protest and the Federated Colored Catholics 1917-1933: Three Perspectives on Racial Justice*, New York: Garland Publishing, Inc., 1988, 286-287.
4. Liptak, 181; Davis, 252-253; Liptak, 183.
5. Davis,"The American Catholic Bishops and Racism, November 14, 1958," *Documents of American Catholic History* 2:646-52," 255, en. 51.
6. Harold Isaacs, "Basic Group Identity: The Idols of the Tribe," *Ethnicity: Theory and Experience*, eds Nathan Glazer and Daniel Moynihan, Cambridge: Harvard University Press, 1975, 30, in Conwill, fn 10.
7. "Industrial Possibilities in Metropolitan Cincinnati," prepared by the special committee for economic Research of the Cincinnati Committee for Economic Development, Frederick V. Geier, Chairman, Cincinnati, June, 1946, 67-70, 151-152, 153, 156, 165.
8. *Redevelopment of Blighted Areas*, Cincinnati City Planning Commission, September, 1951, 23-2; *The Ladislas Segoe Tapes*, a transcript of an interview with Ladislas Segoe conducted on May 22-24, 1978 in Cincinnati, Ohio by Sydney H. Williams, AICP, Washington, D.C.: The American Planning Association, 1980, (Available also at the Public Library of Cincinnati), Tape 3, 39-40.
9. *Cincinnati Enquirer*, April 22, 1948, in Fairbanks, *Making Better Citizens*, 167; Fairbanks, 171-172, 170-174.
10. See John T. Gillard, *The Catholic Church and the American Negro*, Baltimore: St. Joseph's Society Press, 1929, opposite 179.
11. "Hire by Skill, Not by Color,"*The Apostolate" of the Negro*, vol 4, no 3, 1950, 2-3; "Our Catholic Public Schools,""*The Apostolate" of the Negro*, vol 4, no 3, 1950, 2; "Welcome!", "*The Apostolate" of the Negro*, vol 4, no 3, 1950, 2.
12. LaVerne Muldrow Summerlin to author, January 17, 1994.
13. Melvin C. Grier, in interview with author, July, 1994.
14. Conway, *Chronology*, 68, 72, 76.
15. Al Neyer to Chancery Office, March 26, 1953, Holy Trinity file B, HACAC; Nardi to Paul F. Leibold, April 24, 1953, Holy Trinity file B, HACAC.

16. Leibold to Nardi, May 2, 1953, Holy Trinity file folder B, HACAC; *Catholic Telegraph-Register*, May 22, 1953, Holy Trinity file folder C, HACAC; *Catholic Telegraph-Register*, July 19, 1954, Holy Trinity file folder C, HACAC.
17. "Holy Trinity Church to Be Torn Down," unknown newspaper, May 22, 1953, copied on letterhead of The Archdiocese of Cincinnati, HACAC.
18. Conway, *Chronology*, 96, 100; Melvin Grier, in interview with author, 1994, 4.
19. Conway, Chronology, 102-103, 107-108; Alter to Branchesi, May 6, 1955, Holy Trinity file folder B, HACAC.
20. From chancery memo, Leibold to Issenmann, August 9, 1955, Holy Trinity file folder B, HACAC.
21. Grier, 9, 13; Conway, *Chronology*, 162; "History is made at Holy Trinity," *Frontier Call*, July/August, 1955, 62, CMAC; Conway, *Chronology*, 114; "Father Gilbert Tarlton Who Joined Church at 9, To Offer 1st Solemn Mass," *Catholic Telegraph-Register*, May 2?, 1955.
22. Branchesi in letter to author, February 2, 1993; Accorsi to Todesco, September 11, 1958, CMAR; Leibold to Branchesi, September 13, 1958, Holy Trinity file folder C, HACAC.
23. "Old Holy Trinity's Church Property is Bought by City," Holy Trinity file folder C (probably from *Catholic Telegraph-Register*) dated November 4, 1960, HACAC; Conway, *Chronology*, 177.
24. "Urban Renewal Project will Raze Old Church," *Catholic Telegraph*, September 7, 1962, HACAC.
25. Ladislas Segoe, Tape 3, 40-4; Zane L. Miller, "Queensgate II: A History of the Neighborhood," *The Planning Partnership: Views of Urban Renewal*, ed Zane L. Miller and Thomas H. Jenkins, Beverly Hills: Sage Publications, 1983, 73.
26. Melvin Grier, interview with author, 9-10.
27. Father Timothy McNicholas to author, April 5, 1994; Grier, 13.

Chapter 8. Opening in Louisville

1. Memo discusses Autheman's connection and Rizzi's discussion with Maloney at the Louisville chancery, on May 23 (1952), CMAC; *Chronology*, 67.
2. Floersh to Autheman, November 2, 1952, AAL; Floersh to Rizzi, December 17, 1952; Conway, *Chronology*, 67; Robert Erbisti to Dennis Conway, *Interviews*, vol 1, 224-226.
3. Floersh to Rizzi, November 3, 1952, CMAC; Maloney to Rizzi, April 20, 1953, AAL; Decree dated September 7, 1953; Floersh to "Dear Reverend Father," August 31, 1953; James J. Maloney to Floersh, September 2, 1953; AAL.
4. Cyprian Davis, *The History of Black Catholics*, 89, 283 (ft 99).Nathaniel E. Green, *The Silent Believers*, Louisville: West End Catholic Council of Louisville, Kentucky, 1972, 20.
5. Green., 31; Davis, 118.
6. The pastoral letter of 1866 appears in *The National Pastorals of the American Hierarchy (1792-1919)*, ed. Peter Guilday (Washington, D.C.: National Catholic Welfare Council, 1923, 198-225, quotation from pp. 220-21, found in Davis, 121,

ft 26; Davis, 133; Green, 45.

7. Green, 49-58.

8. Clyde F. Crews, *An American Holy Land, A History of the Archdiocese of Louisville,* Louisville: Ikonographics, Inc., 1987, 302, 303; "Catholic Colleges in Louisville Accept Negroes, Lead Fight on Segregation," *Catholic Witness,* April 27, 1950, JA.

9. Mary Luella Conwill interview with author, November 25, 1994.

10. Paolucci, *The First Twenty Years,*" 133; Floersh to Mondini, September 7,1953, AAL; W. Conwill to author, November, 1994; A. Heitzman to author, December, 1994.

11. M. Conwill to author, November, 1994; "Twenty-five Years - Immaculate Heart of Mary... Still Growing in God's Care," a commemorative history published on the 25th anniversary of IHM Parish, a copy from Mrs. Mary Luella Conwill, 5.

12. *Frontier Call,* November, 1955, 93-94; M. Conwill to author, November 25, 1994.

13. "New Parish Grows from Humble Start," *The Record,* August 6, 1954; Charles G. Maloney to City of Louisville, October 23, 1953, AAL; N.H. Dosker to Maloney, October 28, 1953, AAL; Conway, *Chronology* 93, 87, 88; Conway, *Interviews,* vol ii, 35; Mattiato, letter to author, Easter, 1993.

14. W. Conwill to author, November 25, 1994; "Twenty-five Years..." 6; Guy Compisano to Floersh, February 2, 1954, AAL; Floersh to Mondini, November 2, 1955, AAL; Conway, *Chronology,* 93, 95.

15. Paolucci, *"The First Twenty Years,"* 133-134; Conway, *Interviews,* vol 1, 182, CMAC; Conway, *Chronology,* 128.

16. Chancellor to Mondini, November 11, 1953, AAL; Charles G. Maloney [chancellor] to Louisville Gas & Electric, January 1, 1953, AAL; Undated memo in file, AAL.

17. Anselm to Mondini, December 4, 1953, AAL; Conway, *Chronology,* 101-102; "The Church That Started in a Barn," from Mary Luella Conwill; Accorsi to Floersh, September 9, 1954, AAL.

18. *Frontier Call,* November, 1955, 102; Conway, *Chronology,* 110-112; Aldo Cescatti, "God Goes to Little Africa," *Frontier Call,* 95-98, 102; Conway, *Chronology,* 118.

19. Conway, *Chronology,* 119; "The Church That Started in a Barn, 1; Conway, *Chronology,* 124; Mattiato to author, Easter, 1993.

20. Unsigned handwritten letter to Archdiocese, undated, in mid 1956 section of IHM file, AAL; Mondini to Floersh, December 31, 1957, AAL.

21. W. Conwill to author, November 25, 1994.

22. Paolucci, *The First Twenty Years,* 141-143; Conway, *Chronology,* 146.

23. Mondini to Charles G. Maloney, January 7, 1957, AAL; Maloney to Mondini, January 28, 1957, AAL.

24. Mondini to Maloney, February 24, 1958, AAL; Maloney to Schneider, March 5, 1958, AAL, Maloney to Mondini, December 4, 1958, AAL; Conway, *Chronology,* 168.

25. Conway, *Chronology,* 183; 191-192.

26. W. Conwill to author, November 1994.

27. Heitzman to author, December, 1994; Ongaro to author.

Chapter 9. Pursuit of a Dream: The Pala Indian School

1. Margaret Connell Szasz and Carmelita S. Ryan, "American Indian Education," in *Handbook of North American Indians*, vol 4, *History of Indian-White Relations*, gen ed William C. Sturtevant, vol ed Wilcomb E. Washburn, Washington: Smithsonian Institution, 1978, 290-291.
2. ARCIA, Commissioner of Indian Affairs; Annual Reports to the Secretary of the Interior, Washington: U.S. Government Printing Office, (Reprinted: AMS Press, New York, 1976-1977), 1891:220, in Edward D. Castillo, "The Impact of Euro-American Exploration and Settlement," *Handbook of North American Indians*, vol 8, *California*, vol ed Robert F. Heizer, 115-116.
3. Castillo, "Impact," 120; Szasz and Ryan, 294-295; See also Lewis Meriam, "The Problem of Indian Administration, Baltimore, Maryland: John Hopkins Press, 1928, 11 (Reprinted: Johnson Reprint, New York, 1971).
4. California Department of Industrial Relations, Division of Labor Statistics and Research, 1965:10, *American Indians in California*, 1965, San Francisco: Fair Employment Practices Commission, Division of Fair Employment Practices; U.S. Congress, Senate, Special Subcommittee on Indian Education, 1969:75, "A National Tragedy, A National Challenge,"91st Cong., 1st sess., Senate Report No. 501 (Serial No. 12834-1), Washington, U.S. Government Printing Office.
5. Conway, *Interviews*, vol 1, 79; Carillo, interview with author, 4; Conway, *Interviews*, 79-80; Conway, *Chronology*, 96, 105.
6. Aldo Cescatti, "Rebuilding an Indian Mission," *Frontier Call*, July-August, 1955, 59-61; J.M. Carillo, *The Story of Mission San Antonio de Pala*, Cincinnati: Comboni Mission Center, 1959, 32-33, CMAC.
7. Carillo to Buddy, November 2, 1954; Buddy to Carillo, November 5, 1954, SDDA.
8. Katharine Luomala, "Tipai-Ipai," *Handbook of North American Indians*, vol 8, *California*, gen ed William C. Sturtevant, vol ed Robert F. Heizer, Washington: Smithsonian Institution, 1978, 595.
9. J.M. Carillo, *Mission San Antonio de Pala*, *29-31*, 33; Carillo to Buddy, June 27, 1955; Carillo to James Booth, March 8, 1954, SDDA; Buddy to Carillo, July 6, 1955, SDDA; Carillo to Buddy, July 12, 1955, SDDA; author's conversation with Carillo, September, 1994.
10. Carillo, *Mission San Antonio de Pala*, 33-34; Conway, Chronology, 118; *Diary of the Sons of the Sacred Heart of Jesus, Pala, California*, January 1951-February, 1962, CMAC, 271-272.
11. Conway, *Chronology*, 124; *Diary of...Pala*, 279, 281, 282-284; Conway, *Chronology*, 138-139, 140; *Diary of...Pala*, 285.
12. Earl G. Brooks to Buddy, March 15, 1957, SDDA; Buddy to Leavey, January 20, 1957; Carillo to Buddy, February 3, 1957, SDDA; *Diary of...Pala*, 287, 288, 289.
13. *Diary of...Pala*, 291-292, 293, 296; Carillo to Booth, February 24, 1957, SDDA; Buddy to Carillo, June 22, 1957, SDDA.

14. *Diary of...Pala*, 296-300; Carillo to Buddy, July 18, 1957, SDDA; Conway, *Chronology*, 161; *Diary of...Pala*, 298-300.
15. *Diary of...Pala*, 302-304; *Variety Obituaries, vol 6 1964-1968*, November 6, 1968.
16. Carillo, *The Story of Mission San Antonio de Pala*, 35-36; *Diary of...Pala, 303, 305-306;* Carillo to Buddy, May 21, 1958, SDDA; Michael J. Byrne to Carillo, May 26, 1958, SDDA.
17. *Diary of...Pala,* 306-308, 309-312; Carillo to Buddy, September 25, 1958, SDDA.
18. *Diary of...Pala,* 312, 313, 314; Carillo to Anselm, December 6, 1958, SBS. *Diary of...Pala*, 315-315.
19. Byrnes to Carillo, January 20, 1959, SDDA; *Diary of...Pala*, 317-319; Carillo to Buddy, April 13, 1959, SDDA.
20. *Diary of ...Pala,* 320-321, 336, 322, 326, 328, 332, 333, 325, 329; Carillo to Anselm, December 5, 1959, SBS.
21. *Diary of Pala. 327;* Carillo in conversation with author, September 10, 1994; Carillo to Anselm, April 11, 1960, SB; *Diary of...Pala*, 343.
22. Salomon to Buddy, June 28, 1960, SDDA; Byrne to Carillo, July 1, 1960, SDDA; Carillo to Buddy, July 2, 1960, SDDA; Buddy to Carillo, July 18, 1960, SDDA; Byrne to Salomon, July 6, 1960, SDDA.
23. Todesco to Buddy, July 15, 1960, CMAC; Todesco to Buddy, July 25, 1960 [On copy, July 26 is also visible], CMAC; Carillo to Anselm, July 28, 1960, SBS; *Diary of...Pala*, 345-346; author's conversation with Mr. Ray Considine, September, 1994.
24. Carillo to Buddy, September 19, 1960, SDDA; Booth to Carillo, September 23, 1960, SDDA; Carillo to Booth, September 25, 1960, SDDA; *Diary of...Pala*, 347-348; *Diary of...Pala*, 347-348.
25. Carillo to Buddy, December 1, 1960, SDDA; Buddy to Carillo, December 2, 1960, SDDA.

Chapter 10. The Founder as Provincial

1. Conway, *Chronology*, 86.
2. Accorsi to Todesco, November 24, 1953, CMAR.
3. Accorsi to Todesco, September 27, 1953, CMAR; Accorsi to Todesco, October, 19, 1954, CMAR; Todesco to Accorsi, November 14, 1954, CMAR.
4. Accorsi to Todesco, September 27, 1953, CMAR; Rizzi to Hyland, December 5, 1952, CMAC; Hyland to Rizzi, March 9, 1953, CMAC.
5. Accorsi to Hyland, October 27, 1953, CMAC; Accorsi to Hyland, November 1, 1953, CMAC; Hyland to Accorsi, November 11, 1953, CMAC; Conway, *Chronology*, 96-104, CMAC.
6. Hyland to Accorsi, November 1, 1954, CMAC; Accorsi to Todesco, October r 19, 1954, CMAR.
7. Todesco to Accorsi, November 14, 1954, CMAR; Accorsi to Todesco, October 19, 1954, CMAR; Dennis Conway, *Interviews*, vol ii, 2, CMAC.
8. Conway, *Chronology*, 117, 123; Accorsi to Hyland, December 15, 1955, CMAC; Hyland to Accorsi, December 19, 1955, CMAC; Hyland to Accorsi, March 29, 1956, with Accorsi's handwritten note on it, CMAC.

9. Conway, *Chronology*, 142.
10. Todesco, written at Pala, California, December 27, 1955, CMAR, 6.
11. Rizzi to McIntyre, March 14, 1952, CMAC; Accorsi to McIntyre, July 24, 1954, CMAC.
12. Manning to Accorsi, September 9, 1954, CMAC; Accorsi to Manning, September 21, 1954, CMAC; Accorsi to McIntyre, July 30, 1955, CMAC; Manning to Accorsi, August 16, 1955, CMAC.
13. Manning to Accorsi, March 16, 1956, CMAC.
14. Conway, *Chronology*, 1310132.
15. Accorsi to Todesco, July 12, 1957, CMAR; Todesco to Accorsi, July 25, 1957, CMAR.
16. Conway, *Interviews*, vol 2, 3; Conway *Chronology*, 156-157.
17. Chancery memo, April 29, 1953, AAN; Accorsi to James A. Hughes, October 2, 1953, with handwritten memo by Archbishop Bland, October 8, 1953, AAN; Accorsi toBland, June 8, 1954, AAN.
18. Accorsi to Bland, May 7, 1955, AAN; Accorsi to Looney, October 1, 1955, AAN; Gallagher to Looney, October 13, 1955 (two letters), AAN; Accorsi to Bland, November 21, 1955, AAN.
19. Bland to Accorsi, November 29, 1955, AAN.
20. Accorsi to Bland, December 19, 1955, AAN; Memorandum on front of envelope addressed to Bland with return address of Sacred heart Seminary, Cincinnati, initialed "A.B." May 15, 1956, AAN; Todesco to Accorsi, June 12, 1956, CMAR; Accorsi to Bland, August 16, 1956, AAN.

Chapter 11. Accorsi and the Houses of Formation

1. Accorsi to Todesco, October 19, 1954, CMAR; Accorsi to Todesco, February 22, 1955, CMAR.
2. Accorsi to Todesco, October 11, 1954, CMAR.
3. Conway, *Chronology*, 39, 40, 42.
4. ibid., 45, 52, 60, 73, 85, 101.
5. David Baltz, interview with author, May 5, 1992.
6. William Jansen, "Our Man in Rome Comes Home," *Verona Missionaries*, vol 32, no 2, 27, CMAC.
7. Mattiato to author, 1993.
8. Paolucci, *The First 20 Years*, 60-63.
9. Mario Ongaro, *An Historical Outline and Some Dreams*, Cincinnati: Comboni Mission Center, 1983, CMAC, 3; Conway, *Chronology*, 101.
10. Accorsi to Todesco, March 5, 1955, CMAR; Todesco to Accorsi, March 17, 1955, CMAR.
11. Conway, Chronology.
12. *Family News:* vol 1, no 3, 1; vol 1, no 4, 3, vol 1, no 8, 2, vol 1, no 11, 2, vol 1, no 14, 2.
13. Accorsi to Todesco, November 24, 1953, CMAR; Accorsi to Todesco, October 19, 1954, CMAR; Todesco to Accorsi, November 14, 1954, CMAR.

14. Paolucci, *The First Twenty Years,* 82, 80, 85.
15. Conway, *Chronology*, 137.
16. Accorsi to Todesco, August 20, 1957, CMAR; Accorsi to Todesco, November 19, 1957, CMAR; Todesco to Accorsi, November 27, 1957, CMAR.
17. Paolucci, *The First Twenty Years*, 90, 91, 92.
18. Accorsi to Todesco, October 19, 1954, CMAR; Todesco to Accorsi, November 14, 1954, CMAR.
19. Accorsi to Todesco, January 14, 1955, CMAR; Accorsi to Todesco, February 22, 1955, CMAR.
20. Medeghini to Accorsi, July 20, 1955, CMAR; Luibel to Accorsi, July 21, 1955, CMAR; Medeghini to Accorsi, July 30, 1955, CMAC.
21. Accorsi to Luibel, August 16, 1955, CMAC; Accorsi to Todesco, August 17, 1955, CMAR.
22. Accorsi to Wilt, September 10, 1955, CMAC; Wilt to Accorsi, September, 17, 1955, CMAC.
23. Accorsi to Todesco, January 16, 1956, CMAR; Accorsi to Todesco, February 16, 1956, CMAR.
24. Accorsi to Todesco, May 29, 1956, CMAR.
25. Luibel to Accorsi, May 15, 1956, CMAC; Accorsi to Luibel, May 25, 1956, CMAC; Accorsi to Todesco, May 29, 1956, CMAR.
26. Hyland to Lamb, July 9, 1956, CMAC; Todesco to Accorsi, September 21, 1956, CMAR; Hyland to Accorsi, October 1, 1956, CMAC.
27. Accorsi to Bevilacqua, October 5, 1956, CMAR; Accorsi to Todesco, October 5, 1956, CMAR; Todesco to Accorsi, October 16, 1956, CMAR.
28. Accorsi to Francis Costa, S.S.S., November 16, 1956, CMAC; Accorsi to Todesco, October 24, 1956, CMAR.
29. Todesco to Accorsi, November 17, 1956, CMAR.
30. Accorsi to Todesco, December 30, 1956, CMAR; Todesco to Accorsi, January 16, 1957, CMAR; Accorsi to Todesco, June 17, 1957, CMAR.
31. Todesco to Accorsi, July 11, 1957, CMAR; Accorsi to Todesco, July 12, 1957, CMAR; Todesco to Accorsi, July 25, 1957, CMAR.
32. Todesco to Accorsi, October 25, 1957, CMAR; Todesco to Accorsi, November 27, 1957, CMAR; Accorsi to Todesco, December 1, 1957, CMAR.
33. Conway, *Chronology*, 163; Accorsi to Todesco, December 29, 1957, CMAR.
34. Accorsi to Todesco, January 13, 1958, CMAR; Todesco to Accorsi, February 11, 1958, CMAR.
35. Accorsi to Todesco, September 11, 1958, CMAR.
36. "The Generous Lender," *Time Magazine*, vol 72, September 8, 1958, 25.
37. Accorsi to Todesco, September 11, 1958, CMAR; Accorsi to Todesco, December 12, 1958, CMAR; Accorsi to Todesco, February 10, 1959, CMAR.
38. "The Report of the Provincial Superior of the U.S. to the Chapter, 1959," trans Dennis Conway and Mario Ongaro, CMAC; the report is dated June 8, 1959, but given sometime after the Chapter opened in July, the interim period required in order for the superiors of the society to review it along with others.

39. Accorsi to Chiodi, August 1, 1959, CMAC; Accorsi to Chiodi, October 10, 1959.

Chapter 12. A Change of Direction, 1960-1961

1. *Paolucci, Life Journey,* vol ii, 252.
2. ibid.
3. John Tracy Ellis,"The Formation of the American Priest: An Historical Perspective," in *The Catholic Priest in the United States: Historical Investigations,* ed John Tracy Ellis, Collegeville, Minnesota: Saint John's University Press, 1971, 79, 88.
4. "The Report of the Provincial Superior of the U.S. to the Chapter, 1959," CMAC.
5. *Todesco's Diary,* April 10, 1960; Father Victor Turchetti, named provincial of Mexico shortly after these events, told the author this entire loan was repaid.
6. *Todesco's Diary,* January 9, February 14, March 21, February 11, 1960.
7. *Todesco's Diary,* February 24, 1960; while Ackerman publicly expressed support for a San Diego scholasticate, one who was there at the meeting with Ackerman said he privately advised continuing to send scholastics to Mount St. Mary's.
8. *Todesco's Diary,,* February 9, 1960, March 25, 1960.; *Todesco's Diary,* May 27, 1960.
9. *Todesco's Diary,* September 26, 1960, September 30, 1960; Conway, *Chronology,* 199; *Todesco's Diary,* October 6, 1960.
10. *Todesco's Diary,* November 27, 1960, December 5, 1960, January 16, 1961, January 20, 1961.
11. *Todesco's Diary,* February 15, 1961, February 16, 1961.
12. Todesco to Buddy, April 27, 1961, SDDA; Buddy to Todesco, May 4, 1961, SDDA.
13. Conway, *Chronology,* 200, 199.
14. *Yorkville Diary,* November 15 to December 28, 1960; CMAC; *Yorkville Diary,* January 2, 1960 - June 18, 1960; *The Family News of the U.S. Province,* vol 1, no 6, July 5, 1961, CMAC, 4.
15. *Family News,* vol 1, no 7, August 26, 1961; *Yorkville Diary,* August 27, 1961 - November 28, 1961.
16. *Todesco's Diary,* April 29, 1962; *Family News,* vol 1, no 10, 2; Conway, *Interviews,* vol 1, 88-89; Carillo to author, 1995.
17. Jerry Charbonneau, interview with author, April, 1993.
18. Todesco to Accorsi, March 17, 1955, CMAR.
19. *Todesco's Diary,* June 26, 1961 to July 3, 1961; Rouillard to Todesco, June 29, 1961, CMAC; McCarihy to Todesco, July 8, 1961, CMAC.
20. Todesco to Desrochers, August 10, 1961, CMAC; *Todesco's Diary,* November 22, 1961; Todesco to Battelli, November 23, 1961, CMAC.
21. *Todesco's Diary,* December 4, 1961; Todesco to Battelli, January 8, 1962, CMAR; Accorsi to Marie Buse, January 3, 1962, CMAC.
22. Todesco to Battelli, January 12, 1962, CMAR; Battelli to Todesco, January 17, 1962, CMAR; Accorsi to Marie and Carl Buse, January 23, 1962, CMAC.
23. Conway, *Chronology,* 180, 195-196.
24. See letters between Bishop Bell and Father Albert Duggan, March 31, 1957 to January 20, 1958, AALA; Bell to Duggan, December 14, 1959, AALA.

25. Anthony Z. Marigo, *Our Lady of Guadalupe Mission: Irwindale, California*; La Paz, B.C. Mexico: (written and published after Marigo was transferred to Boys' Town at La Paz in 1968), 29-35, CMAC. This pamphlet was made available to the author through the generosity of the present pastor of the Irwindale Church.

26. Conway, *Chronology*, 201.

27. Marigo, *Our Lady of Guadalupe*.

28. Paolucci, *My Stars*, 113, 114, 116-117.

29. ibid., 122.

30. Paolucci, *The First 20 Years*, 167-170.

31. Turchetti to Hyland, February 28, 1960, AAA.

32. Hyland to Todesco, April 6, 1960, AAA.

33. Todesco to Hyland, April 12, 1960, AAA; Hyland to Doniney, October 14, 1960, AAA; Conway, *Interviews*, vol ii, 7, CMAC.

34. Letter from a Comboni priest to author, 1993.

35. *Todesco's Diary*, May 22, 1962, CMAC; Hallinan to Briani, June 15, 1962, AAA.

36. Hallinan to Todesco, June 15, 1962, AAA; Todesco to Hallinan, June 19, 1962, AAA; Briani to Hallinan, June 30, 1962, AAA.

Chapter 13. Seminary Growth/Leadership Change, 1962-1964

1. *Todesco's Diary*, July 6, 1961 and August 29, 1961; Conway, *Chronology, 204; Family News*, vol 1, no 8, 2; Author's interview with a Comboni Missionary, 1994.

2. *Todesco's Diary*, September 1, September 4, September 9, 1961.

3. Virtually all those the author interviewed about this period were from "the early days;" this largely due to the decrease in vocations later.

4. Author's interview with a Comboni missionary, February, 1993, 112-13.

5. Gabriel Chiodi to author, February 9, 1996; Raymond Pax, interview with author, 14-15.

6. *Todesco's Diary*, September 19, 1961 and October 4, 1961; Letter from Chiodi to author, February 9, 1996; Author's interview with a Comboni missionary, January 6, 1993; 6.

7. Todesco to Buddy, December 1, 1961, SDDA; Buddy to Todesco, December 28, 1961, CMAC; Conway, *Chronology*, 206; *Todesco's Diary*, March 26, April 13, February 26, March 8, April 26, and June 23, 1962.

8. *Todesco's Diary*, June 25, June 26, July 5, 1962; *Todesco's Diary*, August 22, September 5, October 9, October 17, December 16, 1962.

9. Todesco to "Dear and Reverend Father Superior," December 21, 1962, CMAC.

10. The most consistent set of statistics on this information is in *The Family News* volumes; figures quoted here are taken from vol 1, nos 3, 6, 7, 8, 10, 11, and 14.

11. *Family News*, vol 1, nos 5 and 9.

12. Todesco to Buddy, August 31, 1962, CMAC; Booth to Todesco, September 5, 1962, CMAC.

13. *Todesco's Diary*, March 18, 1963.

14. Charles Walter, in interview with author, January 6, 1993, 14-15.

15. Ongaro to author, August, 1995 and January, 1996; *Family News*, vol 1, no 10, 4; Ongaro to author, January 6, 1996; *Family News*, vol 1, no 13, 3; Remus Catellani, "Report to 1969 General Chapter," CMAC.
16. *Todesco's Diary*, June 18, June 30, July 1, July 12, July 17, and July 29, 1963.
17. Remus Catellani, in interview with author, April 29, 1992, 3-4.
18. Denis Wilkinson, in conversation with author, June, 1995.
19. Joseph Bragotti in interview with author, March 2, 1995.
20. Accorsi to Carl and Marie Buse, November 23, 1963; Accorsi to Marie Buse, March 16, 1964; *Family News*, vol 1, no 16; *Todesco's Diary*, July 1, 1964.
21. Briani to Accorsi, July 15, 1964, CMAC; Todesco to Accorsi, July 20, 1964, CMAC.
22. Accorsi to Briani, July 21, 1964, CMAC.
23. Briani to Accorsi, August 1, 1964, CMAC.
24. *Todesco's Diary*, February 1, 1964;
25. *Family News*, vol 1, no 17; *Todesco's Diary*, February 28, 1964.
26. Harley and LaCoste, 83-84, 64.
27. Frontier Call, September/October 1961, 97-99; *Family News*, vol 1, no 17, 4.
28. *Mission San Antonio de Pala Corpus Christi* brochures, 1961-1967 (made available by Mrs. Frank Hernandez, Pala, California); *Frontier Call*, January/February, 1967, 212-217; *Verona Fathers Mission Magazine*, Fall, 1969, 12; Conway, Interviews, vol ii, 148-149.
29. *Family News*, vol I, no 4, 4; *Todesco's Diary*, May 8, 1960.
30. *Family News*, vol I, no 4, 4; *Todesco's Diary*, May 8, 1960; Paolucci, *My Stars*, 127-129.
31. Todesco to Leibold, July 11, 1962, HACAC.
32. Alter to Briani, September 22, 1962, HACAC; Briani to Alter, October 30, 1962, HACAC.
33. Paolucci, *My Stars*, 133, 129-130; *Todesco's Diary*, September 20, 1964.
34. *Todesco's Diary*, May 11, 1964.
35. *Family News*, vol 1, no 14; *Family News*, vol 1, no 17; Conway, *Chronology*, 210; *Todesco's Diary*, October 17, 1963, July 11, 1964, August 26, 1964, September 5, 1964.
36. Paolucci, *My Stars*, 127, 130, 131-132.

Chapter 14. Seminaries in Transition, 1965-1966

1. *Family News*, vol 1, no 21, CMAC, 1-2; *Frontier Call*, July/August, 1965, 99-103.
2. Alter to Todesco, February 25, 1965, *Frontier Call,*. vol 18, no 3, May-June, 1965, 61; Briani to Todesco, undated, *Frontier Call,*. vol 18, n o 3, May-June, 1965, 62; Message from Todesco, *Frontier Call,*. vol 18, no 3, May-June, 1965, 58-59.
3. See also Anthony Vignato, To Whom It May Concern, September 29, 1939, CMAR; Todesco, written at Pala, California, December 27, 1955, CMAR, 6.
4. Paolucci, *Life Journey,*, vol iii, 231.
5. Davis, *The History of Black Catholics*, 1993, 256.
6. Ongaro to author, August, 1995.
7. *Todesco's Diary*, March 11, 1966.

8. A Comboni missionary's interview with author, February, 1993, 15; A Comboni missionary's interview with author, July, 1993.
9. Mario Ongaro, "Novitiate-to-Ordination Withdrawal Rates/Verona Fathers United States Province," October 29, 1971, CMAC, 2.
10. Todesco to Father Superior and Confreres, January 1, 1966, CMAC; Frank B. Norris, S.S., "Introduction," *Seminary Education in the Time of Change*, eds James Michael Lee and Louis J. Putz, C.S.C., Notre Dame, Indiana: Fides Publishers, Inc.,1965,xi-xii.
11. Ongaro to author, August 13, 1995; Stafford Poole C.M., *Seminary in Crisis*, New York: Herder and Herder, 1965, 18.
12. Todesco to Chiodi, July 15, 1967, CMAC.
13. Todesco to Chiodi, July 27, 1967, CMAC.
14. From a Comboni missionary's interview with author, March, 1995. A Euro-centeredness that created problems was mentioned by many younger priests.
15. C. Joseph O'Hara and Thomas P. Ferguson, "Seminary Enrollment Statistics: A review of the Past Quarter Century (1966-1991)," *The New CARA Seminary Forum*, vol 1, no 2, Fall, 1992, fig 2, p 10; published by the Center for Applied Research in the Apostolate, Georgetown University; *Family News*, vol 1, no 26, 2; no 27, 4.
16. Conway, *Interviews*, vol 1, 207-208 and vol 2, 119-120, CMAC; *Family News*, vol 1, no 20, 4.
17. *Family News*, vol 1, no 22, 1; Conway, *Interviews*, vol 1, 209; Battelli to Todesco, January 7, 1966, CMAR.
18. Conway, *Interviews*, vol 1, 207; *Todesco's Diary*, January 17-28, 1966.
19. Battelli to Todesco, February 25, 1966, CMAR; Todesco to Battelli, March 2, 1966, CMAR.
20. Todesco to Battelli, March 21, 1966, CMAR.
21. *Todesco's Diary*, May 22, 1966; *Family News*, vol 1, no 23, 4; *Family News*, vol 1, no 23, 4; *Todesco's Diary*, June 27, 1966 to July 4, 1966.
22. *Family News*, vol 1, no 24, 3.
23. Branchesi to James A. Hughes, October 25, 1965, CMAC; "He is Ready... The Seminary is Not," a brochure printed at Montclair in 1965, AAN.
24. "Seminary Fund Begun; 7 Businessmen Form Group to Build for Verona Fathers," Newark Evening News, February 24, 1967, AAN; Shriver to Branchesi, undated, in "He is Ready... " brochure, 12, AAN.
25. *Family News*, vol 1, no 26, 2; *Todesco's Diary*, July 4, 1968.
26. Conway, *Interviews*, vol 2; Carillo to author, August 23, 1995.
27. *Todesco's Diary*, December 10, 1966; Remus Catellani's "Report to the 1969 General Chapter," CMAC.

Chapter 15. Years of Crisis, 1967-1969

1. Todesco to Battelli, May 31, 1967, CMAC.
2. *Family News*, vol 1, no 24; Todesco to Battelli, May 31, 1967, CMAC; Battelli to Todesco, June 13, 1967, CMAC.
3. *Todesco's Diary*, June 16, 1967; *Family News*, vol 1, no 25, 2.

4. *Family News*, vol 1, no 25, 2,; Todesco to Battelli, June 24, 1967, CMAC; Todesco to Battelli, July 7, 1967, CMAC.
5. Todesco to Battelli, July 7, 1967, CMAC; Battelli to Todesco, July 25, 1967, CMAC.
6. Todesco to Battelli, August 13, 1967, CMAC; *Todesco's Diary*, December 19 and 30, 1967; Battelli to Todesco, January 3, 1968, CMAC; Todesco to Battelli, January 27, 1968, CMAC; Battelli to Todesco, April 26, 1968, CMAC.
7. Todesco to Battelli, January 27, 1968, CMAC; Todesco to Chiodi, April 10, 1968, CMAC.
8. Chiesa to Todesco, March 5, 1968, CMAC.
9. Todesco to Battelli, April 22, 1968, CMAC; *Todesco's Diary*, April 25, 1968.
10. Battelli to Todesco, April 26, 1968, CMAC; Chiodi to Todesco, April 14, 1968, CMAC.
11. Todesco to Battelli, May 17, 1968, CMAC; *Todesco's Diary*, May 28, 1968; Todesco to Furey, June 10, 1968, CMAC.
12. Furey to Todesco, June 13, 1968, CMAC.
13. James Michael Lee, "Overview of Educational Problems in Seminaries: I- Objectives and Administration," *Seminary Education in a Time of Change*, 97-98; Todesco to Alter, June 10, 1968, HACAC; Alter to Todesco, June 12, 1968, HACAC.
14. *Family News*, vol 20, no 27, 4.
15. From a Comboni missionary's interview with author.
16. *Todesco's Diary*, June 1 and June 2, 1968; *Family News*, vol 20, no 27, 3; *Todesco's Diary*, August 15, 1968.
17. "Points of Discussion," November 27, 1968, CMAC, 1, 2, 5, 8.
18. ibid., 3, 2, 10.
19. ibid., 8-9, 4, 8.
20. ibid., 5.
21. ibid., 8, 9.
22. *Todesco's Diary*, September 5, 1967, January 1, 1968, July 4, 1968, September, 1968, November 9, 1968, January 20, 1969, February 17, 1969.
23. Todesco to Battelli, January 27, 1968, CMAC; Todesco to Battelli, July 14, 1968, CMAC.
24. Battelli to Todesco, April 26, 1969, CMAC; Todesco to Battelli, May 17, 1968, CMAC.
25. Battelli to Todesco, September 19, 1968, CMAC; Todesco to Battelli, September 26, 1968, CMAC; Paolucci, *Life Journey*, vol ii, 41.
26. Battelli to Todesco, January 3, 1968, CMAC; Battelli to Todesco, April 26, 1968; Todesco to Battelli, May 17, 1968, CMAC; Paolucci, *Life Journey*, vol ii, 47.
27. *Todesco's Diary*, March 28-31, 1967.
28. *Family News*, vol I, no 25, 2; *Todesco's Diary*, October 28, 1967; *Family News*, vol I, no 26, 4; Todesco to "Father Superior and Confreres," July 10, 1967, CMAC.
29. *Verona Fathers' Missions*, vol 21, no 1, January/February, 1969, 6-9.
30. *Todesco's Diary*, January 30, March 8, April 29, and June 12, 1968; Dennis Conway, *Interviews*, vol I, CMAC. 267; *Verona Fathers Missions*, (formerly *Frontier Call*), vol 21, no 22, CMAC, 22-23.

31. *Todesco's Diary*, March 8- March 19, 1969; Catellani, "Financial Report to the 1969 General Chapter," 1969, CMAC.

32. Joseph Bragotti, interview with author, 14-15; Todesco to Busetti, March 11, 1969, CMAC; Busetti to Todesco, April 17, 1969, CMAC.

Chapter 16. Renewal and Choice

1. Karl Rahner, *Concern for the Church*, New York: Crossroad, 1981, p152fn in Gerald A. Arbuckle, *Out of Chaos: Refounding Religious Congregations*, New York: Paulist Press, 1988, 77.

2. Mario Ongaro, "Constitutional History of the Comboni Missionaries of the Heart of Jesus," Rome, 1990, CMAC, 2-5; John Manuel Lozano, *The Spirituality of Daniel Comboni*, Chicago: Claret Center for Resources in Spirituality, 1989, 129, 142.

3. Ongaro, "Constitutional History," 6-7.

4. ibid., 8-10.

5. "Verona Fathers Renewal: A New Life Style," *Verona Fathers Missions*, vol 22, no 2, Spring, 1970, 22-23; *Capitolo Aperto* (The Open Chapter), a bulletin of information about the Tenth General Chapter sent to all Comboni Missionary communities during the chapter, no 1, Rome: May 20, 1969, CMAC, 5-7.

6. *Capitolo Aperto, No. 2, May 27, 1969, 2-4.*

7. *Capitolo Aperto*, no 6, 1-5.

8. Fornasari to author, February, 1997.

9. *Capitolo Aperto*, no 7, July 2, 1969, 1-4; 9-10.

10. *Chapter Documents*, Rome: Verona Fathers, December 8, 1969, 240.

11. *Capitolo Aperto*, no 7, 13-16.

12. *Verona Fathers Missions*, vol 21, no 3, Summer, 1969, 4-7; Charles Walter, interview with author, May 7, 1996.

13. From two undated reports by the Procurator of the North American Province, Father Remus Catellani, CMAC.

14. *Capitolo Aperto*, no 18, 21-23, 23-25.

15. Planning addendum, *Capitolo Aperto*, no 18, 5.

16. Ochs, *Desegregating the Altar*, 447.

Chapter 17. Expanding Black Ministry

1. *Verona Fathers Missions*, vol 22, no 1, 5.

2. From author's interviews with five Comboni priests; *Family News*, vol 2, no 29, March-April, 125.

3. *Chapter Documents, 274*, 278, 282.

4. *Violence in the City - - An End or a Beginning?* A Report by the Governor's Commission on the Los Angeles Riots, December 2, 1965, 1; Rhoda Lois Blumberg, *Civil Rights: The 1960s Freedom Struggle*, 163; Harvard Sitkoff, *The Struggle for Black Equality, 1954-1980*, Toronto: Collins Publishers, 1981, 200, 202-203.

5. Blumberg, *Civil Rights: The 1960s Freedom Struggle*, rev ed, Boston: Twayne Publishers, A Division of G.K. Hall & Co., 1991, 164.

6. David O. Sears and John B. McConahay, *The Politics of Violence-the New Urban Blacks and the Watts Riot,* Boston, Houghton Mifflin, 1973, 158.
7. Sitkoff, 169, 172-185, 146, 218.
8. "Historic Sketch of Holy Cross Parish and Church," a two-page copy of document found at the parish, undated, with note that the information came from *Tidings,* the archdiocesan newspaper. Duplicate in Holy Cross file, CMAC; to Clyne, April 15, 1964, Holy Cross File, 1961-1976, AALA; Rev. Lake Lynch, pastor to Chancery, June 3, 1965, Holy Cross File, AALA.
9. Todesco to Hawkes, January 30, 1969, AALA; Contran to Hawkes, March 17, 1970, CMAC.
10. Contran to Hawkes, June 3, 1970, CMAC.
11. Alexander Nardi, in interview with Dennis Conway, 1988, vol 1, 382-385; "The Center for Brotherly Love," by Joan Wilcoxon, *Verona Fathers Missions,* vol 24, no 2, 14-17.
12. ibid., 16.
13. *Family News,* vol 2, no 37; Nardi interview with Conway, 385-387.
14. Thomas Clagett, "Colleoni," *Verona Missions,* vol 31, no 6, November/December, 1979, 3-7.
15. Xavier Colleoni, in interview with author, June, 1996; Largely, but not totally, taken from interview with Colleoni, November 2, 1996.
16. ibid.
17. Unsigned memo, July 1, 1956, St. Pius File, HACAC.
18. Berning to Chancellor, September 12, 1956, HACAC; Chancellor to Berning, September 14, 1956, HACAC.
19. *The Catholic Sun,* Syracuse, New York, June 22, 1967, JA.
20. *The Catholic Standard and Times,* Philadelphia, Pennsylvania, June 23, 1967, 8, JA; *National Catholic Reporter,* July 19, 1967, JA.
21. *Long Island Catholic,* Rockville Center, New York, July 6, 1967, JA.
22. *Hartford Catholic Transcript,* July 21, 1967, JA; *The Catholic Review,* Baltimore, Maryland, August 4, 1967, JA.
23. *The Catholic Sun,* Syracuse, New York, October 5, 1967, JA; *The Record,* Louisville, Kentucky, May 16, 1968, JA; *The Catholic Virginian,* Richmond, Virginia, February 13, 1970, JA.
24. McCarthy to Berning, March 15, 1967, HACAC; McCarthy to Krusling, June 9, 1969, HACAC; Leibold to Catellani, November 12, 1970, HACAC.
25. Catellani to Leibold, November 17, 1970, HACAC; Contran to Leibold, December 21, 1970, HACAC; Contran to Leibold, January 8, 1970, HACAC.
26. Premarini to Leibold, October 25, 1970, HACAC; Leibold to Premarini, October 28, 1970, HACAC; Contran to Leibold, December 21, 1970, HACAC; "A Proposal with Regard to St. Pius Parish," with a cover letter to Paul F. Leibold from Malcolm Grad, Office of Social Action, Archdiocese of Cincinnati, January 27, 1971, HACAC; Leibold to Grad, February 9, 1971, HACAC.
27. PFL (Paul F. Leibold) to Asplan, July 2, 1971, HACAC; ibid., bottom and reverse of letter.

28. Premarini to Ralph A. Asplan, July 22, 1971, HACAC; Schaefer to Premarini, August 19, 1971, HACAC.
29. Premarini to Leibold, November 10, 1971, HACAC; "We've Only Just Begun," William Jansen, *Verona Fathers Missions*, vol 24, no 3, 1972, 3-6.
30. "We've Only Just Begun," *Verona Fathers Missions*; Premarini in interview with author, 1993.
31. Premarini to Ralph A. Asplan, July 22, 1971, HACAC; "Forecast Budget for the School Year of 1968-1969," [Immaculate Heart of Mary], AAL.
32. Clyde F. Crews, *An American Holy Land*, 316-317.
33. "Commission Head Wants Enforceable Ordinance," *Catholic Record*, March 2, 1967, JA; Crews, 326-327; "A Night in Jail 'Without My Rights,'" *Catholic Record*, May 4, 1967, JA; Carillo, interview with author, November 2, 1996.
34. Crews, 318-319, 327.
35. Heitzman, in interview with author, 1975; Crews, 328.
36. "West End Priest Wages War; Poverty Bombarded with Zeal," *Catholic Record*, February 8, 1968, JA; "Archbishop Assigns Four Priests to West end Team Ministry," *Catholic Record*, April 18, 1968, JA; Carillo to McDonough, August 15, 1968, AAL; [Chancellor] John Hanrahan to Carillo, August 16, 1968, AAL; Carillo to McDonough, November 14, 1968, AAL.
37. McDonough to Todesco, August 23, 1969, CMAC.
38. "Varied Jobs Seen for New 'Action' Unit," *Catholic Record*, January 29, 1970, JA; "West End Priests See Varied Priorities," *Catholic Record*, April 30, 1970, JA.
39. Crews, 328-329; Carillo to McDonough, December 9, 1970, AAL; Carillo to McDonough, February 20, 1971, AAL; Charles G. Maloney, "Memorandum," June 18, 1971, AAL.
40. Contran to Maloney, June 19, 1971, AAL; Maloney to Contran, June 24, 1971, AAL; Archbishop McDonough and Bishop Maloney to "The Members of Immaculate Heart of Mary Parish," June 24, 1971, AAL.
41. Maloney to Contran, July 20, 1971, CMAC.
42. McDonough to Contran, July 23, 1971, CMAC; Contran to McDonough, August 18, 1971, CMAC; McDonough to Contran, August 20, 1971, CMAC; Boldrick to Genaro [Carillo], September 13, 1971.
43. Contran to Rawden, August 2, 1973, CMAC; Rawden to Contran, September 6, 1973, CMAC; Contran to Rawden, October 8, 1973, CMAC.

Chapter 18. Formation: Hope and Despair

1. Minutes of the Meeting of the U.S. Provincial Council, March 10, 1970, 1, 2, CMAC.
2. John W. Padberg, S.J., "Jesuit Higher Education: Too Abstract?" *National Jesuit News*, December, 1983, 7, in Peter McDonough's *Men Astutely Trained: A History of the Jesuits in the American Century*, New York: The Free Press, A Division of Macmillan, Inc., 1992, 458.

3.   *Family News*, vol 2, no 29, 135; *Vatican Council II: The Conciliar and Post Conciliar Documents*, gen ed Austin Flannery, O.P., Collegeville, Minnesota: Liturgical Press, 1975; "Norms for Implementing the Decree: On the Up-To-Date Renewal of Religious Life," (from Paul VI, *Ecclesiae Sanctae* II, 6 August, 1966) 639; and "Decree on the Training of Priests," (from Vatican II, *Optatum Totius*, 28 October, 1965), 717.

4.   *Chapter Documents*, Verona Fathers, December 8, 1969, Part 3, Missionary Formation, 49-53, 380-384; *Family News*, vol 2, no 29, 2.; Provincial Council Meeting, Cincinnati, Ohio, June 9-10, 1970, 1-2.

5.   *Chapter Documents*, sec ii, Ch ii, 428.

6.   Minutes of "Preliminary Meeting of U.S. Formation Secretariat," Sacred Heart Seminary, Monday, March 30, 1970, 2-5, CMAC.

7.   *Family News*, vol 2, no 30, 1 and vol 2, no 31, 1; *Verona Fathers Missions*, vol 22, no 4, 4-6.

8.   For more on prefects, see Ongaro's "The Decalogue of the Prefect," 1965, CMAC.

9.   "U.S. Council Meeting, July 8, 1971, Cincinnati, Ohio," CMAC; *Family News*, vol 2, no 37, 1.

10. David Baltz, in interview with author, March 5, 1992.

11. *Family News*, "From the Secretary's Desk," vol 2, no 39, 2.

12. Minutes of the "Conference on Education," Cincinnati, Ohio, December 2,1971, CMAC; U.S. Province Council Meeting, May 15-16, 1972, CMAC, 2.

13. *Family News*, vol 2, no 35, 2, and vol 2, no 36, 2.

14. Minutes, "Conference on Education," Cincinnati, June 6, 1972, CMAC.

15. Albert Dilanni, S.M., "Religious Life and Modernity," *Review for Religious*," vol 50, no 3, May/June 1991, 339-352.

16. U.S. Provincial Council Meeting, September 5, 1973, CMAC, 2; "Provincial Council Meeting," March 25, 1974, Sacred Heart Seminary, CMAC; "United States Province - Council Meeting," Cincinnati - May 21, 1974, CMAC.

17. "United States Province Council Meeting," February 4-6, 1975, CMAC.

18. Provincial Council Meeting, March 10, 1970; *Family News*, vol 2, no 32, 2; *Family News*, vol 2, no 33, 2.

19. Provincial Council Meeting, March 10, 1970, CMAC, 2; U.S. Provincial Council Meeting, Monroe, Michigan, September 21, 1970, CMAC, 1; U.S. Council Meeting with Superior General, November 16, 1970, CMAC, 3.

20. Angelo Biancalana, in interview with author, April, 1992, 10, 11.

21. *Family News*, vol 2, no 36, 1; *Family News*, vol 2, no 37, 2; *Family News*, vol 2, no 37, 1; *Family News*, vol 2, no 39, 2.

22. U.S. Province Council Meeting, February 28-March 1, 1972, CMAC, 1, 2; U.S. Province Council Meeting, May 15-16, 1972, CMAC, 2; *Family News*, vol 2, no 41, 2; *Family News*, vol 2, no 42, 1.

23. U.S. Provincial Council Meeting: February 7-9, 1973, CMAC, 4; *Family News*, vol 2, no 43, 1; *Family News*, vol 2, no 44, 1.

24. U.S. Provincial Council Meeting, May 21, 1973, CMAC.

25. Ongaro, interview with author, April 9, 1992, 2-3; U.S. Provincial Council Meeting, September 5, 1973, CMAC.

26. "Who Me?", *Verona Fathers Missions*, vol 23, no 4, 11; 19.
27. U.S. Provincial Council Meeting, September 5, 1973, CMAC, 1; *Family News*, vol 2, no 45, 2, 3; "Vocations: A Trust Committed to Us," *Family News*, vol 2, no 46, 3.
28. David Baltz, interview with author; United States Province Council Meeting, Sacred Heart Seminary, Cincinnati, Ohio, October 15, 1974, CMAC, 3.
29. John Staudenmaier, S.J., "Religious Formation in a Time of Cultural Turbulence," paper presented at the 1981 Religious Formation Conference, Washington, D.C., 105; 106-107.
30. ibid., 114-115, 117-118.

Chapter 19. Renewal and Reaction

1. Contran to Leo T. Maher, August 22, 1970, SDDA.
2. Robert P. McDonald to O'Neill P. Martin, August 28, 1970, SDDA.
3. Contran to Maher, August 29, 1970, SDDA; Martin to McDonald, September 3, 1970, SDDA, 2.
4. John E. Baer to Leo T. Maher, December 16, 1969, SDDA.
5. *Family News*, vol 2, no 40, 1-2; Provincial Council Minutes, August 30, 1972, CMAC; Provincial Council Minutes, October 25, 1972, CMAC.
6. *Family News*, vol 2, no 44.
7. "Provincial Directory of the United States, 1973," (Draft), with accompanying responses from members of the province., CMAC.
8. Gerald A. Arbuckle, *Out of Chaos: Refounding Religious Congregations*, New York: Paulist Press, 1988, 79-84.
9. U.S. Provincial Council Minutes, May 21, 1973, 5, CMAC.
10. *Family News*, vol 2, no 33, CMAC, 2; Provincial Council Meeting Minutes and Addenda, November 16, 1970, CMAC.
11. U.S. Council Meeting, February 3, 1971, CMAC; U.S. Council Meeting Minutes, April 12, 1972, CMAC.
12. U.S. Provincial Council Minutes, February 7-9, 1973, CMAC.
13. Provincial Council Meeting Minutes, June 9-10, 1970, CMAC.
14. Provincial Council meeting Minutes, November 16, 1970, CMAC.
15. Provincial Council Meeting Minutes, July 8, 1971, CMAC; Provincial Council Meeting Minutes, October 5-6, 1971, CMAC; *Family News*, vol 2, no 38, 1.
16. Provincial Council Meeting Minutes, August 30, 1972, CMAC, 2; Provincial Council Meeting Minutes, February 7-9, 1973, CMAC, 1.
17. Provincial Council Meeting Minutes, May 21, 1973, CMAC.
18. Tarcisio Agostoni, "Crisis in the Church" and "Independence Era in Africa" in *History of the Institute of the Comboni Missionaries: Outlines*, Rome, Comboni Missionaries of the Heart of Jesus, 1996, 174
19. ibid., 175-179.
20. ibid., 170-171.
21. Provincial Council Minutes, September 5, 1973, CMAC; Paolucci, *Life Journeys*, vol ii, 95.

22. "The Province of the United States - the Last Four Years, 1970-1973," undated, unsigned; a handwritten note reads: "Copy of this was given to the General, January, 1974"; CMAC.
23. U.S. Council Meeting Minutes, January 7-8, 1974, CMAC, 3.
24. ibid., 2.
25. *Family News*, vol 2, no 46, 2.
26. U.S. Provincial Council Meeting Minutes, July 29, 1974; February 4-6, 1975; April 9-10, 1975; *Family News*, vol 2, no 51, 1.
27. United States Province - Council Meeting, July 29, 1974, 2; United States Province Council Meeting, February 4-6, 1975, 1.
28. United States Province -- Report to the General Chapter, [1975] CMAC.

Chapter 20. Working to Survive

1. *Family News*, vol 2, no 52, 1-2.
2. Contran to "Dear Confreres," December 30, 1975, CMAC; Provincial Council Meeting Minutes, February 18-19, 1976, CMAC.
3. Paul Bechtold, C.P., *Catholic Theological Union at Chicago, The Founding Years*, Chicago: Catholic Theological Union, 1993, 3-5; Charles Walter, in interview with author, January, 1993; *Family News*, vol 2, no 52, 3.
4. Bechtold, 17-20, 22, 25; Walter to author, June 16, 1998.
5. Walter, interview with author, January, 1993; *Family News*, vol 2, no 52, 3; Bechtold, 260-262; Walter interview, 1993; *Family News*, vol 2, no 52, 3.
6. Walter to author, June 16, 1998; Provincial Council Meeting Minutes, February 18, 19, 1976, CMAC, 2; *Family News*, vol 3, no 53, 2.
7. *Family News*, December 1, 1979, vol 3, December 1, 1979, 10.
8. "Secretariat for Formation United States Province, Results of the Questionnaire for the V General Assembly," April 15, 1976, Formation Folder, CMAC; *Family News*, vol 3, no 53, 2.
9. Minutes of the Provincial Assembly for Formation, September 7-9, 1976, Formation Folder, CMAC.
10. Provincial Council Minutes, February 2, 1979, V, XIV, in *Family News*, vol 3, no 63, 4-5.; *Family News*, vol 3, no 66, 10 (13.5).
11. Provincial Mission Promotion Assembly Minutes, October 23-25, 1979, in *Family News*, December 1, 1979, 8, (10.2); 14, (18.2).
12. Provincial Assembly of Formation, October 16-17, 1978, in the *Family News*, November, 1978, vol 3, no 62.
13. Provincial Assembly of the North American Province, January 8-11, 1979, in *Family News*, vol 3, no 63; Provincial Council Minutes, April 17-18, 1979, 1.
14. Provincial Council Minutes, July 13, 14, 1976, CMAC, 2.
15. *Family News*, vol 3, no 58, 2; *Family News*, vol 3, no 60, 3; *Family News*, vol 3, no 61, 1; Provincial Assembly of the North American Province, January 8-11, 1979, in *Family News*, vol 3, no 63, 13.
16. Provincial News in *Family News*, December 1, 1979, 8; Provincial Mission Promotion Assembly, October 23-25, 1979, in *Family News*, December 1, 1979, 8-9.

17. Minutes of the Mission Animation Assembly, July 6-7, 1976 in Formation Folder, CMAC; *Family News*, vol 3, no 61, 3-3; *Family News*, vol 3, no 60, 3..
18. Ongaro, "An Historical Outline and Some Dreams," CMAC, 5.
19. Sergio Contran, in interview with author, 7.
20. Provincial News in *Family News*, vol 3, no 64, 6; Provincial Council Meeting, April 17-18, 1979, in *Family News*, vol 3, no 65, 14.
21. *Family News*. vol 3, no 64, 8-12.
22. *Family News*, vol 3, no 55, December, 1976, 1.
23. Busetti to Manning, October 18, 1976, CMAC; Busetti to Manning, February 24, 1977; Rawden to Wright, June 24, 1977, AALA; AGREEMENT between THE ARCHDIOCESE OF LOS ANGELES IN CALIFORNIA and THE VERONA FATHERS Sons of the Sacred Heart, August 1, 1977, CMAC; Busetti to Manning, May 30, 1977.
24. Hugo Riva, in interview with author, fall, 1993.
25. *Family News*, vol 2, no 52, 3; Provincial Council Meeting, July 13, 14, 1976, 3-4.
26. *Family News*, vol 3, no 58, 2; *Family News*, vol 3, no 60, 3; *Family News*, vol 3, no 61, 1; *Family News*, vol 3, no 61, 3; Provincial Council Meeting, November 6, 1978, 3; "Provincial News," in *Family News*, vol 3, no 62, 1.
27. Paolucci, *Life Journey*, vol iii, 39-41.
28. Accorsi to Marie Buse, April 8, 1976; Accorsi to Marie Buse, May 19, 1977.
29. Bollettino FSCJ. #121mp. 77, reprinted in Paolucci, *Life Journey*, vol ii, 195.

Chapter 21. Setting Priorities: Ministry and Vocations

1. Provincial Council Meeting: November 15-16, 1979, *Family News*, vol 3, no 66, 2.0; *Comboni Missions*, March-April, 1980, 29.
2. Pierli to Confreres, Easter, 1981, *Family News*, no 70, April, 1981, 2.
3. Jensen, in interview with Dennis Conway, 300-303.
4. Jensen, interview with Conway, 300-303, 307-308. Provincial Council Meetings: December 2-6, 1980, 35; February 9-11, 1981, 1; July 27-31, 1981, 13; October 12-16, 1981, 25.
5. Jensen interview with Conway, 308-309; Provincial Council Meeting, August 3, 1982, 1.
6. Ongaro to author, 1997.
7. Jensen interview with Conway, 311-312.
8. Jon Jensen and Mario Ongaro,"Casa Comboni," An Evaluation (Revised), Los Angeles, 1984.
9. "Visitation of the Seminaries in the United States Mandated by His Holiness, Pope John Paul II," June 22, 1981, "Casa Comboni," Los Angeles, California, March 27, 1987," 1-13.
10. Provincial Council Meeting, June 16-20, 1980, 2.1.
11. *Family News*, no 72, 3-4.
12. Gasparini, in interview with author, 1992, 6.
13. *Family News*, no 88, 12.
14. Gasparini, in interview with author, 12-14.

15. *Verona Fathers' Missions*, vol 22, no 5, winter, 1970, 8-12.
16. Charles Walter in Eulogy for Dahlen, in Paolucci, *Life Journeys*, vol iii, 83.
17. Caesar Mazzolari, "St. Pius Church: The Growth of a Christian Community," *Family News*, no 71, Christmas, 1981, 18-35.
18. Dahlen to Walter, February 24, 1976, CMAC.
19. Mazzolari's Eulogy for Father Dahlen, January 9, 1981, *Family News*, no 70, 4-6.
20. *Family News*, no 71, 2. and no 73, 6.
21. ibid., no 77, 7.
22. ibid., no 79, 11.
23. ibid., no 81, 6-7.
24. ibid., no 73, 6-7.
25. Provincial Council Meeting, April 11-15, 1983, 12.1, 12.6, 9.0.
26. *Family News*, no 77, 8-9.
27. Jansen, in interview with author, July 14, 1993, 39-41.
28. ibid., 46-52.
29. ibid., 54-57.
30. Provincial Council Meeting, August 3, 1982, con. 11.0.
31. Provincial Council Meetings on: December 13-17, 1982, 2.0; April 11-15,1983, 13.0; June 27-July 1, 1983, 1.2; December 5-9, 1983, 16.1.3; September 23-27, 1985, 6.5, 6.4.

Chapter 22. An American Perspective

1. Seán Sammon, "Making Sense of a Revolution," *Review for Religious*, January-February, 1992, vol 51, no 1, 64-77.
2. Pierli to Confreres, Easter, 1981, *Family News*, no 70, April, 1981, 2.
3. Provincial Council Meeting, March 27, 1980; Provincial Council Meeting, June 16-20, 1980, 15-16.
4. GROW Meeting June 25 and July 23, 1980, *Family News* no 68, Appendix III and IV; Provincial Council Meeting, September 11-14, 1980, 25, 26-28.
5. Walter to Brothers, September 24, 1980, *Family News* no 68, 2-3; Walter to Brothers, December, 1980, *Family News* no 68, 2.
6. *Provincial Directory Survey, Comboni Missionaries of the Heart of Jesus, North American Province*, Washington, D.C., Center for Applied Research in the Apostolate, October, 1981, 1-2.
7. *Provincial Directory Survey...CARA*, 6-14.
8. ibid., 31-33.
9. ibid., 53-56.
10. ibid., 26.
11. Provincial Council Meetings: October 12-16, 1981, 26; January 18-22, 1982, 1-2.
12. Calvia to Confreres, Rome, March 25, 1982, *Family News*, no 73, 3-4.
13. "Report on Personnel for the 1982 Intercapitular Assembly," *Family News*, no 72, March, 1982.

14. Provincial Council Meeting, March 27-April 2, 1980, 3; *Rule of Life: Constitutions and General Directory of the Comboni Missionaries of the Heart of Jesus*, Rome, 1988, #31; Provincial Council Meetings: March 27-April 2, 1980, 3; May 4-8, 1981; February 9-11, 1981, 2, 5.2.
15. Walter, in interview with author, 34.
16. Provincial Council Meetings: December 13-17, 1982, 4.0; March 26-29, 1984, 4.0.
17. Provincial Council Meetings: December 12, 2-6, 3.4; February 9-14, con. 2.0; Provincial Council Meetings: July 5-9, 1982, 13.5; October 20-21, 1982, 3.3.
18. Walter to "All Members of the NAP," August 23, 1982, *Family News*, no 74, 3-4.
19. Walter, in interview with author, 29.
20. Provincial Council Meeting, September 23-27, 1985, 1.5; Provincial Council Meetings: June 16, 1980, con. 2.14; June 16-20, 1980, con. 2.7.
21. Busetti to Maher, February 24, 1977, CMAC; Maher to Busetti, February 28, 1977, CMAC.
22. Gino Doniney, June 14, 1984, *Family News*, no 80, October, 1984, 14.
23. "Report on Personnel for the 1982 Intercapitular Assembly," Easter, 1982, *Family News*, no 72, 2.7.4; Provincial Council Meeting, October 8-9, 1983, 1.1.
24. CARA Report, 94.
25. Provincial Council Meetings: March 26-29, 1984, con. 5.1; October 24-27, 1984, 9.1; May 6-7, 1985 and May 8-10, 1985, 1.1; September 23-27, 1985, 1.1; December 2-5, 1985, 1.3.
26. *Family News*, no 72, March, 1982, 5; "Report on Personnel for Intercapitular Assembly," 19-21; Provincial Council Meetings: October 24-27, 1984, con. 4.0; January 22-26 and February 4-5, 1985, 16.0; May 6-7 & May 8-10, 1985, 11.0; September 23-27, 1985, con. 8.0.
27. Provincial Council Meeting, October 20-21, 1982, con. 8.0; CARA Report, 94.
28. Provincial Council Meetings: June 27-July 1, 1983, con. 8.0; May 21-25, 1984, 5.0; August 4-7, 1984, con. 3.0.; Provincial Council Meeting, January 22-26 and February 4-5, 1985, 3.0.
29. Provincial Council Meetings: January 22-26 and February 4-5, 1985, 6.6, con. 6.1; May 6-7, 1985 and May 8-10, 1985, 3.0; Provincial Council Meeting, September 23-27, Appendix I & II.
30. Provincial Council Meetings: May 19-22, 1986, 14.1 and con. 6.8; August 25-29, 1986, 11.1.3 and 13.1; December 10-12, 1986, 35.3, 37.2.1, and 18.11.
31. Provincial Council Meetings: October 8-9, 1983, 3.4; May 21-25, 1984, 4.4; January 22-26 and February 4-5, 1985, 6.8, con. 6.2; May 6-10, 1985, 6.1, 6.3; September 23-27. 1985, con. 5.0, con. 10.5; Provincial Council Meetings: May 19-22, 1986, 14.6; 8/25/86, 23.4.
32. Calvia to Confreres, Rome, March 25, 1982, *Family News*, no 73, 3-4; Pierli to Confreres, *Family News*, no 79, June, 1984, 1-2.
33. Provincial Council Meeting, October 24-27, 1984, 2.0, also an addendum to the minutes of this meeting due to its being received after the meeting, 25.
34. Provincial Council Meeting, January 22-26 and February 4-5, 1985, con. 2.2; con. 3.0; con. 5.1.3.
35. Provincial Council Meeting, September 23-27, 1985, con. 2.1.1, 2.1.2.

36. Provincial Council Meeting, December 2-5, 1985, 2.0, 6.0.
37. Provincial Council Meeting, April 3-4, 1986, 7.0; May 19-22, 1986, 21.0; *Family News* no 87, September, 1986, Fuchs to Fr. Charles and confreres, Rome, July 4, 1986, 1-4.
38. Charlie to Brothers, *Family News* no 86, July, 1986; Quigley to Brothers, December 1, 1986, *Family News* no 88, December, 1986, 5-6.

INDEX